ORGANIZING
FOR
SOCIAL CHANGE

MIDWEST ACADEMY
MANUAL FOR ACTIVISTS

Kim Bobo   **Jackie Kendall**   **Steve Max**

D1319058

SEVEN LOCKS PRESS

Santa Ana, California
Minneapolis, Minnesota
Washington, D.C.

Library of Congress Cataloging-in-Publication Data
   Bobo, Kimberley A.
   Organizing for Social Change: a manual for activists/Kim Bobo, Jackie Kendall, and Steve Max.
       p. cm.
   Includes index.
   ISBN 0-929765-41-9
       1. Direct action—Handbooks, manuals, etc. I. Kendall, Jackie. II. Max, Steve. III. Title.
   JC328.3.B63   1991
   322.4'3'068—dc20

                                                    90-47467
                                                    CIP

Manufactured in the United States of America

Seven Locks Press is a formerly Washington-based book publisher of non-fiction works on social, political, and cultural issues. It takes its name from a series of lift locks on the Chesapeake and Ohio Canal. Seven Locks Press relocated to California in 1994.

For more information, call or write:
Seven Locks Press
P.O. Box 25689
Santa Ana, CA 92799
800-354-5348

Let me give you a word on the philosophy of reform. The whole history of the progress of human liberty shows that all concessions yet made to her august claims have been born of earnest struggle. The conflict has been exciting, agitating, all absorbing, and for the time being putting all other tumults to silence. It must do this or it does nothing. If there is no struggle there is no progress. Those who profess to favor freedom, and yet depreciate agitation, are men who want crops without plowing up the ground. They want rain without thunder and lightning. They want the ocean without the awful roar of its many waters. This struggle may be a moral one; or it may be a physical one; or it may be both moral and physical; but it must be a struggle. Power concedes nothing without a demand. It never did and it never will. Find out just what people will submit to, and you have found the exact amount of injustice and wrong which will be imposed upon them; and these will continue until they are resisted with either words or blows, or with both. The limits of tyrants are prescribed by the endurance of those whom they oppress.

—Frederick Douglass
Letter to an abolitionist associate, 1849

Dedication

This book is dedicated to the founder of the Midwest Academy, Heather Booth.

Heather wrote the first Academy curriculum. Others have contributed to the training over the years, but the single most useful tool has been the Strategy Chart. Because the Midwest Academy Strategy Chart is so useful and so much used, we thought it important to emphasize here the role Heather Booth played in developing it.

In the years before the Academy started, the conventional organizing wisdom was that leaders could be entrusted to plan tactics, but overall campaign strategy could come only from professional organizers. This division, the development of strategy by organizers and of tactics by leaders, had a basis in reality. By virtue of long experience, many organizers had gained an implicit understanding of the elements of strategy and how to apply them, but they were unable to make that understanding clear enough to transfer it to leaders. The Strategy Chart solved that problem. It made strategy planning explicit. The steps became obvious, and all could participate on an equal basis. Use of the chart not only continues to lead to better strategy, but it is a great equalizer and democratizer within citizen organizations.

Thank you, Heather, for your wisdom, leadership, and vision.

Contents

Preface

Inspired by years of organizing in the student, Labor, women's, and civil rights movements, and funded by a back-pay award in an unfair labor practice suit, Heather Booth founded the Midwest Academy in 1973. With Steve Max, the Academy's first trainer and current Training Director, Heather developed a curriculum to pass on the lessons learned in these movements, provide organizers with a political and economic context, and teach the skills necessary for effective organizing.

The Academy was founded on three principles. For people to organize effectively for social and economic justice, they must

1. Win real improvements in people's lives
2. Get a sense of their own power
3. Alter the relations of power

The Academy's program was premised on building a network across many different kinds of organizations in which activists could share their experiences, develop relationships, and shape a vision not bound by the limitations of any one form of organizing.

In its early years, the Academy trained many leaders of the women's movement. Here they found a place where they could be reinforced as organizers. As word of the training spread, both experienced and would-be organizers came, bringing a diversity to each session that has allowed activists from all parts of the country to benefit from each other's experience.

Over the years, the Academy has been instrumental in helping to build statewide citizen action organizations in many states.

Today, the Academy continues to provide training to these multi-issue, statewide organizations (now part of a national organization—USAction) as well as to numerous other groups, ranging from students to senior citizens and from neighborhood to national organizations.

The common thread connecting all of the Academy's work is the value placed on developing individuals so that they can build powerful organizations that work for a more just society. In our training sessions it is inspiring to watch a low-income mother working on school issues in rural Virginia share her experiences and expertise with an environmental researcher from Washington, D.C., and a housing organizer from Chicago or to hear a New York student deep in conversation with a senior citizen from New Orleans and a trade unionist from Los Angeles. The point is not that diverse people get to know each other but that in doing so, they realize that their problems, though different, have common causes and common solutions. They begin to see the connections between their issues and the economic and political system. They recognize that what unites them is greater than what divides them and that indeed trying to divide them is a main tactic of their opponents.

The vision for which we work must be broad enough to make small victories significant. As people participate in our organizations and gain power, self-confidence, and dignity, they must also share a common vision of a country and world in which they would like to live. The issues on which we organize today may not lead directly to the achievement of that vision, but building up the power of citizen organizations is a necessary step. People can't begin to envision basic social change when the means to achieve it are lacking. Whenever changes for the better occur, it is fundamentally because people have taken charge of their own lives, transforming society as well as themselves.

Although much progress has been made, a great deal more remains to be done. Money and private special interests dominate the way laws are made. Voter participation is at its lowest in the history of the United States, indicating a lack of trust in the political process. Yet in the midst of this, we see where people have organized and won. The Academy has been a part of many of these efforts, training and building organizations and networks, learning and passing on knowledge to others.

It has been my privilege to direct the Midwest Academy since 1982. Under the leadership of Heather Booth and Steve Max, and with trainers including David Hunt, Judy Hertz, Juan Carlos Ruiz, John Cameron, Kim Bobo, Alicia Ybarra,

Paul Booth, Ron Charity, Barry Greever, and Karen Thomas, we have conducted thousands of training sessions. We have had the distinct pleasure of working with some of the best organizers in the country. So many have come through the Academy and gone on to organize and direct today's major progressive institutions. All have contributed something of themselves to make the Midwest Academy one of the best progressive organizer training centers in the United States.

As you read this book, keep in mind that the "steps," the "lists," and the "charts" are tools to help us do a better job. Coupled with a shared progressive vision and values that foster community, these tools help us develop the strategic framework for successful citizens' organizations and active participation in a democracy. Use the manual well, and organize!

Jackie Kendall
Executive Director

Acknowledgments

This manual draws on the experience of many organizers. Many of the concepts, principles, and charts were first developed by Heather Booth, the Midwest Academy's founder and first Executive Director.

We are also indebted to Steve Askin and Jane Hunter, whose revisions of the Tactical Investigations chapter have made it an extraordinary tool for online research. Thanks go to the many people who commented on all or parts of the manual and helped strengthen this and past editions: Jean Allison, Ira Arlook, Heather Booth, Regina Botterill, Harry Boyt, Robert Brandon, Stephen Coats, Rochelle Davis, Mark Dyen, Joan Flanagan, Judy Hertz, Jerry Kendall, Paul Lawrence, Joy Marshall, Judy Maslen, Kim Max, Lynn Max, Amy Neill, Donna Parson, Shelby Pera, Trelinda Pitchford, John Pomerantz, Jamie Pullen, Allan St. John, Barbara Samson, Kim Simmons, Arlette Slachmuylder, Marilyn Sneiderman, Delores Travis, Charles Vestal, Therese Volini, David West, and Marc Wetherhorn.

It was a pleasure to work with the staff of Seven Locks Press. Wynne Cougill and Roberta Shepherd's meticulous editing greatly improved the book's readability. For the third edition we would like to thank Bud Sperry for his assistance. The enthusiasm of our past and present publishers, James Morris and Jim Riordan, encouraged us throughout its writing.

We thank all of you who have read and recommended this manual to activists around the world. Portions of the book have been translated into several languages.

Finally, we would like to express our appreciation to all the fine community organizers and activists we have worked with over the years, particularly our training session participants. We've learned organizing from those with whom we've worked.

PART I
Direct Action
Organizing

1

The new millennium began well. First there was New Year's Eve itself, when, for the first time in history, people the world over participated in one grand televised celebration that added a new dimension to the word "globalization."

Then came a series of remarkable events. The Seattle demonstration against the World Trade Organization, while it marked the end of the 1990s, was very much part of the spirit of a new era in which people of many political persuasions, from militant trade unionists to militant vegetarians, made common cause against a common enemy. In South Carolina, mass action for civil rights re-emerged in the victorious demonstrations to remove the Confederate flag that had been flying above the State Capitol. During this time, demonstrations and sit-ins and fasts were taking place on many college campuses to end the purchase of school-logo garments made in sweatshops or by child labor, and to support janitors and cafeteria workers seeking living wages.

Tens of thousands of janitors and building service union members took to the streets of the West Coast, the Midwest, and the East Coast demanding union contracts. The new wave of union organizing drives is of great long-term importance. These efforts to organize low-wage service workers often have broad community and religious support

**Becoming a National Majority
Movement**

About This Book

2001 Edition Introduction

through organizations such as the National Interfaith Committee for Worker Justice.

In response to a series of brutal racist murders of unarmed citizens by the New York City Police, people of all races, incomes, and ages and from all parts of the city participated in marches, prayer vigils, and demonstrations. The events organized by college and high-school students were among the most dramatic. These events coincided with successful campaigns by anti-death-penalty groups to win moratoria on executions.

Also during this time, senior citizen organizations and groups such as USAction began organizing nationally and state by state to demand prescription drug coverage for those who find that they must choose between buying medicine and buying food.

All of these activities show that we are entering a period when, for many people, perceived self-interest is moving from narrow issues that bring immediate benefits to broader conceptions of human rights and environmental concerns.

Becoming a National Majority Movement

What has been missing, so far, is the emergence of a strategy to move this new energy into the national political arena, either by forcing elected officials and their parties to confront the issues or by posing an electoral alternative. Three factors seem to be slowing the development of a more unified social movement.

First, the language of globalization, while it has its unifying and mobilizing aspects, can also be disempowering. If we are now held captive to a global economy, then what good is national government, and is struggling to gain power over it still worthwhile? In reality, the question now is no different than it was at the dawn of the commercial revolution: will government be made an ally of working people or continue to be an arm of international and domestic corporate power? Globalization complicates the matter but does not fundamentally change our need to organize for control of the democratic political structure.

Second, the '90s was a decade in which progressive people tended to emphasize the particularity of social struggle rather than its universality. Among the powerless, each group tended to focus on the history and sources of its own particular oppression rather than looking for ways to coalesce and create majorities. We have seen healthy signs that this is changing, and more people are recognizing that social struggle can be both particular and universal at the same time. One need not choose.

The third and most important factor is that much of the new momentum is not based in national organizations that can sit down and negotiate a common strategy. Notable exceptions include the role of the AFL-CIO (American Federation of Labor and Congress of Industrial Organizations) in the Seattle demonstrations and the NAACP (National Association for the Advancement of Colored People) in South Carolina, but generally speaking, a major organizing job needs to be done. The Web and e-mail are fine tools for mobilization, but they can't substitute for building actual self-conscious organizational structures that can join together to carry out a campaign to win changes in public policy.

In 1991 the introduction to the first edition of this book noted, and it is worth repeating here, that we Americans have an unbroken history of organizing for social, economic, and political justice. The generation following the men and women who had been inspired by the words of Tom Paine, and who had fought alongside George Washington, made up abolitionist and feminist organizations that worked to extend the liberties of the American Revolution to the whole population. Often, those two movements were intertwined and mutually supportive. Feminist leaders such as Lucretia Mott, Elizabeth Cady Stanton, Lucy Stone, and Susan B. Anthony and abolitionist leaders like Frederick Douglass, Sojourner Truth, Harriet Tubman, William Lloyd Garrison, James Birney, and Sarah and Angelina Grimke now occupy separate chapters of the history books. But in life they knew each other, worked together, and shared the same platforms, debates, and sense of mission.

After the Civil War, the veterans of Gettysburg and newly arrived immigrants worked as long as sixteen hours a day in the country's factories, mines, and mills. Hundreds of thousands of them joined the 1886 nationwide strike for the eight-hour workday. As their movement rose and faced fierce opposition, Eugene Victor Debs was already organizing and would eventually assume the leadership of growing national trade union and socialist movements. In the Western states the seeds of populism, which influenced Debs, were being sown. Turn-of-the-century populism, socialism, and trade unionism shared a common language of economic democracy, and the movements often connected.

Many of the generation that had organized with Debs lived to see the success of the Congress of Industrial Organizations in the 1930s. The CIO strengthened the New Deal of Franklin Roosevelt and helped to ensure the passage of legislation for the right to organize, the minimum wage, social security, unemployment compensation, and the eight-hour workday. The stalwarts of the 1930s generation taught and inspired civil rights workers in the 1950s, as well as activists of the movements of the 1960s, and are now part of the senior citizens' movement. Many of those who first joined the movements for peace and social justice during the turbulent sixties went on to become the leaders of the movements of the next three decades and are now mobilizing women; environmentalists; People of Color; Labor activists; citizen action activists; industrial, social, and agricultural workers; citizens with disabilities; and people struggling for peace, disarmament, social and economic justice, education, health, family issues, and the revitalization of the electoral system. Today, many of the children of the activists of the sixties are leaders of the antiglobalization and antisweatshop movements.

As the 1980s unfolded, a powerful grassroots Right Wing movement emerged. Cloaking itself in the legitimacy of religion and the flag while carrying out the political program of multinational corporations, this movement challenged us for the loyalty of Middle America. At the same time, many of the progressive forces fragmented, and some moved away from majority themes to issues that addressed the needs of more limited constituencies, again posing the old problem of how to defend particular interests while fighting collectively for common goals.

Today, it is clear that the Right Wing economic policies have failed. "Getting government off our backs" and "freeing business to do its job" merely intensify the loss of our industries and farms and their replacement with new low-wage jobs. While the Right destroys environmental protection, a tide of toxic chemicals, nuclear waste, pesticides, sewage, and garbage ruins the quality of life in communities across the country. Deregulation of the airlines leads to higher fares, worse service, and unsafe flights. Deregulated banks collapse in huge numbers and require massive bailouts with public money. Unbridled unregulated greed on Wall Street brings on an orgy of speculation. Our leading corporations are allowed to become truly transnational, and while they flood our markets with foreign products, they are not required to put back into this economy what they take out. Poverty goes unabated. Homelessness, hunger, and inequality rise. Drugs and crime reach epidemic levels, and indications are that the government itself has cooperated with international drug dealers to promote its foreign policy and even to finance unofficial wars.

The paragraphs above were written as a commentary on the 1980s, and it appears that little changed in the decade that followed. Yet we now stand at the start of the new millennium with far brighter prospects.

The tide of the ultra-Right has run out, at least for now, leaving disarray and disillusionment among many of its followers. While the Right searches for its next opening, official Liberalism is just coasting on the high economy. It has no particular plan or direction other than speeding free trade and deregulation. No talk is heard of a pending New Deal or a Great Society. No one is being asked to consider "what you can do for your country." There is no sense of seizing the moment to accomplish something really splendid. If Liberalism is abdicating leadership, then it is creating an opening for a new progressive movement.

The Right still holds one advantage, however. The Right thinks in terms of ideology while we progressives think in terms of issues. The Right Wing ideology holds that government is bad and ought to be done away with to the greatest extent possible. This leads to a simple, easy-to-understand program:

1. Cut the federal budget.
2. Cut the taxes that finance the budget.
3. Privatize government functions. (Vouchers)
4. Deregulate. (Utilities)
5. Foster states' rights legal challenges. (School prayer)

Within this framework Right Wing groups and individuals can take on whatever issues they like. It all leads to reducing government and, coincidentally, leaving corporate power uncontested.

Progressives, on the other hand, have no single overriding objective. Instead, thousands of non-profit groups compete with each other. Some fight for funding for education, others for healthcare; electric-car research; clean air, clean water, and toxic material removal; national forests; recycling; renewable energy; early childhood education; affordable housing; college scholarships; public transportation; social security; Medicaid; Alzheimer's research; heart research; cancer research; research on AIDS, blindness, deafness, arthritis, and developmental disabilities; preservation of endangered species; law enforcement; and much more. We advocate for the rights of women, African Americans, Latinos, gays, workers, Jews, people with disabilities, Asians, seniors, Arabs, the poor, the adopted, the undocumented, the unskilled, the underpaid, children, the unemployed, the sexually harassed, or those in prison. These are fine things to do, necessary things to do. We are not suggesting that anyone stop doing them. Indeed, this book is about how to do them better. We are saying only that a series of issues is not a social program. They may be the building blocks of a program, but even taken all together, they are not a program.

When we compare the program of the Right to the issues of the progressives, we are clearly looking at two totally different approaches to organizing and to the larger process of social change. Of course, we understand that certain values underlie our issues, but we don't organize to promote the values; we promote the issues, and in so doing we are less than we could be if we did both.

Today, everyone understands the meaning of slogans such as "shrink government," "get government off our backs," "fight bureaucracy" "states' rights," "federal interference," and the like. The Right has gotten them into the popular consciousness. Phrases such as "economic justice," "environmental justice," or "equality" are more poorly understood if they are heard at all. Although we are close to it, we are not yet expressing what we are for in a way that presents a broad social vision uniting the many strands of our organizing work. We need a vision with a name that everyone knows and a definition that everyone understands. We have yet to develop the organization or political party that people will join to promote the whole vision, not just its individual parts. These are the tasks for the new millennium.

Let us therefore resolve to focus on what unites us, to turn outward, to build broadly, to make ourselves the voice of the majority, and to always consider how what we are doing today leads to the next steps.

About This Book

This is a handbook on the fundamentals of direct action organizing. Direct action implies a majority strategy. Much of its power derives from the fear haunting all elected officials that they will be defeated at the polls by angry citizens, or a corporation's fear that it will face massive consumer pressure. This means that direct action works best with issues that a majority of the population would support or at least not actively oppose. Nonetheless, most of this book's guidelines for thinking and acting strategically and its recommendations on organizing skills are also useful for working on other, less popular, justice issues. We focus on direct action because we believe it is the best method for building local activist-based membership organizations as well as larger state and national coalitions.

Direct action is not the only form, or the only "correct" form, of organizing. Electoral, union, social service, public interest, advocacy, educational, and legal organizing all play a role in advancing progressive goals. The principles of direct action have applications in many other kinds of organizing, particularly electoral campaigns, advocacy, and union organizing.

We have no illusions that community-based organizations alone are sufficient to win lasting social change, no matter how strong or numerous they become. However, citizen organizations and electoral coalitions, statewide or national, need community-based strength and vitality at their roots if they are truly to represent their base and be able to win victories.

This book will use broadly applicable examples from different types of direct action organizations and issues. Readers who don't see their particular type of organization or issue mentioned should not assume that our approach does not apply to them. The sections on strategy, including criteria for choosing issues and mapping issue campaigns, can be directly applied to a wide range of constituencies, issues, and organizations from the local to the national level.

We treat issue organizing and elections as part of a single process. Although many organizations do not endorse candidates, an election is nonetheless part of the political environment in which an issue campaign takes place.

From this manual you will learn a systematic approach to the techniques of organizing, of building and using power, and of creating lasting institutions that are both self-defense organizations and avenues for citizen participation in public life. You can treat this volume like a cookbook and go directly to the chapter that has the recipe for whatever you are doing at the moment. We urge you not to do this, though, because you will miss the two underlying themes of the book: First, all aspects of organizing are related, making an organization the sum total of what it actually does, not of what you intended it to be at the start, and second, the real goals of organizing go beyond the immediate issues; they are to build the unity and power of all who want control over their own lives.

August 20, 2000

2

How many times have you heard an organizer say something like "People around here are so apathetic, no one wants to do anything." Yet if you walk around the block, you will find that everyone is out industriously doing what they need to do. Most are hard at work or going to school. A few are searching for deposit cans or hustling. Hardly any are apathetically sitting around waiting for good things to come to them. If organizers encounter people who seem apathetic, it is because we haven't been able to convince them that organizing is one way to get what they need. In fact, we usually don't know what they need because we don't understand their self-interest. For that reason, this chapter on the fundamentals of organizing starts with a discussion of self-interest.

Understanding Self-Interest

An underlying assumption behind direct action organizing is that you, the leader or organizer, are working with people who are primarily motivated by self-interest. That is, they are making the effort to organize in order to get something out of it for themselves, their families, or their community. The concept of self-interest also includes motivation by a sense of moral justice or by an ideology that

The Fundamentals of Direct Action Organizing

leads people to want to help the poor or to seek opportunities to fight racism, curb the power of transnational corporations, or protect the environment, among many other things.

Self-interest is one of the most important and misunderstood concepts in direct action organizing. It is sometimes thought of in the most narrow sense: people want more "stuff" and will organize to get it (often to get it away from someone else). But self-interest is actually a much broader concept. The word "interest" comes from the Latin *inter esse,* which means "to be among." (There is a similar word in Spanish.) So, self-interest is self among others. That is, where do my needs fit into those of the larger society?

The concept of self-interest applies to an individual's material needs, such as better housing, education, healthcare, or wages, but it also applies to the need for friends, for respect, for recognition, for being useful, for feeling important, or for feeling part of a larger community. Self-interest generalized is often class interest. Self-interest can mean the good feeling that comes from getting back at the landlord, standing up to the boss, or knocking an unaccountable politician out of office. Self-interest also applies across generational lines as people are motivated to fight for what helps their children or grandchildren. Self-interest, then, applies to what makes people feel good about themselves, as well as to what materially benefits them.

More broadly still, many people feel a need to take on the responsibilities of citizenship and to play a role in shaping public affairs. People want interaction with the larger community and often enjoy working collectively for the common good. Sometimes self-interest is a desire to work with people of a different race or culture in order to broaden one's own perspective or to combat prejudice. Other people may be drawn to an international project, such as fighting foreign sweatshops, because they want to make a global difference.

The point here is not to make a list of all the forms of self-interest and particularly not to imply that all of them apply to everyone. As an organizer, you can assume *nothing* about a person's self-interest that isn't actually expressed to you by that person. One of the worst mistakes an organizer can make is to say, "This is an issue about which everyone must care" or "This is an issue about which you must care because you are a _____ (vegetarian, ballet dancer—fill in the blank)." It is risky enough to act on what the polls tell you people care about. Caring is one thing; acting on it is quite another. Understanding self-interest is the key to getting people to take that step. Listening is an essential way for an organizer to learn what people's self-interest truly is. One-on-one interviews are an excellent way to get to know the values and concerns that motivate people. However you do it, organizing is the process of finding out what people want as individuals and then helping them find *collective* ways of getting it.

The Importance of Relationships

The personal is political: Organizing is overwhelmingly about personal relationships. It is about changing the world and changing how individuals act together. The relationships organizers develop are their most important resource and forming relationships their most important talent. To form good relationships, an organizer must like people. A good organizer is motivated by strong feelings of love and caring. This should not be forgotten because a good organizer is motivated as well by strong feelings of outrage and anger at how people are treated. Forming relationships with people is based on trust and respect. It is based on doing what you commit to do and being honest and straightforward in order to advance the members' goals through building an organization.

One's ability to build relationships reflects one's basic values. In the long term, you will be known by your values. Characteristics that will enable you to build strong relationships include

- Caring about others. People around you can tell if you really care about them or just view them as a means to do your job.

- Treating everyone respectfully, regardless of status or lack thereof. Those who are gracious only to the powerful will be noticed.

- Judging not. ("Judge not that ye be not judged.") Give everyone the benefit of the doubt. Try to understand why people act cer-

tain ways. Develop a reputation as someone who refuses to talk negatively about other people and other organizations. (It's OK to talk negatively about the target of your campaign; in fact, it's necessary.)

Relationships between organization members are also critical. The long-term lesson that successful direct action and Labor organizing teaches is that everyday people can make their own decisions, manage their own organizations, and rely on each other to work for the common good and that they can do it across lines of race, ethnicity, and gender. This is just the opposite of the view that we must all be guided by the economic and intellectual elite. All too often, a bad organizational experience reinforces the wrong lesson. Anyone who sets out to organize others should remember that the political implications go far beyond the immediate issues.

All organizing, then, is based on relationships and self-interest, broadly defined. With this foundation, we will proceed to the ways in which direct action organizing differs from other forms because not only is the personal political, the political is also political.

How Direct Action Differs from Other Types of Organizing

Different types of organizations are like different tools. Each tool is best suited to a particular task, although sometimes more than one tool will do the job. The main types of citizen organizations are shown in the chart:

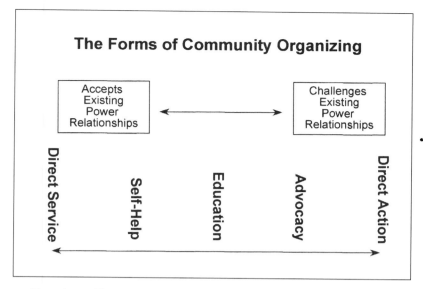

The Forms of Community Organizing

Accepts Existing Power Relationships ←——————→ Challenges Existing Power Relationships

Direct Service — Self-Help — Education — Advocacy — Direct Action

Here is an illustration of the differences using the example of unaffordable prescription drugs. People who can't afford prescription drugs could get them in many ways.

Direct Service. A service organization such as a senior organization could provide discounts to its members by buying in bulk.

Self-Help. People who need the drugs could form their own buying cooperatives to get lower prices.

Education. An education organization could do a study of the cost of prescription drugs or the lack of insurance coverage. A different type of education organization might prepare materials on how to find the lowest cost sources.

Advocacy. An organization might advocate for people who need prescription drugs—victims of a specific disease, for example—by giving testimony about the problem to a committee of Congress or the CEO of a pharmaceutical company. The people who need the prescription drugs might or might not know that an advocacy organization is doing this.

Public Interest. A public interest organization might go beyond advocacy and actually write the legislation for a state or national drug insurance plan that the group would attempt to get passed.

Neither the advocacy organization nor the public interest organization is necessarily made up of the people who actually have the problem, but it works on their behalf.

Direct Action. The people with the problem organize. They agree on a solution that meets their needs and, with the strength of their numbers, pressure the politicians and officials responsible. The people directly affected by the problem take action to solve it.

As the chart indicates, the forms of organizing on the left-hand side tend to accept existing power relationships as they are. The forms further to the right-hand side challenge power relationships.

The Three Principles of Direct Action

Direct action organizing is based on three principles that give it its character and distinguish it from other forms. These three principles will be referred to throughout the manual.

Win Real, Immediate, Concrete Improvements in People's Lives

SMART goals.

Whether the improvement is better health-care, lower auto insurance rates, street lighting, or police protection, the direct action organization attempts to win it for large numbers of people. Even when the problem being addressed is very large or long term—crime, unemployment, discrimination, or world hunger, for example—it must be broken down into short-term, attainable goals, called issues. Without winnable issue goals, there is no reality principle, no way to measure success. If the goal of an organization is educating people, changing the framework of their thinking, or working only for very long-term goals, there is rarely a way to measure progress or even to determine if it is relevant at all. How many people had their thinking changed and by how much? How do you know?

Give People a Sense of Their Own Power

Direct action organizations mobilize the power that people have. In doing so, they teach the value of united action through real-life examples, and they build the self-confidence of both the organization and the individuals in it. Direct action organizations avoid shortcuts that don't build people's power, such as bringing in a lawyer to handle the problem, asking a friendly politician to take care of it, or turning it over to a government agency. Giving people a sense of their own power is as much a part of the organizing goal as is solving the problem.

Alter the Relations of Power

Takes org to alter power relations

Building a strong, lasting, and staffed organization alters the relations of power. Once such an organization exists, people on the "other side" must always consider the organization when making decisions. When the organization is strong enough, it will have to be consulted about decisions that affect its members. The organization further strives to alter power relations by passing laws and regulations that give it power and by putting into public office its own people or close allies (although groups to which contributions are tax deductible are prevented by law from endorsing candidates). Winning on issues is never enough. The organization itself must be built up so that it can take on larger issues and play a political role.

Community and citizen organizations are democratic institutions; their very existence helps to make the whole system work better and opens avenues for ongoing participation. Without such democratic institutions, our concept of politics would be limited to voting every few years, a necessary but often uninspiring activity.

Building an organization is not a natural byproduct of good programs. Groups cannot assume that their organization will grow if they just win on issues. There is a difference between mobilizing people during a campaign and actually organizing them into an ongoing structure for which they take responsibility. Concrete plans must be made and steps taken to assure that the organization grows (e.g., money is raised and members are recruited and retained). This point is particularly important in light of the growing use of e-mail mobilization.

The question of the importance of direct service work, such as feeding the homeless or caring for the aged, comes up repeatedly when direct action organizing is discussed. Often the point of an issue campaign is to win just such programs. In general, we do not recommend combining service delivery with direct action in the same organization. Funding for the service often must come from sources such as a Mayor or County Executive, who are targets of direct action campaigns on issues that may be unrelated to the funding. The officials then use withdrawal of the funding as a threat against the organization, and it may well be lost. Often in such organizations, a split develops between those who see the service aspect as most important (or whose jobs depend on it) and those who see the direct action part of the program as being most important. Both are needed but not as functions of the same group.

How a Direct Action Organizing Issue Campaign Works

In organizing, the word "campaign" has many meanings. An *issue campaign* is waged to win a victory on a particular issue. It is different from an election campaign, which might happen to be fought on issues. It is also different from an education campaign to raise public awareness, a fundraising campaign to support a cause, or a service delivery campaign such as providing the homeless with shelter. An issue campaign ends in a specific victory. People get something they didn't have before. Someone with power agrees to do something that he or she previously refused to do. Implied in the word "campaign" is a series of connected events over a period of time, each of which builds the strength of the organization and brings it closer to victory. Few organizations are strong enough to win a major demand just by asking.

When used in organizing, the word "issue" has meaning that is different from everyday usage. *An issue is a specific solution to a problem.* For example, passing a law requiring sewage treatment is one solution to the problem of water pollution. The law is the issue. The distinction between the problem (what is wrong) and the issue (a solution to the problem) is made to keep the group focused on winning something and not merely expounding upon the problem. An issue campaign has a beginning, a middle, and an end. It is seldom a one-shot event, nor is it simply a series of events linked by a common theme. It is a method of building power and building organization.

The Use of Power in an Issue Campaign

Power generally consists of having a lot of money or a lot of people. Citizen organizations tend to have people, not money. Thus, our ability to win depends on our being able to do with people what the other side is able to do with money. For citizen organizations, power usually takes one of three forms:

1. *You Can Deprive the Other Side of Something It Wants.* Examples: A public official is directly or indirectly deprived of votes. A corporate executive is deprived of a promotion because you cost the company money when you forced a regulatory agency to come into the picture. A landlord is deprived of rent because of a rent strike. A city department head is deprived of a job when you show him or her to be incompetent. Conflict of interest is exposed, and corrupt people are deprived of the ability to do business as usual—or better, sent to jail.

2. *You Can Give the Other Side Something It Wants.* Examples: Senior citizens sign pledges to use a hospital that accepts Medicare assignment as payment in full. Your organization's approval counts with key groups of voters. Your voter registration work creates a base of support for specific issues or candidates.

3. *Your Organization Can Elect Someone Who Supports Your Issues.*

Often, having power means that your organization finds a way to stand on someone's foot until you are paid (by being given what you want) to go away. This isn't a shakedown, nor do we enjoy treating people in such a fashion. But the targets of these tactics are people who have shown a serious disregard for our well-being—or worse, are doing us actual harm.

Of course, a real-life issue campaign doesn't start out with high-pressure activities. It starts out with reasonable people asking nicely for things to which they feel entitled. Efforts are made to persuade on the merits, facts, and morality of the issue. It is after people are refused things, for which they shouldn't even have had to ask in the first place, that power must be applied.

A Tactical Guide to Power

While consulting with many groups over the years, we on the Midwest Academy staff have often heard organizers make shaky assumptions about the power of their own organizations. "We have people power." "We have consumer power." "The law is on our side." Such assumptions are made on the basis of principles that are true in general but that may not hold up when applied to a particular situation. Here are some brief guidelines for measuring the power that you actually have.

Political/Legislative Power: Getting Something Passed by an Elected Body

Many local groups work to pressure unelected government, administrators, or regulators to do what is needed. Their success depends, in large part, on how such people perceive the group's ability to bypass them and take the case directly to the elected officials who appoint them. It also depends on their estimation of the organization's ability to directly or indirectly influence the outcome of elections.

What matters:

- *Primarily:* Voters, especially those who care strongly enough about an issue to vote for candidates on the basis of their position on that issue.
- *Secondarily:* Money that can influence votes. Media that can influence votes.
- *Timing:* Most effective prior to an election.
- *Key Questions to Ask:*

  Regarding the legislative body as a whole:
  - Is the decision made in committee or by the leadership or on the floor?
  - If the decision is made by leadership, how strong are you in their home districts, are they seeking to run for higher office, and will they someday need votes in areas where you are strong?

  - If the decision is not made by leadership but by a vote, then you need half plus one of the voting members. Count up how many are firmly with you and how many will never support you. Look at who is left. Are there enough voting members for a majority? Where do they come from? Can you influence them?
  - Do term limits apply? How many people can't run again in the next election? (It is difficult to influence legislators who aren't running for re-election; that is why term limits is a profoundly antidemocratic idea. Increasingly, legislators simply run for the other house when limits are applied.)

  Regarding a single elected official
  - How close was the last election?
  - Is this seat usually contested?
  - What is the number of supporters you have in the district?
  - Are there organizations that might cooperate?
  - Whom can you get to lobby the elected official from among
    - Key contributors
    - Leaders of primary voting blocks
    - Religious and opinion leaders
    - Party leadership

Consumer Power: The Ability to Conduct a Boycott

What matters:

- *Primarily:* Cutting profits or demonstrating ability to cut profits by changing consumer choices.
- *Secondarily:* Media coverage that could influence purchasing.
- *Timing:* Most effective during times of stress for a company, such as during a merger, a strike, or tight financial times.
- *Key Questions to Ask:*
  - What is the company's profit margin?

- Is the company's market local, regional, national, or international?
- Who, or what, really owns the company?
- Can you really hurt profits?

Legal/Regulatory Power: The Ability to Win in Court or in a Regulatory Process

What matters:

- *Primarily:* Clear laws and tight regulations.
- *Secondarily:* Money for lawyers, volunteer lawyers, or the ability to get a public agency to carry the case for you. Media to make it a political issue.
- *Timing:* Must be prepared to carry on for several years. Sometimes you do this to delay and actually want the process to last many years.
- *Key Questions to Ask:*
  - Are laws or regulations clearly on your side?
  - Have similar cases been won elsewhere?
  - What are the politics of the judges or regulators who will hear the case? Who appointed them?
  - What are the extra costs (e.g., fees for experts or duplicating thousand-page transcripts)? Who pays?

Strike/Disruptive Power

What matters:

- *Primarily*: Cutting profits or income by stopping a company or agency from functioning.
- *Timing*: Most effective during times of stress for a company or agency. such as during a merger, boycott, or tight financial times.
- *Key Questions to Ask:*
  - What is the company's profit margin?
  - Can you make a significant dent by stopping work (strikes) or disrupting work or customers (usually by civil disobedience)? How costly will it be to replace you or get rid of you?

- Do you have a strike fund sufficient to outlast the company by one day?
- Do you have people willing to get arrested and money to bail them out ?

Illusions about Power

All too often, groups believe that they will win because

- They are morally right.
- Truth is on their side.
- They have the best information and it is all spelled correctly.
- They speak for large numbers of people.

Of course we need all of these working in our favor, but very often our opponents who have none of them win anyway. What matters is the ability to bring direct pressure on decision makers. When we claim to speak for large numbers, we need to show that we can mobilize those people and that they respond to us through rallies and demonstrations, letter-writing campaigns, petitions, and their ballots. At the same time, we need to avoid another common misconception about power, which is that everyday people can never gain power over special interests and large corporations. Underestimating our power is as bad as overestimating it. It is true that the larger battle to secure economic justice and to end exploitation will take the mobilization of forces that cannot even be conceived of today. Nonetheless, we can and do win smaller issues when we mobilize what power we now have.

The Stages of an Issue Campaign

Power is built through issue campaigns. Campaigns last for various lengths of time, and an organization can, by carefully choosing its issue, influence the length of its campaigns. Frequently, new organizations want short campaigns and sometimes choose relatively "fixed fights" for their first issues. They ask for information that they know they are entitled to, or they ask for something to be done that probably would have been done anyway but at a later date. The purpose of the fight is to have a visible win. These quick victories build up the members' confidence in their ability to accomplish something and also gain public recognition for the new organization. Later, longer campaigns, say, of six months' duration, provide an opportunity to recruit volunteers, build a committee structure, or give the organization's leadership experience. Issue campaigns may be timed either to coincide with elections or to avoid them.

Both long and short issue campaigns go through a series of steps, although shorter campaigns involve fewer tactics than described below.

1. *Choose the Issue and Develop a Strategy.* The people who have a problem agree on a solution and how to get it. They may decide to define, or "cut," the issue narrowly: "Make our landlord give us back our rent deposits when we move out." Or they may define it more broadly: "Make the City Council pass a law requiring the return of rent deposits." The strategy is the overall plan for winning the issue, building the organization, and changing the relations of power. A strategy is always about a power equation. It is how you assess the strengths and weaknesses of the target/decision maker. (See chapter 4.)

2. *Open Communication with the Target.* Next, communications are opened with the person who has the power to give the group what it wants. Requests are made and arguments are presented. At this point, the problem is sometimes resolved and the organization's requests

are met. When they are not resolved, however, the person with the power becomes the "target" of an issue campaign. The target, or "decision maker," is always the person who has the power to give you what you want. (If no one has such power, then you haven't cut the issue correctly.)

A decision maker is always a person. It is never an institution such as the government, the corporation, the bank, the legislature, the board, or the agency. Break it down. Even the most powerful institutions are made up of people. Having already addressed the institution itself through official channels, the campaign now moves outside that framework to focus pressure on one or more individuals who make up the institution and have the power to give you what you want. These people are actually the institution's weak point. As individuals, they have goals, aspirations, and interests that don't coincide completely with those of the institution. For example, the state insurance commission may be set up to support the industry, but the commissioner may hope to run for Governor someday and thus want to establish the appearance of independence.

3. *Announce the Campaign.* Frequently, a media event announces the start of the campaign. A study may be released, or people may simply tell of their experiences and their efforts to correct the problem. If the campaign is to be a coalition effort, then most of the coalition's member organizations need to sign on to the campaign before the announcement and be present at the event.

(Note: A coalition is an organization of organizations. The Coalition for Interspecies Relationships does not become a true coalition because one member owns a hamster and another a turtle. Even if the members *are* hamsters and turtles, this is still not a true coalition. Only if the coalition is made up of *organizations* of hamsters and turtles, or *organizations* of their owners, is it a real coalition.)

4. *Begin Outreach Activities.* Because every campaign is an opportunity to reach new people, outreach activities are started now. In a statewide or national campaign, other organizations may be enlisted. When the organization has a local focus, individuals and local groups are brought in. Often a petition drive is used both to find supporters and to build a group of active volunteers who circulate the petition. Speakers may be sent out to meetings of groups such as senior clubs, unions, churches, or PTAs (Parent-Teacher Associations). The kickoff of each of these activities can be a press event in itself, at least in smaller cities where press is easier to get.

The outreach drive builds toward a large turnout event such as a public hearing sponsored by the organization. The event establishes legitimacy and brings in more allies and volunteers. It is also fun and a media event.

5. *Stage Direct Encounters with Decision Makers.* Now the organization is ready for direct encounters with the people who have the power to give it what it wants. Large face-to-face meetings (sometimes called "actions") are set up with the decision maker. At this stage, the organization members carefully consider what power the organization has over the decision maker. It usually has more power over elected officials than over appointed ones, and it usually has more power over anyone in government than in private

[handwritten: where do you start Chief or Councilman?]

corporations, unless the corporations are heavily dependent on local customers.

Although several months may have passed, it is still early in the campaign, and the group is probably too weak to challenge its main decision-maker directly. Attention thus shifts to "secondary targets." These are people over whom the organization has more power than it has over the main target. In turn, the secondary target has more power over the main target than does the organization. For example, the Mayor might be the main target and the local ward leader the secondary target. Because the organization's members are a large percentage of the voters in the ward leader's district but only a small percentage of the voters in a citywide election, the organization usually has more power over the locally elected official than over the one elected citywide. And because the local official helps to get the Mayor elected, she has more influence at City Hall than does the group. The organization therefore puts pressure on the ward leader to get her to pressure the Mayor to meet the group's demands. (The terminology of organizing is often confusing on this point. The "secondary target" is not the same as the second target, the person to whom you would go second when you are done seeing the person to whom you went

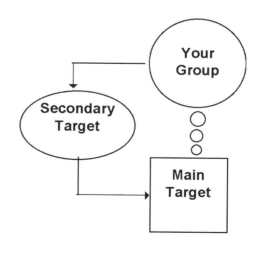

first. A better term for secondary target might be "indirect target"—that is, a person to whom you go to put pressure on someone else indirectly.)

6. *Build the Organization.* A series of meetings with secondary targets builds support for the issue. Each meeting is an opportunity to recruit new supporters, train spokespersons, and try for media coverage. Such meetings are also fun. To demonstrate power, an elected official might be shown more signatures on petitions than the number of votes by which she won in the last election. The Director of a local Housing Authority might be told that he is in violation of HUD (Housing and Urban Development) regulations or local building codes and that outside agencies will be called in to investigate if he doesn't make repairs. At this stage, real power is shown, not just good arguments and facts. (Not every event needs to be a direct confrontation. A community parade, picnic, or even a party to celebrate a victory can also build the group and become a show of numbers. Invite allied elected officials to join you.) But the main reason for holding such events is often to develop the strength of the organization.

Every planning session for an event should include a discussion of how to use the event to build the group. Often people become so focused on what they will say to the decision maker that organization building is forgotten. Planning to build the organization must be specific. How many new people will be recruited, where, how, and by whom? Must the event be held after six o'clock so that working people can come? Must it be before three so that mothers of school-age children can come? How will new people be integrated into the group? How will all the members be told what happened? Perhaps a telephone tree

should be activated or an evening leaflet distribution planned. In general, each event should be larger than the last one. If this isn't happening, then you are not building the organization. Another measure of organizational strength is the experience level of its leaders and members. A local organization that can hold two events at the same time is quite well developed. Plan leadership training into each event. This means practice beforehand and evaluate afterward.

In the course of the issue campaign an election may occur. This offers the organization a fine opportunity to build more strength. (The events described so far have probably taken four to five months to unfold.) During the election season, the organization may do some combination of the following:

- Hold a candidates' night and ask candidates to take a position on the organization's issue. This can be done even if the winner of the election can't really give the group what it wants. Candidates take *symbolic* positions supporting all sorts of things, and an angle for real support can usually be found as well. Members can also attend candidates' nights sponsored by other groups and raise the issue there.

- Allied candidates can be asked to campaign on the issue and mention it in their literature (if it is cut broadly enough to really win votes).

- The organization can register voters as a show of strength in specific areas.

- Some organizations, depending on their IRS (Internal Revenue Service) tax status, can make endorsements and campaign for or against candidates. Others can't.

7. *Win or Regroup.* After a series of successful buildup events, the organization takes on the main decision maker. Sometimes this is done

in an action or confrontation and sometimes in a negotiation. Often a victory is won or a compromise is reached. If not, the organization must be prepared to escalate its tactics. This may mean large demonstrations and picketing, a return to other secondary targets, or the selection of a new main target. Sometimes the issue has to be broadened to attract still more supporters and the campaign taken to a new level. The refusal of a locality to control toxic dumping can lead, for example, to a broader fight for statewide legislation or enforcement. At other times, the organization may decide that it has reached the limit of its strength and that it will have to lower its demand and accept less.

At each of these stages, the organization is being strengthened internally in addition to power being built. The leadership is growing and gaining experience, skill, and media recognition. The membership is growing. Other organizations are moving into closer alliance. Money is being raised. The staff is becoming experienced in organizing and electoral tactics.

Tricks the Other Side Uses

In the years since this manual was first published, citizen organizations have grown more experienced and more creative. At the same time, our opponents have become more skillful at countering our efforts. Here are some of their tricks.

"Let's negotiate." Often, what your opponents most want is to get you to stop organizing in the community and to start spending hours sitting around a table with them. Of course, they say, you can't add new people as the negotiations progress because new people wouldn't know the background. Of course you don't want to talk to the press or anyone else because that would be a breach of confidence. Of course you have to stop doing actions and public events because that creates a bad atmosphere for the negotiations. The campaign comes to a stop. Meanwhile, weeks go by. You lose momentum. Your opponents hire negotiators to sit and talk with you while you must burn up the time of your leaders and organizers. The members who are not "at the table" feel left out and are sure that some awful sellout is developing when they hear you referring to your opponents by their first names. Allies begin to draw back.

What's wrong with this picture? What's wrong is that you began negotiations with no power. Negotiations, by definition, are what goes on between parties of equal power, each of whom has something the other party wants and each of whom is prepared to give up something in order to get something. If that is the real situation, then fine, keep negotiating. In fact, most direct action campaigns do end in some form of negotiation after the organization has actually won. However, when the offer to negotiate comes early in the campaign, it is usually just a tactic to delay and to divide you. It also gives your opponents a chance to size you up, find the weaknesses in your coalition, and buy off your leadership.

"You are invited to the 'stakeholders' meeting." We have seen this one a lot in recent years. Consumer and environmental groups are invited by representatives of the Governor, or a department of the state, to participate in a long series of meetings with other "stakeholders," including representatives of business or industry and state agencies. The goal, you are told, is to frame legislation that will "please everyone" on a particular issue. Why are you invited? Why do they care if you are pleased or not? They don't! They are simply buying your silence for a year, which is about how long it would take to prepare the legislation anyway. You play by their rules in

the hope of getting some small measure of your program into the legislation. You may even succeed, but meanwhile, the time is lost during which you could have been out mobilizing people or spreading the alarm. Then the bill goes to the legislature, but not having built your base during the negotiations, you are unprepared for the fight. Some of your people want to support the bill because of the crumbs you have been given and because they worked so hard on it. Others want to oppose it because the crumbs don't deal with the big picture.

Here is the test of whether you should participate in a process of this type. Tell whoever invites you that you will go to the meetings but that you intend to continue your public campaign on the issue and that because you represent a citizen watchdog group, nothing can be confidential. In fact, you feel it is your *duty* to make public anything and everything you hear at the meetings. If the invitation still stands and you are really able to conduct a public campaign at the same time, then go and participate. An inside/outside strategy can be very powerful if you use the information you get at the "stakeholders" meeting to fuel your campaign. Just remember—and we say this because so many have forgotten—when you get into a room with powerful corporations, you are not one stakeholder among equals and never will be.

"I can get you on the Governor's commission." Commissions, study groups, round tables, and panels exist at every level of government. Many are established to genuinely promote discussions of public policy and reach consensus. Once your organization succeeds in applying pressure to elected officials, it is likely to get offered seats on some such body. Ask yourself, is our opinion genuinely desired, or is this a ploy to swing us over to an insider strategy (trying to influence from within instead of pressuring from without)? Is this yet another way to tie us up in endless deliberations? Sometimes you will be asked not to discuss the work of the commission publicly or even not to comment on its direction. Months can be spent producing a report that then comes to nothing. Your group can be divided between people who think that they are now really making policy and those who want to work independently.

"Go work it out among yourselves." Perhaps you are interested in a patient bill of rights. "So are a lot of other groups," says the chair of the legislative committee, and, "We don't want to bring a bill to the floor and have it lose. So get together with the other interested parties and come up with something you all agree on." The next thing you know, you are meeting with representatives of industry and professional societies, groups over which you have absolutely no power. The elected officials, over whom you do have power, have conveniently gotten rid of you, even though they are the only ones who can actually give you what you want. Your job is to force them to do the right thing or else to get them thrown out of office, not to compromise away your position in meetings with people whose interests are opposed to yours.

"I'm the wrong person." You might be told, "I would love to help you, but I'm not the right person to see." This response is usually a shabby trick to make you feel stupid for having not known whom to see. Often it is the start of a process in which no one will admit to being the right person and you will get sent from one official to the next. The Police will say it is a Parks Department problem. The Parks Department will say it's really a Traffic Department problem, and so on. Some groups have responded by holding a community meeting and inviting all of the "wrong" people. Once they're in the same room, it is harder for them to pass the buck. Usually, though, this response indicates that you are talking

to appointed rather than elected officials. The City Council member from your neighborhood may not alone be able to deliver what you want but can't claim to be the "wrong person."

"*This could affect your funding*." Perhaps this line ought not be listed under "tricks" because it may very well be true. Organizations that receive money from any level of government, often in the form of a contract for some community service or education program, will quickly have the money taken away if they "rock the boat." It is very difficult to combine service and direct action in the same organization. Often these two functions need to be divided out. Foundations will also pull your funding if you venture into policy areas of which they do not approve.

"*You are reasonable but your allies aren't. Can't we just deal with you?*" This should be seen for just what it is, an attempt to divide your coalition and make you think you will win something if you dump your more militant partners.

A consultant speaking to a group of corporate executives once laid out how this trick works:

"Activists fall into three basic categories: radicals, idealists, and realists. The first step is to isolate and marginalize the radicals. They're the ones who see inherent structural problems that need remedying if indeed a particular change is to occur. To isolate them, try to create the perception in the public mind that people advocating fundamental solutions are terrorists, extremists, fear mongers, outsiders, communists, or whatever. After marginalizing the radicals, then identify and educate the idealists—concerned and sympathetic members of the public—by convincing them that changes advocated by the radicals would hurt people.

The goal is to sour the idealists on the idea of working with the radicals. Instead, get them working with the realists. Realists are people who want reform but don't really want to upset the status quo; big public-interest organizations that rely on foundation grants and corporate contributions are a prime example. With correct handling, realists can be counted on to cut a deal with industry that can be touted as a 'win-win' solution but that is actually an industry victory."

3

Problems Are Different from Issues

In direct action organizing, there is a difference between an issue and a problem. A *problem* is a broad area of concern. For example, unaffordable healthcare, pollution, racism, and unemployment are all problems. An *issue* is a solution or partial solution to a problem. National healthcare, green energy, affirmative action, and a federal jobs program are all issues.

Defining a Solution to the Problem

Because direct action organizing is about winning issues, the first step is to analyze the problem and decide what kind of solution to work toward. Some people have the luxury of choosing the problems on which they work. For others, the problem chooses them and can't be avoided no matter how long or difficult the effort. Drugs, an oil spill, or racial discrimination are examples of problems that choose people. In both cases, however, organizations and individuals must still choose the issue. That is, they must define the solution to the problem.

Many approaches can be taken to solving any problem, and the implications of each must be thought through carefully. It isn't enough to ask

Choosing an Issue

which is the most far-reaching solution (or for that matter, which is the most serious problem).

Cutting the Issue

Equally as important is "cutting the issue," that is, deciding how to frame the issue in a way that will gain the most support. For example, an organization was working to get the city to build more low-income housing. The group members realized that if they demanded housing only for people with the greatest need, those with the lowest incomes, they couldn't gain the necessary political support. Instead, they spoke of "affordable" housing and wrote their proposed bill to benefit lower wage working people in addition to the poor. Because the construction would create many jobs, some of which could go to community people, they called their campaign the "Affordable Housing and Jobs Campaign." They won $750 million for housing over five years, which represented a 50 percent increase. Money was targeted for very low income families. The program was so successful that the Mayor proposed a five-year extension.

An organization in a conservative farm state was working for a program to foster the development of electricity from wind power. Its members could have spoken of this as a purely environmental issue stressing the air quality benefits of burning less coal. However, other groups had tried and had not made progress on that basis. Instead, the organization talked about the economic benefits of using a native resource, wind, instead of importing out-of-state coal. They said that the money spent on importing coal should be kept in the local economy, and they highlighted the advantages to farmers of being able to rent out their land for wind turbines. The first commercial wind turbines in the state are now in operation.

An organization was working to have a vast tract of timberland converted into a national park. The issue was cut as one of restoring the woods to their former beauty, but much of the local population sided with the timber companies against the environmentalists. Had the organization been more sensitive to people's fear of job loss, they could have shown that the cutting practices of the timber companies would inevitably lead to the end of both the sawmill and logging jobs, whereas a national park would create a whole new tourist industry. What's more, the park could be developed in stages so that those currently employed in logging could remain so for many years.

The Impact of the Issue on the Organization

The organizational implications of any approach must be carefully thought through. To put it another way, think organizationally. Ask: What impact will taking up this issue have on our organization? What will happen to the organization if we ignore the problem? Don't think only about problems and solutions.

The ability of leaders to think *organizationally* in addition to thinking about *issues* is a major factor in the group's development. It is also a major cause of internal friction between members who come at things from these two different directions. In general, new members are attracted to an organization because of the issues and are not particularly conscious of the structure and mechanics of organizing. One volunteer in a neighborhood organization, after three months of faithfully coming twice a week to the office to make phone calls, looked up and asked, "What did you say the name of this group was?" She was probably asked the question by someone on the phone, but it was nonetheless the first step toward thinking organizationally.

Members who think only about issues are often frustrated by the amount of time and effort that goes into organizational maintenance. Occasionally you will hear leaders accused of being "empire builders." While that may be the case, more often they are organization builders being criticized by someone who hasn't yet learned to value organization. An organization is able to win victory after victory, to protect victories already won from being taken away, and to build political power so that winning becomes easier. Building an organization and winning issues are two interdependent sides of the same process.

It is necessary to consider the impact of the issue on the organization separately from the social value of the issue itself. For any given organization at a particular stage in its development, some issues will be better for organizational development and more winnable than others. For example, a group trying to get a progressive income tax law through the state legislature found that it lacked a sufficient base in the legislative districts to pass the bill. It put the state bill temporarily on hold and, in order to build local committees, shifted to more winnable city and county tax issues. This detour, while necessary, created two challenges. The members who joined to work for the state bill had to be reoriented to a local issue, and, in the future, people who joined because of their interest in the local issues will have to be refocused on the state bill. This example also shows how the choice of issue can change the nature of the organization.

Evaluating Issues

The following checklist is an aid for evaluating issues. We recommend that before a group starts to choose among issues, the members be asked, "What are the criteria for a good issue for our organization?" List what people say on a blackboard or large sheet of paper and try to develop a mutually agreed upon list similar to this one. The choice of an issue will be made much easier, and it will be a sounder choice as well.

A good issue is one that matches most of these criteria. The issue should

1. **Result in a Real Improvement in People's Lives**

    If you can see and feel the improvement, then you can be sure that it has actually been won. For example, a transit rider organization won a commitment for more frequent equipment inspections. Perhaps this led to improved service over a period of years but perhaps not. Riders could not tell. On the other hand, when the group asked for and won printed train schedules, they had a visible victory and also a performance standard to which they could hold the Transit Authority accountable.

2. Give People a Sense of Their Own Power

People should come away from the campaign feeling that the victory was won by them, not by experts, lawyers, or politicians. This builds both their confidence to take on larger issues and their loyalty to the organization. The word "empowerment" is often used in this context, but actually it implies a different concept. Empowerment implies giving people power, but only someone very powerful, surely not an organizer, has power to give away. Citizens either have power in a particular situation or they don't. If they do, they can be made aware of it. If they don't, they can be shown how to gain it. It is very rarely given to them.

3. Alter the Relations of Power

Power relations between citizens and decision makers can be changed in three ways:

- Building a strong, ongoing staffed organization to create a new center of power that changes the way the other side makes decisions.
- Changing laws and regulations in ways that increase our power or diminish that of the other side.
- Electing people to office who support our positions.

4. Be Worthwhile

Members should feel that they are fighting for something about which they feel good and that merits the effort. It is better to end the campaign having won less than you wanted than to scale back your demands from the start and ask for too little. Groups often make this mistake in the name of "realism" when they depend on the advice of professional lobbyists or elected officials who know how to measure the legislative support for a particular measure but don't understand the ability of grassroots pressure to change the picture.

5. Be Winnable

The problem must not be so large or the solution so remote that the organization is overwhelmed. The members must be able to see from the start that they have a good chance of winning, or at least a good strategy exists for winning. Ask who else has won on a similar issue and how. Then call on people with experience and ask for advice. Ask what their strategy was, not just what they did.

It is useful to figure out how much money your victory will cost the people on the other side. Will their additional non-monetary costs make them want to hold out against you? This gives you an idea of how hard they will work to defeat you and how much money they are likely to spend.

6. Be Widely Felt

Many people must feel that this is a real problem and must agree with your solution. It is not enough that a few people feel strongly about it.

7. Be Deeply Felt

Some people must not only agree with you but feel strongly enough to do something about it. It is not enough that many people agree about the issue if none feel strongly.

8. Be Easy to Understand

It is preferable that you don't have to convince people that the problem exists, that your solution is good, and that they want to help win it. However, such convincing is sometimes necessary, particularly with those environmental issues where the source of the problem can't be seen or smelled, or with economic problems where the basic cause is not always obvious. In general, a good issue does not require a lengthy and difficult explanation. One should simply be able to say something like "Look at all those dead fish floating in the water. That didn't happen before the chemical plant opened."

9. Have a Clear Target—Decision Maker

The target, or decision maker as he or she is often called, is the person who can give you what you want. A more difficult campaign usually requires several clear targets. This allows the campaign a longer time to build up strength, even if some of the targets refuse your demands in the early months. If you can't figure out who the decision maker is, either you don't have the right issue or you may be addressing a problem, not an issue. Remember that the decision maker is always a person or a number of people, such as the Mayor, not an institution, corporation, or elected body. The public is never the target. The Mayor, not the public, can give what you want.

10. Have a Clear Time Frame That Works for You

An issue campaign has a beginning, a middle, and an end. You should have an idea of the approximate dates on which those points will fall.

Some key dates for events are *internal*, that is, set by your organization. Some are *external*, set by someone else. The timetable of a campaign to win legislation is almost entirely external, as is the timetable of an election. The timetable for a campaign to get a stop sign in your community is almost totally internal.

Do the dates of major efforts in your campaign fall at particularly difficult parts of the year, such as mid-August or Christmas week? The spring and fall are best for most groups in most places.

Even if your organization does not have specific electoral goals, you want the time frame to fit the electoral calendar. You usually have more power just before an election than just after one. Consider how the issue's timetable can be aligned with the electoral timetable.

11. Be Non-Divisive

Avoid issues that divide your present constituency. Don't pit neighbor against neighbor, old against young, race against race. Don't be content to get traffic or the local drug pusher off your block and onto the next block. (This is not just being "liberal"; both will soon be back on your doorstep.)

Look down the road several years. Whom will you eventually need to bring into your organization? Will this issue help or hinder you in reaching them?

12. Build Leadership

The campaign should have many roles that people can play. Issue campaigns that meet most of the other criteria also build leadership if they are planned to do so. In a coalition organization, building leadership has a different meaning than in a neighborhood group because the people who represent organizations in the coalition already are leaders. They don't need or want you to develop them. Often, however, they do need to learn to work with each other, to use direct action, and to align electoral and issue campaigns where appropriate.

13. Set Up Your Organization for the Next Campaign

A campaign requiring employers to provide health insurance leads to new campaigns on other health issues or employee benefits. On the other hand, a campaign to make the city catch stray dogs generally leads only to catching stray dogs. People who have problems paying for healthcare are likely to have other economic problems in common. People whose link to each other is a dislike of stray dogs may not have a second issue in common and will fall to arguing when the dogs are gone.

In addition to thinking about future issue directions, consider the skills the group will develop in the campaign and the contacts it will make for the next one.

14. Have a Pocketbook Angle

Issues that gain people money or save people money are usually widely and deeply felt.

15. Raise Money

One big test of an issue is whether your constituents will contribute to the campaign. Also ask, What problem is the hot item in the foundation world? It changes almost from year to year.

16. Be Consistent with Your Values and Vision

The issues we choose to work on must reflect our values and our vision. For example, we do want less crime, but is an endlessly increasing number of police and prisons the direction in which we want our society to go?

In addition to these, you may very well have organization-specific criteria. For example, if your area has many new Latino residents who are not represented in your organization, one criterion may be that the issue have strong appeal to the Latino community.

After developing your list of criteria, review the issues under consideration. Some issues will drop from the list very quickly. For the remaining two or three, indicate whether each criterion has a high, medium, or low application to the issue. Then, take a vote. Of course you can always work on the second most popular issue after you win the first, but if the vote is close, more discussion may be needed to avoid splitting the group. In general, at least two-thirds of the group needs to be enthusiastic about any issue chosen.

Checklist for Choosing an Issue

A good issue is one that matches most of these criteria. Use this checklist to compare issues, or develop your own criteria and chart for choosing an issue.

Issue 1	Issue 2	Issue 3	Will the Issue
			1. Result in a real improvement in people's lives?
			2. Give people a sense of their own power?
			3. Alter the relations of power?
			4. Be worthwhile?
			5. Be winnable?
			6. Be widely felt?
			7. Be deeply felt?
			8. Be easy to understand?
			9. Have a clear target?
			10. Have a clear time frame that works for you?
			11. Be non-divisive?
			12. Build leadership?
			13. Set your organization up for the next campaign?
			14. Have a pocketbook angle?
			15. Raise money?
			16. Be consistent with your values and vision?

© Midwest Academy

28 E. Jackson Blvd. #605, Chicago, IL 60604

(312) 427-2304   mwacademy1@aol.com   www.midwestacademy.com

The word "strategy" is so much in use these days that it can mean almost anything. Little children are taught "strategies" for shoe tying and later for doing homework. As life progresses, we learn "strategies" for success in marriage, finding work, Chinese cooking, and breeding tropical fish. No wonder the word is confusing. Even in the more limited arena of citizen organizing, the language often causes confusion. People talk about a "media strategy," a "legal strategy," an "electoral strategy," or a "public education strategy," but all of these are actually tactics, not strategies. We can use the media, the courts, the electoral system, or public education as specific ways to apply pressure to someone, but a strategy is the design of the campaign combined with an analysis of power relationships. Tactics are the individual steps in carrying out a strategy.

In direct action organizing, "strategy" is given a more precise definition.

Strategy
An approach to making a government or corporate official do something in the public interest that he or she does not otherwise wish to do.

The Difference between a Strategy and a Plan

If your objective is anything other than making an official do something, then you don't need a *strategy*; you only need a *plan*. The difference is that a plan is about the steps you will need to take for any project, while a strategy is about the relationship of power between you and the official. In fact, the word "strategy" comes from the Greek *strategos,* meaning the rank of General in the army.

Developing a Strategy

Whatever you are trying to win, or however you want an elected official to vote on a bill, it is always better if the decision maker voluntarily agrees and doesn't need to be pressured. For that reason, the initial tactics in any campaign usually start with writing a letter and trying to have a meeting and a conversation. Explain how the facts are on your side, why you are morally right, and how much people need the change you are advocating. Even talk about how much it will advance the elected official's career to see the matter your way. Sometimes this works. Often it does not.

When persuasion fails, it may be because the decision maker simply holds a strong opinion that is contrary to yours, but more often, it is because as you were going into his or her office, another group was coming out that was applying pressure from the opposite side. More than likely, the other group represented some private interest. As much as public officials like to pretend that they make up their own minds on policy issues, they are usually bowing to the wishes of special interests that can spend large sums of money to get what they want. When pressure is applied to prevent justice from being done, we must apply counterpressure to ensure that justice prevails. For this, you need more than a plan; you need a strategy.

A strategy is the overall design for building the power to compel someone to give your organization what it wants. Short-term strategies can cover a period of days or weeks; long-term strategies can continue for many years.

The strategy chart that follows is an extremely useful tool for campaign planning. It lends itself both to overall campaign strategy and to planning of specific tactics such as a public hearing or an accountability session with an elected official. (Yes, you can have a smaller strategy for carrying out a particular tactic.) The chart is valuable as the focal point of a group planning process because it poses the necessary questions in a logical order and moves people through the planning process step by step.

When *Not* to Use the Chart

The chart is intended for campaigns aimed at winning something from someone. It is not useful for election campaigns or referenda where the goal is to get a majority of voters to vote a certain way or for educational campaigns the goals of which are to get people to think a certain way. If, when using the chart, you find yourself writing "the public" or "voters" in the Targets column, you are probably using the chart for the wrong purpose. The chart is also not intended for dealing with the internal problems of your own organization, where its use will exacerbate conflict and lead to a major meltdown.

Preparing to Make a Chart

Developing a strategy chart assumes that your group has already chosen an issue (see previous chapter). In your strategy planning meetings, display the chart prominently on a blackboard or large sheet of paper in the front of the room. Have the following resources on hand to complement the chart:

1. A large map of the area, city, or state in which the campaign will take place. Critical relationships often exist among issues, groups, neighborhoods, geography, and political districts that become apparent only when you look at a map.
2. Overlays for the map (or separate district maps) to show political districts.
3. Election returns for relevant races for the last several years. Knowing voting patterns and totals in primaries and general elections is important to understanding the strength of allies and opponents, even if your organization is not involved in electoral work.
4. When the decision maker, or target, is a member of an elected body it is necessary to have

someone on hand who knows how that body is actually organized internally and how it works. For example, does your City Council member really have any influence or the ability to move a bill, or is he or she just one vote among many?
5. The Yellow Pages to identify potential constituent and opponent organizations.
6. A list of your own board members and, if you are a coalition, your affiliates by address. This suggests people to involve at different points in the campaign.
7. Someone who knows the major institutions in the area, major employers, banks, corporations, public buildings, etc.

Allow several hours to systematically go through the chart, filling in the required information. Some groups take half a day or longer. A good facilitator is important.

If the group is large, split into a few smaller groups. Ask each group to develop a strategy and then incorporate the best ideas from each group in the final chart.

The Five Columns of the Strategy Chart

There are five major strategy elements to consider. Each has a column to fill in on the chart.
1. Long-Term, Intermediate, and Short-Term Goals
2. Organizational Considerations
3. Constituents, Allies, and Opponents
4. Targets (who can give you what you want)
5. Tactics

At first glance, the chart appears to be a series of lists. What we are unable to show on paper, but what becomes clear when you actually use the chart in planning, is that it is more like a computer

Midwest Academy Strategy Chart

After choosing your issue, fill in this chart as a guide to developing strategy. Be specific. List all the possibilities.

Goals	Organizational Considerations	Constituents, Allies, and Opponents	Targets	Tactics
1. List the long-term objectives of your campaign. 2. State the intermediate goals for this issue campaign. What constitutes victory? *How will the campaign* • Win concrete improvement in people's lives? • Give people a sense of their own power? • Alter the relations of power? 3. What short-term or partial victories can you win as steps toward your long-term goal?	1. List the resources that your organization brings to the campaign. Include money, number of staff, facilities, reputation, canvass, etc. What is the budget, including in-kind contributions, for this campaign? 2. List the specific ways in which you want your organization to be strengthened by this campaign. Fill in numbers for each: • Expand leadership group • Increase experience of existing leadership • Build membership base • Expand into new constituencies • Raise more money 3. List internal problems that have to be considered if the campaign is to succeed.	1. Who cares about this issue enough to join in or help the organization? • Whose problem is it? • What do they gain if they win? • What risks are they taking? • What power do they have over the target? • Into what groups are they organized? 2. Who are your opponents? • What will your victory cost them? • What will they do/spend to oppose you? • How strong are they?	1. Primary Targets A target is always a person. It is never an institution or elected body. • Who has the power to give you what you want? • What power do you have over them? 2. Secondary Targets • Who has power over the people with the power to give you what you want? • What power do you have over them?	For each target, list the tactics that each constituent group can best use to make its power felt. Tactics must be • In context. • Flexible and creative. • Directed at a specific target. • Make sense to the membership. • Be backed up by a specific form of power. Tactics include • Media events • Actions for information and demands • Public hearings • Strikes • Voter registration and voter education • Lawsuits • Accountability sessions • Elections • Negotiations

© Midwest Academy

28 E. Jackson Blvd. #605, Chicago, IL 60604

(312) 427-2304   mwacademy1@aol.com   www.midwestacademy.com

spreadsheet. Whenever you change anything in one column, corresponding changes need to be made in the others. For example, adding another goal may require finding a different type of constituent group that would employ a different tactic against a new target. Mathematical relationships also exist in the chart. Goals must equal power, and tactics must have a cost to the target, for example.

To help illustrate the use of the chart, we will use, among other examples, a hypothetical campaign to win tax reform on the state level.

Let's say that you are the organizer in charge of the campaign. Like many other states, yours has seen a major economic upturn in recent years, but services that were cut during the last recession still have not been restored and the boom is benefiting mainly the rich. The Governor, a middle-of-the-road Democrat, would favor improving services, particularly education, but a large portion of state revenue is coming from regressive sales and excise taxes, which no one wants to increase. Neither is there a desire to raise property taxes, which would fall mainly on the working poor and middle class.

Your organization, the State Citizens Alliance, is a coalition. It includes unions, senior citizen groups, environmentalists, community organizations, low-income organizations, women's organizations, and organizations of People of Color. In addition, the organization has an individual membership of 20,000 people maintained by a professional telephone canvass. It has a fine track record, having won many statewide legislative battles.

Your organization supports increasing taxes, but you want it done in a progressive way, which puts the burden on large corporations and the rich. You have obtained the assistance of a public interest organization to draft your own tax proposal—the Citizens' Fair Tax Plan—so your technical presentation will be as good as anyone

can produce. You are now ready to plan how to get your proposal passed.

Column 1: Goals

Long-Term Goals

These are the goals that you eventually hope to win and toward which the current campaign is a step. Using our example, your long-term goals might be to have the state budget well funded, to provide the services that the people of the state require, and to obtain this funding through a progressive tax system based on the ability to pay.

The legislation you are now sponsoring won't accomplish all of that; it will only close the budget gap in the short run. Many regressive taxes will still be on the books and the schools will still have problems, but it is a good step.

Intermediate Issue Goals

These are the goals that you hope to win in this campaign. In this example, the intermediate issue goal is the passage of the Citizens' Fair Tax Plan.

Goals must be very specific. If members of a housing group said their goal was fair housing or an environmental organization said ending toxic dumping, such goals would be so general that they only restate the problem. Saying that the goal is "to educate the public" is to mistake a goal for a tactic. Public education is really a tactic and goes in the last column.

(Note: Educating the public can be a deceptive concept. How do you know when you have accomplished it? When is the public educated and how educated has it become? Beware of any activity that requires spending money with no way to measure the result.)

Remember, a goal is always something that you win from someone. Test the intermediate goal— are they specific steps toward your long-term goals? Do they meet the three major criteria for choosing an issue? Do they:

1. Win real improvements in people's lives?
2. Give people a sense of their own power?
3. Alter the relations of power?

What does it mean to win? How will you know when you have won?

Short-Term Issue Goals

Short-term issue goals are steps toward your intermediate goals. You don't always necessarily have to have short-term issue goals, but in big issue campaigns they are useful for two reasons: First, few groups are strong enough to win a major campaign without a period of building power. They must win the support of individual officials and increase power at local levels of government. Second, just to sustain your organization in a long campaign, people must see small victories along the way.

Short-term issue goals for the Citizens' Fair Tax Plan campaign might be to obtain the endorsement of City Councils or County Commissions around the state and to move from there to asking members of the legislature to pledge that they agree in principle with the idea of progressive taxation before your bill comes out. Or you might launch a campaign for twenty-five cosponsors from targeted districts.

For a local community organization working on a neighborhood issue, the short-term issue goal might be just to get a meeting with the City Council member. When people see that the organization can do that much, they will be ready for the next step, perhaps a meeting with the Mayor. (If someone gets up at your first meeting and says, "Oh, the Mayor is a friend of mine; I can get you a meeting anytime," don't accept. The point is that the group must feel that it collectively won the meeting because of its strength. If the meeting comes about because of one person's personal relationship, the stature of that individual is built up, but the group isn't

---

Sample Goals Column

1. Long-Term Goals
- State budget well funded by a progressive tax system.
- Full funding of schools by the state.

2. Intermediate Goals
- Pass the Citizens' Fair Tax Plan.
- Win support of key legislative leaders from the 5th, 7th and 14th districts, or develop an anti–Fair Tax record for future races.

3. Short-Term Goals
- Public support from local officials.
- Line up influential sponsors in House and Senate by April.
- 25 cosponsors by June 1.

---

strengthened. And it is likely that nothing will come of the meeting.)

Sometimes, before you can even decide on the intermediate goals, more information about a problem is needed. Then, short-term goals might consist of making an agency compile or release information. For example, a citizen organization concerned about crime against seniors had to make the Police Department keep crime statistics by age just to prove that the problem existed. Sometimes, short-term goals will be electoral. For example, a specific person must be removed or more forceful leadership elected.

While listing goals, consider what the cost to the target will be if you win. Who will pay? What is it worth to someone to defeat you? Knowing this helps you to get a sense of how much money is likely to be spent on defeating you. It also gives you a better idea of who will end up as allies or opponents.

When you are finished listing your goals, have the group put them more or less in the order in which they will have to be achieved.

Sample Organizational Considerations Column

1. Resources To Put In

- Salaries and expenses for six months = $45,000. On hand = $10,000. To raise = $35,000.
- Staff
  Mary—Lead Organizer, full time
  Fred—Organizer, half time
  Sam—Support Staff, 1 day a week
  Liz—College intern, 1 day a week
  Kate—Supervisor, 4 hrs a week
  (cash value of staff time = $40,000)

- Phone canvass. Approx. 5 canvassers.
- 7 board members on the tax committee. Each represents an affiliate organization.
- Committee chair. Very active. Good spokesperson.
- Lobbyist from allied union.
- Tax expert contributed to us by Citizens for Tax Neatness.
- Office space and phones for all staff (cash value = $700).
- 1 Xerox that works, 1 that sort of works. 2 computers. (cash value for use = $200)
- Good relations with press. Abner Berry at the *Sentinel* and Al Ferman at the *Herald*.

[handwritten: regular mtgs, news cvg, mailings]

[handwritten left margin: leaflets, phones, copying, paying would solidify org]

[handwritten: Historical society – historic pres; Church]

2. What We Want to Get Out of It

- Make back all expenses ($45,000) through contributions from affiliates and campaign fund-raising.
- 4 new affiliates. Most likely choices are Carver City Taxpayers Against Waste, Newton Teachers Local 310, Association of Child Service Providers, Gotham City Save Our Schools Committee
- Build a base in the 5th, 7th, and 14th districts. Promote George, Frieda, and Kim as respective spokespersons.
- Develop 15 active volunteers.
- Develop ways to activate 15,000 canvass members in key districts.

3. Problems to Solve *[handwritten: internal]*

- Rivalry between teachers' unions may erupt.
  —Meet with them. Ask them to keep turf fight out of it.
- Uptown Seniors don't like Downtown Seniors.
  —Hold separate meetings in each community.
- Fred says that Mary whistles through her nose all day and he can't work in the same office with her.
  —Seek treatment for Fred since no one else ever hears Mary do this.

Column 2: Organizational Considerations

This column is essentially an organizational expense and income statement. You will list what resources you have to put into the campaign (expenses), what organizational gains you want to come out of the campaign (income), and internal problems that have to be solved.

Start with resources. This is essentially your campaign budget. Consider these to be expenses or, better yet, investments. Be very specific, particularly about staff time and money. List names.

Make sure that the people working on your campaign are in the room when you talk about how much of their time is going into the campaign. "Full time" for example, means that a person has no other responsibilities. Don't be one of those groups where the organizer works "full time" on each of five campaigns at once.

List the amount of money you are putting into the campaign and the amount that needs to be raised. Then, put a fair market cash value on the in-kind contributions you are making, including staff time, rent, and postage. Unless you do this, your allies, affiliates, and members will never have any idea of the size of your real contribution, and neither will you.

In the second part of the column, list everything that the organization wants to get out of the campaign, in addition to winning the issue. Consider this income, and plan to make a "profit" that is to build your organization through both internal development and fundraising. Again, the point here is to be very specific. How many new affiliates, new members, or leaders? Name them if possible. How much money raised? Put in an amount. Do you want more media recognition for your group? Where? How often? The purpose of being specific goes beyond setting objectives. To reach the objectives, you will need corresponding tactics and sometimes corresponding targets and constituencies. If one organizational objective is to get into the newspapers once a week for a month, then in the Tactics column you will have to plan to have at least one media hit a week. If the local paper is strongly Republican and so is the Mayor, then your attacks on the Mayor may not be covered. You will have to find an additional target, perhaps a City Council committee chair, in order to meet the objective of increased media coverage. If another organizational objective is to increase by four the number of People of Color in leadership, then more organizations to which People of Color belong may need to be added to the Constituents column. All of the columns of the chart are wired together in these ways.

The last part of this column lists internal problems that will have to be considered or solved in the course of the campaign. Here, "internal" implies problems within your organization (e.g., staff relationships), problems within your coalition, and problems within constituent organizations.

Column 3: Constituents, Allies, and Opponents

Constituents and Allies

This column is where you answer the questions, who cares about this issue, what do they stand to win or lose, what power do they have, and how are they organized? A constituency is a group of people, hopefully already organized, whom you can contact and bring into the campaign. In filling out this column, be expansive, even far-fetched. The idea is to come up with a long list of potential constituents. During the campaign you may not contact all of them, but you can come back to the list later if events bog down and you need additional support. The difference between *constituents* and *allies* is that constituents are potential members of your organization, while allies are not. Students might be allies in a senior-led campaign for more frequent bus service. Other senior clubs would be constituents.

When you start drawing up the list for the Citizens' Fair Tax Plan campaign, the first groups that come to mind are public employee organizations. Some taxpayer groups will be very Right Wing, but some could join you. Clearly, organizations that receive services or funding from the state will also be interested in improved funding. Examples include seniors and day-care providers.

The problem is that in the face of a general sentiment in the state that favors sales taxes over income taxes, this list is too short. Additional constituents will be homeowners and parents, but to bring them in, the goals of the campaign will have to be expanded to include property tax relief and school funding. (This is another example of how the chart is like a computer spreadsheet. When you change one column, changes are required in others, but they don't happen automatically as they do in a spreadsheet.) The next question is, how are homeowners and parents

Sample Constituents, Allies, and Opponents Column

1. Constituents and Allies
- State Teachers Union: 7,000 members
  Local 210 Gotham City
  Local 113 Newton
  Local 69 Butler
  Local 666 Spuyten Duyvil
- State Teachers Association:
  12,000 members
  List locals
- State Public Employees Union:
  14,000 members
  List locals
- State Labor Federation:
  40,000 members
  List active locals and labor councils
- Association of Day Care Centers: 1,200 members
- State Senior Council: 3,000 members
  Clubs in
  Parker (5th District)
  Gotham
  Newton (7th District)
  Salem
  Winchester (14th District)
  Westchester
- Council of Home Health Care Providers
- Newton Council of Civic Associations
- State Alliance of PTAs
- Taxpayers Union: 2,000 members

2. Opponents
- Chamber of Commerce
- Bankers Association
- Insurance Industry Council
- Johnson Corp.
- Taxpayers Association of Hatemail
- etc., etc.

owners. PTAs are the logical place to find parents, but larger numbers of parents may be found in religious congregations.

Even if your organization has individual members rather than being a coalition, it is still useful to think of people as parts of groups. For example, say that you are working on a public transportation issue and decide that senior citizens are a possible constituency. You could list seniors on the chart, but that won't tell you how to reach them. Instead, be more specific. Say, "Seniors who ride the #1 and #2 buses." That, at least, leads you to leafleting bus stops on those lines. It would be much better, however, to look at the transit map or the Yellow Pages to see what senior centers are served by those lines. Don't overlook congregations that might have senior clubs. Mark them on a map. Put them on the chart by name. Go and visit them.

Look for constituencies that are less than obvious. On the tax issue, realtors or real estate associations might join with you because value is added to the houses they sell if property taxes don't rise and the school system is good.

Think of each constituent group as the hub of a wheel. Then look at the spokes. Who cares about these people? Who does business with them? Who provides services to them? Who lends them money? Who borrows their money (banks, insurance companies)? For whom do they vote? If they had more money to spend, where would they spend it? Who would get it (local merchants or Swiss banks)? What organizations or congregations do they belong to? Looking at your possible constituents in this way, it is easy to see that the self-interest of one group affects the self-interest of many others and may create still more constituents for the campaign.

While it is necessary to think about potential areas of conflict between the groups, remember that people don't all have to love each other, agree on tactics, or even sit in the same room in

organized? Condo associations, particularly those with many seniors, could be an important constituency and are often better organized than neighborhood civic associations. You would have to be sure that your proposed legislation's benefits for homeowners included condominium order to support the same issue. In fact, sometimes the issue brings them together. This was the case in the classic campaign against the Chicago Crosstown Expressway. The proposed expressway route ran through different ethnic communities. One White group came with signs saying "Black Roads, White Lines United Against the Crosstown."

Mark your list according to whether the constituency is organized or unorganized—that is, homeowners associations in the Humboldt Park area, as opposed to individual homeowners. Then rank the groups according to the power they bring to the campaign. Consider the following:

- How many members do they have?
- Did they work or vote for the incumbent office holder?
- Do they make political campaign contributions?
- Will they give money to your issue campaign?
- Do they bring special credibility? (Clergy)
- Do they have special appeal? (Children)
- Are they part of a larger organized network? (Veterans)
- Do they have a reputation for being tough? (Unions)
- Do they have special skills? (Lawyers)
- Are they considered particularly newsworthy? (Penguins)

Last, examine the weaknesses of each constituency. Look at their reputations, past history, and the enemies that you might inherit by linking up with them. If the target is an elected official, then constituents will have very little power who never voted for her and never will. If consumer power is to be used against a corporation, then constituents must be customers of that company.

Opponents

List all the groups, individuals, and institutions that stand to lose or be very upset if you win. What will your victory cost them? Try to evaluate how actively each will oppose you and what they will do or spend to defeat you. In a few cases you may find ways to neutralize them, but even if you can do nothing, it is best to have some idea of what to expect as the campaign unfolds. List the power of each opponent. How does the strength of your constituents stack up against the strength of your opponents in the eyes of the people who can give you what you want? Generally avoid engaging opponents during the campaign. They can't give you what you want, and you have no influence over them anyway. Don't even hold debates with them unless you expect to win over larger numbers of their base. In most campaigns, your opponents have you outspent and outstaffed; spending time on them just diverts you from the real targets. This is not to say that opponents don't matter or that we should not be concerned about their strength, only that challenging them directly can be a diversion.

Column 4: Decision Makers (Targets)
Primary Decision Makers

The person with the power to give you what you want is often referred to as the "target" of the campaign. This does not necessarily imply that the person is evil. It simply means that by virtue of having the power to give you what you want, that person is the focus of the campaign. Some groups prefer to say "decision maker."

The decision maker is always a person. "Personalize the target" is a fundamental rule of organizing. Even if the power to give you what you want is actually held by an institution such as a City Council, a board of directors, the legislature, the Police Department, or the Environmental Protection Agency (EPA), personalize it. Find out the name of the person(s) who can make the decision or at least strongly influence it. Make that person the target. Not only does this help to narrow the focus of the campaign, but it makes your

> ## Sample Targets Column
>
> **1. Primary Targets**
> - Governor Winthrop
> - House Tax Committee Chair Rep. Bacon (5th District)
> - Senate Committee Chair Rep. Lax
> - Committee members, to be determined
> - Other legislators, to be determined
>
> **2. Secondary Targets**
> - G. Groggy—Union County Dem. Chairman—includes 14th Dist.
> - R. Waterdown—Kent County Dem. Chairman—includes 7th Dist.
> - Selected campaign contributors to individuals listed above
> - County Commissioners in the counties containing target districts

[handwritten margin notes: Councilman, Drug Task Force, Neighborhood Police - liaison, Mayor, Committee Chair, Trash collr.]

handed down. List the reasons that each target has to oppose you as well as to agree with you. List your power over each target. Go back to the constituency list and consider how to match the power of each constituency against the vulnerabilities of the targets. In campaigns aimed at legislators, think about who are the pro and anti swing voters. Sometimes it is sufficient to win over the swing voters if they represent the balance of power. In that case, you don't have to reach everyone.

Secondary Targets

A secondary target is a person who has more power over the primary decision maker than you do but whom you have more power over than you have over the primary decision maker.

Tenants in public housing wanted their buildings painted. The tenants made several members of the City Housing Authority their primary targets. When the tenants discovered that old lead paint was peeling off the walls, they made the head of the Health Department a secondary target. She didn't care about the tenants' dispute with the Housing Authority, but lead was a health hazard that had to be corrected. She told the Housing Authority that the walls must be scraped and repainted.

When you list secondary targets, write down what power you have over them and what power they have over the primary target.

In the Fair Tax campaign, the targets are determined by an analysis of the legislature. Clearly, the Governor will be a target, as will the heads of key committees. Once the legislation is introduced and a head count taken of committee members and the legislature as a whole, specific members will be targeted as well. Secondary targets for this campaign might include officials such as county chairs of the Democratic and Republican parties, lower-level elected officials,

members feel that winning is possible. A campaign to change a person's mind is much more believable than one to change the policy of a big institution. In addition, individual decision makers have human responses such as fairness, guilt, fear, ambition, vanity, or loyalty. These do not exist in institutions or formal bodies as a whole. Such responses can only come into play if you personalize the target.

When filling out this column, list all the possible people who can give you what you want. Try to include more than one of them because where power is divided, usually more weak spots and openings exist. Also, multiple targets provide an opportunity to sustain the campaign over a longer time. This allows you to build strength. In many types of campaigns, time is on your side if you can hold out. This is particularly true if you are trying to stop expensive structures from being built or large sums of money from being spent. A long campaign may also help you to keep the issue alive until an election intervenes or a court decision is campaign contributors, or volunteer coordinators, provided they either agree with you or you have some power over the target.

When dealing with corporations, a large purchaser can be a good secondary target. Look to see if the corporation has government contracts. If so, the public officials who can end the contracts become secondary targets.

You may not need to have a secondary target if you have power over the primary one.

Column 5: Tactics

Tactics are steps in carrying out your overall plan. They are the specific things that the people in the Constituency column do to the people in the Targets column to put pressure on them. When you list tactics, write down who will do what and to whom.

The Tactics column is always filled out last to avoid the common tendency to jump to tactics as soon as the issue is chosen. ("Let's all go to Mayor Gold's office with a goldfish and a sign that says 'All that glitters is not Gold.'") Tactics should never be planned in isolation from the larger strategy of which they must be a part. One statewide healthcare advocacy group heard that its counterpart in another state had held a very successful statewide lobby day that helped to pass a piece of legislation. The group decided that it too should host a lobby day, but when the time came it had no bill to support and nothing to advocate for. A lobby day without a bill is a classic example of a tactic without a strategy.

For every tactic, there must be

- Someone who does it.
- Someone to whom it is done.
- Some reason why the person to whom it is done doesn't want it done and will make a concession to you if you stop doing it.

Sample Tactics Column

(Listed more or less in the order in which they might actually be used)

- Media hits. Feature unjust tax distribution between homeowners and EXXON refinery.
- More media hits. Spotlight education cuts. Kids come with symbols of cut programs, e.g., sports equipment, musical instruments.
- Do same day in four cities with teacher organizations and PTAs.
- Make this an issue in the next gubernatorial primary.
- Start postcard campaign for fair taxes. "Dear Gov., When my income goes over $200,000, I will happily pay higher taxes if you enact them now."
- Media hit in capital to release detailed Fair Tax Plan. Sponsors and cosponsors on hand.
- Canvassers start petition drive in targeted districts.
- Media hits in targeted districts to announce formation of district Fair Tax committees to put legislature on the spot. Show petitions.
- Delegation meetings to get position of targeted legislators.
- Local hearings. Either sponsors hold them officially or we hold them. Aim for high turnout.
- Additional delegation meetings in target district. Service providers, seniors, clients of programs are included.
- Save our school. Rallies and picnics. Fund-raiser.
- TV debate between our leader and legislative opponents.
- Tax bill burning day when tax bills are sent out.
- Accountability sessions in targeted districts, particularly the 5th, 7th, and 14th districts.
- Mass lobby day in capital when bill comes up for vote. Governor invited to speak for the bill. Empty chair if he doesn't. Invite potential opponents.

Tactics should be fun. They should be within the experience of your members but outside the experience of your targets. Every tactic has an element of power behind it. None should be purely symbolic. Different tactics require different levels of organizational strength and sophistication to use. For that reason, some work better at the beginning of a campaign and some can be used only later, after a certain level of strength is reached.

Notes on Tactics

Media Events

Media events are designed to get press and TV coverage. As stand-alone events, they are usually used at the start of the campaign to dramatize the issue and announce that the organization is working on it. Later in the campaign, the media will be used in conjunction with other tactics. A media event might consist of releasing information or a study, demanding information, having victims tell their stories, and making demands on the target.

For the Fair Tax Campaign, an opening media event might be held in front of property owned by a large corporation. The percentage of income paid in taxes by the corporation could be contrasted to that paid by nearby homeowners, who would bring big enlargements of their tax bills to display to the press. The media event should not simply be an attempt to educate the public. Remember, it is a tactic and tactics are done to someone. If the legislators in whose district the corporation is located don't support the Fair Tax Bill, make that part of the media hit. If the corporation gave them campaign contributions, that is also news.

The press usually responds well to something visual and funny or dramatic. One citizen organization wanted to dramatize that the rising cost of auto insurance was forcing people to choose between paying for their homes or their cars. The

group built a home inside a car with the toilet in the trunk. The press loved it.

If the media event features groups such as low-income people, the homeless, the unemployed, or striking workers, be sure that they are presented with dignity and as whole people asking for the same rights that others enjoy. They are not objects of pity, nor are they looking for a handout.

Actions

Actions are a particularly useful tactic for local organizations, especially toward the start of a campaign. In an action, a group of people confront a target and make specific demands. They expect to get an answer on the spot. Organizations usually start with procedural demands such as asking for an appointment with someone or that a hearing be held. They also might ask for the release of information, the publication of rules, or time on the agenda. Later, when the group is stronger, actions might be used to win some of its main demands.

Actions often involve the media, but they are not media events. That is, the objective is not simply to get covered in the media but to use additional power to win something. The organization's power may be the number of participants or the size of the constituency they represent, their ability to embarrass the target with information they have uncovered, or their ability to cause the target political harm if the target is a public official, or financial harm if a business.

Public Hearings

You might demand that the target hold an official public hearing, but consider holding your own hearing in which a panel of community leaders and allied political leaders listens to testimony from your constituency. Often a report is issued. The hearing serves to educate, get publicity, put opponents on the spot, and establish your organization as a leading force on the issue.

Accountability Sessions

Accountability sessions are large meetings with elected officials. They are sponsored by you and held on your turf. Several hundred people come to tell the official what they want done. The official is asked to respond at once.

Elections

Depending on what type of organization you are, you may actually endorse candidates. Even if you don't, you usually have more leverage in the weeks before an election because candidates are more vulnerable then.

Negotiations

Issue campaigns usually end in some form of negotiation. You must have shown considerable power to get the other side to agree to talk. If your target offers to negotiate too easily or too soon, watch out! It may be a device to make the other side look reasonable without any serious concessions being made. (But don't automatically assume that every offer is some kind of trick. Some groups "snatch defeat out of the jaws of victory" because they can never believe that they actually won.)

The next chapter explores some of these and other tactics in greater detail.

Using the Chart

The strategy chart can be used to plan organizational development as well as issue campaigns. The starting point in the chart is determined by the type of planning you are doing. For example, to plan an issue campaign, work from left to right. To plan the start-up of a new organization, say, a new senior citizen coalition, begin at the lower half of the Organizational Considerations column. Write down how many senior clubs you want to have affiliated and specific goals to make the coalition diverse and inclusive. Then, skip to the Constituents column and list all the existing clubs that could potentially join the coalition. Note the ethnic characteristics of each. Next, go back to the Goals column and with the objective of diversity in mind, decide what issues would appeal to the clubs. From there, go to the Targets and then to the Tactics columns.

One reason that the chart works in so many ways is that an organization is literally the product of what it does. Once you are clear on what you want your organization to be, you can work backward toward shaping the group in the desired direction.

An example of a complete strategy chart that shows all five of the sample columns presented earlier for the tax campaign appears at the end of this chapter.

The two questions most frequently asked about the strategy chart:

Question: In which column do I put an activity such as getting more publicity for my organization? Is that a Goal, an Organizational Consideration, or a Tactic?

Answer: Nothing goes in the Goals column unless you intend to win it from someone. Tactics are always done by someone to someone, so a media event aimed at a target goes under Tactics. Getting publicity in general is an Organizational Consideration.

Question: Exactly what is the relationship between the columns of the chart?

Answer: Tactics are what people in the Constituency column do to the people in the Targets column to make them give the organization the things in the Goals column so as to build the organization as outlined in the Organizational Considerations column.

Timelines

To finish the planning process, make timelines for the campaign. Include all the major campaign events and deadlines for preparing the publicity for each. Be sure to include the key dates in the electoral process. Even if you are not involved with candidates, note information such as when voter registration starts and ends, when nominating petitions start circulating, when petitions must be filed for major party candidates and independents, when candidate fundraising reports must be filed (you may want to look at them), and of course, all election dates. Also note when appropriate legislative bodies are in session, when members of Congress and the legislature are home for recess, and when major civil, religious, and school holidays occur. Timelines also help you sort through too many good ideas. The first tactics list that most groups create is a brainstorm list with little relationship to a group's limited resources. A timeline that includes "who will do what by when" helps the group be more realistic about what it can do.

You might want to develop a multitiered timeline, which can help in planning activities that build on something already scheduled or indicate where too much is going on at one time and something needs to be rescheduled. An example of such a timeline is as follows:

	Jan	Feb	Mar	Apr	May	June	July	Aug	Sep	Oct	Nov	Dec
Organization												
City Council												
State Leg.												
Congress												
Elections												
Fundraising												
Other												

Midwest Academy Strategy Chart for "Fair Tax Campaign"

Goals	Organizational Considerations	Constituents, Allies, and Opponents	Targets	Tactics
1. Long-Term Goals • State budget well funded by a progressive tax system. • Full funding of schools by the state. **2. Intermediate Goals** • Pass the Citizens' Fair Tax Plan. • Win support of key legislative leaders from the 5th, 7th and 14th districts, or develop an anti-Fair Tax record for future races. **3. Short-Term Goals** • Public support from local officials. • Line up influential sponsors in House and Senate by April. • 25 cosponsors by June 1.	**1. Resources to put in** • Salaries and expenses for six months = $45,000. On hand = $10,000. To raise = $35,000. • Staff Mary—Lead Organizer, full time Fred—Organizer, half time Sam—Support Staff, 1 day a week Liz—College intern, 1 day a week Kate—Supervisor, 4 hrs a week (cash value of staff time = $40,000) • Phone canvass. Approx. 5 canvassers. • 7 board members on the tax committee. Each represents an affiliate organization. • Committee chair. Very active. Good spokesperson • Lobbyist from allied union • Tax expert contributed to us by Citizens for Tax Neatness. • Office space and phones for all staff (cash value = $700). • 1 Xerox that works, 1 that sort of works. 2 computers. (cash value for use = $200) • Good relations with press. Abner Berry at the *Sentinel* and Al Ferman at the *Herald*. **2. What We Want to Get Out of It** • Make back all expenses ($45,000) through contributions from affiliates and campaign fund-raising. • 4 new affiliates. Most likely choices are Carver City Taxpayers Against Waste, Newton Teachers Local 310, Association of Child Service Providers, Gotham City Save Our Schools Committee • Build a base in the 5th, 7th, and 14th districts. Promote George, Frieda, and Kim as respective spokespersons. • Develop 15 active volunteers. • Develop ways to activate 15,000 canvass members in key districts. **3. Problems to Solve** • Rivalry between teachers' unions may erupt. —Meet with them. Ask them to keep turf fight out of it. • Uptown Seniors don't like Downtown Seniors. —Hold separate meetings in each community. • Fred says that Mary whistles through her nose all day and he can't work in the same office with her. —Seek treatment for Fred since no one else ever hears Mary do this.	**1. Constituents and Allies** • State Teachers Union: 7,000 members Local 210 Gotham City Local 113 Newton Local 69 Butler Local 666 Spuyten Duyvil • State Teachers Association: 12,000 members List locals • State Public Employees Union: 14,000 members List locals • State Labor Federation: 40,000 members List active locals and labor councils • Association of Day Care Centers: 1,200 members • State Senior Council: 3,000 members Clubs in Parker (5th District) Gotham Newton (7th District) Salem Winchester (14th District) Westchester • Council of Home Health Care Providers • Newton Council of Civic Associations • State Alliance of PTAs • Taxpayers Union: 2,000 members **2. Opponents** • Chamber of Commerce • Bankers Association • Insurance Industry Council • Johnson Corp. • Taxpayers Association of Hatemail	**1. Primary Targets** • Governor Winthrop • House Tax Committee Chair Rep. Bacon (5th District) • Senate Committee Chair Rep. Lax • Committee members, to be determined • Other legislators, to be determined **2. Secondary Targets** • G. Groggy—Union County Dem. Chairman—includes 14th Dist. • R. Waterdown—Kent County Dem. Chairman—includes 7th Dist. • Selected campaign contributors to individuals listed above • County Commissioners in the counties containing target districts	(Listed more or less in the order in which they might actually be used) • Media hits. Feature unjust tax distribution between homeowners and EXXON refinery. • More media hits. Spotlight education cuts. Kids come with symbols of cut programs, e.g., sports equipment, musical instruments. • Do same day in four cities with teacher organizations and PTAs. • Make this an issue in the next gubernatorial primary. • Start postcard campaign for fair taxes. • "Dear Gov. When my income goes over $200,000, I will happily pay higher taxes if you enact them now." • Media hit in capital to release detailed Fair Tax Plan. Sponsors and cosponsors on hand. • Canvassers start petition drive in targeted districts. • Media hits in targeted districts to announce formation of district Fair Tax committees to put legislature on the spot. Show petitions. • Delegation meetings to get position of targeted legislators. • Local hearings. Either sponsors hold them officially or we hold them. Aim for high turnout. • Additional delegation meetings in target district. Service providers, seniors, clients of programs are included. • Save our school. Rallies and picnics. Fundraiser. • TV debate between our leader and legislative opponents. • Tax bill burning day when tax bills are sent out. • Accountability sessions in targeted districts, particularly the 5th, 7th, and 14th districts. • Mass lobby day in capital when bill comes up for vote. Governor invited to speak for the bill. Empty chair if he doesn't. Invite potential opponents.

© Midwest Academy

28 E. Jackson Blvd. #605, Chicago, IL 60604

(312) 427-2304   mwacademy1@aol.com   www.midwestacademy.com

Midwest Academy Strategy Chart

Goals	Organizational Considerations	Constituents, Allies, and Opponents	Targets	Tactics

Training participants to develop a strategy chart.

5

We are somewhat reluctant to present a guide to tactics for the same reason that we would not print biographies of characters in movies. The characters have no real existence that is independent of the movie script. Similarly, tactics have no meaningful existence outside the strategy of which they are a part. When a given tactic is standing alone, it is impossible to say that it is right or wrong, good or bad, clever or dumb. That's why tactics come at the end of the strategy chart.

All too often, organizations allow a tactic to take on a life of its own, independent of any strategic context. A group will hear of a clever tactic that worked someplace else and use it without considering either why it worked the first time or how the current situation might be different. For example, word arrived from a nearby state that because people had mailed Band-Aids to their legislators, progress was made on a bill to lower auto insurance rates. Mailing Band-Aids became the new "in" tactic. All sorts of groups started doing it. No one realized that in the nearby state, the legislature was up for election, while their own state elections had been completed just before the Band-Aid frenzy began. Tactics do not work just because they are smart or funny, although it helps.

A Guide to Tactics

The worst mistake an organizer can make is to act tactically instead of strategically.

Criteria for Tactics

Once a tactic has been placed in its strategic context, it should be evaluated against five basic criteria for a good tactic.

1. *It Is Focused on the Primary or Secondary Target of the Campaign.* The tactic is not focused on someone else.

2. *It Puts Power behind a Specific Demand.* The weakest tactic is one that is not aimed at anyone and makes no demand, for example, a candlelight vigil to save the whales that doesn't call on anyone to do anything in particular. (If a quarter of a million people show up, as they well might, that is a different story and some politician will rush to implement a measure on behalf of the whales.)

3. *It Meets Your Organizational Goals as Well as Your Issue Goals.* That is, it builds the organization as well as helps to win the issue. As far as we know, the Boston Tea Party dramatized the problem of taxation but did not help to build an organization. No group took credit for it because it was illegal. Since then, many organizations have used the tea party tactic by dumping something into an appropriate body of water. Usually the press is called and the group's name is prominently displayed, indicating that the practice of this tactic has improved over the years.

4. *It Is outside the Experience of the Target.* An organization demanding equal access to Postal Service jobs for Hispanics made hundreds of copies of job application forms for people in the community to fill out. The local Postal Service administrator was taken off guard as this tactic was outside his experience. He blundered by disqualifying the copied forms, insisting that only original Postal Service forms would be considered. This seemed so unfair and so prejudiced that he was forced to back down, thus handing the organization an easy first victory. In another example, the new owners of a hotel laid off workers and refused to honor their union contract. The workers called on the Religion-Labor coalition for help. The coalition decided on a tactic that was definitely outside of the hotel management's experience. They came and prayed in the hotel lobby. After four days of lobby prayer, the hotel manager called the union and asked if recognizing the union would end the praying. The union won and the workers were rehired.

5. *It Is within the Experience of Your Own Members, and They Are Comfortable with It.* A citizen organization brought several hundred members to a meeting at a church, from which they were to march to the office of a state official. The members were not comfortable with the idea of the march, which they associated with "protesters." They refused to leave the church. Had the organizers better understood the members' attitude, they might have arranged to have the state official meet with the group at the church.

Considerations in Using Some Popular Tactics

Petition Drives

If you haven't already heard this, you soon will. A politician will tell you, "Don't bring me petitions. I would rather see one or two well-thought-out, spontaneous, handwritten letters than one thousand signatures from an organized group." This is the truth. In fact, what the politicians would *really* rather see is *no* signatures, *no* handwritten letters, and *no* organized group, because then they could do just as they please. Of course they want you to talk to two or three thoughtful people instead of thousands.

When used properly, petitions are very powerful, and collecting signatures is a good organization builder as well. Petitions and letters in which people pledge to vote on the basis of a politician's stand on your issue are the strongest kind, especially when they are delivered by a large number of people with media coverage. Petitions that are simply mailed to a politician are basically useless.

Where the Power of Petitions Comes From
1. Numbers
2. Strategic Location and Timing

3. Organized Followup
   - Signatures gathered from around the state and sent to the clerk of the legislature have very little impact unless their number is really overwhelming. Signatures gathered in one district where the state Rep. won by a *narrow* margin have considerable impact on that Rep.
   - Signatures presented to an *elected* government official have much more impact than those given to *appointed* officials (unless the person is likely to run for office in the future or was appointed by and is identified with someone elected who will be embarrassed).
   - Signatures presented to a store owner matter a great deal if they come from *customers*. But if the community petitions the owner of a wholesale plumbing supply company, the signatures will have very little impact.
   - Petitions presented a month before an official is up for election are much more powerful than twice as many signatures presented a month after the election.
   - Every official to whom petitions are presented should be made aware that the names come from a well organized group and that the signers will be informed of the response that their petition received.

Petition Tips
- Keep the message short and simple. Just a couple of sentences followed by two or three bullet points is enough. The idea is to enable people to quickly read the petition, not to spell out every detail for the person receiving the signatures. That can be done in a separate letter.
- Have no more than ten signature lines on a page. If you use the petitions in a media event, you will want the pile to look large. This is not the time to save trees by cramming twenty names on one page. In addition, you want the

names to be legible in order to contact those signers interested in volunteering.

- Ask everyone who signs if they want to volunteer. Take phone numbers and e-mail addresses of those who do. (After being called, probably only one in ten will actually show up, but that's fine.) Leave everyone with a piece of literature. You can also ask for a contribution.
- Emphasize quantity, not quality. You are going for numbers, so don't spend a lot time trying to "educate" one person.
- Go out in teams. It's more fun. An organized petition day is much better than asking everyone to do it individually at their own pace. People can meet at a common location, be briefed quickly, go out for a set time, and then meet back for refreshments and to exchange experiences.
- Never give away signed petitions without having made copies. They are useful for follow-up mailings and phone calls. The same petitions can be used again on another occasion with a different decision maker.

Letter Writing

The power of letter writing comes from the same sources as does that of petitions. The letter represents a slightly larger commitment on the part of the writer, and where appropriate, it gives you a longer period of contact in which to recruit the writer as a volunteer or to get a contribution. Whenever you have a meeting with an official, get dozens of letters written beforehand. Mail in half during the week before the meeting and bring the rest with you. This always makes an impression. Remember, though, that many office holders actually answer letters and thus will have the last word with your supporters. They may use it to explain why you are wrong.

Choose letter writing over petitions whenever an audience is sitting down. Congregations, for example, will often agree to do letter writing for you, either in the lobby or actually in the pews. Letter writing also works well on a busy street corner if you set up a card table. By themselves, form letters (on which people sign their names to preprinted letters) have the same impact as petitions. Handwritten letters show a greater commitment by the writer.

Letter-Writing Tips

- Have a sample text of not more than three sentences. Print it on slips of paper with the decision maker's address, and tape it to the clip of the clipboards on which people will write their letters. Tell each person to either use the sample or put it in their own words. When working with a group or congregation, consider bringing a laptop so that people can dictate short letters.
- Tell the writer to include a return address and the decision maker will probably send a reply. This may give the decision maker the last word, but it also keeps people engaged.
- Ask each person to address an envelope after they finish the letter. Then say, "We'll mail it for you. Would you make a contribution for postage?" Many people will give more money than the postage costs. Collect and mail all the letters yourself. Discourage people from walking away with their letters; they won't make it to the mailbox.
- Combine petition and letter-writing drives with selling something such as buttons or T-shirts, and you can keep the petty cash box full. When you mail the letters, spread them out over a week. They are more likely to be noticed.
- An outdoor letter-writing table requires a minimum of three people. More is better. One

person should stand (not sit) behind the table and handle the clipboards. The other two should be in front of the table with leaflets engaging passersby and steering them over to the table.

How Many Is Many?
We say many letters, signatures, or people, but we don't say how many. This number depends on the number of people who voted in the last election and the margin by which the official won. How many signatures do other groups usually get?

Turnout Events

Getting people to come to events is the core of organizing. It doesn't matter how good your ideas are, the groups that attract attention are the ones that get people to come and keep them coming back. For a community group, getting people to turn out is almost entirely a matter of good telephone work. This means developing lists of everyone who has ever shown interest in the organization or its issues and writing down the date and nature of every contact and attempted contact with them. Phoning is best done from an office with several phone lines where you can coach the callers. (Borrow an office for a few hours in the evening if necessary.) Having people call from home will also work as long as everything is explained beforehand, but it is not as good as having a central location.

Every organization develops its own telephone success rate over time. The general rule is that of the people who say on your second (confirming) phone call to them that they will come to an event, half will actually come. The calculations that you need to make for a turnout event appear in the chart that follows. Of course, the number of calls you need to make to get one person to come will be different from group to

Meeting with Council Member	Goal: 60 People
Your regulars	**15**
From other groups	**10**
From phones	**35**
Necessary confirmed twice names	70
Number of calls to get 70 confirmed	490 (70 x 7)
Number of calls per person, per hour	20
Number of person hours calling	25
Number of calling nights and people	5 people a night for 5 nights

group. Seven calls to get one "yes," as shown here, is a good average. Don't count anyone as a "yes" who says, "I'll try to come." That means no. The chart shows the necessity of putting calling on a factory basis. It can't be left to a few people to do when they get a chance. The calling may need to include an appeal for volunteers to make more calls. This is good to do in any case.

Turnout Tips
- Don't start with the words "Hello, Mrs. Smith. Your name appears on a list in our office." This is traditional but deadly. Instead, say something like this:

Hello, Mrs. Smith. This is Steve from United Parents. Two weeks ago you signed our petition to get eye disease screening for the children at Public School 165. As a result of the petition, we have a meeting with a member of the School Board, Mr. Bookish. It will be a chance for you to show him how you feel about the screening having been cut in our community. Of course, the more people who come, the more he will have to listen to us. He'd better listen, he *is* elected. It is next Tuesday, the 17th, at the school. The room is 315. We will all meet outside the building at 5:30 P.M. and go in together. We will be finished by about 6:30. I'll be there, can you come? . . . Oh, that's wonderful. We'll give you a reminder call a day or two beforehand if that's all right.

Notice the following elements in the call:
- Stress the past connection—the petition.
- Mention a previous success of the campaign—getting the meeting.
- Indicate that the person will play a role, even if it is not a speaking role—"By being there, you can show him how you feel."
- Talk about why the person is needed—numbers matter; Mr. Bookish is elected.
- Indicate that everyone will go in together as a group.
- Ask for a definite commitment—"Can you come?"
- Indicate a reminder call and be sure to make one. (Of the people who say *twice* that they will come, half will come.)

- In addition to phoning people, try to get the same message to each individual in at least three other ways. For example, send a mailing, send an e-mail, put up posters, and have someone make an announcement at PTA meetings. Mail, posters, leaflets, advertisements, or public service announcements will reinforce the phone call and remind people, but they are no substitute for the call. The more times people hear the message, the more likely they are to come.
- At the event, all callers should make an effort to meet the people they called and introduce themselves. Nametags help.

- If your events are fun, exciting, and get press, people will come back. For example, you could tape the petitions to the back of a six-foot eye chart and give it to Mr. Bookish. (OK, so doctors don't really screen for eye disease with a chart, but you get the idea. Have something unusual at every event that people will talk about afterward.)

Visits with Public Officials

Nothing beats actual face-to-face meetings between your members and public officials. These can be held with fifteen to twenty-five people. If you can, show larger numbers of supporters through petitions or letters. These meetings are usually held in an official's office. Most elected officials hate these meetings but can't avoid agreeing to hold them if you have sufficient community support.

Famous Elected-Official Lies

"I was just about to do what you want, but because you act like this, now I won't."

"I never respond to pressure. I always make up my own mind."

"Look, I'm your friend."

"I can't vote for money for your disease group. I'd prefer to let the NIH decide. They have a better understanding of the science."

Tips for Visits with Public Officials
- Try to meet with elected officials rather than appointed ones.
- Know what the last election results were (general and primary) so that you have an idea of how secure the official's seat is.
- Because the meeting is small and everyone must be "with the program," don't recruit people whom you don't know.
- Have a single spokesperson who may call on two or three other people to speak. The rest of the group should be introduced, indicating

which other organizations or congregations each person represents. (Don't say, "I'm a homeowner." Say, "I belong to the homeowner's association.")

- Come with a specific demand, usually that the elected official support some legislation. Have a fallback demand (for example, hold a hearing, do a study).
- Think of the forms of power that you have:
  - Numbers
  - Support of campaign contributors or workers
  - Support of influential people in the community
  - Ability to embarrass the official for not acting in the interest of the community
  - Conflict of interest on the part of the official
  - The official is yielding to pressure or money from special interests
- Try to pin down the official to a specific agreement.
- If you can't get an agreement, get another meeting.

Public Hearings

Two kinds of public hearings are held: those that you sponsor and "official" ones held by public agencies.

Holding Your Own Public Hearing

The first victory in holding a public hearing lies in getting the public official to come. The virtue of this tactic is that it is very difficult for an official to refuse such an invitation. To do so would be an admission that the community's opinion doesn't count. To your own members, the appearance of an important decision maker at *their* event is a sign of growing power. Often, a group uses actions and other pressure tactics just to force someone to attend its own hearing. If an official does refuse to come, the hearing can be held anyway with a panel of prestigious allies listening to testimony. These might include members of the clergy, other elected officials, educators, heads of organizations, or people from special fields connected with the issue. Holding your own hearing has several advantages:

- It establishes your group as a force/authority on the issue.
- It is an opportunity to do outreach to other groups, individuals, or neighborhoods.
- It shows off your influential supporters or leaders. They can sit on the hearing panel or testify.
- It can showcase a potential candidate.
- It is a display of numbers.
- You control almost every aspect of it, which makes it a fine forum for your point of view.
- It is fun and not very hard to do.
- It is good training for your own leaders.
- It will probably get media coverage.

In planning your hearing, write and practice all testimony in advance. It need not be "expert" testimony; in fact, it's better that it not be. People telling their own stories of how the issue affects them is just fine so long as each person also represents a larger constituency and says so. Make the physical setting attractive both to participants and to TV. A good job of decorating using banners or signs naming the organizations present is one way of showing strength. As with most tactics, a really large turnout makes up for what is lacking in execution, so don't spend so much time writing testimony that you neglect recruitment.

Hearings, like any other meeting, should be over within two hours. The trick is to avoid having the hearing dribble away at the end. Save your strongest speaker until last, and end with a call to action and an announcement of the next step in the campaign.

Tips for Holding Your Own Hearing

- This is not a "town meeting" where all points of view are represented; it is to present your case to the public, to public officials, and to the media.

- To use this tactic, your group must be able to turn out a crowd of at least 100 people.

- Pick a hall of a size that you know you can fill to overflowing. Take out any extra chairs. The goal is to have every seat filled and a few people standing in the back.

- Get the name, address, phone number, and e-mail address of everyone who comes.

- Testimony should be prepared in advance and given by people who represent organized groups. A few individuals can also be recognized to speak.

- Bring letters and petitions to show support from people who can't come. Conduct voter registration in the back of the room. Read messages and greetings from allied groups.

- Appoint one press person who gives out your release and points the media toward other spokespeople for interviews.

- Close with a rousing statement and give everyone something to do after the event. It could be a leaflet to hand out, a poster to put up, or another event to attend.

A variation on an organization's own hearing is the Workers Rights Board, created by Jobs with Justice to parallel the National Labor Relations Board (NLRB). Workers Boards have no legal authority, but they do have moral authority. Respected community leaders, such as a business ethics professor, a Bishop, or the head of the local League of Women Voters, are recruited to serve on these boards. The boards hear cases and make "rulings" about what should be done. The boards are a tactical vehicle for recruiting new people and helping to publicize worker grievances at specific companies.

Attending an Official Hearing

As a result of organizing activity during the 1970s, a great expansion of legally required citizen participation in government decision-making processes occurred. Often this participation takes the form of an official public hearing. Although the hearing is usually meaningless and the decision makers intend to ignore it, it can still be a useful arena in which to move the campaign forward. Where not required by law, groups often demand hearings as a way of opening the debate, delaying a decision, or creating an arena in which to show their strength.

Try to get the hearing held on your own turf at a time when your people can attend. Most official hearings are held downtown at 9 A.M. Fighting to get evening hearings held in your neighborhood is often a good way to build the campaign. It is the type of demand that is hard for a public agency to refuse. If you win, however, you are obligated to produce a crowd.

When you are stuck with the morning time slot and downtown location, try to get on the agenda at the very opening of the hearing. That is when the media will come, and they will not stay long. Also, your people will get tired. Often you must register to speak weeks or months in advance. (This is particularly true for environmental hearings on big state or federal projects.)

Official hearings are boring. Do not plan on keeping a crowd at one for long. Consider having a picket line, press event, or demonstration outside until it is time for your spokesperson to testify. Technical hearings are super boring. It is often not useful to bring large groups to them.

Use tactics that are humorous but that are also in good taste and make a political point. This is particularly important for gaining media coverage at an otherwise unnewsworthy event. A leader of a citizens' group, for example, appeared at a utility rate hearing dressed as King Com, the

Electric Gorilla (*Com*monwealth Edison). A public housing tenants' organization appeared in the City Council chamber with mice that had been caught in their apartments. Gimmicks like these are good for morale and press but have little inherent power. They are no substitute for large numbers of people.

If the goal of appearing at the hearing is to get media coverage for your position, avoid appearing at a time when opposition groups will also be present. A confrontation between rival organizations will be covered, but the substance of your position is likely to be even more lost than usual. If you want television coverage, you will need to have something "visual" for the cameras.

The assumption here is that hearings are theater. Occasionally this is not true. Some legally mandated hearings can be used to build up a case for later court action or to win major delays. Some technical hearings really can modify the rulings of regulatory agencies. Someone on your team should know how to play it straight, which often requires expert technical and legal advice. If very technical testimony is required, try to find a public interest or advocacy group to provide it. And at any hearing, have printed copies of your testimony available for the media, the official record, and general distribution.

A group fighting a utility rate increase discovered that the hearing was being held so far out in the suburbs that people from the city couldn't even find it. The organization called the press and TV news to an event where it released homing pigeons, which, the media were told, were being sent to search for the hearing. The point was made. The stunt got good coverage and embarrassed the utility.

Tips for Going to an Official Hearing

- Everyone in the group should be easily identified. If your group has buttons, T-shirts, or hats, wear them. Print out your group's name or a slogan in large type on big computer labels that people can stick on their clothing.
- Set up a literature table outside the hearing room or on the street. That way you can find supporters among the crowd whom you did not know. Give them a sticker to identify them as being with your group inside the hearing.
- Prepare a fact sheet or a leaflet to hand out at the hearing in order to explain to everyone just who your group is and what you want. Have the same information in the form of a press statement with quotations from your spokespeople.
- At really big events, appoint one or two "applause managers" to make sure that your people support speakers with whom you agree.
- At events where there are several floor microphones, line your people up at all of them. Give them an index card with talking points or questions to ask. The first person to be called on makes the first point on the list, the next person the second point, and so on.
- If your group feels it appropriate, don't hesitate to bring large signs or posters. The idea is to turn the hearing into *your* event.
- If the crowd is really with you and the decision makers are actually present, try to push them into making commitments on the spot, even though that is not the official purpose of the hearing. Ask that the audience be allowed to go on record by voting on the issue. Let the presiding official tell people that they aren't allowed to vote.

Mass Demonstrations

Mass demonstrations are a good show of numbers, but they are also a lot of work. If you hold more than one during an issue campaign, each must be larger than the preceding one or you will appear to be losing support. This tactic works best when a single individual is the target. When aimed at a legislative body, it can lose focus and fail to apply pressure to individual members. Consequently, such demonstrations should be combined with direct lobbying.

The nice thing about a mass demonstration is that it is like money in the bank. Once you have produced a thousand people, or a million, you do not need to do it again for a long time. Your reputation will carry you.

Location is critical. You want a place where passing street traffic will feed the event. It is cheating, however, to claim that everyone eating lunch on the mall at noon was part of your demonstration. Eventually, the truth will catch up with you. (What is actually considered a large turnout depends on where you live and on how many people usually come to such events.)

Accountability Sessions

An accountability session is a meeting that you hold with an elected official where you control the agenda. During the session, people from your constituency present information and say why they expect the official to support a certain measure. Then, a panel of your leaders makes specific demands on the official. An immediate and positive response is expected. This tactic's ability to succeed is directly proportional to the numerical strength you can show in relation to the elected official's margin of victory in the last election. High numbers count, as does having speakers who represent large groups. Often, petitions or letters are presented to demonstrate even wider support. The assumption, of course, is that the official is vulnerable and that many of your people either voted for him or her or did not vote at all but will now. If all of your people always vote for the opposing party anyway, you will

voter registration

have much less leverage. Because this is such a useful tactic, an entire chapter of this book is devoted to it.

Educational Meetings and Teach-Ins

An educational event should not be designed solely to inform people. It should also generate publicity and show strength. The measure of successful education is that it leads to action, and this should be built into the meeting. One speaker should present the organization's plans and tell the audience how people can become active. Everyone should leave the meeting with something specific to do.

You are under no moral obligation to represent the other side's position at an educational meeting. The only reason to hold a debate is if you think you can trounce an opposition spokesperson or win over his or her followers. And as with all events, whenever you get more than five people in a room, take up a collection.

Civil Disobedience and Arrest

Civil disobedience, like all tactics, should never be seen as an end in itself but always as a way of moving forward a larger strategy. In the early part of this century, when the members of the legendary Industrial Workers of the World (IWW, or "Wobblies") packed the jails of the Northwest during the free speech fights, they were not simply assuming a moral posture. Packing the jails in response to the arrest of their organizers really did create a crisis for many towns that had no place to put additional prisoners and no budgets to cover all the extra food and guards. This tactic also brought publicity and built solidarity among the members, who might otherwise have been isolated and intimidated.

In the civil rights movement, civil disobedience often took the form of exercising legal rights, registering to vote for example, that were recognized nationally but not locally. One part of the movement's strategy was to force the federal government to intervene and protect local activists. When students protesting a tuition increase seized college buildings, their strategy was to force the Governor either to increase funding or to risk violence by causing the arrest of students who were asking for no more than an affordable education. In part, the strategy worked because the Governor had presidential ambitions and was very image conscious. In the Pittston coal miners strike, the miners sat on the road to stop trucks from moving coal. They took over a breaker building to attract national media attention to the injustice of the use of strikebreakers. Both acts of civil disobedience were part of a careful strategy to cut the company's profits and build national support for the miners' demands. Civil disobedience works as part of a well-thought-out strategy. It is not an end in itself, as some romantics might suggest. In fact, in many organizing situations civil disobedience frightens people and may hinder your ability to recruit members and consequently your ability to win on an issue.

America, and other countries as well, has a long history of government agents infiltrating citizen organizations and advocating violence. This is done to create a pretext for arrests or to limit the public appeal of an otherwise popular movement. Civil disobedience and violence are two different things. Civil disobedience is doing something that is morally right and is either legal, or ought to be, but is wrongly interpreted as illegal by the authorities—blocking loggers from clear-cutting a forest, for example. Civil disobedience can also mean challenging the illegitimate authority or immoral acts of the state—for example, by not paying taxes for war. If violence ensues from such challenges, it usually is initiated by the authorities. Legitimate violence by citizens' groups is always

a defensive response. Symbolic demonstrations of violence, such as throwing rocks at the police or breaking windows, are altogether different and seldom justified.

You must carefully consider whether civil disobedience is an appropriate tactic for your group. Civil disobedience can be effective when:

- Your constituency is comfortable with the tactic.
- Visible leadership roles are available for those who don't choose to participate directly in civil disobedience. (Many people can't because of family obligations.)
- The tactic demonstrates power to the target. Civil disobedience shows your power by cutting into a company's profits or demonstrating the ability to do so. Civil disobedience shows power if large numbers of people participate or express support. Politicians realize that if people feel strongly enough about an issue to get arrested, they will feel strongly enough to vote against them on election day.

Legal Disruptive Tactics

With tactics such as strikes, picket lines, or withholding of rent, the power actually lies in the implementation of the tactic itself. Such tactics are qualitatively different from those designed to imply an electoral threat by showing numbers. Picketing, when it succeeds in keeping people out of a place of business, goes beyond the symbolic to create financial loss. These forms of economic/consumer power, rather than political power, must be carefully focused on specific targets.

Boycotts

The popularity of the Montgomery bus boycott, the United Farm Workers' grape boycott, and Infact's boycott of Nestle makes boycotts one of the first tactics that many groups consider.

In general, however, most national or international boycotts against products don't work. A careful analysis of the product and your ability to actually affect the company's profits is required. As corporations merge and become larger, the requirements for a successful boycott are being raised. They include

- A moral issue of national or international importance.
- A product that
  - Everyone buys frequently.
  - Is easily identifiable by a brand name that the company spends a great deal of money promoting or is at least easily identifiable.
  - Is non-essential, or better, for which competing brands or substitutes exist.

It should be clear from the above that if someone suggests that you boycott cement, there is a good chance that you are talking to a silly person.

Boycotts of a local retail business are more manageable than are boycotts of specific products. Communities have successfully taken action, for example, against franchises that put locally owned stores out of business.

A boycott, like a strike, is similar to a revolver with one bullet in the chamber. The threat of using it is more powerful than the weapon itself. But don't make the threat unless you are prepared to carry it out.

A Method for Planning Tactics

The strategy chart is as useful for planning individual tactics as it is for planning your overall campaign. To use it in this way, simply place the tactic (holding your own rally, for example) in the first column (Goals). The Organizational Considerations column becomes the budget and organizational goals for the event itself (organizational goals are always considered separately from issue goals). The Constituents column becomes the turnout plan for the event. The Targets column is used to identify the people with power at whom the event is aimed. Pay particular attention to secondary targets whom you may want to involve. The Tactics column then becomes a list of the things you will do at the event to show your own power, make the target uncomfortable, get media attention, and create an exciting activity.

Checklist for Tactics

All tactics must be considered within an overall strategy. Use this checklist to make sure that each tactic makes sense given your strategy.

_____ Can you really do it? Do you have the needed people, time, and resources?

_____ Is it focused on either the primary or secondary target?

_____ Does it put real power behind a specific demand?

_____ Does it meet your organizational goals as well as your issue goals?

_____ Is it outside the experience of the target?

_____ Is it within the experience of your own members and are they comfortable with it?

_____ Do you have leaders experienced enough to do it?

_____ Will people enjoy working on it or participating in it?

_____ Will it play positively in the media?

© Midwest Academy

28 E. Jackson Blvd. #605, Chicago, IL 60604

(312) 427-2304   mwacademy1@aol.com   www.midwestacademy.com

Using the Strategy Chart to Plan a Tactic
Newton Save Our Schools Rally

After using the strategy chart to plan an overall campaign, any tactic from the last column can become the basis of a new chart that is used to plan that particular tactic. The following chart demonstrates how this works.

Goals	Organizational Considerations	Constituents	Targets	Tactics
1. Long-Term Pass Fair Tax Plan. 2. Intermediate Force Rep. Hide to support the Fair Tax Plan. 3. Short-Range Hold rally of 400 people.	1. Resources to Put In Budget = $300.000 $100.00 from coalition. Rest to be raised locally. Fred: 3 weeks (half time first 2 weeks, full time for 3rd week) Liz: 3 days Board Member—Kim Max (lives in Newton) Newton office—2 phones 2. What We Want to Get Out Closer relations with teachers organization and Newton PTAs. Build toward affiliation of Newton Black Issues Committee.	Teachers organizations (200)* Black Issues Committee (50) Fed. of Puerto Rican Home Town Associations (30) Kensington/Johnston Action Council (40) CWA Local 72 (30) Newton Parents United (45) Newton Real Estate Association (5) Newton Civic Association (20) Individual parents and students (50) Unorganized homeowners (40) *These numbers are the turnout goals for each group.	1. Main Target Rep. Harry Hide 2. Secondary Targets School Board Members: Penny Black, Allison Vandyke Judge Thomas—strong school supporter Sarah Kendall—Hide contributor, big on education. Has millions of dollars. Melvin Elvin-Rep. candidate for Supervisor. Wants ticket to win.	Hold rally outside Rep. Hide's office. Kids march up with symbols of discontinued school programs drawn on posters, e.g., basketball hoop, band instruments, theater masks, computers, microscopes. Each child calls to Hide through PA system to come down and save program. When he doesn't come, poster is thrown in big trash can labeled "Hide's Hope Chest." Petitions taken up to Hide's office. Speakers: Heads of major groups. Collection taken. Major push for press and TV. Meet with all school board members. Ask them to attend the rally. Promise empty chairs on platform to those who don't show.

© Midwest Academy

28 E. Jackson Blvd. #605, Chicago, IL 60604

(312) 427-2304   mwacademy1@aol.com   www.midwestacademy.com

6

Leaders lead people, but organizers organize organizations. The role of an organizer is to construct an organization. An organizer who neglects the structure and rushes to work with individual people is like a taxi driver who picks up customers in his arms and carries them from place to place without the cab. Some members love to have the organizer carry them because they are relieved of the burden of thinking about and maintaining an organization. Many organizers who do realize the importance of building a structure pay little attention to the model, the architectural plan for the structure.

The Model Is the Architecture of the Organization

Imagine a group of people building a house without a plan. One person lays concrete for the slab under the house, while the next starts digging a basement. The walls go up half of wood and half of brick. Someone is roofing over the second story while another person builds a staircase to the non-existent third story. The toilet is installed in front of the fireplace. Fortunately, the building inspector will quickly call a halt to the construction. Unfortunately, organizational structures don't have building inspectors. Many leaders and staff mem-

The Model Is the Architecture of the Organization

The Model Is a "What," Not a "How" or a "Why"

The Four Elements of the Model

The Model Must Be Clear and Internally Consistent

Organizing Models:
The Underlying Structure of Organizations

bers organize without a building plan. Not only are they unable to say exactly what the structure they are creating should look like when finished, but they often create conflicting structures within their organizations:

- A non-profit community development corporation sets up and staffs a tenant organization in buildings that it owns and manages. The tenants then start to fight "the landlord," and the staff is told to make them stop.

- The board of a disabilities organization includes both representatives of the disabled and their service providers, although many of the disabled consider the providers to be part of the problem.

- A legislative coalition, in order to get funding for a special project, is compelled by the funder to create a whole new project board, which is different from the "real" board.

- A federation of senior clubs organizes a group of seniors who don't belong to any of its member clubs.

- An organization, which operates on both a community *service* model and a community *organizing* model, finds that when it organizes people to fight City Hall, City Hall retaliates by cutting off the funding for the service program.

The Model Is a "What," Not a "How" or a "Why"

The organizing model is the answer to the question, Exactly what are we building? For any organization, many ways can be used to build successfully, but only *one thing* is being built. When asked, "On what model are you building?" people often state the *function* that the group is to serve: "We are building an organization to which environmentalists in the Great Lakes region will turn for coordination." The function is a part of what makes up the model, but they are two different things. If the inquiry is about the model, then the answer should be "We are building a *coalition* of groups that organize on Lakes-related issues" or "We are going to recruit 30,000 *individual members* from around the Lakes" or "We will be a *staff* of four, all of whom will monitor state programs in the Lakes region." Each of these different organizing models could serve the same function of building a group toward which environmentalists look for coordination. Obviously, there is no one right model of organizing, but experience indicates that the range of successful possibilities is more limited than might be imagined, particularly among groups that have survived more than ten years.

An organizational model, or architectural plan, is a conception of the essential skeleton of the organization. It is not necessarily the same as the organizational chart or bylaws, although they are related. The organization's program, its formal leadership bodies, and its staffing pattern are all derived from its basic architecture.

The Four Elements of the Model

An organizational model is composed of the following four elements:

1. *The Function of the Organization.* Is the function to win issues such as getting a traffic light installed? Is it to pass legislation, to win elections, or to provide direct services? Is it to advocate, educate, or some combination of the above?

2. *The Geographic Basis of the Organization.* Is the organization based in a neighborhood, a housing development, or a political district such as a congressional district? Is it citywide, countywide, statewide, regional, or national? Obviously, the geography relates directly to the function.

3. *The Basis of Membership.* Do individual people join, or is the organization a coalition of organizations? If the members are individuals, are they organized into chapters or are they at large? Is the organization a formal coalition that groups actually vote to join and put their names on the letterhead? If so, then those groups are the members. Is it an informal coalition where staff or leaders from other groups join the board as individuals? In that case, the board is usually the membership. In some models, a coalition builds an at-large base of individual members through its door-to-door canvassing. In yet another model, the staff is basically the membership. In another model, the members of the organization are religious congregations that hire an organizer

to work for them. Once again, the point is not that any of these are better or worse than others but simply that the model, the basis of membership, and the location of decision-making power must be clear.

4. *The Funding Base of the Organization.* The funding base is included in the definition of the model because, more than any other single factor, it determines how the organization works and what it does. What percentage of the funds is actually intended to be raised by the members? How much is to come from foundations or outside donors? How much will come from contracts with public agencies? Do many foundations and donors contribute or only a few? Is there a field or phone canvass, and what percentage of the budget comes from it? Many organizations that appear on paper to be controlled by the members are actually controlled by their funders. Will the organization choose a tax status that restricts lobbying or one that doesn't?

The Model Must Be Clear and Internally Consistent

A model is clear when the board and the staff can see what they are building. It is internally consistent when all the pieces fit neatly into the basic concept and reinforce each other. None should appear to have been tacked on like tail fins on a Volkswagen Beetle. The best way to illustrate this point is with case histories that are actual composites of our own experience.

The Case of the Ambiguous Tenant Organization

A housing organization was unclear about the difference between a service model and an organizing model. The staff did a little of both, considering them to be the same thing.

A man from a building to which an organizer had been assigned came into the office. After being interviewed about his problem, he was advised to go to Legal Assistance and get a lawyer. The man said, "That's too much hassle," and he left. The organizer remarked, "See, that's why we can't ever get anything going in the building; nobody cares enough to do anything." She didn't make the distinction between an individual problem requiring a lawyer and a buildingwide issue that could be addressed by organizing. More to the point, the organization as a whole made no such distinction because its underlying model was neither clearly *service* nor clearly *organizing*. If something could be called "housing," the organization did it.

Had there been a clear *organizing* model, the staff member would not have made a referral. Instead, she would have gone back to the building with the man, talked to the other tenants, and seen who had the same problem. Even if the problem was an individual matter such as eviction for non-payment of rent, if many other people were also behind, the tenants might have tried to negotiate a payment plan in exchange for improved conditions. If legal action to improve building services was required, all the tenants, not one individual, should have brought the action. If all else failed, then helping the man to get a lawyer would have been appropriate.

On the other hand, if the organization had a clear *service* model, not an organizing model, then the staff should have phoned Legal Assistance at once, explained the man's case, had the man talk about the case over the phone, and then made an appointment for him. Perhaps someone would even have driven him there.

Unfortunately, because the staff was unclear about what was being built, the man's request for help was handled inappropriately. The result was neither service nor organizing.

The Case of the Superfluous Office

A national organization, based on a model of individual membership in local chapters, had as its major function the passage of national legislation. This required building chapters to lobby in key congressional districts. The organization decided to set up a regional office with organizing staff to service a major metropolitan area in which it had a very large membership. The organization's leaders thought that the members would be enthusiastic about the office and would easily raise the money for it. As it turned out, the members never fully saw what purpose the office served and didn't support it.

A basic problem emerged here because a regional office really had no programmatic role. The efforts of the chapters were focused on the congressional districts in which they were located. Because a region isn't a political district of any kind, there was no regional political decision maker. Without a common target, there was no common regionwide program in which all the chapters could participate together. Without such a program, the only role for regional staff was to help the individual chapter in their own congressional districts. Rightly or wrongly (probably wrongly), the chapter members didn't feel that they needed "outside" help and declined to raise the money to pay for it. Had a critical vote been coming up in the U.S. Senate, they would have given money for a statewide campaign office, but they couldn't see the logic of a regional office.

This is a very typical situation in which the *model* and the *program* do not coincide. In order for them to coincide, some meaningful program must exist at each geographic level of organizational structure, be it a neighborhood chapter, a district committee, a citywide board, or organization by region, county, or state. In direct action organizing, where the purpose is to win something, useful structures can exist only at geographic levels where there is actually something to be won and someone from whom to win it. For example, environmental groups from a number of states could form a regional organization, the target of which was a Regional Director of the Environmental Protection Agency. Setting up unnecessary regional structures is one of the most common ways in which organizations create internal problems for themselves.

The Case of the Statewide Coalition with Local Chapters

A statewide citizen organization had a formal coalition membership model. That is, organizations voted to join the coalition and placed one of their officers on the coalition's board. Its function was to pass legislation and to elect (through a political action committee) legislators who would support its program.

After a number of years, the board voted to set up several community chapters, which were to work on local neighborhood issues. On the surface, little appeared to have changed; however, a second organization with a different model had actually been created within the first.

Eventually, a number of problems became apparent with the dual model structure. Because the chapters dealt with very local issues, they neither strengthened nor drew strength from the statewide campaigns. Had the chapter's turf conformed to legislative districts, and had the chapter members been organized to pressure their legislators to vote for the organization's program, the chapters might have been a better fit.

The local leaders, whom the organizers tried to involve in the statewide coalition, were naturally suspicious. They saw resources coming in but had little interest in the statewide issues. They had been working on local issues all along and didn't want to be diverted to someone else's agenda. Their attitude was to take what they could get from the state organization but to keep

their distance from it. The organizing staff was drawn into the local activities, which took them away from the statewide efforts. Much of the staff's work amounted to a subsidy to neighborhood groups, but when the coalition tried to raise funds for its community work, it found itself in competition with the same local organizations it was helping and was resented for it. Launching the local chapters was a classic case of creating structures and programs that were at odds with the basic model.

The Case of the Coalition That Started a Coalition

A statewide citizen organization had an informal coalition model. That is, leaders of other organizations sat on its board, but their groups did not formally vote to join the coalition. The coalition's function was passing legislation.

When funding became available for a state Family Leave Act campaign, a decision was made to set up a new coalition just for that issue. The hope was that groups not then a part of the state organization would join the campaign through this new structure. Money was channeled through the state organization to the new coalition, and some of the organization's staff members were assigned to the new group, which was called the Family Coalition.

The first task of these staff people was to recruit some of the state organization's own board members to the board of the new Family Coalition. Next, they recruited additional Family Coalition board members from among the leaders of other organizations interested in the issue. The Family Coalition then held media events, published studies, and began lobbying in its own name. It was a big success. Although the state organization had started it, raised funds for it, and staffed it, the Family Coalition listed the parent organization on the letterhead as just another of seventeen member groups. Before long, the board of the Family Coalition asked the organizers if they could apply for foundation grants independently so that funds would no longer come through the state organization. The board members said they wanted to hire their own staff and go their own way.

When the state organization's leaders started the Family Coalition, they thought they were simply creating another program and another campaign. But by not respecting the integrity of its own model, the state organization had set up another coalition that could and did become a competitor. Their model could not accommodate a coalition within a coalition.

Because the board created a free-floating, self-governing program not anchored into its underlying coalition board structure, a typical result occurred. The program took on a life of its own. It happens every time. Committees, locals, chapters, regions, temporary coalitions, and special programs all naturally tend toward having an independent existence. Even field offices that are not closely supervised do this.

Setting up any structure that is not integral to your organizing model or that doesn't use your group's own name is generally a bad idea. The same principle applies to setting up independent organizations that you intend, someday, to absorb or merge into your own group. For example, an organization built local committees to campaign for a specific piece of state legislation. The connection between the committees and the organization was left ambiguous. Each was, in effect, independent of the other. If such organizations have real people in them, they will develop their own identities and will resist change. People who would have readily joined you had they been asked to do so in the first place will become suspicious and hostile if, after setting up an independent group, you then suggest a merger. Often, the fact that you raised the money

and staffed the independent group only deepens their resentment and fear of a hidden agenda. Never expect ambiguity to lead to gratitude.

Another organization, let's call it the Great Plains Citizens Network, handled this type of situation with far better results. Great Plains was *not* designed to be a coalition, but it needed to build a coalition structure through which other groups could support its renewable energy program. Avoiding the word "coalition," which implied a more formal structure than was needed, Great Plains created the "Sustainable Power for Economic Development" ("SPEED") Campaign. Over twenty groups joined. The SPEED Campaign's letterhead and literature always contained the line "A project of the Great Plains Citizens Network," with the Great Plains address. In this way, the organizational relationship was always kept clear and open. The SPEED Campaign affiliates knew that they weren't joining Great Plains itself, nor were they setting up something independent. They were part of a single-purpose, time-limited, issue campaign sponsored by another group. The model was clean.

The Case of the Inconsistent Board

A community-based organization described itself as an alliance of organizations and service agencies dealing with poor people. Its model was that of a very, very informal coalition.

As the group expanded, it added to the board individuals who were active in its programs but who did not come from any organization. It also kept on the board people who had once represented organizations but who were no longer connected with those groups. Everything went well enough until the organization received a very large grant. The board at once fell to fighting over how and where the money would be spent. In the process, board members from real organizations found themselves being outvoted by people representing no one but themselves. They complained that they had joined an alliance of *organizations,* and now the rules were changed. The alliance didn't last a moment longer than the money did; then it self-destructed.

This organization was unclear about the basis of its membership, a critical aspect of the model. A group is either an organization of *individuals* or an organization of *organizations*. Trying to be both, a mixed model, can create problems in many kinds of organizations. (Service agencies seem to be an exception and are often well served by boards composed of people from allied groups, funders, and prominent individuals.)

In direct action organizations, such mixed boards may work until a crunch comes. Then, be the conflict over a program, finances, or politics, different categories of board members are likely to question the legitimacy of decisions made by others. Structure matters most when the chips are down and the question is, who has the votes?

Another difficulty in mixing individuals with group representatives on the board of a coalition is that they come with different viewpoints and are subject to different pressures. For example, an individual board member may have nothing to lose by attacking the Mayor or taking on an unpopular issue, but an organizational board member may fear losing city funding or dividing the membership of the group he or she represents. Similarly, an organizational member may want the coalition to target someone with whom an individual board member happens to have an important business relationship. Of course, the same problems can and do occur on boards with either all individual or all organizational members, but they are less likely to get out of hand when all voting members have the same institutional relationship to the group.

Organizations that deal with the needs of constituencies such as seniors, children, the disabled, or the homeless often have boards composed of representatives of the particular constituency, service providers, and government agencies. Such groups are supposedly united in their desire to work for their constituents and get programs funded, but because their institutional interests are so different, they tend to block each other and allow the government agencies and service providers to keep the actual constituents under control. For example, a coalition of disabilities groups wanted to start a campaign to win the right of the disabled to fire their own home health aides. The agencies that provided the aides sat on the coalition's board and blocked the campaign.

Concluding Thoughts

Each of these cases has been presented to emphasize flaws in the conception of the model. In day-to-day organizing, such flaws may not be so obvious. Problems with the model can come disguised as personality conflicts, feuding between member organizations, financial trouble, debates over philosophy, political rifts, and criticism of the Director. The role of the organizer is to look past the surface problems, no matter how serious, and determine if these are symptoms of a discordant model.

Model-related problems are present in every organization. Like the flu, they lurk about, looking for a chance to strike. Unlike the flu, they often appear as something else. For example, staff members will complain that the Director does not spend enough time with them and therefore they don't understand what they are supposed to be *doing.* Frequently, what they are really saying is that they don't understand what they are supposed to be *building.* They sense that the model isn't clear, even though they may not say it that way. When the model isn't clear, no amount of time with a Director can compensate for it.

An unclear model results in day-to-day organizing tasks becoming complicated policy matters instead of being part of a repeatable plan. If, for example, a clear individual-membership chapter model is in place, then when the chapter holds a media event, the elected leaders of the chapter are *always* the main speakers. But if the group is made up of some individual members, some institutional members, some people with a real base in the community and others with none, a member of the clergy to whom everyone defers, a candidate for City Council, and a college professor who really knows the issue, then who speaks at the media event? The answer differs according to the day of the week, and no one is ever happy with it. No wonder the staff never seems to get enough direction and the Director never has enough time. When the model is not clear, very little else will be clear.

Board members will complain that there is not enough communication and they no longer know what is going on in the organization. They may be right, but sometimes this is a symptom of the program having moved away from the basic model so that board leadership is less directly involved. This often occurs in a coalition where the program is supposed to be carried out through the affiliates but, usually in response to a funding opportunity, the staff has started some other project involving different people. Once that happens, increased communication will seldom bring the original affiliates closer to a program that isn't theirs. People hear what they want to hear. No matter how much an organization communicates with affiliates or board members, if the communication isn't about something they are actually doing or want to do, they won't hear it. Then they will complain that there isn't enough communication. The program must either be brought back in line with the model—that is, with the way the organization was set up to operate—or the model itself must be changed to integrate the new activity.

In a similar way, organizational problems are often attributed to a lack of training. The Midwest Academy staff is frequently called upon for training, only to find that over the years a group has added so many bits and pieces of program and structure that no one understands any longer where everything is going. Training will help only after the program has been realigned with the model.

Any given model affects an organization's program. It makes some types of campaigns easier to win and some harder. It encourages the participation of some groups while discouraging others. It either enhances or diminishes the political power of the organization. It advances certain types of fundraising and holds back others.

Some organizers say that they believe in free-form organizing. They have no model, want no model, and need no model. They are wrong. *There is always a model.* If you don't create it, it evolves on its own, often influenced by funding. It will always operate just as the force of gravity always operates, even upon those who believe that they have transcended it. Organizers, you have a choice: learn to understand and use the concept of the model or be blindly led by it.

7

An action is a tactic in which an organized group of people with a common grievance meet with the person who has the power to give them what they want. At the meeting, they place their demands before that person and expect to gain a victory on the spot. The person is often called the "decision maker" or "target" of the action.

This tactic is used after "proper channels" have been tried and failed. Your group has already written letters, filled out forms, left messages, and attempted to be heard. In the course of those activities you recruited additional people into your campaign. Now people are getting a little mad and it is time to move to the next step.

An action is a tactic. In organizing, the word "action" has a special meaning for reasons that have been lost to history. While other people might take action or get a piece of the action, organizers *"do"* an action. Worse yet, we do it *"on"* someone. Don't blame the Midwest Academy—we didn't invent this language. We are merely reluctant to change it, so great is the burden of tradition. As with other tactics, actions come at the end of the strategy chart. Actions are one of the things that the people listed in the Constituency column do to the people listed in the Targets column. The key to successful actions

Why Actions Work

When to Use Actions

Action Planning

Checklist for Planning an Action

Designing Actions

is for people to develop real power over the target and show that power during the action.

No other tactic does as much to win short- and medium-range demands or to build the organization. In days, the use of actions can cut through months, and sometimes years, of bureaucratic red tape. Equally as important is the impact on the participants. People come away with a heightened sense of their own power and dignity, while their opponents are made to appear smaller and more vulnerable. At the same time, relationships of power are clarified because problems that might have been attributed to misunderstanding or lack of communication are seen sharply for what they really are—the conflicting interests of public good against private greed. In the process, loyalty to the organization is built up because people see it actually working for them and realize that their participation is essential to its success.

Why Actions Work

The principle of this tactic is deceptively simple and direct. You ask for something, and more often than not, you get it. It's like magic and you say, "Why didn't we do this months ago?" The answer is that it probably wouldn't have worked

months ago because you hadn't built up your organized strength, nor had you made the necessary strategic calculations.

The real reason that actions work arises from a set of calculations about the relationship between your group and the target. It can best be described, from the target's point of view, as a cost-benefit analysis. The target, the decision maker, considers the expense of giving you what you want and the damage you can cause if you don't get it.

The damage might be that pressure from your organization would result in a loss of votes or that the target fears a problem that was supposed to be kept quiet will make it into the media. Perhaps the target's company will lose business or government contracts, a regulatory agency will step in, or an official investigation will be launched. If you are able to make anything like this happen, there is a clear and measurable benefit to the target in giving you what you want and getting rid of you.

What you want has a cost to the target. It might be a financial cost like the expense of removing asbestos from a school, cleaning up a toxic dump, or providing childcare. It might be a loss of campaign contributions from people who oppose the position you are trying to get the decision maker to take. It might mean lost credibility if giving in means admitting a mistake was made. The target is therefore put in the position of having to balance the two sets of costs: the cost of giving you what you want versus the cost of not giving it to you. Your strategy is to raise the cost of not giving you what you want so that the benefit to the decision maker of having you go away happy is greater than the cost of what you are asking for. The whole process is a bit like finding a way to stand on someone's foot until they pay you to leave.

Fortunately, most of the time the target is a public official who doesn't have to spend his or her own money to meet your demand. Actions usually don't work in situations where the target must personally pay any financial cost. (Actions on landlords are an exception. Often, tenants don't fully realize the extent of the landlord's vulnerability because of violations, illegalities, bribery, or financial manipulation. The landlord may therefore decide it's cheaper to meet tenant demands for a specific repair or service than to risk greater exposure.) Sometimes workers conduct actions on employers, making demands such as bathroom breaks, clean restrooms, safety equipment, or fairer treatment. Actions on employers are most effective on issues that will not cost large amounts of money or when the actions are about violations for which the company could be fined by a government agency or taken to court. (We are using the direct action organizing definition of "action." A boycott against an employer or a strike are different *tactics*.)

Public officials usually expect that your group will give them something in return for the concession they make to you. They'll want a positive gesture, usually a public affirmation that they did the right thing, not in response to pressure but because they are such good people. Negotiating on these lines is not necessarily bad. You are,

after all, trying to convince elected officials that they have more to gain by cooperating with your group than by opposing you. If you really don't want a particular elected official to seek public favor by taking credit for doing what you demand, then don't ask in the first place. If the official is one whom you ultimately hope to see out of office, make demands you know you can't win, or raise the issue in other ways.

Actions can also be used to pressure a target indirectly. For example, when a bank foreclosed on one local company, the company closed down owing two weeks of back pay to 450 minimum-wage workers. A community organization that was helping the workers collect their pay, wanted to meet with bank officials but couldn't get the meeting. Upon finding that the bank had a branch in the neighborhood, the group "did an action" on the local branch manager. Members of the group marched into the bank, demanding that the manager ask the bank president to talk with the group. The branch manager called the president, and the group eventually met with the bank's top executives. Eventually, after pressuring the bank president, the local Department of Labor, and the former owner, the workers got the back wages owed them.

When to Use Actions

Tactics are rated from weak to strong according to how much pressure they put on the target. Of course, the more pressure the tactic applies, the more powerful the organization using it must be.

An action is a low- to medium-power tactic. It has more power than a few hours of picketing a building but less power than a strike or a boycott. It is most useful in the opening phases of a campaign, when you need to assemble a core group and get it moving quickly. An action can be done with fewer than fifteen people, but more is better. Successful actions are great organization builders because after the first one, the members will want to do more, and they will see the need to bring in larger numbers of people. Actions are also fun.

Actions are a good measure of an organization's ability to turn out people, and they test the ability of the leadership. This gives the members a criterion for judging leaders other than by how well they speak at meetings. In addition, publicity from actions will bring in new recruits. The expectation should be that over a period of months as you take on more important targets, each action will be a little larger than the one preceding it. Actions are used to build up to large turnout events of your own, such as public hearings or accountability sessions.

One of the reasons that actions work is that they take the organization outside established channels for getting things done and move it to terrain where officials are less sure of how to handle the situation. It is always wise to make the effort of going through the proper channels first. Send letters, fill out the proper forms, file formal complaints, and generally do whatever is necessary to establish that you tried the "normal" way and it didn't work. If this step is skipped, some of your members may feel that the action is not appropriate. Most people want to give the other person the benefit of the doubt.

The strategy chart is an excellent tool for planning a single action as well as a whole campaign. Just plug in the information that is relevant to this particular activity. Here are some considerations for each column of the chart.

Action Planning

Goals (Demands)

Success in formulating demands depends on understanding the power relationships involved. This means not only accurately assessing the strength of your forces but also understanding the self-interest of the other side. Knowing what the cost of a citizen victory will be to the other side and who will have to pay it brings you to an estimation of the amount of opposition that your organization will receive. This, in turn, is the basis for deciding what demands you will make. Every increase in the cost of the organization's demands must be matched by a corresponding increase in the organization's power.

Because the whole process is logical, an underlying assumption is that the target is rational and will act in his or her self-interest. If the target is not a rational person or reacts to pressure by stonewalling, or if the citizens make it clear that their negative view of the target will never improve no matter what, then this tactic is short-circuited and will probably not work. A short-circuited action can have some advantages, however. After dealing with a target over a period of time, you may learn what makes that person "pop," that is, go berserk or act inappropriately in public. Such a display of odd behavior can discredit a public official, but be sure that you have another target to move on to, and remember that officials are often trying to do the same thing to you.

Demands are ranked according to whether they are main demands or fallback demands. A fallback demand means asking for something that is useful but less than you wanted. Often, procedural and information demands are used as fallbacks. Every action should have one main or substantive demand (for example, "Clean up the dump") and several fallbacks ("Hold hearings on cleaning up the dump" "Release your study on dump site hazards"). Part of the role of the spokesperson is to decide when to switch from one to another.

The information demand is the easiest to win and is a good type of demand for your first action. In later actions, it would probably be a fallback. Your final fallback demand, if you get nothing else, should always be a commitment to another meeting. This gives you an opportunity to regroup and increase your strength.

Any agreement that is reached should include these specifics:

- How much will be done.
- When it will be done.
- Who will do it.
- What the review process is if it isn't done or is done improperly.

In addition, longer-term changes can be won and included in the agreement. Some are administrative: "Inspections must be done every six months forever." Others involve a structural reform that increases citizen power: "A permanent citizen oversight board will be established."

Organizational Considerations

An action, like every other event, should be assigned its own budget and staff. Because recruitment is done by word of mouth and by phones, the biggest expense will usually be staff time.

In addition to bringing victory on the issue, an action will strengthen the organization if you build that into the plan. Actions are most useful for leadership development. Speaking to the target or the press develops leadership skills, and the planning process teaches strategy as well. As a rule, speaking roles should be awarded to those who bring out the most people. The long-term result will be a leadership composed of people who actually have a base rather than of people who merely speak well. The ability to mobilize people, be it six friends or stewards from a union local, is the most important criterion for leadership in a citizens' organization.

As with other events, the organizer should know who the potential leaders are and build action roles around them. During the planning process, the group should set modest goals for the number of leaders it would like to see gain experience, as well as for the number of new people who ought to be recruited from the membership.

Constituency (Turnout)

The people who come to an action should be active members of your organization or coalition. Because the event needs to be tightly controlled, this is not the time to advertise publicly. Participants should be representative of all of the different types of people who are affected by the problem and who will benefit from the solution. If your organization is a coalition, the heads of member groups should be clearly visible at the action.

Consider bringing people who are influential in the community, such as clergy, political supporters, or heads of major civic organizations or unions. Always be sure to explain the nature of the action to them first. No one should be surprised by unusual tactics. People who are surprised sometimes start apologizing to the target or criticizing the organization.

If you invite sympathetic office holders to join you, figure out a way that they will get recognition in the media because what they most want is publicity. Discuss this with them in advance. If you don't, the moment a TV camera shows up they will try to grab the spokesperson role, which should always go to a leader of your own group. The media have a tendency to focus on "important" people. Think twice before you invite one.

The Target (Decision Maker)

The decision maker is always a person who has the power to give you what you want. In real life, several such people often exist for an issue. For example, in public housing, a building manager could order repairs, as could someone at the Housing Authority or a higher-up at the federal level. In this case, the choice of target is usually made according to what is most convenient for the group and what location will favor the strongest turnout. People usually want to stay close to home in their own neighborhood; as the group gains experience, it becomes an adventure to go to City Hall, the Capitol, or some agency's regional headquarters. The problem in the above example is that none of the potential targets are elected. The question is, What power might a tenant group have over appointed officials? Here are some possibilities:

- Money was already allocated for the repairs but the person in charge failed to spend it or misspent it.
- The repair involves health issues such as lead paint or lack of heat, which can bring into question the competence of the administrator.
- The administrator was appointed by an elected official who needs to cultivate a "liberal" image.
- Other political forces are out to get the job of the head of the agency and this problem just adds fuel to the fire.
- The repair or service was subcontracted to a company that has political connections or that gave campaign contributions and failed to perform the work.

Because for them, as for us, there is safety in numbers, at any action there should be only one target. The exception is that if at several previous actions the targets all denied responsibility and pointed to some other official, then getting them all in the same room can end buck passing. (Some community-based organizations will hold a neighborhood meeting and invite several local officials to come. These events are not actions but accountability sessions, and while it is better to have just one target, inviting several can bring together people from different parts of the neighborhood that have different problems.)

Direct action organizing has two types of targets: "primary" and "secondary." The primary target, such as the Mayor, can give you what you want, but you may not have enough power to challenge him or her directly. The secondary target is a person who can't deliver what you want but who can pressure the main target better than you can. The secondary target must either want to cooperate or be someone over whom you have a degree of power, such as a campaign contributor to the elected official whose position you want to change, a state representative who is on the committee that approves the budget of the university where you are organizing, or a local business owner who belongs to a trade association you are trying to influence. Individuals such as elected officials' staffers or corporate executives' assistants are not secondary targets. They may have some influence over the target, but as employees they do not have actual power. Consider them to be allies if they are willing to cooperate. Remember, though, that often the job of such people is to try to influence you or to gather information on you while pretending to help.

Actions may be used against secondary targets to secure their help in pressuring the main target. You might say to the ward (district) leader, "We have come to ask you to pick up the phone and tell the Mayor that next November your party is going to have a revolt on its hands in this district unless she sets up a meeting this week to hear our complaints." (The fallback demand in this case is, "Would you send a letter to the Mayor making this point and send a copy to us?") Your power in this situation comes from the fact that the ward leader is responsible for getting out the vote in your neighborhood and is more sensitive to public opinion than is someone elected citywide. The ward leader will also look bad if the Mayor's vote drops in that ward, even if the Mayor wins anyway. Of course the ward leader has no direct power over the Mayor, but because the Mayor relies on the ward leaders for voter turnout, she is apt to try to help one of them, at least to the extent of giving you a meeting.

Tactics

Every action must meet two requirements:
- It must be fun.
- It must demonstrate real *power.*

Tactics used during an action should reflect these goals. You may be saying "Wait a minute! You said that an action is a tactic. Can a tactic have tactics?" Can a flea have fleas? Yes, and not only that, but a tactic can have a strategy. An action is a tactic in a larger campaign, but a ministrategy is needed to carry out each tactic. As a particular tactic becomes your goal for the day, the steps to carrying it out become the tactics for the day.

Note: Readers of past editions have been perplexed by the reference to fleas. We therefore quote the passage in full.

*So, Nat'ralists observe, a Flea
Hath smaller Fleas that on him prey:
And these have smaller fleas to bite 'em
And so proceed* ad infinitum.
　　　　　　　　—*Jonathan Swift, 1733*
Swift also commented that "Elephants are always drawn smaller than life, but a flea always larger."
Actions, like fleas, should always be drawn larger than life.

Tactics for use in actions fall into three categories:

Tactics Aimed at the Target That Show Your Power. These include presenting petitions, letters, voter registration forms, and statements of support from important people in the community.

Other power tactics include demonstrating the size of your organization by a large turnout or showing the media-worthy nature of the issue by using clever visual props. Controlling the agenda and setting the tone of a meeting demonstrate the internal strength of your group.

Tactics Aimed at Raising the Morale of Your Members. These include singing or chanting, standing rather than sitting, displaying signs or funny props, and, when appropriate, displaying anger at the target. Tactics in this category, while important, must always be subordinate to those that show power and to the overall goal of the action. Actions have fallen apart over side issues such as a test of the democratic right to chant in someone's office. If you don't have real power, these tactics are not a substitute.

Tactics Aimed at Getting Media Coverage. Understanding the self-interest of the media is important in getting coverage. Editors want a short, punchy event in which everyday people, who are like their own audience, do something visually interesting. In other words, you gotta have a gimmick. This doesn't always have to be funny. A dramatic way of showing the seriousness of the problem or the toll it is taking on its victims is very effective.

A song, chant, emotional speech, or animal will get covered whereas someone just talking won't. Challenging the target to actually "drink this cup of polluted water" will get covered, whereas saying "I'll bet you don't drink the water at home" won't. Bringing a seven-foot thermometer showing the rising anger of the community as the action progresses will get covered, whereas saying "People are really hot about this" won't. Because the media usually dislike mentioning the names of citizen organizations, be sure that yours is prominently displayed on a sign with someone assigned to hold it where the camera can't avoid including it in the scene.

Tactics give you a small edge during the action, but gimmicks don't give you a win. You win because of your power, based on the size of your support. If you lose, it is because you either didn't have the power or failed to show it. Perhaps your costume was lost on the way to the action and when the spokesperson said, "It was so cold without any heat that the cat froze," you got up looking frozen but not at all like a cat. The lost costume was not the reason you failed to win and get the heat turned on. Winning does not depend on your degree of resemblance to any particular species.

The tone of the action must be appropriate to your community and constituency. People in small towns and suburbs are often much more polite to the target than are city dwellers. The key factor is that everyone must feel comfortable about what occurs.

Action Planning Reminders

The following paragraphs include some helpful guidelines for planning an action.

Stay within the Experience of Your Group. Don't confuse loudness, rudeness, or vulgarity with power. Don't suggest that, as a sign of contempt, your spokesperson sit at the target's desk and eat the target's lunch unless there is some purpose to it. (If your issue is about hunger and homelessness, you actually might make a point this way if everyone will go along and understand why it is being done.) Never make your own people feel uncomfortable at an action.

Try to Get outside the Experience of the Target. The fact that you have come in person and are no longer just sending letters is a good start. The target is usually not accustomed to losing control of a meeting or to seeing confident, articulate, and knowledgeable people who will not be intimidated. If the action occurs on your own turf, all

the better; your neighborhood itself is often outside the target's experience. Media that respond to you, not to the target, is also outside the target's experience, as is showing up with a group at the target's home. Publicizing that the law has not been followed or that the job someone is paid to do is not being done is often, but not always, outside the target's experience.

Try to Make an Appointment to See the Target Rather Than to Try for a Surprise Encounter. If you try for a surprise encounter, the target may not be there and your group members will feel dumb and get mad at you.

"Case the Joint." Organizers should look over the building and make a floor plan. Check the location of the target's office as well as elevators, stairs, bathrooms, pay telephones, and parking/transit facilities. Is the location accessible to disabled members?

Hold a Dress Rehearsal for Participants. You play the role of the target. Keep the action short (about twenty minutes, sometimes less). Remember that an action is not a negotiation. You can tell the target why you are morally right, but being right is rarely a substitute for power.

Have Only One Spokesperson in an Action. That person may call on a small number of others to present specific information. Have the group decide beforehand on the one or two people authorized to make decisions during the action. Inform everyone of this. If your organization believes in decision making by consensus or that everyone has the right to say anything at any time, forget about doing actions until the members are willing to delegate responsibility during an action to one or two trusted leaders.

Ask People to Come to the Action Fifteen Minutes Early. Have a quick briefing meeting outside the building.

If Media Are Wanted (They Aren't Always), Send a Press Release a Week Ahead of Time. Include a "notice of photo opportunity" highlighting your gimmick ("Councilman Jones will be presented with a three-foot apple symbolizing his inability to resist the temptation of commercial development"). Phone all assignment editors (City Desks, daybooks) the night before. Hold the action in the morning and at a place convenient to the media if you have a choice. Assign someone to speak with the press and provide a press release describing what you are doing and why.

Keep Your Demands Clear and Simple. Be ready with both main demands and fallback demands. Have a note taker write down the positive and negative responses. Try to get any agreement signed.

At the end of the action, use the notes to summarize what has been agreed to. Hold a short debriefing outside after the action to fill in everyone who couldn't hear, take attendance, thank people, and announce the next event.

For action planning, be sure to use the media information in chapter 14 in conjunction with this one.

Checklist for Planning an Action

_____ Will your action be both fun and based on real power?

_____ Is everyone in your group comfortable with the plan? (Is it within the experience of your group?)

_____ Will the plan be outside the experience of the target? Are you going outside the "official channels"?

_____ Are your demands clear and simple?

_____ Do you have several fallback demands?

_____ Do you have an appointment?

_____ Have you scouted the building and made a floor plan? Do you know where to find

    _____ Elevator and stairs?

    _____ Bathrooms?

    _____ Pay phone?

    _____ Parking or nearest transit stops?

    _____ The target's office?

_____ Can the site accommodate disabled members?

_____ Has the group selected who will present information at the action? Are people prepared for their roles?

_____ Has the group selected its spokesperson for the action?

_____ Have you held a dress rehearsal for the spokesperson and the participants?

_____ Have you calculated how you will demonstrate your power? Do you plan to have symbols with you (letters, petitions)?

_____ Do you have a good turnout plan for the action, including last-minute reminder phone calls?

_____ If you want the media, have they been notified? Have you

    _____ Sent a release, including a notice of your photo opportunity highlighting your gimmick, a week ahead of time?

    _____ Called the daybook a week ahead of time?

    _____ Called assignment editors the day before the action?

    _____ Prepared a release for distribution on the day of the action?

    _____ Assigned someone to talk with the media at the action itself? (Your spokesperson may be busy.)

_____ Have you selected someone to take notes during the action and write the confirmation letter to the target?

_____ Do you know who will debrief the action with participants and where the debriefing will occur?

©The Midwest Academy

28 E. Jackson Blvd. #605, Chicago, IL 60604

(312) 427-2304   mwacademy1@aol.com   www.midwestacademy.com

PART II
Organizing Skills

8

An accountability session is a large community meeting at which an elected official, or sometimes a high-level public administrator (the "decision maker" or "target"), is held accountable to the community. Because accountability sessions ultimately rely on political pressure, they are rarely used against corporate targets. They may, however, be used to force regulators to hold corporations accountable. At the meeting, very specific demands are made about matters such as legislation, funding, code enforcement, or community services, and the organization(s) holding the meeting expects a positive response on the spot.

An accountability session is a high-power tactic. It is usually used toward the end of an issue campaign after a great deal of strength has been built up. It requires the ability to turn out hundreds of people, as well as a sophisticated leadership that can run the meeting and put heat on the target. Like other tactics, it is placed in the last column of the strategy chart.

An accountability session is not simply a community "speak-out" or legislator's town meeting, although the community does speak out and the official is invited to speak briefly. It is a much more rehearsed and controlled event, but the real difference is that it is a big show of organizational

Holding Accountability Sessions

power. It is your organization's event, and there is no reason to present the other side or give time to opposing opinions.

"Power" is always a relative term. An assessment of how much power your group has is the starting point for planning an accountability session. Begin with an analysis of the target, the person who can give you what you want. (To avoid modern literary ambiguities such as "he/she," we will refer to the decision maker as "she" in this chapter.) Ask these questions:

- What is her political strength?
- How close were the last primary and general elections?
- Were they landslides or cliffhangers?
- What is her ability to raise campaign money, and has she a big debt?
- Is she up for re-election in three weeks or three years?
- Is an opponent waiting in the wings, or is she considered unbeatable?
- Has she ambitions for higher office?

If the target is a non-elected official, the task of estimating power is harder. It is approached by asking three questions:

1. What are the person's political connections? All appointed public officials are ultimately answerable to some elected person, and part of their job is to protect that person from criticism. An accountability session can be used to embarrass the elected employer of the appointed official or to hold the elected official responsible for the actions of a civil servant.

2. What is the person's career self-interest? No official wants to be publicly embarrassed. All officials want to appear to have good relations with the community and to be keeping matters under control. Some officials are taking bribes or drugs, giving jobs to friends, or being generally incompetent. Such people don't want to draw attention to themselves. They have an interest in keeping everything nice and quiet.

3. What are the person's business and social connections? Where has she worked? Where does her spouse work? Is she old money or new money? Are there potential conflicts of interest between past employers and the person's present position? For instance, did the Commissioner of Streets previously work for an asphalt paving company that does work for the city? Knowing these facts will often suggest secondary targets and additional pressure points.

Having established this background reading of the target's power and vulnerability to pressure, gauge the strength of your organization in relation to it. If you are a turf-based group, look at the political map and see how much of your territory is really in the target's district. If you are a coalition, you should know roughly how many of the individual members of the member organizations live in her district. (A look at the zip codes of member organizations' mailing lists will give you a rough idea of this.) How important are your members to her? Did they vote for her? Might they? If all of your people backed the other candidate or party and will probably do so again, then it won't mean a whole lot when you threaten not to vote for her. You will have to broaden your base. On the other hand, if you represent a strong body of support for her, which will appear to be going soft during the session, you are in a very good position. If some of her campaign contributors are in your group, all the better. Seat them in the front row. A potential opponent or two working the crowd is a nice touch.

If your conclusion is that you do have power over this person, test it out by sending her an invitation to your meeting. What is the response? Does a high-level staff person get back to you at once, or does an assistant make a call after a few weeks? Do you get a firm commitment, or is the decision left a bit vague until closer to the meeting date? Schedulers rarely say, "Well, if no one more important than you calls, she'll be there," but you can tell this from the tone of voice. Later, when you start to frame your demands, return to this question of power and begin by asking, "Why did she accept the invitation in the first place? What is she afraid of?" All of this supposes that eventually you do get a commitment *in writing* that she will come.

If you are refused the meeting, it is probably a good thing because it shows that you didn't have the power to win in the first place. A series of buildup tactics is now needed to increase your strength and visibility in order to get the official to come to the meeting. These tactics might include press "hits" (press conferences, releases of studies, or media stunts) or letter-writing drives or actions against the main target or secondary targets. Avoid taking shortcuts. If someone says, "Oh, the Senator is a friend of mine; I'll invite her for you," don't accept! You want her to come because of your group's strength or not at all. What's more, if you accept, you will then have to contend with the friend saying, "No, you can't ask her that; it will embarrass me."

(Note: The term "accountability session" is organizing language and would not generally be used in a letter. Instead, say something like "We invite you to attend a community meeting in order to tell us what you plan to do about . . .")

Demands: The Heart of the Matter

As with actions and other tactics, use a slightly modified version of the strategy chart to plan the accountability session. The five columns of the chart are used as described in the following sections.

Goals

Goals become Demands when planning the session. Instead of long, intermediate, and short-term goals, we talk about *main* demands and *fallback* demands.

Figuring out what you can ask for takes some practice. As with actions, you are setting up an equation in which you ask for something that has a monetary or political cost to the target. If the target gives it to you, she is rewarded with the valuable goodwill of the community or organization (at least until the next time). If she doesn't give it to you, the bad feeling and adverse publicity will cost her more than giving you what you want. If this last condition isn't true, you are unlikely to get much.

The specifics of the demands also determine, in part, who will come to the accountability session. For example, a community group that was asking for greater police protection increased turnout by extending its demands to include an adjoining neighborhood. This allowed the group to make alliances with civic associations in that area. Of course, each time the stakes are raised, the cost of what you are asking for goes up as well, and so does the amount of power required to win it.

An added complication is that the more demands you have and the more diverse items they cover, the greater the danger of becoming whipsawed or divided. Once the group feels that it got part of what it wanted, it is harder to get people to keep up the pressure for the rest. Worse, the target can divide the community by offering more police protection in one place and a study of the need for it in the other place. The target may tell you that she will support one piece of legislation you are trying to win but not another, or even that she will work for one section of your bill but not all of it. While your active members may see through such ploys. Others might not and believe that they should take whatever they can get. Indeed, organizations often have to make some close judgment calls in such cases.

In terms of the whole campaign, can this person really give you what you want, or is she only part of the process of getting it? For example, a member of the City Council can give you only one vote; she can't pass your bill. What else can you ask for in this situation? Will she go with you to talk to other council members? Will she talk to the Mayor? Will she come to a joint media event with you? Will she trade her vote and support someone else's bill if that person supports yours?

The point of an accountability session is to win. When you win, the organization grows. People see results. If you don't win anything, folks become discouraged and consider it all to have been a waste of time. In the future they won't work as hard for the organization, give as much money, or be there for the next fight.

Because accountability sessions need to end with a win, you must have at least one demand that you are quite sure you will get. You don't have to call attention to the fact that this is the bottom line. You can even try to hide it among more ambitious proposals, but it has to be there. What this means, however, is that just as there is pressure on the target to settle with you, there is also some need for you to settle with her.

Demands fall into two broad categories, *substantive* and *procedural*. "Substantive" refers to actually getting something of substance, such as five more patrol cars. "Procedural" can involve getting a bill out of committee, a public hearing, or a study. This distinction is a useful basis for analyzing your demands. *Main* demands are usually substantive, and *fallback* demands, which are made after a main demand is refused, are often procedural. Sometimes the best fallback is simply to ask for less: "Well, if you won't give us five patrol cars by May, how about three by August?" If that doesn't work, switch to a procedural demand: "Our members will find this disregard for their safety very disappointing. Will the Police Chief come to our community and hold an official hearing and bring members of the City Council's Law Enforcement Committee with him?" This fallback, a public hearing, is really a way to keep the issue alive and buy time to build up your campaign. To the target it says, "You shouldn't have to take all the heat alone;

bring those other turkeys around for a roasting." You each gain something.

In general, you should have three or four of each type of demand. Each fallback is attached to a main demand and is made by the same person making the main demand. Also, have a few escalation demands ready in case you get what you want too easily. If you do, it is a sign that you didn't ask for enough. Escalation demands should not be simply numerical increases in what you first asked for: "We are very happy that you agreed to five cars. How about nine?" That is too obvious and is considered very bad form. You might say, "And we would like you to ensure that the five cars will be used on all four shifts."

These, then, are the factors that go into the demand equation. You will have to figure out how to solve the equation on a case-by-case basis. We wish there were a magic formula for it. If you hear of one, write to us at once.

Organizational Considerations

Start with the resources to put into the accountability session:

- *Budget*. Any large event should cover its own costs, but an initial cash outlay will be necessary. Put down the overall cost of the accountability session, how much money you have on hand, and how much you need to raise. A collection should be taken at the event. In addition, you can sell raffle tickets, hold a cash drawing (where allowed by law), sell sponsorships to neighborhood merchants and even to elected officials, or ask for contributions from allied groups that are participating.
- *Staff and Leadership Time*. Put down who will have major responsibility for the event and how much time they are expected to spend on it. Other assignments may have to be adjusted to make this possible.

- *Members*. List the names of active members and the committees you will invite them to serve on. Note special talents such as poster making, singing, and so on. Put down the number of less active people who will probably come.
- *Equipment*. List all the office equipment that can be used in the event. This is done partly to ensure that no one plans to use the same items for other activities at the same time. Include phones, computers, copiers, and even video equipment.
- *Access to Media*. List media contacts, people who have covered you in the past, stations that run PSAs (public service announcements), and so on.
- *Reputation*, and anything else that you now have that will be useful in turning out a crowd and making this a successful event.

In the second half of this column, list all the organizational gains that you want to make during this event *other than the issue demands*. Be very specific about the numbers. For example:

- 25 new members.
- Higher visibility in the community. (Measured by what?)
- More power in relation to the target. (Measured by the number of people who come.)
- 7 more experienced leaders. (Who?)
- Closer relations with 3 specific community groups and 1 local union.
- Media coverage. (Where?)
- Money raised. (How much?)
- New voters registered at the event. (How many?)

Constituency

This column becomes the turnout plan for the event. It includes getting your own members to come, getting people from allied organizations, recruiting off the street, and using the media.

Ask who cares about this issue and how you can reach them. Are they organized in any way? Can you contact them through unions, churches, or civic associations? Who has mailing and e-mail lists? Are there gathering points such as rush-hour bus stops or shopping malls? The main part of the plan will consist of your own volunteers contacting your members individually by phone. List other groups and set a turnout goal for each along with the contact person and phone number. Review your own lists. How many names with numbers do you have? How current is the list?

Targets/Decision Maker

Of course, you already know who the decision maker is, and you have a sense of what power you have. Go over these additional questions: Are there other people (secondary targets) whose participation would make a difference? What happens if the decision maker doesn't show up? Will you accept an aide as a substitute? It is generally unwise to accept an aide of local elected officials unless the person is specifically authorized to make a commitment. Try insisting that the aide get the official on a cell phone. If a member of Congress gets stuck in Washington, an aide might be acceptable. In most states, the aide of a U.S. Senator is as close as you will get. If the decision maker fails to show up after making a commitment, consider busing or marching the whole crowd to the target's house to leaflet the neighbors.

Tactics

Tactics are all the things that you will do during the accountability session to show your strength, weaken your target, and build the morale of your members. Tactics include using signs to decorate the hall, singing songs, bringing in petitions, reading letters of support, hearing testimony from the floor, and so on. As with actions, some tactics primarily put pressure on the target, some are essentially for the morale of your own group, and some are for the benefit of the media. For each tactic you use, be aware of who it is aimed at and what its purpose is. Ask yourself if anyone will be offended by it.

The stance that you take toward the target is also a tactic. Are you going to be friendly, neutral, or angry? High key or low key? Will the target be given a comfortable chair behind a table or just a wooden folding chair? It is OK if members show more anger when speaking than the chair does. ("Look, these are your constituents— they are really mad.") Remember, though, the successful use of the accountability session is based on the assumption that the target is reacting rationally. If you make the target so angry that you get an emotional response instead of a calculated response, you will probably lose.

Any event with an elected official comes down to the power of votes. The target is sizing you up to see your numbers and whether you and your issue can gain support in the larger community. You, in turn, are putting on a bit of a demonstration of the negative campaign you will run in the community if you don't get what you want.

Rule: An accountability session works only if the elected official believes that she has more to gain by cooperating with you than opposing you.

Planning

The following paragraphs include guidelines for planning a successful accountability session:

Organize a Planning Committee. Your organization's key leaders should be on it.

Start with a Discussion of the Organizational Considerations. This is laid out in the second column of the strategy chart. Decide who will take responsibility for which aspects of the plan.

Decide on Demands. Agree on what your main demands will be. You should have at least three, usually substantive, main demands. Then decide on escalation demands and fallback demands, which are usually procedural.

Propose Dates. Contact the target with as many potential meeting dates as possible so that she can't say, "I'd love to, but I can't do it then." For example, tell the target that anytime in the last two weeks of May is fine, although you would prefer a Tuesday evening (or whatever the case may be). If the date has been set by phone, confirm it with a letter and keep copies.

Develop an Agenda. Do this after you have an idea of how many people are coming and from which groups. Groups that do strong turnout often want to have one of their own people in a speaking position. Developing the agenda is very political. You will have to strike some balance among the people who are needed to show power, allies wanting visibility, and general community members. The total time for this event, and most meetings, should be limited to two hours. A sample agenda is presented in the next section.

Plan the Logistics and Spirit of the Event. These are essentially tactics that you use at the accountability session to show more power and to make the group more cohesive. They are listed in column five of the strategy chart and include everything from decorating the hall to dramatic representations of the issue. Someone needs to be put in charge of each tactic.

Rehearse. People speaking or presenting demands should all rehearse or role-play beforehand.

Hold the Meeting.

Follow Up. If the meeting was a success but media were not present, publicize the results yourselves. In some cases you may want to do this jointly with the target. It gives the target some credit while locking her into the agreement publicly. If no public statement is made, then immediately after the meeting send a letter to the target restating the agreement.

Thank Everyone and Celebrate. Send personal thank-you notes to everyone who helped in the planning and implementation of the meeting. Be sure to thank the legislator for coming; this letter should again confirm the agreement that was reached and review implementation steps. Find a way to celebrate with the key people.

Evaluate. Call a meeting of the planning committee to review the original plan, and then evaluate how it was carried out. This is most valuable for building leadership. Pay particular attention to your turnout plan. Check attendance sheets (sign-in sheets) from the event against lists of people who said they would come. Did individuals and other organizations produce the people they were committed to bring? Did people come off the street in response to leaflets, posters, or advance media coverage?

Sample Agenda

An accountability session is a tightly controlled meeting, with a clear purpose and clear demands that are formally conveyed to the target. Below is a sample agenda.

Welcome and Purpose: 5–10 Minutes

The moderator welcomes everyone to the meeting with a brief talk about the importance of the issue and the goals for the evening. This sets the spirit of the meeting and starts applause. The audience is reminded not to ask the target questions:

"Representative Smith has had two years to tell us what she thinks, but we have only two hours to tell her what we think, so please don't ask her questions or bring up other subjects. She has a few minutes on the agenda to say what is on her mind after she responds to our requests."

Since this is not a spontaneous outpouring of community residents it is not necessary to pretend that it is. The chair should make clear that this meeting is an organized event. The organization has been preparing for it by meeting with many different individuals and groups in the community, and those speaking have been chosen to reflect the concerns of the broader community. If your leaders feel strongly that some time should be given to people who want to speak from the floor, then call on one or two and follow up with two strong speakers from your organization who will end on message.

Opening Prayer or Song: 5 Minutes

In many community meetings, a local religious leader leads an opening (ecumenical) prayer, or else a patriotic observance is held. In other communities, a song about the issue is appropriate. It's nice to have some sort of "opening." The decision on how to open should reflect the community's customs, not the organizer's biases.

Community Residents Speak: 45–60 Minutes

Community residents or coalition members speak about why they want the target to respond in a certain fashion. The presentations are prearranged, but they can be interspersed with a few spontaneous remarks from the floor. The speakers should represent major organizations or institutions in the community that have political clout.

The purpose of their talks is less to persuade by logic and more to show numbers and strength. Be sure that people stress numbers—how many folks they represent either organizationally or by

category: "Those of us who rent our homes make up half of the voters in this district. We are 14,000 voters, and we want rent control." It is always good to have people speak who are known contributors to the legislator's campaign if they're supporters of your position. A time limit of two minutes a person should be set.

Collection: 10 Minutes

Pass the hat to raise money to win the campaign. After an officer of the organization makes a pitch, have a local musician entertain the group during the collection. This is a good opportunity for the leadership to caucus and tie up any loose ends. This item is always placed on the agenda before the main event (making the demands on the target) because if it is done after the main event, many people will get up and leave.

What We Expect of the Target: 15–20 Minutes

This is when the demands are made, but since "demands" is organizer talk and not an everyday word, call it something else, such as "Our organization's questions to Senator Smith." A panel of three or four people makes the demands, which, of course, have been decided upon and written out in advance. Everyone on the panel should have a script showing the order of the questions and which fallback and escalation demands go with which question. Each panel member is assigned one or two main demands with their fallbacks. The target should be asked to respond to each demand before the next one is made. Generally, you are asking for "yes" or "no" responses, but allow the person some flexibility in answering the questions.

Some groups make a scoreboard for the responses with "yes," "no," and "waffle" categories. Others hand a scorecard to all meeting participants. Because fallback or escalation questions will be based upon the initial responses, the whole list of questions is not distributed or posted.

Summary Statement: 5 Minutes

The moderator should summarize the outcome of the meeting and express the group's pleasure or disappointment with the commitments. If the meeting has not gone well, the moderator should nonetheless avoid the temptation to say, "We are livid with rage." (In most halls, "livid" sounds like "liver.")

Adjournment

The chair or another leader closes the meeting with a song, prayer, or parting word. Outline the next steps in the campaign and the next event the organization is holding. Everyone should leave with an assignment of something to do—a petition to circulate, a letter to write, leaflets to give out, or posters to put up. Try to avoid announcing upcoming events of other groups. A barrage of meeting notices tends to diffuse the impact of the ending. Besides, half of the announcements are usually silly: "Citizens Opposed to Canned Food is holding an international convention to form a worldwide third party at the Parks Department field house."

Key Roles

Part of the process of leadership development is training leaders in visible, public roles. Generally, it's better to have more roles and jobs than fewer. Here are some of the key roles you will want in the meeting:

Chair. The person who chairs the meeting should be a respected leader of your organization. The job requires being prepared to keep the audience focused on the issue and to keep the target from taking over the meeting. The chair should have a detailed agenda that includes who is speaking and what group each speaker is from, the exact demands from the panel, and the times for each agenda item. The chair needs to be able to jump in and improvise if something goes wrong. The chair is assigned a small staff during the meeting.

Chair's Messenger. Particularly if the room is large, the chair needs a way of communicating with other leaders and staff, finding the next speaker, and dealing with unanticipated problems. The messenger, who needs to be able to recognize everyone, stays near the chair.

Scorekeeper. If a scoreboard is used to record target's responses, a scorekeeper is assigned to the chair and marks the board only at the chair's direction.

Chair's Organizer. An organizer should stay close by the chair to discuss unexpected proposals or developments.

General or Lead Organizer. The general or lead organizer should remain in the back of the room, dealing with problems. This person can double as the "celebrity spotter," looking for other elected officials and leaders of organizations whose presence the chair should announce.

Panel Members. The members of the panel who make the demands should be people from your planning committee who are familiar with the issue and politics of the situation. If the meeting is a coalition effort, they can come from different organizations, but this increases the need for a group rehearsal.

Official Target Greeter. One person should be assigned to greet the decision maker and keep her occupied until the meeting begins. This prevents her working the crowd, shaking hands, and acting nice. Ideally, the greeter should have met the target before. The greeter should not be on the panel. It's too hard to lean on someone after chatting with them for fifteen minutes.

Press Contact. If you expect the press, assign one person to meet and greet the media, and hand out a press statement. Some meetings have a press table to which press people are directed. It is fine for the press to interview people in the crowd, but the press contact needs to be sure that the organization's view of the issues is accurately expressed. The press greeter should make sure that the press is introduced to "our official spokesperson." Get a list of all press people who attend. Follow up with them as the campaign unfolds. Remember that if someone you have never seen before shows up with a chicken tied to his head and a sign saying "Roast 'Em Now," that is the person the press will want to interview. Unless you act quickly, he will end up being quoted as the spokesperson for your group.

Ushers. They run the sign-in table, help people get seated, pass out any materials, take the collection and help with the refreshments. Have an armband or some other identification for them. Ushers should be prepared to handle disruptive people. Sitting next to them or engaging them in conversation often distracts them. Never actually touch a disruptive person. That can quickly escalate the disruption into a fight or charges of assault. When not working, ushers can sit in the audience and encourage clapping and other audience participation.

Microphone Holder. Never leave a live mike unattended. It is a sure way to lose control. If you use a mike in the center of the room for audience participation, take away the stand, and assign a person to hold the mike for the speakers. This ensures control and allows the chair to maintain time limits.

Facilities Coordinator. Put someone in charge of the hall itself. This includes knowing how to work the lights, heat, air conditioning, and sound, as well as maintaining relations with the building staff.

Signer. Very large meetings often have a person signing for those with hearing impairment.

Translators. Many groups now provide simultaneous translation by either buying or renting headset equipment. In our experience, this equipment is never as easy to use or as convenient as one would think. Practice with it. Make sure that the translators are fully briefed on the political context of the situation and any technical or idiomatic language involved ("My house is in the way of the highway right of way, and I want it moved away right away"). It is not enough to just speak the language.

Logistics and Spirit

As with any public meeting, it's hard to anticipate all logistical matters, but the better planning you do, the fewer last-minute crises you will face. Consider the following:

Room Setup. Map out where you want everything before you get to the meeting. (See the diagram on the next page.) Visit the hall to see and hear it in use and make a floor plan. If the chairs are movable or the room can be partitioned, be sure that you have fewer chairs than needed rather than many empty chairs.

Generally, you want the chair (standing at a podium) and the target (seated) in the front of the room with the target on the chair's left. The panel members should be seated at a table off to the side somewhat and on the chair's right. There should be an easy way for the organizer to move from the front to other parts of the room.

Microphones. Do you need them? If so, where should they be placed? One for the chair, one or two for the panel, one for the target, and one for the audience adds up to more than many halls have. The cheap solution is to borrow small

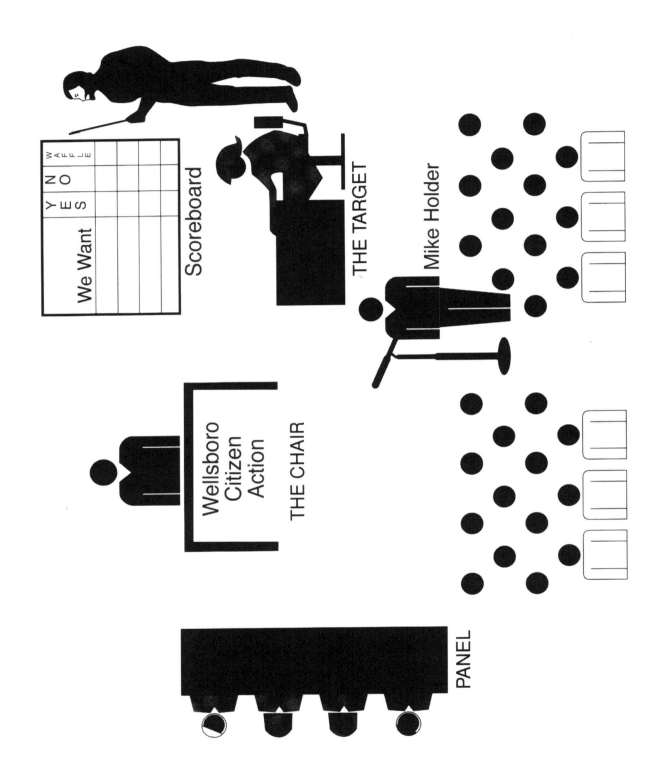

Organizing for Social Change

amplifiers. Even boom boxes have been used—most have a mike jack. Buying the cheapest Radio Shack mike to plug in is still cheaper than renting. Test the equipment before the meeting begins.

Sign-In Sheets. Do you have enough? Do you want special forms so you can get more information than just name, address, phone number, and e-mail? Will the names need to be in a certain format to be entered into a computer database? If so, design the sign-in form to correspond to your database format. The goal is to get a complete list of everyone who comes, so you need lots of sign-in sheets to avoid a bottleneck at the door.

Set up tables outside in the hall that everyone must pass, and assign ushers to stand next to them and steer people over. If you give out nametags and programs at the table, people are more likely to stop. Another method is to offer a door prize. People must fill out a card and drop it in a box to win. Sign-in sheets tend to disappear, so make sure that they are given to the organizer as soon as they are filled out.

Handouts. Do you plan to hand out any materials, including a printed agenda? Do you need press materials? Is someone responsible for preparing and copying the materials? Do you need signs on the front of the building directing people to the right room? Do you want posters hung around the room?

Historical Note: a Greek named Socrates invented the practice of making statements into questions like these. If the answer to any of these questions is no, you are probably making a big mistake. Call him and talk it over.

Scoreboard. Often a huge scoreboard is placed next to the target. The demands are listed on it and next to each one are spaces to check "Yes," "No," and "Waffle." This device helps pin down the target. A scorekeeper marks the board at the direction of the chair. In addition, you can print the scorecard and hand it out so that people can mark it themselves. The target knows that they will take it home and show everyone.

Fun Activities. Build in dramatic activities that also make a point. For example, when a target waffled on a question, one group brought out a plate of waffles. Another group had a large cardboard waffle. A Deputy Mayor was presented with a small violin reminiscent of another politician, Nero, who fiddled while Rome burned. After the head of a Transit Authority had finished speaking, an organization concerned with transit safety lowered a graphic mural depicting a subway disaster. Visuals such as these are a key to getting TV coverage.

Other techniques include connecting an absent political figure through an amplified telephone to lend support. Very short (under five minutes) slide shows and videos have also been used to help an audience visualize the problem. Longer slide shows have been used to everyone's sorrow. One organization fearing that the target would not show up hired a band to lead the audience to the target's house. The target came, but the band stayed to play "Happy Days Are Here Again" after the opening speech and drum rolls to emphasize important points thereafter. Large bunches of helium balloons make great decorations.

You can think of better ideas than these. You want to be known as the group that puts on the greatest events that are less expensive than a movie. Have fun while remembering that there is a fine line between clever and silly.

Money Collection. Bring cans or containers for the collection. Or stop at a take-out Chinese food place and buy a dozen soup containers. Wrap leaflets around them, slit the lids, and tape the containers shut. Provide armbands for ushers. In some African-American communities, the churches have made it traditional to ask the audience to come forward and put their donations in a central collection plate. An experienced collection speaker is required.

Refreshments. Will there be any? If so, be sure that several people who have no other major jobs are responsible for them. Members and local merchants can be asked to donate stuff. Be sure to recognize them publicly.

Fill-ins. What happens if your target is late or your panel needs a few minutes to discuss matters? Plan some "fill-ins" such as music, songs, or bird imitations. Try to use leaders for this who will be there anyway. Few things are worse than inviting a musician for a fill-in and then having neither the need nor time for a performance.

Turnout, Publicity, and Transportation/Facilities

Turnout

Getting large numbers of people to the accountability session is critical for demonstrating your power. Of course, the meaning of "large numbers" varies greatly based on the size and nature of your community. Getting 200 people to an accountability session in a small town might be terrific, whereas getting that many to an accountability session with the Mayor of a major city would be dreadful. On the other hand, getting 200 people to a session with a local City Council person, even within a large city, is probably fine. Whatever will suffice as "large" should be your attendance goal. Identify all the possible groups and people who might be interested.

For a community group, getting people to turn out is almost entirely a matter of good telephone work. Develop lists of everyone who has ever shown an interest and write down the date and nature of every attempted contact with them. Phoning is best done from your own or a borrowed office with several phones lines where you can coach the callers from a short script and also make it into a social evening. As the first step is putting together an adequate calling list, start with your group's own membership list and ask allies for the use of theirs. Add names from petitions you have gathered. For the main calling effort, set up regular telephone nights in the office, put someone in charge, and have volunteers come in to call the organizational lists. If you don't have enough phone lines, several locations may be required. Avoid having people make cold calls alone at home. It isn't any fun, so people tend not to make these calls. E-mail should augment the phone calls, not substitute for them.

In addition, at a meeting, ask all your volunteers to make a list of the friends they will personally invite to the accountability session. Make copies so the organization can keep a list for last-minute reminder calls. (This list is also a good guide to future leadership because it shows who can get people to come.) Check back to see that the calls have been made.

Every organization develops its own telephone success rate over time. The general rule is that of the people who say twice that they will come to a session, half will come. Of course, the number of calls you need to make to get one person will be different from group to group. Five to seven calls to get one "yes" from a general contact list is a very good average, but it may take a while to work up to. Calling should be put on a factory basis and may need to include an appeal for volunteers to make more calls.

The main goal of your turnout plan should be to make at least five times as many phone calls as you need people to come. Fewer calls may do if you have a particularly hot issue and an active list or have been regularly turning out crowds. Remember, every person who says "Yes, I'll come" must be called a *second time* to reconfirm within a week of the event. Once again, no matter what allied groups promise, your own organization should be responsible for producing at least two-thirds of the minimum number of people needed from its own phone operation. The rest of the crowd can be recruited by other groups and "off the street."

Save your phone list and check it against the sign-in sheets after the event. You need to know how many of those called actually came and which of your leaders and allies really produced.

Calling Tips

• Don't start calls with the words "Hello, Mrs. Warbash, did you get our mailing?" The answer is usually no, which creates an awkward moment. Instead, say:

"Hello, Mrs. Warbash, this is Jackie from the Campaign for Clean Elections. Two weeks ago you signed our petition to get Assemblyman Smith to sponsor our bill to replace private campaign contributions with limited public funds. As a result of the petition, Mr. Smith has agreed to come to a meeting we are holding. It will be a chance for you to show him how strongly you feel about wealthy people and corporations buying elections, and of course the more voters who come, the more he will have to listen to us. It is next Tuesday, the 17th, at the school, Intermediate School 54, room 131, 7:30 P.M. We will be done by about 9:30. Will I see you there? Oh that's wonderful. We'll give you a reminder call a day or two beforehand if that's all right?"

Notice the following elements in the call:
- Stress the past connection, the petition.
- Mention a success of the campaign, getting the meeting.
- Indicate that the person will play a role, even if it is not a speaking role. By being there you can show him how you feel.
- Talk about why the person is needed, voters matter.
- Ask for a definite commitment, will I see you there? (Can you come?)
- Indicate a reminder call and be sure to make one. (Of the people who say twice that they will come, half will come.)

• In addition to phoning people, try to get the message to them in at least three other ways. For example, send a mailing, put up posters, and send someone to make an announcement at the PTA meeting. Mail, posters, e-mail, leaflets, advertisements, or public service announcements will reinforce the call, and remind people, but are no substitute for the call. The more times people hear the message, the more likely they are to come.

• At events, every caller should make an effort to meet the people they called and introduce themselves.

Publicity

Make lists of all the other community meetings that are being held, and send people to them to make announcements. Don't overlook senior centers, political clubs, union meetings, and "official" meetings like school boards. Try to get announcements made in churches. Leaflet and talk to people outside grade schools when school dismisses. If your organization has a door-to-door canvass, concentrate it in the area of the event a few weeks ahead of time. Canvassers should bring in names of interested people whom you can call. Leaflet commuter lines, shopping centers, and malls. Combine leafleting with a petition or letter writing.

Transportation/Facilities

Is transportation to the session a problem? If so, arrange for carpools or special transportation. Sometimes, social service agencies or churches are willing to loan their buses or vans to bring people to special community events.

You may want to offer childcare if you hope to attract many families with young children. Make sure to arrange for adequate adult supervision of children, facilities for infants, and toys for children. You will want your childcare providers to look at the space ahead of time to identify any possible difficulties. If transportation and/or childcare are provided, be sure to mention these in all your promotional materials and announcements along with information on accessibility for the disabled and signing for the deaf.

Press Plan

Your press plan should include the following:
- Trying to get advance publicity. If the issue is not of citywide interest, maybe a community weekly will carry the story. Sometimes releasing a study on the subject or even a clever media stunt may get the event mentioned, whereas a straight press release won't.
- Sending a media advisory to key media contacts a week before the meeting. Consider inviting area college media classes to videotape your event.
- Making follow-up calls to media people, City Desks, daybooks, and assignment editors a day or two before the meeting.
- Preparing a press packet for distribution to press people at the meeting. It should include another press release and background information on your issue and your organization.

- Preparing visuals. Both newspapers and television prefer taking interesting pictures rather than pictures of talking heads. Prepare some visuals, charts, banners, or stunts that you think might be interesting. The visual should not just be "catchy" but should convey your message. The name of the organization should be visible everywhere, especially on the front of the podium.
- Talking with press people at the event. One person should be assigned to greet the press. Your planning group should clarify who your spokespersons are so that the press greeter can direct the media to the proper people for interviews.
- Calling the press people who didn't come to tell them what happened or sending a follow-up press release if you don't expect to get much media coverage.
- Thanking the press people for covering your event, even if you don't like how they covered it. (If there was a really negative article don't thank the reporter.)
- Working closely with all your speakers to help them deliver tight messages in ten-second sound bites for television use. In some large media events, the television and radio press people are handed copies of speeches with the ten-second sound bites indicated, so the crews can be sure to have their television cameras running at the proper time.

If you expect lots of people and lots of press at the accountability session, you must be concerned with where they will be located. Consider roping off a special set of seats up front for the press and selecting a good spot for television cameras.

For more information on using the media, see chapter 14.

Tone of the Meeting

The tone of the meeting should be upbeat but serious, professional but fun, and controlled but not too much so. It should always end positively, looking forward to future action.

Upbeat but Serious. The issue about which the meeting is organized is serious. The people who attend are serious about the issue. Nonetheless, the meeting must be run in a very positive fashion, assuming that a positive outcome will emerge from the meeting.

Professional but Fun. The meeting needs to be run professionally. Agendas should be prepared, leaders should have practiced their speaking parts, the room should be set up, time limits should be held to, and logistics should run smoothly. No one should know about last-minute crises but the organizer and key leaders. The event should not be conducted like a business meeting. It is a community accountability session. It should be fun. People should be encouraged to sing songs, hold up signs, join in chants, or participate in other "fun" activities that express concern about the issue and demonstrate the group's organizational ability. (Being organized enough to get everyone to chant the same thing is worth something.)

Controlled but Not Too Much. The chair must control the agenda and is responsible for making sure that the meeting's goals are accomplished and that the target doesn't take over the meeting. However, sometimes chairs feel so compelled to control a meeting that they become shrill and tyrannical. Control is important; too much control is not welcome. Tyrannical chairs cause audiences to sympathize with targets—not with what you want.

End Positively with Action. Make sure that the close of a meeting is positive and leads to the next action. Prepare the meeting chair to give a rousing closing and send people off prepared to fight another battle—whether it be on this issue or the next.

Checklist for Holding an Accountability Session

_____ Are your key leaders on the planning committee?

_____ Have you used the strategy chart to plan the accountability session, being sure to take into account your power?

_____ Do you have main demands (usually substantive), a list of escalation demands, and some fallback demands (usually procedural)?

_____ Are the proposed date and time for the accountability session suitable for your constituency?

_____ Have you confirmed the date with the target?

_____ Do you have an appropriate site that is accessible, centrally located, and equipped to handle your needs?

_____ Have you made a realistic turnout plan? Are enough people assigned to work on turnout?

_____ Do you have a good press plan? Have you arranged for

    _____ The initial media advisory and notice of photo opportunity?

    _____ Follow-up calls to media to get them to come?

    _____ The press release in press packets with supporting materials?

    _____ Visuals for TV and still photographers?

    _____ A press table and person staffing it?

    _____ A special area for television crews?

    _____ Calls to press people who didn't attend?

    _____ Thank-yous to press people who covered the session?

_____ Does the agenda demonstrate power over the target and give your leadership visible roles?

_____ Does the agenda include the following components:

    _____ Welcome and purpose?

    _____ Opening prayer, song, or Pledge of Allegiance?

    _____ Community residents speaking?

    _____ Collection?

    _____ Demands and target's responses?

    _____ Summary statement?

    _____ Adjournment?

_____ Have you taken care of logistics? Have you arranged for

    _____ Refreshments?

    _____ Room setup?

    _____ Room decorations (posters, banners)?

    _____ Music or entertainment?

    _____ Baskets or buckets for collecting money?

    _____ Words for chants or songs?

    _____ Demands scoreboard?

    _____ Audiovisual equipment?

_____ Microphones?

_____ Extension cords (power strips)?

_____ Sign-in sheets and sign-in table?

_____ Room cleanup?

_____ Will you provide childcare? Is a good room available?

_____ Are carpools or transportation arrangements available?

_____ Do you have a dress rehearsal scheduled?

_____ Is someone assigned to greet the target as she or he enters the building?

_____ Are your key leaders and staff assigned to the following roles:

    _____ Chair (leader)?

    _____ Chair's messenger (leader or staff)?

    _____ Scorekeeper (leader)?

    _____ Chair's organizer (leader or staff)?

    _____ General organizer (leader or staff)?

    _____ Target greeter (leader)?

    _____ Press contact (leader or staff)?

    _____ Press spokesperson(s) (leader)?

    _____ Speakers on the program (leaders)?

_____ Have you recruited other volunteers and emerging leaders for the following roles:

    _____ Ushers?

    _____ Microphone holder?

    _____ Person with the sign-in sheets?

    _____ Person to distribute handouts?

    _____ People to collect money?

    _____ Refreshment servers?

    _____ Music or entertainment fill-ins?

    _____ Childcare?

    _____ Applause and audience participation starters?

_____ Does your follow-up plan include

    _____ Sending a confirmation letter to the target?

    _____ Sending thank-you notes to everyone who helped?

    _____ Celebrating with key people?

    _____ Checking attendance lists against those who said they would come and/or deliver people?

    _____ Meeting with the planning committee to evaluate the session?

©The Midwest Academy

28 E. Jackson Blvd. #605, Chicago, IL 60604

(312) 427-2304   mwacademy1@aol.com   www.midwestacademy.com

9

"Wouldn't It Be Loverly?" If you find yourself humming this tune as you think about building a coalition, beware! Coalitions are not built because it is good, moral, or nice to get everyone working together. Coalitions are about building power. The only reason to spend the time and energy building a coalition is to amass the power necessary to do something you cannot do through one organization.

A coalition is an organization of organizations working together for a common goal. An individual membership organization cannot technically be a coalition, although the term is used more loosely in common parlance.

Coalitions come in a variety of forms. They can be permanent or temporary, single- or multi-issue, geographically defined, limited to certain constituencies (such as a coalition of women's organizations), or a combination of some of the above (e.g., a Midwestern coalition of farm organizations). Some coalitions are permanent and multi-issue. Their goal is often to bring together major progressive organizations to build a base of power capable of winning on issues of mutual concern. Other coalitions are best set up on a temporary basis—an environmental coalition to increase funding for the state EPA, for

Advantages and Disadvantages of Working in Coalitions

Principles for Successful Coalitions

Do You Really Want to Join or Form a Coalition?

Questions to Consider before Joining a Coalition

Working for and Building the Coalition: The Organizer's Job

Building and Joining Coalitions

example. The reason for this is that apart from a common interest in this one issue, the programs and constituents of the member groups could be very different. One of them might be working on wildlife preservation, another on blocking construction of an incinerator, and the third on preventing the use of pesticides.

Advantages and Disadvantages of Working in Coalitions

In Midwest Academy training sessions, participants are asked about their coalition experiences. Below are some common responses.

Advantages
- *Win what couldn't be won alone.* Many issues require large numbers of people and many resources to win. Coalitions can pool people and resources to win important victories.
- *Build an ongoing power base.*
- *Increase the impact of an individual organization's efforts.* Not only does your involvement help win a campaign, but you make the work you undertake more effective.
- *Develop new leaders.* Experienced leaders can be asked to take on coalition leadership roles, thereby opening up slots for new leaders.
- *Increase resources.* If the coalition's issue is central to your organization, you may directly benefit from additional staff and money.
- *Broaden scope.* A coalition may provide the opportunity for your group to work on state or national issues, making the scope of your work more exciting and important.

Disadvantages
- *Distracts from other work.* If the coalition issue is not your main agenda item, it can divert your time and resources.
- *Weak members can't deliver.* Organizations providing leadership and resources may get impatient with some of the weaker groups' inexperience and inability to deliver on commitments.
- *Too many compromises.* To keep the coalition together, it is often necessary to play to the least common denominator, especially on tactics.
- *Inequality of power.* The range of experience, resources, and power can create internal problems. One group, one vote does not work for groups with wide ranges of power and resources.

- *Individual organizations may not get credit.* If all activities are done in the name of the coalition, groups that contribute a lot often feel they do not get enough credit.
- *Dull tactics.* Groups that like more confrontational, highly visible tactics may feel that the more subdued tactics of a coalition are not exciting enough to activate their members.

Obviously, not all of the experiences are positive, but almost everyone agrees that when an important shared goal exists, the benefits can outweigh the problems. Recently, it has become fashionable in the foundation world to insist that groups form coalitions in order to get funding. While this has proven positive in many cases, it has also forced groups with little in common to try to work together. Before accepting funding on such a basis, ask yourself, "Is there any reason to form an alliance with these groups *other* than for money?" The rest of this chapter will look at ways to emphasize the advantages and minimize the disadvantages of working in coalitions.

Principles for Successful Coalitions

Choose Unifying Issues

A common issue, not just a desire to work together on each other's separate agendas, is a must. A shopping list of issues will result in chaos and bad feelings. For example, a coalition of groups representing people with particular disabilities can be built around issues involving the civil rights of all the disabled. But an issue that meets the needs of people with only one type of disability may be of no interest to other participants in the coalition.

If your goal is to build a permanent coalition, you may be willing to make short-term compromises. For example, you may agree that the coalition will not work on certain specific issues that divide the coalition's membership and prevent unity on other issues.

Hire Neutral Coalition Staff

It must be someone's primary responsibility to work for the whole coalition, and that person needs to be politically astute and understand the organizational self-interest of the member groups. Ideally, money should be raised to hire an impartial, experienced organizer. Limited resources, however, may make it necessary for this staff member to be contributed by one of the member organizations. When this is done, the contributed staff member needs to make every effort to be impartial and not to appear to be acting as the agent of one of the organizations. A staff person running a coalition part time out of a desk drawer while working full time for another organization is headed for trouble.

Understand and Respect Institutional Self-Interest

Each organization brings its own history, structure, agenda, values, culture, leadership, and relationships to a coalition. It is important for all members of the coalition to understand each other in order to build on their strengths and avoid unnecessary conflicts.

Help Organizations to Achieve Their Self-Interest

Organizations need to believe that they are benefiting from a coalition. Many organizations' self-interests are relatively easy to accommodate if they are clearly understood by the coalition's staff. For example, a neighborhood organization working to better its local schools may find it beneficial to join a statewide tax reform coalition in return for the coalition including increased school funding as part of its agenda.

All organizations must accomplish seven basic functions if they are to survive. A coalition can be a help or a detriment. For example, an organization may join a coalition only to find that the funding and publicity that it had previously obtained are going instead to the coalition. The seven basic functions are these:

- Gain new members
- Be perceived as powerful
- Get media coverage
- Build relations with other groups
- Provide the members with an exciting program
- Build internal morale
- Give its leaders a public role

A successful coalition works to help the members accomplish these seven functions and avoids competing with its own members as much as possible.

Develop a Realistic Coalition Budget

The coalition's budget should include all of the anticipated expenses and income necessary to carry out the coalition's agenda. If staff is being contributed by a member organization, their salary should be included on the expense side and listed as an in-kind contribution on the income side. This will give members a better understanding of the real cost of the campaign and the real contribution that each group is making.

Agree to Disagree

Seldom do all member organizations of a coalition agree on all issues. Focus on your common agenda, the issues on which you agree. Agree to avoid the issues on which you do not agree. If disagreements are so fundamental that they color everything else, then working together may be impossible.

Play to the Center with Tactics

When developing tactics for a coalition, it is usually necessary to play to the groups that are toward the middle. At certain points in an issue campaign, the coalition's strategy may be to encourage the appropriate organizations to act independently and in their own names, utilizing more militant tactics. This can make the coalition appear more reasonable.

Recognize That Contributions Vary

Organizations will bring different strengths and weaknesses to the coalition. As long as each member understands and accepts what other members bring, problems should be minimal. For example, one organization may be able to contribute large sums of money but be unable to turn out its membership, while the opposite would be true of another member organization. A third group might have members in a critical legislative district where no other group does. All can be essential to the success of the coalition effort and should be valued for the resources they bring.

Structure Decision Making Carefully

Unless all groups contribute relatively equally, decision making cannot simply be one vote per organization. Those contributing the most usually want the most say in decisions. This is often done through an informal understanding among the leaders, but some coalitions write it into the rules and give weighted votes to the more important organizations on the basis of size or some other characteristic.

Achieve Significant Victories

Although it's obvious, coalitions must achieve important victories if they are to be successful. Groups will continue contributing only if they see concrete, measurable results.

Urge Stable, Senior Board Representatives

As organizations join the coalition, their choice of representatives to the board is an indication of how seriously they take the coalition. If the presidents of the respective organizations do not participate, they should send a high-ranking board member or staff person as their regular representative. Some coalitions make participation dependent on sending an "important" representative.

Having a series of individuals "fill in" for the president is very disruptive. It is enough of a problem that organizations in a coalition may be of very unequal strength and that their levels of participation may vary widely without compounding that difficulty by having inappropriate representatives at board meetings.

If high-ranking officers of major organizations don't see their peers at meetings, they will drop out and start sending lower-level staff or interns who lack the power to represent the organization. This in turn lengthens the time it takes for the coalition to make a decision because many board members must report back to someone in authority and wait for an answer.

Clarify Decision-Making Procedures

Depending on the level of the coalition, different working arrangements are necessary. For example, in a large national coalition, and even in statewide coalitions in large states, it is very cumbersome and expensive to bring the whole board together regularly. Such coalitions often choose a working group or committee to meet with the staff to develop strategy. As long as the board is clear on how policy is set and trusts the working group to check back at appropriate points, this method can be useful. Whatever the structure, it should be clear to all coalition board members.

Distribute Credit Fairly

One of the most frequent problems of coalition building is that of giving and receiving credit. To those who haven't had the experience of working in a grassroots organization, all of the fighting and jockeying over who gets recognition and for what often seems petty, vulgar, and mindless. Some coalition organizers may feel that this is something that groups need to be cured of and that the proper "attitudes" will make it go away. Quite the contrary. These problems are rooted in basic survival instinct. They will never go away, nor should they. An organization's ability to raise money, recruit members, build power, attract staff, develop leaders, and fulfill its mission depends directly on the amount of public credit it receives, particularly in the media. Coalitions that lose sight of credit concerns don't last long.

When the issue of the coalition is of only secondary importance to a particular affiliate, then credit is less of a problem. But when the issue of the coalition is also the main issue of the affiliate, then credit is a big problem. The program needs to be structured so that the affiliates do some things jointly as a coalition and the coalition helps them do other things in their own names. For example, a study done by the coalition can be released to local papers by local groups in their own names at the same time that it is released to the statewide media in the name of the coalition. Each local release features the impact of the problem on that particular area. This is much more work for the coalition staff, but it keeps the affiliates happy and, above all, healthy. Organizational self-interest is legitimate, and a saying among organizers is that "Groups join coalitions to gain power, not to give it away."

Do You Really Want to Join or Form a Coalition?

Before joining a coalition, determine if it is appropriate for what you want to accomplish. Will you be able to advance your own organizational agenda? If yours is a new organization that needs to establish an independent identity, avoid coalitions for at least a year. Instead, choose smaller issues that you can win on your own. This leads to a strong membership-based organization that can eventually work in a coalition when necessary.

Is your group strong enough, with a well enough developed leadership structure, to carry on two campaigns at once? If it is, then working in a coalition may be appropriate for you. If not, if you can do only one thing at a time, then there is a danger that the coalition's program will become your only activity. Of course, you could join a "letterhead" coalition that makes very few demands on the members.

When considering building a coalition, remember that this creates another level of organization or bureaucracy that requires separate resources. It is certainly not in your organizational self-interest to develop a separate entity with which you will later have to compete for resources. Nor do you want to devote scarce staff time to building a coalition instead of your own organization.

Questions to Consider before Joining a Coalition

Is It Permanent or Temporary?

When you decide that your group should form or join a new coalition, determine whether it should be permanent or temporary. If temporary, consider calling it something other than a coalition.

Using a more temporary-sounding term, such as "campaign" or "Countdown 2004," connotes a shorter lifespan. The reason for giving a temporary coalition a temporary-sounding name is that coalitions tend to take on lives of their own. This is particularly true of coalitions with paid staff, who will find new functions to keep the group alive after its initial purpose has been served.

Organizations do not have to join every coalition that is formed. Many organizations develop formal policies for joining coalitions and criteria for different levels of participation. Some organizations will agree to participate in a coalition only if they are actually prepared to work on the coalition's issues. Others are willing to endorse a coalition, by lending it their name and stature, without participating in its program. Below are some questions to consider before joining a coalition.

Who Is behind the Coalition?

If you have been invited to participate in a coalition, approach the table understanding that you will have to give something to get something. The question, then, is to whom are you giving it and who is responsible for what you get back? Look around. Who else is participating? Who called all of you to this meeting? Why? Where are the expenses of the meeting coming from (e.g., staff time, travel, room rental)? It is important to know the driving force behind the formation of the coalition. If it is funder driven, is the funder committed for the long haul or just willing to give enough to get the work started? If led by a few organizations, will they get the bulk of the benefits and credit? In return, will they do the bulk of the work? All of this information helps to determine not only if the effort is worthwhile but also if an organization of your size can benefit by being in it. If you are participating in a coalition you consider a priority, make sure that a critical number of other organizations are also participating so your efforts will not be in vain.

What's Your Organizational Self-Interest?

It is important to assess whether you should play a leadership role or merely be a member. Both leaders and members are essential, but decide where you want to fit in. If you intend to be a leader of the coalition and to have your own members participate in its program, then make sure the coalition's issue affects your membership deeply. If the coalition's issue is also one of your main issues, it is essential that you play a leadership role.

Be up-front and clear about what you expect in exchange for your participation. For example, a local community group in a large city joined a citywide coalition to improve mass transportation. The group set the following conditions for joining the coalition: (1) It was to be the only affiliate in its geographic area. This gave it a sort of exclusive franchise on citywide transit activity, and people wishing to participate in the campaign had to join the group in order to do so. (2) Its leaders were to be among the principal spokespersons for the coalition. (3) It was to be the host organization for the coalition's first major citywide event, with people from other neighborhoods being bused into its community. Needless to say, the community organization had to be quite strong and capable of significant turnout in order to negotiate this arrangement.

How Can Your Members Participate?

Make sure that coalition tactics or activities will be designed so that your members can and will want to participate. Decide where you are most comfortable in the range, from low key to militant, and make sure there is agreement from the other organizations that they will stay within that range.

How Will Participating in the Coalition Build Your Organization?

Because participating in a coalition will mean more work for your organization, it should also help you build your organization. You will want credit for your work whenever possible. If your members will serve as spokespersons, you will want their organizational identity made known. In reality, all members of a coalition can't and won't get equal credit. The media, always reluctant to use the names of organizations, may pick up the coalition's name but will rarely list all its members.

For example, when two prominent statewide organizations agreed to combine in a coalition to win auto insurance reform, the subsequent campaign received a flood of media coverage. But a survey of the newspaper clips showed that in articles where the name of the coalition itself was mentioned, the names of the two coalition partners were mentioned only 40 percent of the time, despite the fact that all coalition materials consistently used the names of the partners in conjunction with the name of the coalition (i.e., "Citizens Auto Revolt, a joint campaign of New Jersey Citizen Action and New Jersey Public Interest Research Group"). This problem would have been compounded in a coalition of ten groups instead of only two.

Generally, the organizations that are the strongest and that have the most visibility independent of the coalition will also tend to get the most recognition. If your organization has a spokesperson who is clearly identified with you in the public mind, you will get some indirect credit when that person appears for the coalition, even if your group's name isn't mentioned by the media.

Is It a Letterhead Coalition?

Often the board members of a coalition represent no one but themselves. This is what is known as a letterhead coalition. The telltale indicator is an asterisk after the board members' names that indicates "organizations listed for identification purposes only." There is nothing wrong with a letterhead coalition; however, it usually means that resources will not be coming from the coalition members, and another plan needs to be in place. Your organization's participation should be on the same basis as the other groups'.

Working for and Building the Coalition: The Organizer's Job

There is a difference between organizing an individual membership organization and a coalition. With a coalition, you are not creating an entity in which anyone who so desires may participate. You are carefully pulling together the appropriate groups, in the appropriate order, to ensure that all who "should" be in "on the ground floor" are invited, seemingly simultaneously. This must be done carefully, and it requires a skilled organizer who can juggle a number of things at once. You must talk to all the key players at about the same time to avoid anyone feeling as if they are "the last" to be consulted or invited.

Staffing a coalition board is different from staffing a community organization's board. Your job is not to develop "new leadership." Rather, it is to figure out how to work with the leaders who are sent from the member organizations and to help them participate fully. It is also to minimize tensions among board members. Most of the people you will deal with already know how to be leaders. What they may not know is how to work with each other and how to function in a coalition so that it both builds the coalition and builds their own organizations. Often you will need to demonstrate how to do this.

Never become involved in the internal politics of any coalition member organization! This is a cardinal rule. Because you will have to work with the winners, stay neutral during members' internal election campaigns or fights. Be particularly careful not to become involved in jurisdictional fights between rival unions on your board or in turf battles between community groups. If you are unaware of these problems, it is easy to fall into the trap of having the coalition take an action that favors one side or the other (or that the other side thinks does).

The program of the coalition should be carried out by and through the affiliates. The staff should be getting information to the affiliates and helping them to mobilize their own members to support the issue. Staff should avoid the temptation to set up another operation on the side or to start organizing individuals unless this is explicitly part of the strategy.

In addition to knowing the principles of building successful coalitions and guidelines for joining coalitions, before beginning your organizing, you should ask yourself the following questions:

Who Hired You? If your answer is "The coalition board or steering committee," then who is on the steering committee? How did they get there? What do they want collectively and what is the organizational self-interest of each member? The mere fact that there is a beginning "core" group will give you some sense of who will control the coalition. If the core is too narrow and you must broaden the base to win, will the founding board agree? All organizations are not created equal. Which organizations are playing the leadership roles in the coalition? The lead organizations will probably have the most to say. You have to decide if you agree with their perspectives and will be able to work with them.

Who Makes Decisions? Do any organizations have a veto? Why? In some coalitions, member groups look fairly equal on the surface until you discover that some groups have a veto. This veto power usually indicates that they are making extraordinary contributions and therefore want some ability to control the direction of the coalition. This may be fine, but you need to understand the self-interest of the controlling members if you are to help build the coalition.

To Whom Do You Report? Who's the boss? It is almost inevitable that you will get requests from many board members to do too many things, some of them conflicting at least to the extent that they all take time. All board members should clearly understand to whom you report (for example, to the Executive Director if you are a staff member or to a top elected officer if you are the Director). All requests for your time should go through that person. A written campaign strategy and clear workplan will ensure that all board members understand what you are doing.

All too often, a coalition board member will try to involve the coalition staff in some extra project for the member's own organization. This amounts to a subsidy from the coalition as a whole to that group. The group may feel justified in making such requests because of what it gives to the coalition, but this practice should be against the rules. An executive committee that meets at least monthly and reviews the staff's work can protect against this to some degree.

What Competing Organizational Self-Interests Exist between Members? This is important to know before any strategy decisions can be made. For instance, some homeowner groups may want to defeat a proposed property tax increase, but the public employees union may be for it because the tax increase will provide money for better salaries.

Which Organizations Are Contributing the Most, and Which Are Gaining the Most by Participating? If those contributing the bulk of

the resources are not getting what they want, eventually they will resent seeing their resources go for items that are not a high priority for them and will stop participating.

Where Is the Money Coming From? All of the questions surrounding money are critical to understanding who has influence within the coalition. If the bulk of the income is raised from the coalition partners, they will have the most control. More often, additional money will have to be raised to support the coalition.

If the money is coming in from outside (e.g., a foundation), whose money is it? Who is actually raising it? What is the interest of the funding source, and what role will that source have in the coalition, both formally and informally?

Who Is Being Excluded and Why? If certain groups are being excluded, this may be fine, but you want to understand why to help you better understand the politics and self-interest surrounding the issue.

Coalition building is a skill that an organizer can develop. If there is adequate commitment to a coalition and a clear understanding of the self-interests and relationships of the member organizations, one can build powerful coalitions capable of accomplishing what none of the parts can do alone.

Coalitions in and of themselves are not "the answer" for progressives. Strong individual membership organizations must be built that mobilize large numbers of citizens on progressive issues. Nonetheless, major social issues, particularly at the state and national levels, require broad-based coalitions in order to win. Building coalitions that are strong enough to challenge political structures and making them work effectively requires tough, analytical, strategic thinking, a clear understanding about how coalitions work, savvy staff, hard work, and tender loving care. With such attention, coalitions can change the political landscape for this new century.

10

"How come I do all the work around here?" Well, either you're being punished, or you're not recruiting members and volunteers. Every task that an organizer does alone—every envelope stuffed, every phone call made, every page typed—is a lost opportunity to recruit someone else to do that job. Many organizations would be far stronger if their staff and leaders resolved to do nothing else but find others to volunteer for all the jobs.

In some ways, recruitment is the most important subject we deal with in this manual. If we had entitled this chapter "Organizing" instead of "Recruiting," that would have given it the proper emphasis. We know organizers who are always surrounded by people because they instinctively draw people into their work. Other organizers function alone. Perhaps they are excellent at all the technical skills, but they don't involve anyone. Indeed, they often consider members a bother and seem to believe that the goal is to present the perfect testimony at a hearing or to write the world's finest press release. What such people do may be very valuable, but it isn't organizing. Recruiting and involving people comes naturally to some, but all can learn to do it by incorporating the techniques outlined here. Of course, this isn't a contest to see how much work

Basic Recruitment Principles

Your Image as a Recruiter

Six Steps toward Successful Recruitment

Tips on Keeping Volunteers

Practice Makes Perfect

Recruiting

you can get out of doing; it is the way that organizations are built. More and more people take on more and more responsibility (including financial responsibility). This makes them feel that they own the organization and that it is the product of their efforts. The more that staff and leaders do for members, the less ownership the members feel and the less commitment they have. You can produce the best array of services, projects, activities, or publications for your members, but if they haven't been involved in the planning, making it happen, and paying for it, they will say, "What, is that all?"

Basic Recruitment Principles

In addition to recruiting individual members, canvassing, fundraising, and coalition building are forms of recruitment. This chapter deals with recruiting individual members, but its basic principles apply to all forms of recruitment.

Often, but not always, the first step in getting new people or groups to help is asking them to join. People want to join and to be active; they want to put time and effort and money into useful projects.

In 1832, when the Frenchman Alexis de Tocqueville came to America to chronicle life in the "New World," he marveled at the way Americans set up voluntary organizations for every form of social betterment. "Americans of all ages, all conditions, and all dispositions constantly form associations," he observed.[1] Comparing America to Europe, de Tocqueville noted that projects undertaken by the government in France or the nobility in England were done by citizens' associations in America. This tradition is no less strong in America today.

Your job isn't as hard as it may seem. You don't have to figure out how to get people to be active, to care about their community, or to be concerned with larger issues. They are already doing that. Your job is mainly to make sure that your organization gets its fair share of all the volunteer activity that is going on. Yes, that requires a special skill, but you don't have to change human nature. It is already working with you on this one. Once your group starts getting results, you will have more members from among the ranks of those who wanted to be active but stayed home because they thought that nothing they could do mattered. (Although most individuals

---

1. *Democracy in America*, vol. 2. (New York: Vintage Books, 1945).

are joiners by nature, there is no indication that organizations have the same tendency to join coalitions.)

Appeal to People's Self-Interest

If I am not for myself who is for me?
And if I am only for myself, what am I?
And if not now, when?

—Hillel

Giving time, money, and loyalty to an organization involves giving so much of one's self that saying it is motivated by self-interest seems not only a contradiction but slightly mean. In fact, it is neither. People do the most selfless acts out of self-interest, including joining unions, voting, inventing computer chips, and walking dogs. Indeed, self-interest generalized becomes class interest, and few things beat class interest for making history, but that is another story.

If you want to move people, it has to be toward a vision that's positive for them, that taps important values, that gets them something they desire, and it has to be presented in a compelling way that they feel inspired to follow.

— Martin Luther King

By self-interest we don't mean being selfish. The word "interest" comes from two Latin words, *inter esse*, meaning "to be between or among." So self-interest means self among others or how we are aware of our selves and our own needs in the context of our relationships with others.

When recruiting people, always appeal to their self-interest. This is very different from telling them why it is in your self-interest for them to help you. (In truth, certain kinds of people just want to help you, but they are more like groupies than members. The problem with groupies is that they get jealous if you have more than three.) Self-interest takes several forms, which together with values, vision, and relationships underpin most organizational involvement:

Personal. People join organizations working on issues that personally affect them. Lower utility rates or lower taxes are examples of immediate self-interest, while global warming or disarmament exemplifies longer-term self-interest. People join to stop the oppression, prejudice, and discrimination that affect their lives. Such activities are often accompanied by the feeling that they are doing it for their children or grandchildren, which brings a kind of satisfaction beyond the issue itself.

Senior citizens often join groups for companionship and a desire to continue to be useful after retirement. They enjoy an opportunity to apply the skills of their former occupations. They often seek activities that are multigenerational rather than confined to seniors. Then there are people who volunteer for additional social self-interest reasons such as meeting people, making new friends with similar values, getting out of the house, taking a break from young children, just having fun, or even dating. A few people join for all of these reasons.

People also volunteer because organizations are fun. They are exciting and, particularly with direct action, very often a form of theater.

Professional. Many people volunteer for career self-interest reasons. They want to develop new skills that can enhance their resumes, or they want to test out possible new career options. They may want to make contacts that lead to jobs. Members of certain professions sometimes join organizations in the hope of finding clients. You will also meet people who are looking for work experience, such as students, or homemakers trying to get back into the workplace. A chance to learn word processing or spreadsheets, which may be a chore for you, can be a real inducement for them.

Power. Some people volunteer for the power that comes from being part of an organization. They are interested in revenge against political crooks, landlords, and polluters of the environment. They enjoy the opportunity to be a spokesperson, to get on TV, or to speak at a rally. Some are considering running for office.

Moral. To sustain commitment, people must volunteer based on their values and vision. They believe that using their time to help bring justice to the world is the right thing to do. They think that "Faith without works is dead." Many people feel that they have a civic responsibility to do something for their community and that this is indeed a lifelong obligation, along with voting or paying taxes. In fact, moral values usually go along with all of the other reasons that people join groups. Moral values can be religious, ethical, or ideological.

Negative Forms of Self-Interest. A few individuals become identified with an organization in order to sell out for a price, to promote their own interests at the expense of the community, or simply to provide themselves with an audience for crackpot ideas or abnormal behavior.

Ninety-nine percent of the time, however, self-interest works on the side of the organization, and if you understand what people desire, you can structure your recruitment appeal and your program accordingly. Self-interest is rarely one-dimensional. People are motivated by combinations of needs, wants, and rewards. They join and stay with the organization that reflects their humanity and values and addresses specific forms of self-interest.

Fire a Shot over the Water

Outreach needs to be built into every aspect of an issue campaign. An organization should be regularly doing things that raise its public visibility and at the same time give people an opportunity to join. In fact, in any place on any issue, a number of people are actually looking for you.

Mark Twain, in writing about his boyhood on the Mississippi, spoke of the practice of firing a cannon over the water to raise the victims of drowning. Particularly at the beginning of a campaign, but also later on, the organization should fire a shot over the water to bring to the surface those who are just looking for a chance to participate. This takes the form of holding publicly advertised events such as hearings, teach-ins, accountability sessions, rallies, and marches. People will come to support the issue but also to check out the group. Sign-in sheets and follow-up recruitment calls should be standard procedure.

Smaller activities also work well. Petition drives and letter-writing campaigns can bring the organization into contact with hundreds of people in a short time, and each person should be asked to volunteer. Experience indicates that if one out of ten who volunteer actually shows up, you are doing well. The point is to have an ongoing activity that generates a constant inflow of new people.

Recruit to an Activity, Not a Business Meeting

Organizations often try to build their recruitment around meetings. This is probably the least effective method for drawing people in, and if meetings are the only activity of your group, they may be a cause of dwindling membership.

Most of the time we are looking for people who want to do something more than come to a business meeting. What organizer has not offered prayers to be saved from the person who says, "I have no time to do anything, but I'd love to help you make policy. When is your next meeting?" By recruiting to an activity, you get action-oriented people rather than chronic meeting-goers.

Some very successful organizations rely on a program of house meetings as their major outreach method. This is not at all the same as recruiting to a business meeting and has produced dramatic results. House meetings are action oriented. Those attending hear a brief talk on the issue, then they are asked to write a letter, give money, and sponsor a meeting in their own home. The follow-up involves recruitment to other activities.

Have an Ongoing Entry-Level Program for New People

A major obstacle to successful recruitment is that new people feel that they are arriving in the middle of a party. Everyone knows so much about the issues and has learned all the jargon. They can talk about the "bimodal split," "Mr. Parker at CHA," or "parts of particulate matter per billion." No one wants to be around folks who talk in code. It creates an instant in-group, with all the new people automatically excluded. For this reason, when you recruit new members it is important to involve them in something in which they can immediately feel useful. For example, one successful community organization maintained a regular program of weekend letter writing at street tables. Because the issue was very popular and the tables were highly successful, working at them was a fine entry-level activity. Anyone could do it. New volunteers worked as equals alongside the organization's veterans. Passersby put dollar bills in the donation can, the weather was fine, and everyone felt good. All letter writers were also asked to volunteer for an hour. They knew what would be expected of them because they saw the activity going on. They knew that they could successfully get others to write letters because they themselves had written

one. Maintaining this operation required that several nights each week be spent contacting volunteers. Coming in and making calls was seen as a next step of organizational involvement. Although this particular issue campaign dragged on for ten years before victory, the outreach program ensured a small but steady stream of recruits.

Offer Childcare

Increasingly, the strongest volunteer programs in the country are addressing the obstacles to volunteering and are adjusting to reach the changing face of volunteers. A key issue is childcare. Consider ways your organization can coordinate a childcare program at certain times to enable parents of small children to participate as active volunteers. Some volunteers may be interested in providing childcare.

Your Image as a Recruiter

Because the best recruitment is done in person, your image is important. Try to look as much as possible like the people you are trying to recruit. If this is impossible, then try to look like someone they would want to bring home to dinner. (No, you do not have to wear the national costume of another culture unless it truly becomes you.) The rule of thumb on appearance is that people shouldn't be able to remember what you looked like. Remembering, regardless of whether it was good or bad, means that your appearance distracted from the message instead of blending in with it.

> "What did that young man in the three-piece suit want?"

> "You mean the young man in the pin-stripe and red tie?"

> "Yes, the one with the crimson pocket handkerchief and alligator Guccis."

"I don't know. He said something about the world coming to an end. I didn't really get it. The handkerchief clashed with the tie."

Of course, eye contact is important, and language, like dress, should be appropriate, but the rules for many of these factors change with the constituency you are organizing. In some ethnic communities, averting the eyes, not eye contact, is a sign of respect. So do what everyone else does. However, you must still be yourself. The goal is to adopt the behavior and customs that help you gain acceptance, but don't try to "become" the people you are organizing.

Sound confident by knowing the subject, but don't try to impress with a blizzard of facts. Most important, be enthusiastic. This will happen naturally if you are recruiting to an important activity. Convey urgency. Avoid starting with history. Don't say "Our organization was formed in 2000 because in 1998, the City Council passed a master zoning plan for the year 2010. In section III (b) there was a major flaw that wasn't noticed until 1999 during the Streetfogle Commission hearings when . . ." Instead, start with the main point: "They are building a sewage treatment plant right in this community, and our homes won't be worth. . . !"

Practice explaining your organization's issue in a concise, upbeat fashion. In a few sentences, you should be able to convey the essence of the organization, the issue, and how you intend to win. Having a clear message is as important for recruiting people as it is for speaking to the media.

Six Steps toward Successful Recruitment

The following sections discuss the six steps you need to take to successfully recruit volunteers for your organization.

1. Be Prepared

Recruitment requires solid preparation. Have in your mind how you will explain your goal and what you want the recruit to do. Consider areas of self-interest to which you will appeal. Have a few fallback requests as well. These are jobs that need to be done but require less of a commitment: "If you can't chair the newsletter committee, can you help with the layout? Of course, we can list you on the masthead: Layout and design by . . ."

When you are acquainted with your potential recruit, review what you know about the person— his or her interests, experience, past activities, family, and anything else that will help you identify self-interest. If this is a "cold contact," someone you have never met and don't know anything about, then prepare some questions to bring up in the conversation that will get the person talking about himself or herself. Look for visual clues, for example, parents of small children usually have stains on their clothing. This can lead you into a discussion of day care, baby-sitting, schools, taxes, playgrounds, traffic lights, crime, housing, and almost anything else. You might observe that a person's clothing is covered with cat hair. This leads to a more limited range of social issues.

If you are recruiting an organization to join a coalition, research its history and program. Know its funding sources and tax status.

Whether recruiting an individual or an organization, you should approach the first meeting as if it is the beginning of what you hope will be a long-term relationship. You really want to get to know the individual and bring him or her into the organization in a way that benefits both of you. Preparing for the meeting with this mind-set will help shape your recruitment strategy.

2. Legitimize Yourself

Particularly with people you don't know, you need to gain quick credibility. You can do this in several ways.

First, if it is true, explain that you are from the same community, workplace, school, ethnic group, or whatever the appropriate division is and that you have the same problem that they do. It is important to show that you are not using their problem to advance some other agenda (e.g., "We can get this toxic dump cleaned up if all functions of government are assumed by one big industrial union of all workers regardless of craft").

Second, be able to say that you got a person's name from a mutual friend, church leader, or public figure in the community who suggested that you contact him or her.

Third, mention other people on the block (in the office, etc.) who have already agreed to join, sign, or come to the event.

Last, remind people that they really have heard of your organization. For example, you were the group that blocked McDonald's from coming in.

A key part of your recruitment strategy is explaining why that person's participation will make a difference. What is the unique role they can play that someone else can't? Even if it is just a matter of boosting turnout, explain why turnout is important: "Representative Smith won by only 150 votes. If 76 votes had gone the other way, she would have lost. We need 76 people who voted for her to get up and say that they are now ready to switch. We have 75. Will you do it?" (OK, so things really aren't made to order like this, but you get the idea.)

3. Listen

Think long-term relationship! Draw people out, identify their self-interests, clarify their concerns, and establish rapport. If you are whizzing along telling your story, you won't be able to do any of this. Listening is how you get information and show your concern. It is not simply the absence of talking, it is asking people good questions and providing encouraging remarks and body language

to convey your interest in them. It is also polite.

Listen to the responses when you legitimize yourself. If you mention a person, what is the reaction to that name? If you mention a past campaign of your group's, has the person really heard of it? If you feel that you are not connecting, ask an open-ended question like, "How long have you lived in the neighborhood? What changes have you seen?" Or ask about children or grandchildren.

Other details to listen for include special skills the person might have, useful contacts, and organizational networks such as a civic club or synagogue. Perhaps a meeting with other groups can be arranged for you.

4. Agitate

When you agitate, you are trying, as Webster's defines the word, "to stir up people so as to produce changes." You are not trying to offend or be obnoxious, but neither will you passively accept excuses for people not getting involved.

If someone says, "Oh well, I don't like the idea of a gas pipeline coming through here, but it has to go someplace, and we all have to accept these things. That's progress," then you agitate by saying, "Yes, but it was originally designed to go through vacant land that happened to belong to a wealthy contributor to U.S. Senator Jones. The contributor went to Jones, who leaned on the gas company to move the pipeline into our neighborhood. That guy didn't think it was progress, and he's a millionaire, so he should know. Here is the clipping that tells the whole story."

By agitating, you make people angry. Not only is the thing bad, but it's unfair. You can say, "No, schools are not closing all over town, just in certain places. Some schools with far fewer students than we have will stay open because those communities have more pull than we do. Is that fair to our kids?"

5. Get a Commitment

Don't leave a conversation open-ended. Get a commitment. Remember, you are trying to match the organization's needs to the person's self-interest and talents. If you can't get an actual agreement, at least try for a date by which the person will decide. If you do get an agreement, it should be to do a specific task on a specific day. Write it down. Make a note to call and remind the person. Clarify what will happen next, who will call, who will drop off any materials, and when the briefing will be.

6. Follow Up

Nothing impresses people more than timely follow-up because few of us actually do it. Make sure that your administrative systems are in place to keep track of people and get back to them as scheduled. When people you recruited do come to an event or meeting, be sure to greet them and introduce them around. Nothing is more demoralizing than making a big fuss over people while recruiting them and then ignoring them when they actually show up. If you worked on turnout for an event, try to free yourself from logistical responsibilities on that day so that you can pay attention to the new people. Write the names of those you really want to spend time with on an index card and keep it in your pocket. Refer to it throughout the event and seek out those you listed. It is too easy to get caught up talking to old friends and acquaintances and ignore the newcomers.

Tips on Keeping Volunteers

Recruitment has to be backed up by an organizational plan, with clear goals and expectations of what volunteers will do. For this to work, training and supervision are needed. People should be set to work as soon as they arrive, but first, take the time to explain the organizational importance of the task and how it fits into winning on the issue. Ask people how long they can stay and assign tasks accordingly. Never allow people to feel that you wasted their time or didn't really need them. Have a variety of things to do. Provide coffee. Celebrate birthdays of office regulars. Bring in champagne to toast even small victories. Provide ways that those who want to can move up in the structure of the organization, and don't high-pressure those who are happy with the level they are at. Maintain regular volunteer hours at different times of the day. Keep the schedule the same so that people can plan around it. Thank people and give public recognition. Don't look disappointed when they go home. In short, make an evening in the office more interesting than staying home and watching TV.

Practice Makes Perfect

At the Midwest Academy, students often role-play situations in which they recruit people. Consider having your staff and leaders practice on one another. Work on a few opening lines because getting started is the hardest part. Don't forget, most normal conversations begin by talking about the weather, sports, kids, or some other everyday subject. Practice answers to typical questions that you will be asked. If you can't adequately explain the program in role-playing, consider the possibility that you don't have a recruitment problem but an organizational problem, because your program, solution, or strategy really isn't clear enough to appeal to anyone.

Recruitment is the lifeblood of an organization. What kills groups fastest is that they stop recruiting new people. Growing, thriving organizations must train staff and leaders on how to recruit others and build recruitment strategies into their ongoing program work.

11

Principles for Leadership Development

The Leadership Development Process

Guidelines for Leadership Maintenance and Growth

Leaders and Organizers

All organizing is about the development of leadership, although this takes place in many different ways. Some organizations, particularly community and church-based groups, consider leadership development to be the real purpose of their work. To them, while issues are meaningful, they are mainly a means to developing a large pool of self-conscious, skilled leaders, without which people can never win power for themselves. The transformation of individuals into an organization of motivated progressive social-change activists is as important as any single victory that can be won. In other organizations, such as state and national coalitions, the leaders are often persons who have already risen to the top of their own organizations—trade unions, for example—and who have many years of experience in positions of some power.

While the experience level in each of these situations is very different, leadership development is nonetheless a critical element in making the organizations work. Community people may need to learn basic leadership skills such as writing a press release, analyzing the strength of an elected official, speaking publicly, and running a meeting. The union leader may have learned those skills many years ago but may be unaccustomed to working in

Developing Leadership

coalition with environmentalists and consumer groups or integrating direct action campaigns into the union's electoral agenda.

For most community organizers, leadership development poses a set of basic questions: how do we get people to feel that they own this organization, raise money for it, recruit to it, and work to keep it going? If these points aren't attended to, it won't be possible to reach the level of raising political consciousness that many organizers consider to be their long-term mission.

Principles for Leadership Development

In established organizations, paid staff are responsible to their elected leadership or to a board chosen with input from the members. In new organizations, the staff is often out looking for potential leaders. In both types of groups, the task of replenishing the leadership core tends to fall mostly to the staff. This actually puts the staff in a more powerful position than is implied in the group's bylaws, and the success of the organization very much depends on the good judgment of the staff in finding potential leaders.

Leaders Have Followers

How do you know who is a good potential leader? Who among the membership should be encouraged to be more active and take on more responsibility? The basic guideline is that leaders have followers, people they can bring to events. It might be a neighborhood person who can bring friends from her building or, in a coalition, the head of another organization who can bring his members. In any case, a leader has followers. Not only that, but the followers are typical of the community or constituency that your organization represents. The person who brings people from the Society for Freeze-Dried Pets may not be whom you are looking for.

The importance of understanding that leaders have followers can't be overemphasized because it creates a reality principle for the organization. People who can motivate and move others are basically in tune with the community or constituency. They talk the language, they are trusted, they understand what others want or expect, and they know how to get along with others. Therefore, the decisions that they make as leaders are likely to be sound ones, and the organization is likely to grow. A person who comes to every meeting and has a strong opinion on every subject but who never can bring another individual is likely to be out of sync with the community.

In the course of time, it may be useful to add to the leadership people who have special skills or special training the organization may need (e.g., someone who understands the banking regulations on community reinvestment). But these folks, useful as they are, should not make up the majority of the leadership.

To develop the leadership of people—those who can bring out other people—the organization needs a program that includes many public events and opportunities to do turnout. It also needs to find ways to spotlight those who do the best turnout, such as praising them at meetings. Unless this principle is followed and events are managed to encourage leadership by people with a base, top positions will end up going to those who talk the best game at meetings or who are known because they run a local business or have ties to the political machine. A few such people are fine, but if they are the majority of an organization's main leaders, this can be a problem. (There are exceptions, however. One of our staff recalls organizing in rural Kentucky where, in three communities, the owners of the general stores became the main leaders. It worked out well. Meetings were held in the stores, people were used to coming there, they all knew the owners, and owed them money. Those storekeepers had a real base.)

In coalitions, the principle of having a base takes on an added dimension. One leader may represent an organization with 7,000 members, none of whom ever come to anything, while another may have 70 members and always brings 20 of them. Who gets a seat on the executive committee? Well, they both do, but the one with the bigger group goes on first. The power of such an organization is both important and useful, even if the members are not seen. Perhaps later you will find the key to involving some of them.

Start with a Balanced Ticket

The balanced ticket is an old urban political concept. To get the votes of all ethnic groups, have one candidate from each group running on the party ticket. The same applies to organizations. If you want racial, ethnic, gender, and class integration, the leadership must reflect this from the very start. Once the leaders are established as being one kind of person, other kinds of people will stay away.

Many groups don't have an integrated leadership, just as most institutions and communities in our country are not integrated. We don't mean only racial integration, although that is often the case. Avoid trying to remedy this deficiency with tokenism. If people of a particular race, ethnicity, gender, or class are staying away in droves, don't go out and find the one person from that constituency who is so atypical that he or she agrees at once to become a leader in your group *unless that person has a real base and can bring other people along.* Instead, add to your issues. Find out what is of concern to the group you want to recruit, and start a campaign that will bring you in contact with its real leaders.

Don't Rush the Leadership Process

Because of the need for balance and for knowing who can bring out folks, it is wise for a new group to delay its first elections for six months or even a year. Set a date, of course, but in the meantime operate with a temporary steering committee open to all.

A pattern we have seen repeatedly is that at the first meeting of a new group, someone says, "We can't operate without bylaws." There are always a few people whose main interest in life is bylaws. They immediately start a series of long and boring debates on the subject, which drive away everyone else. Months later, when the bylaws are finished, no one is left to run for office but the bylaw crowd. Once in leadership, they say, "The reason that no one comes to meetings anymore is that we need to revise the bylaws." Start with action and stay flexible.

Both Task and Maintenance Leadership Are Needed

One helpful social work concept is that of *task* leadership and *maintenance* (or emotional) leadership. Task leadership is the kind of leadership that gets "tasks" accomplished. Maintenance leadership is the kind that cares about the emotional strength of the group and the people involved in it. Every successful organization has a healthy balance of both types of leadership. The task leader says, "I want to get this done now." The maintenance leader says, "I want people to feel good about getting it done."

While most of us consciously try to develop skills in both areas, our personalities and innate characteristics lead us to be stronger in one area than the other. Someone who is stronger in task leadership is probably pushing through the program but making people mad all along the way. Someone stronger in maintenance leadership probably gets along well with everyone but has trouble moving a program forward. The point is not that one kind of leadership is better than the other but that both are needed for a healthy organization.

If this concept is unclear to you, think about any group with which you are familiar that has functioned well over a long period of time. See if you can identify a mixture of people who provide task and maintenance leadership. Or you can observe any meeting. Typical task leadership functions are

- Preparing an agenda
- Recommending objectives
- Determining key questions
- Suggesting ways to accomplish specific objectives

- Clarifying information, moving the group to action or decision making
- Recording information and decisions
- Opening and closing meetings

Typical maintenance (emotional) leadership functions are

- Welcoming and introducing people
- Actively listening to people's ideas
- Including everyone in discussions
- Encouraging shy and quiet people to speak
- Thanking people for contributions and coming to meetings
- Giving positive feedback to speakers

If you suspect that your organization does not have a good balance between task and maintenance leaders, watch a few meetings to observe the dynamics. If the group seems to be short on one kind of leader, actively seek people who provide a balance.

Seek Qualities and Develop Skills

All good leaders possess both personal *qualities* and specific *skills* that make them respected. The easiest way to distinguish between skills and qualities (or characteristics) is to say, "Susie is . . ." (a quality) or "Susie is good at . . ." (a skill). A quality is something you "are" intrinsically. A skill is something you learn. It is important in identifying potential leaders that you distinguish between skills and qualities. We have to find people who have the qualities that are needed. We can always train people in particular skills. For example, if we are looking for a volunteer treasurer, we are looking for someone with the characteristics of honesty, attentiveness to details, thoroughness, good follow-through, and commitment to the organization. These characteristics can't be "taught," at least not very easily. We must find someone who already has them. Obviously, we'd like that person to also have bookkeeping experience. But if the person doesn't, we can offer training in bookkeeping.

Although the qualities and skills needed for every position vary, there are some typical ones that leaders need in most roles. The *qualities* all leaders need are described below.

Commitment. If they are not committed to what they are doing, it will show. The leader needs a commitment to the particular organization, a long-term commitment to social change, and a vision of what the future can be.

Honesty. Honesty, tempered with tactfulness, is always the best policy.

Positive Outlook. The world is full of negative people and negative situations. A leader must radiate positiveness and look for solutions to problems instead of focusing on the difficulties.

Confidence/Self-Assurance. A leader must have confidence in himself or herself. This does not mean that the person knows everything but rather that he or she is self-assured enough to ask for help and to admit weaknesses. The confident, self-assured person accepts compliments as well as criticism. Confidence is not only important in individual dealings and relationships but also when the organization is facing an adversarial person who represents an unjust institution. The leader must have the confidence to hold firm in a position based on the planned strategy.

Trust in People. Leaders must fundamentally trust and like people. They must draw out the best in people and urge them to live up to high standards, as opposed to waiting for people to falter. Most people live up to the high standards and trust placed in them.

Mistrust of Unaccountable Institutions. Although leaders must trust people, they must mistrust institutions that are not accountable to people. Leaders are frequently the people who ask "why?" or "why not?" A healthy skepticism is a useful quality for a leader.

Some of the *skills* almost all leaders need to develop include

Listening. Leaders need to be able to listen to others. Good listening means not only opening one's ears but also really concentrating on what someone else is saying.

Diplomacy. All leaders find themselves in situations where they must use diplomacy. They must learn to be direct, assertive, and yet tactful— unless a group has consciously decided in a particular situation not to be diplomatic.

Recruitment. Almost all leaders need to recruit others to work with them in some capacity or other. Thus, they must clearly understand how to recruit and to develop experience in recruiting others.

Personal Organization. Leaders need to be personally organized. They need good systems for keeping track of meetings, following up with people, making calls, and so forth. Without good administrative systems for organizing oneself, a leader does not follow through with tasks and commitments as promised.

Goal Setting. All leaders need to develop skills in setting measurable and realistic goals. Without such goals, we are unclear about where we are going. If we get there, we don't know to congratulate ourselves. Learning to set such goals helps avoid leadership burnout. The skills of goal setting are needed at all levels of the organization, from the board to the staff, committee, and individual levels.

The Leadership Development Process

Start with Self-Interest

There is a saying in community organizing that leadership is developed, not found. Very few "natural leaders" are sitting around not doing anything but waiting for you to call. Your group may be lucky and find a person whose leadership experience was developed in another organization, perhaps a congregation, or who is one of those rare people to whom others in the community turn in time of crisis. But for the most part, organizations develop their own leaders. (As noted previously, in coalitions, the people who come are already leaders, but they develop coalition skills.) Developing leadership on any level starts with understanding the self-interest of the potential leader. A person who is going to put in long hours, work hard, and take real risks has to get something back in return. Of course, there is commitment to the issue itself, but issues are won and lost. There has to be more. Think for a moment about all the benefits a person can get out of being a leader in your organization. Here are just a few:

- Recognition
- New skills
- Respect
- Excitement
- Social activity
- A chance to make history
- A seat on the dais
- An opportunity to start a new career
- The pleasure of "sticking it" to enemies of the community

A coalition leader may already have all these but can gain

- New allies
- A wider circle of influential contacts
- New ways to be more effective in his or her own organization
- Even greater contact with the media
- An opportunity to run for office

Of course, not everyone wants all of this. The point is to listen and figure out what the potential leader's self-interest actually is and then shape the position in ways that help the leader achieve those personal goals.

Create Positions in Which Leaders Can Develop

A true story illustrates this point. Many years ago, a popular figure in both the women's movement and the peace movement ran for Mayor of New York City. The campaign attracted hundreds of volunteers who were deployed on weekends at street tables up and down the main avenues. The volunteers, sometimes numbering as many as 300 in a single weekend, gave out literature, sold buttons, and publicized issues.

The paid campaign staff ran the whole street table operation. There was no leadership among the volunteers until the staff decided to create it. They invented the position of "corner captain" and invited volunteers who had come regularly to be corner captains. Their responsibilities included arriving early to receive the table from the truck and then instructing other volunteers in their duties.

It worked. People began to take responsibility. Special training sessions were held at headquarters for the captains, and they felt more a part of the campaign. Later, the staff who had been making the weekly phone calls to all of the volunteers told certain captains, "We have six people for your location on Saturday. Ten more volunteers live in your area, but we don't have the time to call them. Could you call?" Before long, a number of the captains were calling their own volunteer lists.

A niche was thus created in which leadership could develop. A strong motivation was provided by the candidate and the issues. There was a title, a short list of time-limited responsibilities, other people to help, and someone higher in the group to step in if problems occurred. It turned out that all the elements for beginning leadership development had come together at dozens of street corners.

In many organizations, the same type of niche is provided by a committee structure. People can start on the path to leadership by chairing a committee or even a subcommittee that has a specific task to carry out. It gives newer members a place to do something without being overshadowed by older leaders. The reason for having a formal committee structure isn't necessarily that it is more efficient; it is a way to develop leaders.

Another example of creating niches was illustrated by the program for a dinner given by a congregation to honor a civil rights leader. The program listed the names of the members of all the committees. One committee was in charge of floral arrangements for the head table and another committee for floral arrangements for the other tables. There was even a committee to print the program listing the dozen or so committees. In all, over a hundred people were listed on that program as having had some part in organizing the dinner. You can bet that they all showed up at the event and sold a lot of tickets as well. That's leadership development! In most groups, the organizer would have just picked up the phone and ordered the flowers, or more likely, there would have been no flowers.

As this indicates, one of the secrets of leadership development is breaking big projects down into manageable pieces and then finding someone to take responsibility for each piece. It will work if the goals are clear, the piece is really manageable, there is someone experienced to fall back on for advice or help, and doing the job brings some satisfaction and reward.

Guidelines for Leadership Maintenance and Growth

Here are some ways to maintain leaders and help them develop their leadership skills.

Practice Evaluations. Look for and give positive, as well as growth-producing, feedback. Regular group evaluations at meetings are good.

Institute the Rotation of Roles, and Develop Systems for Training People for New Roles. Few of us want to remain doing the same job forever.

Make Sure Leaders Are Enjoying Their Positions. If leaders are not enjoying their positions, they will either get frustrated and quit or make themselves and those around them miserable.

Use Strong, Skilled Leaders to Train Others. Every strong leader should be training others. No one should become "irreplaceable." Build leadership development into every position.

Ask Leaders to Set Personal Leadership Development Goals as Part of Your Annual Goal-Setting Session. Provide needed support and training to help leaders achieve their goals, as long as they don't conflict with the organization's goals.

Leaders and Organizers

Some schools of organizing stress that a leader is one thing and an organizer is another. Conceptually, it is not clear that this is true. In a coalition, the leaders may all be the paid staff of other groups, and in many organizations that have no staff, volunteer leaders do much the same job that paid staff would do. What is clear is that in local organizations with both paid staff and volunteer leaders, certain roles are appropriate for each.

One of the first lessons that most new organizers are taught is that in the absence of a salary, leaders get certain "perks": being quoted in the newspaper or interviewed on TV, representing the organization publicly, and receiving praise and recognition. This is not just a matter of rewarding leaders. It is important to the organization as a whole that its leaders become widely known personalities who enhance the group's power. For that reason, organizers are warned not to get in the spotlight themselves. Every time the paid staff is interviewed on TV, an opportunity is lost to strengthen the leadership. Worse, resentment is created and leaders ask, "Why should I help him run his organization; that's what he's paid for."

The situation is somewhat different in statewide and national coalitions. It is not always possible to have volunteer leaders on hand where and when the media want them. In addition, the coalition as a whole needs to receive a large amount of the recognition rather than have it go to the head of one group within the coalition. In such situations, Executive Directors and other staff more often play the role of spokesperson.

The second lesson that organizers should be taught, but many aren't, is not to do anything for leaders that leaders can do for themselves. The job of leaders is to build the organization. The job of organizers is to get others to build the organization.

One community organization had no staff at one time. Often, leaflets had to be taken to the printer, who was located in another neighborhood and closed at five o'clock. The leaders worked out a system to get their copy to the printer. The woman who did the layout brought it with her when she took her child to school. There, she gave it to another member who had a child in the same class. That member took the layout home and gave it to his wife, who took it to work the next day. At lunch, she gave it to another member, who worked near her. He took it home, and the next day his wife, who worked

near the printer, took it in on her lunch hour. Now, it was true that getting the leaflet to the printer took two days and involved six people, but that was really fine. It kept the people in touch with each other, and with the organization, and it gave them a way of helping the organization that didn't take them much out of their way.

Later, when the group hired an organizer, she said, "I'll just pick up the layout and take it to the printer." Wrong! The organizer is a paid professional. Her job is to get people to build the organization, not to run errands. That organizer was taking roles away from members and wasting time that she should have spent finding new people to help out.

Here are some of the roles that are appropriate for paid organizers and for volunteer leaders. For most community organizations, *organizers* should

- Make proposals for action
- Develop workplans based on board decisions
- Identify leadership roles and training needed
- Help recruit new leaders
- Ensure honest evaluations
- Help people assume leadership tasks
- Coordinate information flow between boards and committees

Volunteer *leaders* should

- Represent the constituency, which means speaking in public forums and providing interviews for the media
- Take the lead in actions or confrontations with decision makers
- Maintain the organization by forming a board that is responsible for raising money, setting policies, hiring and evaluating the Executive Director (or firing if need be)
- Do as much of the actual physical work of the organization as possible.

Sometimes problems arise within organizations that hire community leaders to serve as organizers. Even if the leaders have good organizing skills, they may not understand that their roles have changed and that they are now to develop the leadership of others and drop the up-front spokesperson role that they might have played in the past.

Another problem arises when someone is hired to function as an organizer but really has no experience in organizing. Leaders become frustrated and wonder why they aren't getting paid if that person is. If the organizer is not looked to for providing professional organizing skills, then the leaders will tend to give the staff all the jobs they don't want to do. The organizer gets frustrated because he doesn't enjoy the work and is learning few new skills. This problem occurs frequently in low-budget organizations that hire young organizers just out of school.

If your organization is in this situation, consider raising additional funds in order to hire a skilled and experienced organizer. Perhaps a person could be hired to train and develop your inexperienced staff. If you are not able to hire an experienced organizer, be sure to provide intensive training and support from an experienced organizing consulting group. A few foundations set aside special technical assistance funds to ensure that community organizations get proper training and consulting.

In ending this chapter, allow us to restate what is really the only point. Volunteer leadership development is about the most important job an organizer has. If you are not developing leaders, then you are not building your organization.

Developing leadership takes practice. Community members role-play a meeting with a public official.

12

Did you ever go to a meeting where the agenda consisted of two items, "old business" and "new business," or worse, where the chair got up and said, "Well, what would you like to talk about?" Were you then assured that such practices were the height of organizational democracy and designed to encourage maximum participation? Don't believe it!

Meetings can make or break an organization. If your meetings are well prepared, focused on planning for action, and facilitated in an efficient yet involving and upbeat manner, they help build your organization. On the other hand, if your meetings are poorly planned, are poorly run, and don't focus on planning for action, it will be difficult, if not impossible, to build an organization.

Rule: The purpose of a meeting is to make decisions. All else is secondary.

All meetings should help meet the basic principles of direct action organizing. First, the meeting should help the organization win concrete improvements in people's lives. Thus, all meetings must have concrete goals that matter and that are accomplished. If you are meeting with

Preparation

Meeting Facilitation

Follow-Up

Participation in Meetings

Meeting Checklist

Planning and Facilitating Meetings

your organization's leadership, your goal is to plan, to make decisions, or to involve people in the work at hand. Few people want to attend a meeting just to hear announcements.

Second, the meeting should give people a sense of their own power. Meetings must be run efficiently and well so that people will gain a sense of their power through participating in an efficient and well-run organization. If members feel that the group can't even get through a meeting, they will doubt that it can do anything even more complicated.

Finally, the meeting should help you plan ways to change the relations of power. You do this when you build or strengthen your organization. Every meeting should strengthen your organization by making plans for raising funds, recruiting volunteers, and training your board to function more effectively or planning other ways to build your organization. Making sure that your organization grows and develops enables you not only to win immediate issue victories but also to build an organization that has real power in the community.

Preparation

Well-run, effective meetings require solid preparation. The hardest part and certainly the

most time-consuming aspect of a meeting is the planning, which takes much longer than the meeting itself. The average business meeting should run no longer than two hours, but planning for it can take up to several days and may require an additional smaller executive committee meeting, which must also be planned. Much of the real work of defining the issues and framing the discussion goes on during the preparation process. Planning means making political judgments about the program alternatives to be presented at the meeting. It also involves arranging for someone to explain each proposal or agenda item and speaking with all the members beforehand so that they know what is on the agenda and what the alternatives are. Sometimes planning requires deciding on the most beneficial way to handle disagreements. By the time of the meeting, all of the group's leadership and most active members will have been consulted, discussed the issues the meeting will deal with, and taken responsibility for various aspects of the event.

This is not to say that all the decisions are made in advance and then "sold" to the members at the meeting. Just the opposite. The members need to be engaged in making the decisions because the members are the ones who will have to carry them out. However, a large group of people, more than twenty meeting monthly, can't make sound decisions in a two-hour period unless alternatives are clearly framed, proposals and background information are distributed on paper, and people who have thought through the matter come prepared to lay out the arguments. This is the role of leadership.

All of this having been said, remember that the purpose of an organization is to do things, not to have meetings. Meetings, no matter how good, will never be the most popular activity and will never attract and hold people the way that action and fun events will. If most of the time of leaders and staff is spent on meetings, then something is wrong with the program.

The meeting planning process includes the following twelve elements:

Goals. Every meeting should have concrete, realistic, and measurable action goals, the things you want to accomplish. Without them, it is difficult to even figure out an agenda. Holding a meeting is not a goal in itself. Even if the bylaws say that there must be a monthly meeting, there still has to be some larger purpose.

Educating people, keeping people in touch, and updating them are not objectives that require a meeting. They can often be achieved just as well through newsletters and phone calls. If people are asked to give up an evening, they need to be offered more. In addition, it's difficult to measure whether or not you've really "educated" or "updated" people. An occasional forum with well-prepared speakers, films, or slides is fine, but if your meetings consist primarily of educational programs or announcements, you will attract a different group of people than would more action-focused meetings.

The main function of an organizational meeting is to make decisions that are required

- To develop a strategy and timeline to implement an issue campaign.

- To develop a strategy and timeline for a specific tactic.
- To recruit volunteers or new members.
- To evaluate goals or programs and to plan for the future.
- To decide upon organizational positions.

Site. The choice of meeting site will affect who comes to a meeting. Criteria for choosing a site include

- *Familiarity*. Is it a place with which people are familiar and comfortable?
- *Accessibility*. Is the meeting site accessible for those you are trying to reach? Make sure that the room is accessible for disabled and elderly people. Central location is important and availability of public transportation may also be important.
- *Safety*. Is the location in a neighborhood or block that the majority of your people feel safe going to?
- *Symbolic Meaning*. Does the site have any symbolic significance that might work for or against you? For example, if you are trying to build a multiracial organization and your meetings are regularly held in a mainly White church, your choice of site might send the wrong message, even though your group has no connection with the church other than to use its rooms.
- *Adequate Facilities*. Different meetings require different facilities. Small meetings need a small cozy room, not a corner of a large empty room. Larger meetings need bigger rooms with more elaborate facilities. Meetings of senior citizens need a good speaker system. Be sure to consider all the things you might need before you choose a site.

Date/Timing. Set the meeting at a time that is most convenient for those whom you want to attend. You may need to call several people and suggest possible options. Would people rather meet early on the way home from work, or would they rather come out again after dinner? Are weekends better than weekdays? Seniors often like to be home before dark. Younger people may have baby-sitters. Check on holidays and Sabbath observance.

Chairperson. Every meeting should have a chairperson whose main job is to facilitate the meeting. The meeting chair is often the top elected officer of the group, but this need not be the case. It is often best to have a chair who does not need to present program suggestions or answer lots of questions. The meeting chair should be free to focus on facilitating the meeting instead of talking. The meeting chair should be involved in setting the agenda so that he or she understands it and thinks it is workable.

Agenda. Who actually plans the agenda depends on the situation. In most organizations, the organizer works with the chairperson or executive committee to plan the agenda. For board meetings, the organization's Director works with the board president to plan the agenda.

The following guidelines apply to the preparation of meeting agendas:

• Participants should receive a printed agenda and attachments that provide some background on the topics for discussion.

• Many facilitators find that it helps to list the objective of each discussion item right on the agenda (e.g., "The objective of this discussion is to decide on our next campaign. The alternatives are . . .").

• Include suggested time limits for each agenda item. This helps the chair to keep the group on schedule and gives an indication of the relative importance of the different agenda items. (It has been observed that people tend to spend the most time discussing the least consequential item or the smallest amount of money.)

• Designate the "action items" on the agenda—those on which the group must take action by making a decision.

• Indicate on the agenda the names of the people who are going to introduce or speak to each agenda item. This not only gives them a recognized role, but they are more likely to show up if everyone is expecting them.

• For each agenda item, include time for getting commitments for work and participation. The link between making decisions and carrying them out needs to be clearly established. This can be difficult because our society teaches people that citizenship means little more than voting. If you are going to pass around sign-up sheets for various activities, do it before people start leaving. Make sure that everyone leaves with something concrete to do.

• For meetings where many decisions will be made, consider ordering the decisions as follows:

- Easy decisions. Ask the group to make a few easy decisions; this gets people off to the right start.

- Hard, controversial decisions. Next, tackle the hard decisions that require lots of discussion. Where a decision is particularly controversial or has a major impact on the organization, you may want to introduce the topic, hand out the background materials, and then give people until the next meeting to think about it.

- Moderate, non-controversial decisions. At the end, include decisions that are of moderate importance but upon which most people will probably agree. People will be tired, so they won't want to debate. And you want to end the meeting on a harmonious note, if at all possible.

Food. Keep people eating. Nothing lifts the spirit and soothes the temper like food. Don't hold all the refreshments until the meeting ends and everyone is rushing out. If people are sitting at a table, have popcorn and lots of little snacks to nibble on during the meeting. At a larger meeting, at least get the coffeepot going early and put out cookies, fruit, and raw vegetables in the back.

Background Materials/Proposals. Whoever plans the agenda should identify materials and proposals that will provide the necessary background for people to make good decisions and will save the group time. In general, people find it easier to respond to proposals than to create programs from scratch, and while small groups may develop plans or strategies, large groups can best alter and choose between alternatives presented to them.

Literacy and Language. Don't assume that everyone can read, or can read English. Some groups make it a practice to read aloud any key documents. Translate documents in advance and prepare to have translation at meetings where needed.

Meeting Roles. Assign all meeting roles before the actual meeting. The five reasons for people to have particular leadership roles in a meeting are as follows:

- Someone has a particular talent that will enhance the meeting—leading a song, facilitating discussion, welcoming people.
- The responsibility is part of someone's job. For example, it is the treasurer's job to give the financial report. Not to have the treasurer give the report would be a slight to the person.
- It would be politically good for your organization to have a particular person play a leadership role in the meeting—a local union leader or member of the clergy, for example.
- People need experience in making presentations and leading discussions in order to develop their leadership.

- People will come to the meeting if they have a role to play. The more roles you have, the better.

Typical roles in meetings include:

- *Facilitator/Chairperson.* This person sees that the meeting moves forward and follows the agenda, unless the agenda is changed by a vote of the group.
- *Note Taker.* The note taker keeps the record of the meeting and may also write the meeting's main points on an easel pad that is placed so that everyone attending can see it.
- *Timekeeper.* The timekeeper reminds the chairperson about time constraints. If there are disagreements in the organization or time limits on speaking, the timekeeper should be a neutral person whose participation in the debate is minimal. This avoids the perception that one side is getting more time. It also takes some of the heat off the chair: "I'm sorry, the *timekeeper* says your three minutes are up."
- *Presenters.* A variety of people can present various programs, ideas, and reports. Avoid having all the presentations made by the facilitator/chairperson. The more people who participate, the more you are building leadership.
- *Tone Setter.* This person can open or close a meeting with a prayer or song, a uniting statement, or an emotional call to action.
- *Greeter.* Ask at least one person to welcome new people and get their names and addresses as they enter.

Room Arrangements/Logistics. Before the meeting, assess the actual room you will use in order to plan the room arrangements and logistical details. Items to consider include:

- *Chair Arrangements.* Chairs in a circle or better, around a table, encourage discussion and cohesiveness. Podiums and theater seating encourage formality and are better for large groups. Decide which arrangements are best for the particular meeting. Set up fewer chairs than the number expected. It's better to add chairs than have chairs sitting empty.

- *Places to Hang Flip-Chart Paper.* Will tape damage the walls? Is an easel available? The newer self-stick chart pads are great, although a bit expensive.
- *Outlets for Audiovisual Equipment.* Always bring extra extension cords and a three-prong plug adapter.
- *Places for People to Sign In.* Where can you place the sign-in table to ensure that you get names, addresses, phone and fax numbers, and e-mail addresses for follow-up?
- *Refreshments.* Who will bring them? Can someone else bring the plates or cups? Do you need outlets for coffeepots? Can the room be arranged such that people can get food without disrupting the meeting? Who will handle cleanup? For smaller groups and board meetings, ask people to volunteer to bake. Some folks enjoy doing this, and occasionally you will find that a person welcomes an opportunity to do something for the group who doesn't otherwise participate a great deal. (A most common problem is plugging in multiple coffeepots and blowing the fuse in a building with which you are unfamiliar. Ask first.)
- *Microphone Setups.* Will you need microphones? Will someone be available to set up and test the equipment? Is there a way to adjust the volume from the back? Is the equipment height adjustable?
- *Translation.* Is there a place in the room to put the translation equipment or a section for specific-language speakers?

Asking people to bring items or to help arrange things for the meeting helps to assure their attendance. Assign people to bring coffee, cups, cookies, tablecloths, agendas, posters, sign-in sheets, tape players, or flowers. Ask different people to set up chairs, sound equipment, or informational displays. Delegating tasks ahead of time, instead of grabbing the first person who walks in, may seem more trouble than it's worth, but it gets people involved in the meeting and the organization. People are more likely to come if they have a job, and this is a particularly good way to integrate new people. It also makes the meeting run smoothly, which people appreciate.

Turnout. If you want your large membership meetings well attended, make plans to remind people. Do not rely on mailings or e-mail to get people to a meeting. If your meeting involves only a few people, one person can call everyone a day or two ahead. If you are hoping for larger numbers of people, recruit a number of people to help call those you want to attend. Calls should be made no more than five days before the meeting, although written notices or public announcements should go out in advance. These calls have an organizing function as well as aiding turnout. Explain the urgent issues that will be discussed at the meeting, and identify points of controversy.

For many groups, childcare, transportation, and language are barriers to people's participation. If you can make arrangements for all, you can increase your participation. Be sure to mention these in calls if they are available. If you provide childcare, some parents will want an indication of the quality of care (e.g., "Professional childcare providers will bring games and activities" as opposed to "Local teenager will sit kids in front of TV").

For large organizational meetings, keep track of what percentage of those who agreed to come actually showed up. This will give you a figure on which to base future turnout projections. You can also compare your meeting sign-in sheets with the lists used by the individual members, leaders, or outside groups who agreed to recruit to the meeting. You will then know who the real leaders are or what organizations are most effective in recruiting people.

Fun. Every meeting should have two or three fun elements built into the agenda. These could be singing or having someone recite a poem, celebrating a birthday or anniversary, giving comic awards or T-shirts to people who helped with the last activity, giving a door prize, showing slides or a video of a past event (including TV coverage), or putting on a short skit.

All your meetings should help move the organization forward. If well organized, with lots of participation, good decisions, and concrete plans for action, then the meetings will increase your members' confidence, support the leadership, build unity, and portray your organization as one that can get things done.

Meeting Facilitation

Every meeting should be enjoyable, run efficiently, and build organizational morale. However, measuring these characteristics may be difficult. Efficient meetings respect people's time as their most valuable resource. They also build organizational morale by generating a sense of unity and helping people respect and support one another.

In order to be adequately prepared, the chairperson must know ahead of time that she or he will facilitate the meeting. There's nothing worse than arriving and asking, "Who's chairing this meeting?" If no one has prepared to facilitate, the meeting will probably be poorly run.

Being a good facilitator is both a skill and an art. It is a skill in that people can learn certain techniques and can improve their ability with practice. It is an art in that some people just have more of a knack for it than others. Unless, as with some board meetings, your bylaws specifically state that a certain officer must chair, you can draw upon members with the requisite skills.

Facilitating a meeting requires someone to

- Understand the goals of the meeting and the organization.
- Keep the group on the agenda and moving forward.
- Involve everyone in the meeting, both controlling the domineering people and drawing out the shy ones.
- Make sure that decisions are made democratically.

The chair must assure that decisions, plans, and commitments are made in a manner enjoyable for all. This means being upbeat, positive, and not critical of the group. ("Well, I can tell by all the talking in the back that no one here really cares that the Northern forests are dying and that you would rather drink coffee than save the planet!") A good chair is concerned about both a meeting's *content* and its *style*. By assigning other roles, such as note takers and timekeepers, the chair has some assistance in moving the agenda along.

Here are some guides for meeting facilitation:

Start the Meeting Promptly. For large group meetings, start within ten to fifteen minutes of the official beginning time, regardless of how many people are late. For smaller meetings, particularly regular organizational meetings, start exactly on time. Don't delay until more people show up. That just penalizes those who come on time and rewards those who come late. If you delay the starting time of this meeting by a half-hour, people will come forty-five minutes late to the next meeting.

Welcome Everyone. Make a point to welcome everyone who comes to the meeting. *Do not, under any circumstance, bemoan the size of the group.* Once you are at a meeting, the people there are the people there. Go with what you have. (You may want to analyze the recruitment plans after the meeting.)

We few, we happy few.
—Shakespeare

Introduce People. If just a few people are new, ask them to introduce themselves. If the group as a whole does not know one another well, ask people to answer a question or tell something about themselves.

The kinds of questions you should ask depend upon the kind of meeting it is, the number of people participating, and the overall goals of the meeting. Sample introductory questions include

- How did you first get involved with our organization? (Ask this question if most people are already involved but don't know one another well.)
- What makes you most angry about this problem? (Ask if the meeting is to focus on a particular problem.)
- Can you mention a recent victory of your group? (Ask if people are from other organizations.)

Avoid asking what animal they would most like to be.

Make everyone feel welcome and listened to at the beginning of a meeting, otherwise participants may feel uncomfortable and unappreciated. In addition, if you don't get basic information from people about their backgrounds and involvement, you may miss golden opportunities. For example, someone at the meeting may be the editor of a regional newspaper, but if you don't find out, you won't be able to make use of the connection. If people don't know the chairperson, she should say who she is and why she is facilitating the meeting. It never hurts for chairs to explain how long they have been a part of an organization, how important the organization is to them, and what outcomes they hope for from the meeting.

Review the Agenda. Go over what's going to happen in the meeting. Ask the group if the agenda is adequate. Ninety percent of the time, people will say yes. Occasionally someone will suggest an additional item. Either the item can be addressed directly in the meeting or you can explain how and when the issue can be addressed.

Explain the Meeting Rules. Most groups need some basic rules of order for meetings. Don't use a very formal system such as *Robert's Rules of Order*, unless everyone understands it. While a few people can dominate a meeting because of their better knowledge of *Robert's Rules,* more likely there will just be confusion and frustration. Some groups follow "Bob's Rules," an improvised and less formal version of *Robert's Rules* that allows for basic motions, amendments, and not much more. You can make up your own version of "Bob's Rules" since it isn't written down anywhere. The AFL-CIO publishes a great pamphlet *How to Run a Union Meeting,* which gives simplified parliamentary rules applicable to any kind of organization. You can get a copy for each member at a nominal price. Many unions have similar booklets.

The philosophy behind all rules of order is this: On any issue that comes before the group, there will be numerical minority and majority positions. The minority has a right to be heard and to try to persuade people in the majority to change their minds. The majority has a right to vote, settle the matter, and move on—but only *after* it becomes clear that a longer debate won't change any more minds. Meeting rules are largely a matter of defining these two sets of rights and establishing the procedures and limits for each.

In common practice, a majority vote, 50 percent plus one of the group, settles any issue. But it is not always best to use this method in a volunteer organization. If the difference of opinion is a serious one and the group is evenly divided, there is a danger of losing half the membership. Some groups make a point of requiring a "supermajority," two-thirds of the votes, in order to pass certain kinds of motions such as adopting a new issue. A few groups try to operate by consensus, talking matters out until everyone agrees without voting. This is fine if you can do it, but it usually requires such long meetings that people with job and family responsibilities can't attend or stay till the end. While it is true that formal rules can be manipulated to dominate a meeting, consensus meetings are even more easily controlled, especially those where the leaders pretend that there are no leaders.

Bring Closure to Discussions. Most groups will discuss items longer than needed unless the facilitator helps them recognize that they are basically in agreement. Formulate a consensus position, or ask someone in the group to formulate a position that reflects the group's general position, and then move forward. If one or two people strongly disagree, state the situation as clearly as you can: "Tom and Livonia disagree on this matter, but everyone else seems to be in agreement to go in this direction. Perhaps we should decide to go in the direction most of the group wants to go, but maybe Tom and Livonia can get back to us on other ways to accommodate their concerns." For most groups to work well,

they should seek consensus where possible but take votes in order to move decisions forward and make leaders accountable.

Stick to the Agenda. If people start to wander from the original agenda, bring it to their attention. You can say, "That's an interesting issue, but perhaps we should get back to the matter under discussion."

Avoid Detailed Decision Making. Frequently, it is easier for a group to discuss the color of napkins than the real issue it is facing. Help a group not to get immersed in details. Instead, suggest, "Perhaps the committee could resolve that matter. You don't really want to be involved in this level of detail, do you?"

Move to Action. Meetings should not only provide an opportunity for people to talk but should also challenge them to plan ways to confront and change injustice, in whatever forms it takes.

Seek Commitments. For small meetings, write people's names on an easel pad next to the tasks they agree to undertake. The chairperson may want to ask each person directly how he or she wants to help. Don't ever close a meeting by saying, "We will get back to you to confirm how you might get involved." Seize the moment. Confirm how people want to get involved right at the meeting.

Encourage Participation and Respect People's Rights. The facilitator is the protector of the weak in meetings. She encourages quiet and shy people to speak and does not allow domineering people to ridicule others' ideas or to embarrass them in any fashion.

Try one of these phrases for encouraging participation: "We've heard a lot from the men this evening; are there women who have additional comments?" "We've heard a lot from the front of the room. Are there people with thoughts in the back of the room?" "Let's hear from someone who hasn't spoken yet."

Sometimes people dominate a discussion because they are really interested in an issue and have lots of ideas. There may be ways to capture their interest and concern without having them continue to dominate the meeting. For example, consider asking them to serve on a task force or committee on that matter. In other situations, people just talk to hear themselves. If a person regularly participates in your organization's meetings and regularly creates problems, a key leader should ask that person to help with involving the new people and drawing out others to speak at meetings.

Be Flexible. Occasionally, issues and concerns arise that are so important you must alter the agenda to discuss them before returning to the prepared agenda. If necessary, ask for a five-minute break in the meeting to discuss with the key leaders how to handle the issue and how to restructure the agenda.

Summarize the Meeting Results and Follow Up. Before closing a meeting, summarize what happened and what follow-up will occur. Review the commitments people made to reinforce them, as well as to remind them how effective the meeting was.

Thank People. Take a moment to thank people who prepared things for the meeting, set up the room, brought refreshments, or typed up the agenda. Also thank everyone for making the meeting a success.

Close the Meeting on or before the Ending Time. Unless a meeting is really exciting, people want it to end on time. And remember, no one minds getting out of a meeting early. In fact, if you end early, people will think you are a terrific facilitator.

Follow-Up

There are two main principles for meeting follow-up: Do it, and do it promptly. If meetings are not followed up promptly, much of the work accomplished at them will be lost. Nothing is more disheartening than holding a good planning meeting and then allowing decisions and plans to fall through the cracks because follow-up was neglected.

Make sure that your note taker prepares the meeting notes soon after the meeting. Otherwise, he or she will forget what the comments mean, and they will be useless later. Organizers should work with the note takers to assure that the meeting notes are clear and produced in a timely fashion.

Call active members who missed the meeting. Tell them you missed them and update them on the meeting's outcome. If you are seeking new members, call anyone who indicated that he or she would come and not just active members.

Again, thank people who helped make the meeting successful, including people who brought refreshments, set up chairs, gave presentations, and played particularly positive roles in the meeting. Don't forget to thank the people "backstage," such as the cleanup crew, childcare workers, or parking lot "security guards."

Call the chairperson. Thank him or her for chairing, and review the outcome of the meeting. If appropriate, discuss ways to improve the next meeting.

Call new people who came to the meeting. Thank them for coming and see about setting up one-on-one meetings with people who look like potential leaders. Be sure to follow up with people while their interest is still fresh.

Once the minutes are prepared, write relevant reminder notes in your calendar. For example, if someone agreed to research something by March 15, jot down a reminder to call the person on

March 7 and inquire about how the research is progressing.

Before the next meeting, the officers and staff should ensure that tasks that were agreed to at the last meeting are accomplished and reports are prepared for the next meeting. It's terrible to have to report that the plans of the previous meeting were not carried out. In fact, those who were supposed to have carried them out won't come. Not doing good follow-up will affect turnout for the next meeting.

Place a copy of the meeting notes in an organizational notebook or file so that everyone knows where the "institutional memory" is kept. For meetings of your board of directors, the minutes are the legal record of the corporation. Minutes record important legal decisions and are reviewed as part of the annual audit.

Participating in Meetings

Everyone who participates in meetings has a responsibility to help make them a success. We can't always control others, but we can control ourselves. Below are some dos and don'ts for participating in meetings:

DO
- Personally welcome new people.
- Actively listen to others.
- Support the facilitator in moving the agenda ahead.
- Recommend ways to resolve differences.
- Participate in discussions.
- Encourage new people to speak and volunteer.
- Help set up and clean up the room.
- Be positive and upbeat throughout the meeting.
- Tell a joke or add a light comment to ease the tension in a difficult discussion.

DON'T
- Dominate the discussion.
- Bring up tangents.
- Dwell on past problems.
- Insist that people support your ideas.
- Gossip about how awful it all is.

If you can't speak well of someone,
come sit by me.

—Alice Roosevelt Longworth

With solid planning, good facilitation, and strong follow-up, an organization can move forward in ways that win real victories, give people a sense of their own power, and change the relations of power. Meetings play a significant role in achieving your goals and deserve your utmost attention. Make your organization the one with the fun, productive meetings.

Meeting Checklist

_____ Have you set concrete, realistic goals?

_____ Is the site familiar, accessible, representative, and adequate?

_____ Are the date and time good for those you want to attend?

_____ Do you have a chairperson for the meeting? Has the chairperson been involved in preparing the agenda or been fully briefed?

_____ Do you have translators?

Does the agenda

        _____ Accomplish the goals?

        _____ Encourage commitment and involvement?

        _____ Provide visible leadership roles?

        _____ Let people have fun?

Do you have

        _____ Printed agendas?

        _____ Background materials?

        _____ Written proposals for action?

Have you asked people to serve as the

        _____ Chairperson/facilitator?

        _____ Note taker?

        _____ Timekeeper?

        _____ Presenters?

        _____ Tone setters? (open and close meetings)

        _____ Greeter? (welcome people and get names and addresses)

        _____ Refreshment servers?

Have you considered the following logistical matters?

        _____ Chair arrangements

        _____ Flip charts, markers, and masking tape

        _____ Easel or chalkboard

        _____ Outlets for audiovisual equipment

        _____ Sign-in sheets and table

        _____ Refreshments

        _____ Microphone setups

        _____ Translation logistics

_____ Do you have a turnout plan and enough people working on making turnout calls? Do you have a system for comparing those who say they will come with those who actually come?

_____ Have you arranged for childcare?

_____ Do you have transportation for those who need it?

©The Midwest Academy

28 E. Jackson Blvd. #605, Chicago, IL 60604

(312) 427-2304   mwacademy1@aol.com   www.midwestacademy.com

13

You should know two astonishing facts about public speaking. First, it is easier to speak to fifty people than to five. This is because when you speak to a very small group of people in an informal setting, each of them expects it to be like holding a personal conversation with you.

You may be giving a report to a committee, but each member wants it to be like a private dialogue. You are supposed to have rapport and to know what's on each person's mind. Although this is very difficult, most people can do it and feel comfortable with it. You have probably done it lots of times without even thinking about it. On the other hand, when speaking to a large group (from 20 to 20,000), no such personal expectations exist. People know that they are going to hear a speech. They know that you have something important to say, otherwise you wouldn't be up there in the first place. They know that they would just die if they had to speak to a group that big. So as long as you don't go blank or throw up, you can't lose. It is only necessary that the material be clearly presented and that you can be heard.

The second astonishing fact: it is easier to speak to strangers than to friends. The trouble with friends is that they know you. They know that you can't remember figures. They know that

A Speech Moves People to Act

Speaking to Create a Mood

Preparing Your Speech

Style

Delivering the Speech

Being a Great Public Speaker

you have a rash behind your knee. They know that you can't pronounce "thesaurus" and that your son won't bathe. Everything you say is evaluated in light of these facts. The great advantage of speaking to strangers is that they know none of this. They form a quick first impression, and then the speech stands on its own. You are even free to do things that you wouldn't do with close friends—to be more forceful, more emotional, or more poetic. The audience will think you're like that all the time. Yet how often have you said, "I can't get up there and talk. I don't know those people"?

A Speech Moves People to Act

Unless you are simply giving information to people who don't read, the purpose of a speech is to move people to action. This doesn't necessarily mean exhorting them to storm the Bastille, although that has worked. The activity might be something as everyday as buying a raffle ticket or coming to the annual picnic.

In general, the more immediate and concrete the activity, the easier the speech is to prepare and deliver. The Germans have the word "*weltverbesserungswahn*," which means "world betterment craze." Speeches on this subject are often dreadful because no amount of brilliant

analysis can compensate for the advocacy of distant, uncertain, and murky solutions. Before you prepare your speech, make a decision about the action that people are to take. Construct the speech using that as the goal. Don't be vague. It's not enough to say, "Go home, talk to your neighbors, write your congressperson, and help in any way you can." Tell the neighbors what? Ask them to do what? What should be said to the member of Congress, and just how many letters are needed by when? List three ways that people can help, one of which is always to give money.

Speaking to Create a Mood

One way a speech moves people to action is by creating a mood. The mood may be one of righteous indignation, making people outraged about the unjust behavior of their opponents. It may be one that expresses their confidence in themselves, their organization, and its leadership. There are moods of faith, determination, or perseverance. There is the exhilaration that people feel when they first see their way through to the solution of a difficult problem. The specific content of the speech is secondary to creating the mood. The very best speakers can take people through a series of moods or emotions.

Creating a mood by speaking is something that we do naturally all the time. Try saying to your child, "Stop that at once, and go to your room," and watch her mood change. A mood can also be created by playing the violin, but that is more difficult. Even the lowly treasurer's report creates a mood: "The organization is in debt, and everyone must help." "The raffle was a great success, this is a great organization, and I'm a great treasurer. The organization is out of debt!" The actual numbers in the report will back this up. Mention a few in the speech, but hand out the rest.

Think of a speech as being like a song. You sing to create a mood, not to transmit data. (The one exception to this is the song "Ninety-nine Bottles of Beer on the Wall.") The written word creates a mood, but a speech is not merely an extension of the written word. It is not the written word read aloud. It is its own separate form of creating and communicating emotion. A speech can be reduced to writing, but it is not the same as writing.

But, you cry, I don't want to create a mood, I just want to announce the annual picnic: "The annual picnic will be April 15th in Riverside Park. Admission is five dollars. Bring your own food, charcoal, starter, and matches. Please, no alcoholic beverages, unleashed pets, or unsupervised children by order of the Park Department. Senior citizen discount is 50 percent. Thank you."

Well, OK, but remember that with us humans, speaking is always an emotional business. You will create a mood whether you want to or not—it can't be helped. Pay attention to it or the mood will come across as "This picnic is organized by a dull and nervous person who will probably forget to bring the park permit, so don't spend a lot on food."

Now if you were to stand up, raise a big striped umbrella, open a huge picnic basket, and with each word, place on a table a delicious-looking item,

this would create a wholly different mood. It wouldn't even matter if you were nervous because people don't notice that when you are waving a ham at them. Purists will argue that this is an example of theater, not speech making. We reject any such distinction. Of course, it is true that in the theater it may be considered sufficient if the audience has a good laugh or a good cry and goes home. But the purpose of a speech is to produce a result, not just a reaction.

Preparing Your Speech

Research the Audience

If there is one single key to success, this is it: Before even researching your topic or sitting down to write, you must know who will be listening. Where do they live and in what kind of houses? What do they do for a living? How old are they? What kinds of families do they have? How much money do they earn? How are they the same as, or different from, the majority of people living in the area, state, or nation? How much school have they attended? What is their race or ethnicity? What has their organization done? In what issues are they interested?

Most of you will be speaking to your own organizations in your own community and will already know the answers to all of these questions but perhaps not be conscious of them. Think about them anyway. Start by asking yourself two sets of questions: First, how am I the same as everyone here? What do we all have in common that I can mention in the speech to draw us together? Second, how am I different? Am I the only person who has or hasn't a job, did or didn't go to college, is or isn't rich, does or doesn't speak with an accent? Are their goals and aspirations and lifestyles the same as mine? Am I taking the same risks that they are? When you call on common experience, make sure it really is common. Once, at a government hearing on a land development project, an organizer attacked the Real Estate Board saying, "Why should we listen to the representatives of our landlords?" The audience laughed. No one else in the room was a renter.

When you speak to groups outside your own community, gathering this preliminary information is important for both style and content. In addition, keep the following guidelines in mind:

- *Language should be appropriate and geared to the audience's actual vocabulary.* Books, songs, or people quoted must be known to the group. (Quoting from the Bible is almost always safe when done respectfully.)
- *Humor must be tailored to the audience.* Clever wordplay or double entendre, much prized by urban intellectuals, falls flat elsewhere.
- *Even factual information is transmitted differently according to class and region.* Some people don't quote statistics to each other; they tell anecdotes that illustrate, in non-quantitative ways, the point being made. Others expect statistics from unimpeachable authorities.
- *The life experience of the audience matters.* The annual convention of a trade union will be little moved by speeches on the promise of trade unionism; the delegates have been hearing them for many years. The same speech delivered on a picket line or to newly organized workers gets an entirely different reception.
- *The geographic location changes the impact of the speech.* Using the insurance industry as an example of corporate greed goes over well among retirees in West Palm Beach, Florida. It bombs in Jacksonville, headquarters to many insurance companies.
- *Age changes perspective.* Talking about social security to older retired people, people just about to retire, and younger working people requires three different approaches. Within the

same generation, the separation of class position can be critical. Financial self-interest issues at a public university are very different from those at a private university.

In summary, the more factual information you have about the audience, the better the speech will be. It even helps to know something of the organizational background of the particular event at which you are speaking. A speaker ought to know what brought this particular audience together. How was the turnout done? Are these the organization's regulars, or did they come off the street in response to a particular crisis? Assume nothing. One of our staff members was the after-dinner speaker at a fund-raiser for a local community group. The speech was addressed directly to the organization's members, but it turned out that few of them were actually in attendance. Tickets, priced out of their reach, had been sold instead to area service agencies, which passed them out to staff. The audience, presumed to be low-income neighborhood people, were really professionals and not exactly "united in our common struggle to save our homes."

Ask about the details of the program. How big is the audience? How long are you expected to speak? What is the rest of the program? It is one matter to be the opening speaker, something else to be on the agenda near the beginning, and a different matter altogether to be the last speaker before dinner. If you are standing between people and their dinner, keep your speech short. While you're asking, find out who else is on the program and what topics they are covering. Are you the only Black or White speaker or the only man or woman on the program? Are you one of five lawyers? Shape your remarks accordingly. Consider what unique contribution you have to offer. For example, if you are speaking at an academic conference and you are the only "practitioner" (person doing real work) on the panel, don't try to give an academic lecture. Rather, focus on your practical experience.

Ask those who know, and ask yourself, what the audience expects you to say. What do they want to hear or hope to hear? Show that you are in tune with this: "I know that you are expecting a talk on sericulture (raising silkworms), and I'm not going to disappointment you." Or "I know that you want to hear more about sericulture. But first allow me to read a poem." More to the point, use this information to strengthen your message: "I know that you all expect me to come before you to urge endorsement of the regular party ticket, so you will realize how serious it is when I say that this year, we should not take a position."

Research Your Topic

What, more research? The point is that you are going to have to condense the topic to bring out two or three essential points. That means you must know a lot just to figure out what those few essential points are. People who know only a little can still fill a speech with facts, but they can't focus it properly. What's worse, they are so afraid of leaving out something important and not knowing it, that they try to cram in everything just to be safe.

Researching and writing a speech are two separate steps. Many people try to combine them, mistakenly thinking that the speech is merely the written word read aloud. If it were a documentary movie and not a speech, the difference between the steps would be clear at once. First you would assemble the information, then you would start filming.

It doesn't matter whether your topic is "The Sorry State of World Trade" or "The Annual Picnic Announcement"; the research process is essentially the same. How do you research the picnic? Start with the location, Riverside Park.

Go over and take a good look at it. Are there bathrooms, drinking fountains, charcoal grills, and ball fields? Are there picnic tables or should people bring blankets? Is there a concession stand where people can buy soda? What about slides, swings, and a sandbox for the little kids? Is there parking or public transportation nearby? Look for beauty as well. Can you see flowers, and how is the view of the river? Take notes. Of course, all of this information won't be in the speech, just a few essential facts.

Even if Riverside Park is right in the neighborhood and everyone knows exactly what it is like, go and do the research anyway. It helps just to be able to say "I was over there yesterday. The grass is bright green and covered with beautiful yellow dandelions. The river was a deeper blue than I ever remember it. We're lucky to have such a great spot for our picnic."

Next, research the organization's program. Five bucks is a lot to charge for a bring-your-own-food picnic, so find out what the money is for. It better be going to fight an important issue campaign and not to pay the electric bill or your salary. (See chapter 21 on grassroots fundraising.) You'll need to know enough about the issue so that you can explain its importance in one or two sentences.

If you haven't already researched the audience, do it now. Is this a ball-playing crowd? Are many seniors present for whom the discount is important and transportation likely to be a problem? Are lots of parents with young children in the group? Now that all the information is together, you can start to write the speech. Of course, had the topic been "The Sorry State of World Trade," the research methodology would be a bit different, but the process is basically the same.

Write the Speech

"Never mind, I'll just get up and wing it." Oh, yeah? Did you ever sit through a rambling speech, and just when you could stand it no longer, the speaker said, "Now I'll pull all these ideas together"? Then he pulled and pulled, but it never did come together. Weren't you insulted that the speaker took your time and hadn't bothered to prepare? Whether you actually deliver your speech by reading it, memorizing it, or something in between is a different matter that we will come to shortly. But in any case, you should have a fully written out second draft or clear notes. Only a few really great orators can come with nothing but three points on the back of an envelope. (They know who they are and may ignore this advice.)

Every speech has a beginning, a middle, and an end. Plan each of these separately following the traditional advice that you should tell the audience what you're going to tell them, then tell it to them, and then remind them of what you just told them. Putting it another way, a speech isn't like a report. A report starts out by stating facts and then logically works toward a conclusion that comes, appropriately, at the end. If you wait until the end of a speech to get to the point, you are likely to lose the audience. Instead, put it near the beginning.

Start with an outline. Write in the headings "Beginning," "Middle," and "End," then list the points to be made under each. You can break it down into smaller parts. For example:

1) Beginning   Half page
   a)
   b)
2) Middle   Two–three pages
   a)
   b)
   c)
3) End   One page
   a)
   b)
   c) Closing   Half page

One trick is to write the beginning last, after you have had a chance to see how the speech unfolds. This lets you use the introduction to focus what you are actually going to say, not what you thought you were going to say when you started. Almost any written work is strengthened by taking the closing paragraph and moving it up to the beginning. Then, write a new closing with more flourish than the old one. None of this is logical or what you are "supposed" to do, but it works.

The beginning or introduction is really a summary of the whole speech. It states the problem and the solution, and it tells people what they have to do to achieve the solution.

The middle of the speech adds more detail. The detail might be supplied by making factual arguments or by telling stories of people's personal experience with the problem. The goal here is to make the problem real to the audience. This is also a good time to go on the attack against the person who caused the problem or the person who holds the key to the solution but won't use it. This might be overkill in the speech about the picnic, but since you are going to mention the issue campaign to which the money is going, it could be worked in at this point.

As you move into the end of the speech, start building the case for the solution you are going to advocate. No solution to any problem should be considered self-evident. If it were self-evident, everyone would have realized it long ago. Try to anticipate some of the major objections that will crop up in the minds of the audience and head them off. It is better to acknowledge up-front that people might have questions about what you are proposing. If you talk to enough people beforehand, you can anticipate the questions: "Some of you remember that at last year's picnic, there was certain evidence that dog walkers had been in the area. This year, our super-heroic-volunteer-cleanup-crew will sweep through just before starting time."

If you haven't been specific about what the group needs to do, now is the time: "Each person in this room must sell five picnic tickets each week for the next two weeks. That's only one ticket a day. I know you can do it."

The closing section of the speech quickly summarizes the steps the organization has to take to make the solution happen. Then it moves on to its real purpose, which is the charge to the audience that closes the speech. It goes along the lines of "We have never failed our community before, and I know that if we each do our part, we will win." Or "Our allies in Labor have always stood by us. Now is the time to walk with them." Or "If we each do our bit, this will be a record-breaking picnic."

Ending the speech can be a combination of words and gestures. Sometimes words alone don't quite convey that the speech is now over. You have probably heard speakers go through three endings without being able to stop. Step back. Take your notes off the podium. Make a dramatic gesture with both arms. Or simply sit down; you can stand up again in a moment to acknowledge applause. Many speakers end by saying "Thank you." This is fine for closing all but the most emotional or dramatic speeches. In any event, don't overstay your welcome. You will be appreciated as much for being brief as for the content of what you said.

Each speaker has a personal speaking rate, and you should know exactly how long it takes to say the equivalent of one double-spaced type-written page. Time yourself until you know this precisely. Then you will always know how long a speech will run.

Use the outline to write the first draft. Plan on writing at least two drafts. The first is just to get the information down and sort out the order of your points. It is like making the initial sketch for a painting. In the second draft, start adding the color, or in this case, the colorful language. Your mind must first be relieved of worrying about the content before you can focus on mood and style. Many will be tempted to simply edit the first draft and call it a second draft. Don't. Start a new file and begin to type in the speech all over again, copying from the first draft. With each sentence ask, How can I say this better? Should I say it at all? Should it go someplace else? Does it need an example? Rewrite as you go. Too many facts and too much detail are the most common problems.

A good book of quotations is useful for speech writing. Use quotes as in a sermon. Start with the quotation, explain what it has to do with the subject, then come back to the quotation several times to emphasize points. Get it right. Remember the mess that former Vice President Quayle made when he addressed the United Negro College Fund? Trying to quote their motto, "A mind is a terrible thing to waste," he said, "What a waste it is to lose one's mind or not to have a mind—how true that is."

A prize-winning painter of landscapes said that he starts by squinting at the scene to be painted. This breaks up the detail so that only the boldest colors and shapes stand out. Mentally squint at your first draft. Let the boldest colors and shapes stand out in your mind. Then find words to express them. Another term for this is "style."

Style

Images and Pictures

Abraham Lincoln once said of an opposing lawyer, "He can compress the most words into the fewest ideas." In public speaking, of course, the goal is to do the opposite. It is to use the fewest words to represent your ideas. A speech is a picture painted with words so that the picture tells the story. The words don't tell the story; they create the picture. The words are like the brush strokes. The brush strokes make the painting, and the painting tells the story. In giving a speech, you can use a very small brush and many fine strokes (words) in order to fill the picture with a lot of detail, or you can use a broader brush with fewer strokes to give the impression of your subject with fewer words. The imagination of the listener will then fill in the details, which makes the details more vivid and the listener more involved. This happens when you read a book and build pictures of the characters in your imagination. Often, when the book is later made into a movie, you are disappointed with the characters as they appear on the screen because the ones in your imagination were more real and vivid.

If you were using a very fine brush, you might say,

> Between 1995 and 2000, contrary to the national trend, the number of poor people in this town rose from 10,153 to 11,239. That's an increase of 10.7 percent. During the same years, 1995 to 2000, the number of homeless rose from 50 to 638, an increase of 963.3 percent. Of those, only an estimated 349 are in charitable facilities, the rest are on the streets.

If you were painting with a broader brush to create a picture and a mood, you could say,

> When I left home to start college, I saw just one homeless person sleeping on a bench at the train station. Coming back here four years later, every bench was filled, the washroom was filled, even the newsstand had become a refuge for someone. In that short time, homelessness had increased by nearly 1,000 percent. Homelessness is in decline all around the country. Why is it rising here?

Of course, this is much less precise, but that is just the point. The exact statistics don't really matter. They are undoubtedly inaccurate anyway.

The years don't matter either; a rise of 850 percent between 1994 and 2000 would be no different. Drop the numbers, and paint a picture of the human magnitude of the problem. (But have the numbers on a card in your pocket because someone will ask during the question period. The picture should be an interpretation of information you have, not a cover-up for what you don't know. People who haven't done their homework eventually get caught.)

Abraham Lincoln himself was a master at painting pictures with words. In the opening of a speech that he thought the world would "little note nor long remember," and doubtless would not be gender-specific if made in modern times, Lincoln said,

> Four score and seven years ago our fathers brought forth upon this continent a new nation, conceived in liberty, and dedicated to the proposition that all men are created equal.

That was one sentence of thirty words, and yet it flashed to the audience four broadly painted, mood-setting pictures:

1. "Four score and seven." Simply saying "eighty-seven years ago" would have been more direct, but Lincoln's audience read the Bible more than most do nowadays. They knew that each person's allotted time on earth is "three score years and ten." Four score and seven, then, starts to paint a picture of the previous generation and separates it from the present one. The words lead directly into "our fathers"—not the founding fathers, not some remote group of people, but the actual parents and grandparents of that very audience. The image Lincoln was conveying was that the

audience and the nation were literally brought forth by the same parents.

2. "Conceived in liberty." This phrase takes first prize for the grandest picture painted with the fewest words. The words themselves, taken literally, don't actually make sense. Only the picture they paint makes sense.

3. "Dedicated to the proposition" paints a different kind of picture, one that helped Lincoln to solve a political problem in the speech. He was heading toward painting the Civil War as a war for equality and wanted to link that idea with the revolutionary heritage of 1776. The problem was that while the Declaration of Independence had said that "all men are created equal," the Constitution had not. Equality, one of the founding principles of the nation, was pointedly omitted when the Constitution was drafted in 1787. Everyone knew this better then than we do today because the matter had been hotly debated in the years leading to the Civil War. The word "proposition" can be read as meaning a proposal, not yet a reality, or an undertaking, not yet an accomplished fact. Thus, in only four words, Lincoln resolved (and fudged) the ambiguity of the founding of America, in which the forces supporting universal human freedom lost out to those opposing it. Again, the words taken literally don't quite make sense. A nation can be dedicated to a principle, but exactly how is it dedicated to a proposition? As a picture, however, it makes perfect sense.

Lincoln might have tried to explain, using a finer brush and more words, that if at the constitutional convention Madison had done more of this, and Hamilton less of that, and

had the northern states gone more strongly this way while the southerners went some other way, and had the yeoman farmers been as well organized as the merchant/planter coalition, it all might have been as he wished it would have been. But that would not have been painting pictures and creating a mood; it would have been writing a report.

4. By saying, in effect, that all people are created equal. Lincoln again accomplished a fine picture. The Declaration had held that common people and kings were equals; slaves were now to be included in that equation. It has been only ten months since the Emancipation Proclamation had gone into effect. Before that time, the war was justified as being fought to preserve the Union. Now, new dimensions of freedom and equality were officially added. This conception was boldly sketched into the speech with only five words.

The entire address is worthy of study. It is like watching a slide show. Image after image flashes by. The images are created by words but are more than words. The desired action, of course, was that the audience rededicate itself to winning the war. Toward that conclusion the speech moved with the cadence of a march: "We can not dedicate, we can not consecrate, we can not hallow this ground . . . Government of the people, by the people and for the people shall not perish from the earth." It carries the audience up past the endless rows of graves that surround them and on to the most lofty aim of the war: the new birth of freedom. So pronounced is the rhythm of the speech that the closing lines were actually later set to music and sung as a march in the stirring "Ballad for Americans," recorded by both Paul Robeson and Odetta.

Humor

It is customary to begin speeches, other than those dedicating cemeteries, with a joke. Follow this tradition as long as the joke has something to do with the topic, is non-offensive, isn't about making a speech, and you can tell a joke. Telling an opening joke is a little like bribing the audience to like you, but that's OK.

Humor has a number of functions in a speech. Most important, it really does make people like you. Speeches in which you take an unpopular position are best cloaked in humor. Getting a group to laugh with you at itself is a good way of giving criticism. Laughter keeps the audience alert. Jokes are the one part of the speech that no one wants to miss. If they know jokes are coming, they will listen for them and catch more of what you are saying. Humor quickly changes the mood, which makes it a good transition from one part of the speech to the next. It also relieves tension. If you are a speaker good enough to create tension, you should also break it occasionally. Laughing wakes people up by causing them to breath deeply and rapidly, thus giving a shot of oxygen to the brain. (In smoke-filled rooms it gets smoke to the brain.) This is why one joke at the start of the speech is not enough. Work humor into the text. Here are a few things that are funny:

An Unusual Invective. When aimed at an opponent, this can be funny: "I have always considered him to be the short end of nothing shaved down to a point." Playing with your opponent's name is also funny: "Here comes Mr. let-them-eat-cake Drake." Lincoln said of an opponent, "His point was as thin as a homeopathic soup made from the shadow of a pigeon that had starved to death." (But be careful not to come off as mean by making fun of everyone but yourself.)

An Allusion to the Forbidden. References that come close to forbidden subjects are funny: "I saw Limburger cheese once. I didn't know whether to eat it or step in it."

Word Games. Word games and quotations that are funny if people get them, are pointless if they don't. For example,

> If there is any doubt in your mind about coming to the picnic, remember the immortal words of the great poet Chaucer:
>
> *Whan that April with his shoures soote*
> *The droghte of March hath perced to the*
> *   roote,*
> *And bathed every veyne in swich licour*
> *Of which vertu engendred is the flour . . .*

Informality. Being less formal in speech or manner than previous speakers, or than the occasion seems to demand, is funny. (But there is a thin line between funny and silly.)

Storytelling. Telling a story about a personally embarrassing situation is funny: "There I was with the grease oozing out of my button holes, the Mayor coming toward me, and the Police behind me, and I know I don't have to tell you what happened next."

The Absurd and the Unexpected. "You should have been at last year's picnic—a parrot won the raffle. I called the number, and this bird flew up with the ticket in its beak. I said, 'Just what are you going to do with a weekend for two in Atlantic City?' The parrot shot back, 'What's the matter, you don't think I can get a date?'"

Of course, the best jokes are the ones you make up, but it helps to clip jokes or funny situations out of newspapers.

Sharing Yourself

In the course of the speech, you need to project yourself as a believable character, someone the audience feels they know. There has to be a personal reason why you are so concerned about the subject. It can't just be your job to get up and say certain words. Talk about yourself, your experience, and how the problem affects you. Tell stories about people you know who are in the same situation, what happened to them, and how you felt about it. Why did you decide to get involved with this? Mention your family and how the situation had an impact on them. Quote your child or your Great-Aunt Tilly.

Delivering the Speech

Deciding How You Will Give the Speech

Very few guidelines exist for deciding *how* to give a speech. It is an individual matter. Some people actually read every speech word for word. This works if you write the way you speak, although it can sound stilted. Most people use an outline, filling in the actual language from memory. A few speakers memorize the whole presentation, but they are often people who use the same material over and over. It is probably easier to learn to read well than to memorize, but it is hard to write the way you speak if you have been encumbered by formal education.

Go back to your outline and try using it to jog your memory while you plug in the language from the final text. If you don't feel comfortable with this, take the fully written speech and highlight the key points. This way, the highlighted points serve as an outline, but the whole text is there if you need it. If you speak from index cards, number them. If you ever drop your cards, you will thank us for telling you this.

You still don't feel that you have it? OK, just read the speech word for word. If you practice, it will come out fine.

Practice

Start with a tape recorder or video camera. Rig up a podium on which to rest your text. Put it six feet from a full-length mirror. Stand up and blast away at yourself. Use the mirror to practice eye contact with the audience as well as hand gestures and, of course, your smile. If you are a beginner, don't worry about gestures at first, but build up to using your whole body in a speech. That's why you were given a body. During practice, look at yourself in the mirror more than at the speech. Read ahead a sentence or two. Put your finger on the next sentence to hold your place. Look up at the audience and speak the sentences. If you are memorizing the speech, you can practice with a tape recorder in your car on the way to work. Don't practice on public transportation. Too many people are doing that already.

Play back the tape, listening for the timing. Most speeches are delivered too fast. Slow down for clarity, and slow down further at certain parts for emphasis. For still greater emphasis, try saying a sentence at normal speed, and then repeat it at half speed with your voice slightly lower. Mark the margins of the speech to indicate places to slow down and raise or lower your voice. As you listen to the tape, think of where you want the audience to participate in the speech by laughing, clapping, or even shouting. Mark pauses in the margin to allow time for this.

Listen for sentences that are too long or involved. Remember that when you speak, the audience can't see the punctuation marks. Don't use anything more complicated than a comma. You can always pause for a comma, but what do you do for a semicolon?

Listen for even volume. You do not want to say everything with the same degree of loudness, but before you can control that, you must eliminate spots where your voice falls off. These are usually caused by running out of breath on sentences that are too long. After shortening all your sentences to a length you can say without gasping for air, look for phrases that should be emphasized by speaking more loudly or more softly.

Put speaking directions in the margin or in the text. A favorite speaking direction is "Logic weak—pound table." When finished, your text might look something like this:

Pause between Words	Sometimes it is said that man can not be trusted to govern himself.
Regular	Can he then be trusted with the government of others?
Hit "Kings"	Or have we found angels in the form of *kings* to govern him?
Soft/ Slow	Let history answer this question.

—Thomas Jefferson's
First Inaugural Address, 1801

An effective speaker we have heard uses a different method. She writes in the margin the type of emotion she wishes to evoke at that point— anger, fear, sadness, or joy, among others. Just seeing the word puts the right tone into her voice. She doesn't know why it works, but we can attest that it does.

When you go to deliver your speech, be sure to arrive early so you will have a chance to stand at the podium, and test the mike. Sometimes you will have to locate the podium, which someone neglected to set up. Make sure the mike is situated at the right height and that you can see over the podium. As you age, having adequate light by which to read your notes becomes critical. Notes that were perfectly legible at home become a blur in the dim light of many halls. You will not actually age during the speech, although it may feel that way.

Audience Involvement

Large Groups. The audience should be as involved in the speech as you are. In large groups, this will occur naturally if you pause to give them a chance to clap after lines with which you know they will agree. Take this a step further and write in applause lines that state the group's sentiment in ways they will want to support: "Year after year we have seen the legislature sold to the highest bidders. Laws were made by people who were nothing but the hired servants of corporate wealth. Now, we *will* pass Public Financing of Campaigns. We *will* drive the big money out of politics."

Enjoying humor is another form of participation. Pausing for laughter not only encourages it but also keeps your next words from being drowned out.

Beyond this, if you want still more participation, you have to build it into the text. In general, the larger the audience, the easier it is to get people to participate because they enjoy the feeling of power that comes from doing something together. A line such as "Will we let them get away with it [pause]?" will bring a resounding "No!" Or "Is it time to fight back?" . . . "Yes!" . . . "I can't hear you." . . . "YES!!"

Any response other than a simple yes or no must first be taught.

"We can't pay these bills. We've got to roll back rates. We're going to tell the Governor, 'Roll back rates.'
What do we want?"
"Roll back rates."
"Say it so he can hear it."
"ROLL BACK RATES!"

Make sure that questions are clearly put so that the audience knows how to respond. Avoid this type of oft-made error: "Do we either sink or swim or not? What do you say?" Avoid trying to get an audience to shout a slogan in a foreign language, no matter what country or movement you are in solidarity with. Be flexible. If you are the third speaker and the other two have already elicited a lot of audience involvement, cut down your amount and save it until near the end.

Small Groups. Speaking to a small group is more like a conversation than a speech. Start by asking people to introduce themselves and tell one thing about themselves such as a recent victory of their organization. Why are they concerned about the issue? The question is an ice breaker and also has something to do with the subject. In the course of the speech, direct other occasional questions to the audience: "Has anyone had experience with this?" Some comments can be directed at specific audience members: "In a minute I'm going to call on Lynn and Dan and ask them to respond to the points we have been discussing, but first I want to say. . ." Then, having given notice to the people on whom you will call, proceed with your speech.

Here are a few tips for speaking informally to small groups when you are unexpectedly called on, or have had no time to prepare, and are casting about for something to say. Size up the group and decide on three points to make. No more, no less. For example, if you are being introduced for the first time and will have an ongoing relationship with the organization, then what are the three things about you that are most important for them to hear? Otherwise, what are the three most important things to do about the issue or the campaign? Or what are the three most important things to tell them about your organization? Then think (or ask) who in the group should get praise or recognition from you? What can the group as a whole be praised for? Is there an unstated sentiment in the room that needs expression? "We

are all frightened." " We are all fighting mad." "We are all relieved, but this must never happen again." Any combination of these will give you a fine off-the-cuff speech.

Being Introduced

"How do you like to be introduced?" "Me? Oh, don't bother. I'll just get up and speak." Bad idea!

Of course, most of us are modest; we don't like being talked about or praised in public, and we certainly don't like telling someone else how to do that. Nonetheless, the introduction matters. As in recruiting volunteers or members, you need to legitimize yourself. The introduction can even make or break the speech. It sets you up with the audience. "Last March was bleak. The organization had debts, and I couldn't find anyone to head up the Picnic Committee. Then I called on Fran. Even though she was home with a new baby, she volunteered, and she has been on the phone every day since, selling tickets and making arrangements. Let's show our appreciation to Fran."

When speaking to a group you don't know, a warm introduction from one of its leaders is like a license to speak. If the leader stumbles over your name and forgets which organization you are from, the audience gets the message that you aren't very important. If the leader says that she met you ten years ago and mentions how helpful you have been ever since then, it's a different story. But even someone who really has known you for ten years can stumble over your name if nervous or unprepared. Most of the time you will be asked for material for the introduction. If not, then offer it. Write it down. Print your name, the name of your group, one or two statements about the importance of the issue, and one or two things that qualify you to speak on this issue. Don't try to pull rank on the audience with your qualifications. "Dr. Max has done postgraduate work in astrophysics and speaks seven languages. He was sent to Europe with the team to save Venice from sinking. His topic today is "The Challenge of Community Gardening."

If, after being introduced, you feel that you still need to make some important points about who you are or why you are there, you can always add them. Don't assume that everyone knows you, no matter how famous you are. Don't let the chair get away with saying "Now, someone who needs no introduction." Every speaker needs an introduction.

Actually Doing It

The rule of thumb in speaking publicly is to dress slightly more formally than the group you are addressing. For many groups, looking more formal and businesslike is a sign of respect for the audience. In any event, you want people to remember what you said, not what you wore.

Nervous? Good. You should be a bit nervous. The old fight-or-flee instinct will pump you up and make your voice sharper and more energetic. If you are completely calm, go out and make yourself nervous by worrying about what can go wrong. Eat chocolate just before the speech. The combination of sugar and natural caffeine will give you a burst of energy. If you are too nervous, actually shaking, talk to a friend about something else until you hear yourself being introduced. It helps to arrive early and stand in the place you will be speaking from. Once you have tried it out, you will feel more comfortable.

Listen carefully to the introduction or to previous speakers and try to see what distance from the microphone works best. Beware of getting too close to the mike as this distorts the sound. Ask a friend in the audience to stand in the back of the room and signal you if you can't be heard. If you are speaking from notes, arrange in advance for a podium. Otherwise, you will be standing up and looking down at the table, a distance usually too far to read comfortably. Worse, you won't be looking at the audience. A podium is a bit formal but necessary.

Always speak standing up. Your lungs won't function properly when you're sitting down. Keep a glass of water on hand. Ask loved ones whether you tend to sway back and forth or to pace when speaking. Both are distracting. If you do, keep one foot on a leg of the podium. This throws you off balance and you have to stand still to keep from falling. Take coins out of your pocket to avoid jingling.

Stage fright, also called tunnel vision, can hit anyone. Your text goes blurry, you can't remember anything, and you freeze. Drink water. That sometimes stops it right away. If not, it buys you some time. Take a tissue from your pocket or purse and wipe your brow. Breath deeply and steadily. Say these words to yourself: "As soon as I finish here I can go to the bathroom." Look out at the expectant faces of your audience, which thinks you have paused for dramatic emphasis, and speak on.

Above all, never apologize for anything. Don't talk about how nervous you are. Don't say that you had to stay up all night and couldn't prepare. Don't say this is your first speech or "they made me do it." One young activist opened a speech with a long sob story about how hard he had been working, how far he had traveled, how tired he was, and how he might be catching a cold. The next speaker was a wizened Vietnamese Buddhist monk who had been fasting for peace for eight months. He didn't apologize. His speech was a perfect jewel. Learn to listen with your "third ear." What you hear when speaking is the sound of your own voice. But hidden inside your head is actually a third ear that is meant for listening to audiences. Although communication is going out from you to the audience, you need to keep a channel open for communication coming back in. How is the audience responding? Are people getting the jokes? Are they restless? If you stop connecting and start to bore those in the audience, they will begin moving their chairs and coughing.

Once the audience's attention goes, it must be brought back. Check your speed and slow down. Going too fast is the easiest way to lose a group. Try speaking very softly so that people strain to catch your words. This usually quiets a room. Slip in a joke if you are able. Try an audience participation gimmick. If all else fails, skip to the last page of your speech and get out of there quickly. No one will even notice.

A very experienced speaker learns to make changes in midspeech according to the feedback. Perhaps people are tired and the speech needs to be shortened or the vocabulary is wrong for the audience. It takes quite a while to develop this ability. Keep it in mind as a goal.

After your speech, no matter how good it was—and it was probably very good—you will feel awful. You will think you did a terrible job, made a fool of yourself, and had a spot on your clothing. This is a natural feeling that always comes when anything taking a great deal of energy is over. The adrenaline goes out of your blood and you feel a letdown. The feeling goes away overnight. Wait until the following day to critique your speech or play back the tape or video.

Your speaking will be improved by critique and practice. Look for speaking opportunities, volunteer, and seek larger audiences. The ability to move an audience to action is one of the most valuable skills you can learn.

Now let it work. Mischief thou art afoot.
Take thou what course thou wilt.
—Anthony's Funeral Oration

USAction members call on Speaker of the House Dennis Hastert to pass a prescription drug bill.

14

Using the media is a direct action organizing tactic that goes in the last column of the strategy chart. As with other tactics, there is always someone who does it and someone to whom it is done. Granting the ungrammatical nature of "doing media to someone," the concept is nonetheless accurate. Using the media is another way to put pressure on the target of a campaign and to build the strength of the organization. Of course, this is not to say that every media activity has to mention the decision maker by name. One might, for example, issue a report proving the target's position wrong. Although the report may be scientific and objective and may make no reference to the target, its release is still a way of applying pressure.

Because the use of the media is a direct action tactic, the phrase "media strategy" is not used. Media work is developed as part of the overall issue campaign strategy. We cannot stress this too much. Unfortunately, it has become quite fashionable to talk about a "media strategy" as a method for winning. To speak of a media strategy implies that the issue can be won through the use of media alone. In the military sense of the word, *strategic* weapons are those that can totally wipe out an opponent and end a war. For example, hydrogen bombs are called *strategic*

Using the Media

weapons. Conventional bombs are called *tactical* weapons because their use has to be part of some larger plan. The concept of a media strategy is valid in fields such as marketing and some electoral campaigns where paid media alone can determine the outcome. This is seldom the case in direct action organizing.

Who Controls the Media?

Increasingly, the print and TV news shows are highly monopolized segments of international conglomerate entertainment empires. They have the same two goals as any other large corporation. They want to make money, and they want to promote a political climate that allows them to make even more money without interference. Unlike other companies, the news media also have corporate sponsors, advertisers whose interests are placed above others. Those companies, like the media, are heavily invested in the careers of certain political figures who do their bidding. Needless to say, the media is not the neutral reporter of the daily lives of average people that it would like to have us believe. It fosters a culture of consumerism and political passivity in which the responsibilities of citizenship are reduced to shopping and voting. Democracy is defined as the right to choose among competing "products" or candidates and sometimes the lesser of two political evils.

Even the television and newspaper personalities who intervene to get people's money back or their heat turned on, contribute to the erosion of democracy. They focus on the problems of single individuals instead of the larger patterns of corporate abuse. They help one person a week when they should be pressuring public agencies to help thousands. They rely on voluntary action instead of law and they make it appear that government isn't necessary because you can always call the TV station. In a recent Chicago newspaper column reporting how current property tax laws were used to "legally" seize an elderly woman's home for "non-payment" of back taxes, the reporter told how his article forced the city to save the woman from this abuse by publicizing her plight. He ended by saying, "I guess everyone needs his/her own newspaper reporter."

Having said all this, we believe the media is nonetheless useful in organizing. Too often groups use "corporate control of the media" as an excuse for not doing good media work. Only after we have done all the relationship building with reporters and taken all the basic public relations steps can we blame the media if we still don't get covered.

Citizens' groups can and do get good media coverage. The secret lies in understanding the narrow self-interest of the media, which is always to increase its audience. It wants to portray what its audience considers to be interesting people doing interesting things. If your activities will sell newspapers, you will get press as long as you aren't threatening any of the media's vital interests.

Your issue campaign timeline should include media work where it will be the most effective. Sometimes groups focus on media work at the beginning of a campaign in order to garner enough support to get a bill introduced into a legislative body. An example is New Jersey Citizen Action's campaign to lower auto insurance rates. As a means of building broad-based support for the campaign and generating enough interest among legislators to introduce strong legislation, a three-month media campaign was developed. To dramatize the point that insurance rates were so high that people were forced to choose between their homes and their cars, the group furnished a car like a home with the toilet in the trunk. This series of media "hits" (stunts, press conferences, and releases of studies) helped build the momentum necessary for getting legislators to introduce legislation.

Of course the legislators didn't just read the papers and decide to introduce the bill. The organization had to write a bill and then go out and find sponsors. It held a petition drive, made personal visits to legislators, and used many other tactics. The role of the media campaign, one tactic among many, was to demonstrate to the legislators that the organization could get the media to cover the insurance issue and that the media would probably note which elected officials led the effort to lower rates and which supported the insurance companies by opposing it.

Frequently, groups seek media coverage in the middle of a campaign to discredit or embarrass a target. This is usually done in the context of political/electoral power. For example, during the campaign for national single-payer healthcare, groups held "Get out of bed" media hits in front of congressional offices. A bed was set up on the street and under the covers was a poster showing the amount of money the particular member of Congress had taken from the healthcare industry. The media were invited to film the covers being turned down to reveal the information. While such events generally got covered, the whole healthcare campaign was one where the media consistently distorted the issues and sided with the health insurance companies. The insurance companies then spent untold millions on a national media campaign to frighten and mislead the public, and it seems that the media threw in a good deal of editorial support for the price.

Options for Using the Media

An organization can get media coverage in many ways. Some are more appropriate than others for particular issues and particular times during an issue campaign. As you plan your organization's issue campaign, consider various ways to use the media to help you win issues, develop leaders, and build the organization.

Events. Sometimes groups plan events, also known as media hits, staged solely for the media's benefit. At other times, the media are invited to cover an action or an accountability session in which specific demands will be made on a decision maker. Regardless of its type, these are opportunities for the organization to make itself and its position known in the community. They are discussed in detail in the "Media Tips" section of this chapter.

Press (News) Conferences. A press conference is similar to a media event, except that it relies primarily upon "talking heads." Many groups find it difficult to draw press to a press conference unless they have really hot news, a national story, or a tie-in to a breaking story. A press conference can also be successful if the spokespeople are famous personalities in their own right. The conference format lends itself best to the release of studies that include a lot of detail, background papers, and visual chart presentations and you really want the reporters to absorb the content rather than take a picture and run.

During a famine in Africa, Bread for the World had been lobbying for increased food and aid to hungry countries but with limited results. All of a sudden, the media "discovered" the famine. Bread for the World knew that a more generous U.S. government response was critical to preventing even wider starvation. It decided to use the opportunity to focus the public's concern on the government's miserly response. Twenty-five chapters volunteered to organize local press conferences within the week. Key religious and Bread for the World leaders were recruited to speak, statements were drafted, media contacted, and successful press conferences held. In spite of the fact that no local Bread for the World chapter had ever held a press conference before, every press conference generated media coverage, most in both print and television. The conferences focused attention on the issue and helped Bread for the World further its strategy to triple the government's contribution to the international relief effort.

The logistics of a press conference are similar to those of a media event (see the checklist at the end of this chapter). If possible, have only a few speakers and don't try to make more than three points. One main spokesperson should make a statement and then introduce the others who are making statements. If you need additional people present for political reasons, have them stand in the background so as to be visible in pictures.

Features. All media regularly run feature stories on specific people and issues. If you are engaged in an issue campaign that you expect to run for several months, check with the local media to see if they have any features scheduled that relate to your situation. You could end up becoming the subject of a lengthy special.

A suburban Chicago group, for example, was trying to get a local school board to start an after-school day-care program in the public schools. The town was too far from the city to attract news crews to a local hearing, but when calls were made to the television stations, one indicated that it was filming a feature on parenting to air the next month. The station was eager to cover the group's work and provided in-depth coverage. The media presence at the hearing strengthened the resolve of the leaders and increased the importance of the event in the eyes of the community and the school board. It also assisted in winning the board's vote because even though the television program was not shown until weeks after the victory, it was just before the school board election.

Simple Press Release. Sometimes a group will get coverage simply by sending a release if it has hard news to announce or a report to issue. Organizations often make it a point to send out a release every month because, in addition to getting into print, it reminds reporters that the organization exists and the organization may get asked to comment on topics related to its issues.

Interviews/Talk Shows. Both radio and television talk shows are always looking for interesting new angles, people, and issues to cover. Local television and radio talk shows are particularly accessible. Get to know the producers and assistants, even if only by phone. If you provide interesting guests and material, they may ask you back regularly. Try to cultivate relationships that cause them to call you when they are looking for the "consumer" or "citizen'" response to events as they happen. Some publications will also interview people for "human interest" angles on stories.

Letters to the Editor. Don't forget letters to the editor. This is the most widely read section of the newspaper, except for the front page. Work with leaders at a meeting to draft your letter. Especially, write them in response to articles about your organization or articles on your issue. Newspapers like to make themselves look fair by running your three-inch letter in response to their misleading front-page story. Look at the letters section to see what the typical length is. Shorter letters have a better chance of being printed, and longer ones are apt to be cut.

Op-Eds. These longer pieces on the editorial page, opposite the editorial, give you a chance to make a more substantive statement than a letter to the editor. However, because you are being given more space, your article needs to be of more general interest. Unlike a letter to the editor, it shouldn't be about how you were misquoted: "I didn't say 'twenty-five cats.' I said '*up to* twenty-five cats.'" Instead, write more broadly (in this case, on a new scientific breakthrough): "Healing with cats—how our municipal housing code can encourage it."

Meetings with Editorial Boards. Small newspapers have an editor who writes the paper's editorials. Large papers have an editorial board that shares the editorial responsibilities. It is always wise to schedule a time to talk with editors about your issue. This is when you pull out the academics and researchers who support your positions. It is a situation in which you have absolutely no power other than the strength of your arguments. Speak from the viewpoint of typical readers of the paper and explain why your position will be good for them. In cities that are

off the celebrity circuit, editors will often appreciate a meeting if your organization brings to town a person of national reputation. Once you build a relationship with editors, send them your press releases. Sometimes they will write an editorial that looks remarkably similar to your release.

Announcements/Bulletin Boards. Both publications and radio stations offer free community bulletin boards or meeting announcement sections. Don't rely on them to draw people, but consider them another means of building name recognition for your group. They will also reinforce your other recruitment efforts. The goal in recruitment is always to have people hear the same information from as many sources as possible.

Video Press Releases (for Big Stories). As TV stations cut back on the number of camera people, the stations are more interested in footage supplied by outside organizations. If you are able to develop a short professional-quality video press release, your issue will have a greater chance of being covered in the television media.

Radio Actualities. These are essentially prepackaged radio interviews that your organization distributes to radio stations. These are inexpensive and very effective for most organizations.

Media Tips

The following points will be useful for planning media hits and press conferences as well as for getting coverage at other events. Keep in mind the distinction. Media hits and press conferences are events held for the media. The media are the audience and the purpose is to get covered. If the media hit is not covered, then it wasn't useful and it is almost as if it didn't happen. Other events such as a rally, a picket line, or a fundraising picnic have a purpose of their own. Although their usefulness will be enhanced by media coverage, they still have a real function without it. This doesn't mean that a media hit can consist of just your group making a statement. It is usually better to try to engage the decision maker in the hit, for example, by holding it in front of the target's office and then going inside to present a petition or make a demand. Usually, you don't expect to win at this point. Rather, you want to increase the pressure by forcing the target to take an unpopular position in public.

Start Planning by Writing a Headline. When you start to plan the media event, ask yourself what you would like the headline to say. Of course, you don't get to write the real headline, and although you put one on the press release it usually isn't used. But to focus the plans for the event ask, What would be the best headline? Then set up the event so that those attending draw the conclusion stated in your headline. (Avoid headlines such as that notorious one from the entertainment industry publication *Variety:* "Hicks Nix Hicks Pix.")

Write a Strong Media Advisory. An advisory is the notice of a media event that goes out in advance. It tells who, what, where, when, and why. Put a prominent subhead in the media advisory that says "Photo opportunity." Then say what the opportunity is: "A working model wind turbine will demonstrate the technology of alternative energy."

Groups often make the mistake of giving out too much information in the media advisory. We have even seen groups that are holding an event to release a study actually mail out the whole study in advance. If you send reporters enough information to write the story without coming to the event, that is what they will do, or they may decide not to cover the story because the study seems uninteresting without the human interest elements, visuals, and your explanation, all of which are presented at the event.

Make Sure Your Event Is Hard News. Unless you are the President, a rock star, or the head of the Mafia, your opinion isn't news. You can't call a media event just to say how upset you are about something. There must be news. News can be any of the following:

- A large number of people come together to do something. The media's view is that if it was interesting enough for these people to come, then more people will want to read about it.

- Someone who is actually news speaks for you. However, using celebrities is not the best idea for groups that are trying to develop their own leadership. You want your leaders to become local celebrities who are considered newsworthy. This will be short-circuited by bringing in outside people.

- People who can actually carry it out announce a new activity: "We are starting a drive to recall the Mayor." Actually being able to create a credible recall threat is the key to making this hard news. If you simply got up and said, "In our opinion, the Mayor ought to be recalled," that would not be news.

- New information is revealed as part of an ongoing story. For example, the construction company that gave the bribe is actually owned by the Mayor's cousin.

- The really unexpected is often news: "Reading scores rise by 10 percent."

- A new treatment of an old story can be news. Taxes are an old story. A 16-foot pyramid of tax forms on April 15 is new news.

- A tie-in with national news makes your local event more newsworthy. For example, your organization is demanding a patient's bill of rights at a local facility while Congress debates a national patient's bill of rights. Try to make the timing coincide, because news editors will often welcome a local tie-in.

Think Pictures. Even the print media are increasingly visual in their writing. Ask yourself, How will this event look? The media hates talking heads, so move the event outdoors and produce interesting visuals and exciting people. Even if a newspaper doesn't run a photo, part of the story will include what the reporter saw. One organization that was trying to pressure a member of Congress into taking a position held a "get off the fence" demonstration at his office. Each person carried a section of white picket fence from the garden store, making a walking fence around the block.

Make sure that signs are everywhere with your organization's name on them. Hang banners behind speakers. Ask people throughout the crowd to hold signs. Place placards on the podium. It is a good investment to have small neat signs made up displaying the name of the organization that fit at the top of a podium. Spokespersons can also wear buttons with the organization's name. If you don't have buttons, bright sheets of paper bearing the organization's name and worn by all attending can be quite noticeable when the cameras scan the crowd.

Good visuals also include a large sign with a slogan and a big drawing or chart or graph to illustrate the main point. Add people with signs with the group's name or slogan. The visual needs to work as a still photo, as a snapshot; it can't be an activity that takes time to unfold. Before the start of a press conference or event, cup your hands around your eyes and pretend you have a camera. What do you see? For a press conference, focus in on the speaker. Too often, the sign you placed behind the speaker is too high to be seen. Or all that is visible are two or three letters surrounding the speaker's head and the "Holiday Inn" plate on the front of the podium. A podium sign with your organization's name is the most important sign in the room!

Have a Quotable Quote or Sound Bite. This is a consistent theme that runs throughout the event and is reflected in the visuals. Each speaker should use the same quote. On National Secretaries Day, a working woman's organization used the quote "Raises not roses."

Help Reporters Do Their Work. Like most everyone else, reporters are overworked and feel underpaid. If they can take your release and run it as their article, they are more likely to use the story than if they have to take notes and write something themselves. Study the length and style of stories in the local paper and learn to write that way. Develop a reputation for issuing factual, well-written material.

Know the Staff. Having a personal relationship with reporters and editors is helpful in many ways. Find out who covers your program area and introduce yourself. Respect reporters' integrity. They want to cover news that is happening. They don't want to feel that you are making up news just to get them to cover it. When you do have a relationship with reporters, remember that nothing is ever really confidential or off the record. If you don't want it printed, don't say it. If you don't want it on TV, don't do it. We usually think that information flows from us to the reporter, but if you can build relationships and reporters decide to help you, they can be great sources of all kinds of information. Reporters who regularly cover your topic will call you for comments if you build an ongoing relationship.

Include Human Interest. A study about toxic emissions is boring. A statement from a family whose child was exposed to the emissions is human interest. Every media event should have a human-interest element, with real people telling their own stories. A media hit that is made up just of experts or politicians can get covered, but it is not part of the direct action organizing philosophy because it doesn't build up the group's own leadership.

Recognize Luck. As in all of life, luck plays a role, good and bad. You may have the greatest story to tell or the best event in town, but if an earthquake strikes San Francisco or new revelations of presidential misconduct surface, you won't be covered that day. On the other hand, you may schedule an event on a slow news day and be the star of the evening news. Such is life.

Be in Control at the Event. You don't have to be a career public relations person to appear professional. Have a press table where reporters, photographers, and camera crews sign in (so you can add them later to your press list). Hand out press kits containing a press statement and background pieces on your organization and the issue. Assign someone to greet the members of the press and direct them to your spokespersons. (Everyone should know who these people are.) Distribute a list of all spokespersons with names spelled correctly and, if part of a coalition, their organizations identified. The media people will take care of their own equipment. If you are using audio or visual equipment, be sure you have spare batteries and projector bulbs. Never go anywhere without an extra extension cord and a three-prong adapter. Some citizen organizations require their staffs to carry a media box of these materials in their cars at all times. They include a folding easel, a large sign with the group's name, copies of the group's basic brochure, markers, and other equipment mentioned above.

Appreciate Reporter's Writing Skill. Some good print reporters have stronger writing skills than personal skills. Don't be offended when you are interrupted midsentence.

Build a Reporter-Friendly Web Site. Increasingly, reporters will go to your organization's Web site for background information and to view past press releases prior to calling you for a statement. The site should include background on the organization and on the issue as well as past releases and links to other resources. The Web site is a necessary part of your overall media plan.

Avoid Getting Sued. The simplest tips we have heard for avoiding getting sued are to use the phrases "according to" or "allegedly" to state things you know or have heard but would be hard-pressed to prove, even though you know you are right. Don't state anything that is gossip and/or untrue.

Developing and Using a Media List

Your press list should be computerized in such a way that you can generate blast faxes, e-mails, or mailing labels at a moment's notice. Divide or code your lists by category. Make sure you have included the personal contacts described above, news reporters, specialty editors or "City Desks" for television (local, network, and cable), radio, daily newspapers, weekly newspapers, ethnic newspapers (Black, Hispanic, or others), student newspapers (if you are in a large college town), and religious and union publications. Large cities will probably have an Associated Press (AP) and United Press International (UPI) reporter and a "daybook." The daybook lists all scheduled events for the day and is used by most media. Organizations are increasingly using faxes and e-mail to send material to the media. Do whatever reporters prefer (some don't like e-mail), but remember that the key to coverage is the follow-up phone call and the personal relationship. Call assignment editors (the City Desk at newspapers) twice for every event: once the day before and once the morning of the event. If you know the reporter, call earlier.

Media advisories (the notice of your media event) should be sent to the wires, daily papers, and television and radio stations two to four days before an event. Weekly newspapers usually have deadlines of three or four days before publication, so check beforehand. If you have control over your timing, schedule your event to maximize coverage by both dailies and weeklies.

Preparing Spokespeople for a Media Event

People love seeing their names in print. Pictures are even better. Nothing gives leaders a stronger sense of power and a conviction that what they are doing is important than to see themselves on television or in the paper. Who gets interviewed and who is photographed matters greatly. For community organizations, the volunteer leaders, not the staff, are usually the people who speak before the media. Leaders sometimes resent staff who "hog" the media.

The person who speaks before the media or gives an interview should be a leader in your organization, someone who does real work, and not simply an articulate person. Don't allow people who do little work to "volunteer" to be the media spokespersons.

Some leaders may be bashful about working with the media, but they should be encouraged to practice (perhaps in special training sessions that are videotaped) and then supported in their initial efforts. Everyone who is good at working with the media was scared the first time. Besides, getting in the media is a small "perk" for longtime committed leaders.

One public housing group was demanding that lead paint be removed from its development. As part of the campaign, the Health Department was asked to test children in the development for lead poisoning. The media was called and asked to cover the testing. The testing and the issue got excellent print and television coverage. The few leaders involved were surprised to find themselves quoted in the paper and began to take their work and the issue much more seriously. The coverage enhanced their self-image and enabled them to talk more freely with their neighbors about the importance of the issue.

In some large organizations, particularly national or large statewide coalitions, the Director is often the spokesperson because it may be impractical, if not impossible, to have the volunteer leaders play this role. In large organizations where press releases are sent to numerous places throughout the country or state, quote local leaders in the releases to media in their area. Be sure to get the leaders to approve the quotes first. This takes a little longer but is well worth it. The local media are more likely to pick up the story, and your leaders and local membership will feel better about being part of a larger organization. The same "mail merge" word processing function that is used to personalize mailings can be set up to customize press releases by inserting local names and addresses. In this way, a statement can be attributed to a different leader in each city. Alternatively, the file can be e-mailed to local leaders who customize it and send the release.

Before the event, practice with the leaders. Assign someone to play the press roles and ask questions. Develop short statements that use your quotable quotes. Encourage people to stick to the script. Remind them that they are representing the organization and should only give the organization's position. If they don't agree with the position, they shouldn't act as spokespersons. They also don't have to answer every question, particularly ones for which they don't have an answer. It's OK to say, "I don't know, I'll get back to you on that" or "our organization has not taken a position on that issue." Anticipate the obvious questions and make sure that all spokespersons have answers. Train leaders in how to stay on message by repeating the basic point instead of answering a question that goes in a different direction. For example:

> *Leader:* The Coalition for Better Transit is here to ask Representative Max to vote for the transit bond issue.
>
> *Reporter:* Isn't it dangerous to ride the bus in high crime neighborhoods?
>
> *Leader:* Representative Max can improve transportation throughout the city by voting for the transit bond issue.

Everyone should be prepared to mention the name of the organization in his or her answer. When asked the question, "Why are you here today?" all organization spokespeople should respond "USAction is here today to . . ." Too often news coverage is generic. How many times have you groaned as you read in the paper "a local citizens group said. . . ." The name of the organization was left out!

In one national membership organization, the volunteer media coordinators were trained on how to get the organization mentioned and how to push membership. Its leaders knew that in the last minute of radio or television interviews, they should give out the organization's address and toll-free membership number. In talking with reporters for print media, they would specifically ask if the address and phone number could be listed at the bottom of the article.

Writing Press Releases and Media Advisories

Anyone who can write a simple declarative sentence can write a good press release, the statement that you hand out at the media event and deliver afterward to reporters who didn't attend. Here are the steps:

1. Make an attractive letterhead on the computer. Put the word "NEWS" on it in very big type or "NEWS FROM" and your organization's name. Add a simple drawing or your logo. Of course, you can use your regular letterhead.

2. Add the traditional heading:
   - Your address and today's date.
   - The words "FOR IMMEDIATE RELEASE" or the words "HOLD UNTIL . . ." followed by a date. Put a "hold" on a press release when you want the story run at a specific time in the future. For example, you are holding your state convention and a famous speaker is coming to talk about toxic chemicals in children's toys. You might prepare an article on the life and work of the speaker and send it to feature editors and columnists a few days in advance so that they know they have it and can plan to use it. But you put a hold on it until the day of the convention. At the convention, you distribute another press release about what the speaker actually said to your group, which you hope will be carried in the press on the following day.
   - "For Further Information Contact . . ." Add the name and phone numbers of your spokesperson. This needs to be someone who will actually be easy to reach and who can field any kind of question. When an organization wants leaders, rather than staff, to be quoted in the press, there can be a problem if the leader can't take calls at work or has to go out to pick up the kids. In that case, put down the name of the leader and the phone number of the organization's office. The staff will answer the call and say, "That person isn't here at the moment. I'll see that she gets right back to you." Then you can hunt down the leader, find another leader, or decide to have staff talk to the reporter. Ask the reporter, "Are you on a

deadline?" If the answer is yes, you have only a few minutes to call back, after which you have blown it. Cell phones can speed this up, but it is still good to have the call come first to the office. Several contact people can be listed. Add daytime and nighttime phone numbers, cell phone numbers, and e-mail addresses if e-mail is checked often.

3. Write a headline. It probably won't be printed. Newspapers usually have a special person to write headlines in order to give each page a consistent style and tone. You are writing the headlines to catch the reporter's eye. Avoid passive headlines such as "The Parents Response to Governor's Statement." Instead say, "Angry Parents Picket Governor."

4. Set your word processor to double space for the body of the release.

5. Write a lead paragraph. This is the most critical paragraph in the whole release. It must grab the attention of the reporter or editor, and if all the rest of the release is cut, this must stand on its own. Start with a dateline, which is simply the name of your city and the date without the year. The lead paragraph answers the questions who, what, when, where, and why? You don't have to do this all in one sentence, but get all the information in quickly:

> Mt. Rushmore, February 24—Seven members of the organization Healing with Cats today picketed the office of Mayor Lincoln protesting the city's newly imposed limit of ten cats to each residential unit. The organization demanded that the limit be raised to twenty-five.

6. Write a second paragraph with quotes from your spokesperson.

> "Ten cats are far below the critical mass needed to cure most diseases, and the Mayor is clearly being influenced by the big pharmaceutical companies," said Healing with Cats President, Felix Domesticus. "By invoking this 1897 ordinance prohibiting raising livestock within the city limits, Mayor Lincoln contravenes the latest scientific evidence that cats do heal," he added.

Put in quotation marks any statement other than completely non-controversial matters of fact. For example, in the lead paragraph above, the point that picketing took place is a matter of fact. In the second paragraph, the point that ten cats is less than a critical mass for healing is really a matter of opinion that is best attributed to a specific person as a quotation. The reason for doing this is that reporters usually feel responsible for the accuracy of all the information that goes into an article under their names. They don't want to print statements that can't be easily verified. However, they are not responsible for the accuracy of material in a quotation, the person quoted is responsible for that. The paper is merely asserting that a certain quotation was made, not that what was said is true. Reporters are therefore much more likely to print your point of view if it is in the form of a quotation. No reporter had any problem printing Richard Nixon's famous statement "I am not a crook," but few reporters wanted to write, "Richard Nixon is not a crook."

7. Continue to develop the story using quotations from the same and other leaders. The third paragraph would be the place to document the

scientific evidence that cats have healing powers: "According to a recently discovered papyrus from an Egyptian tomb. . . ." Mention the name of your group in each paragraph.

8. End the release by trying to get in a plug for your next meeting or activity, or give your phone number or Web site address for more information. Media seldom give the phone number but often give the Web site address. It probably won't be printed, but on a slow news day, you may get lucky.

9. Try to limit the release to two sheets of paper. If you have a report or study to back up your position, hand it out in addition to the release.

In writing a media advisory to notify reporters of your event, use the same heading. Add the words "Media Advisory" or "News Advisory" in large type. Then state the nature of the event, with the time and place. In addition, in bold type say, for example:

NOTICE OF PHOTO OPPORTUNITY
A Mark Twain look-alike will read aloud from the chapter of *Tom Sawyer* in which a dead cat is used to cure warts.

A typical media advisory

The Peoples Insurance Campaign
666 Lower Road Crossing
New York, NY 12345

Feb. 27, 2002

For Further Information
Nick Quick
P (000) 666 6297
F (000) 666 6298
Nicky666@ooo.com

NOTICE OF MEDIA EVENT

The Peoples Insurance Campaign will release a report linking decisions of Insurance Commissioner Mott directly to campaign contributions from the Insurance Industry.

9:00 AM. Monday, March 3rd
666 Lower Crossing Road
New York, NY 12345

Photo Opportunity
See the bent steering column from a totaled car declared "fit to drive" by Commissioner Mott.

It's preferable to get positive media coverage, but don't worry too much if the coverage is not completely flattering (unless it's a complete exposé on how your organization has mismanaged funds). Some people even suggest that "all coverage is good coverage" and that it is always better to be in the news than to be ignored.

Checklist for Press Releases

_____ Is the release on organizational letterhead?

_____ Is the release dated and marked for immediate release or held until a specific day and time?

_____ Is the contact person's name and phone number (day and evening) listed at the top of the release?

_____ Is the headline short and pithy?

_____ Is the copy double-spaced?

_____ Does the first paragraph explain who, what, why, when, and where?

_____ Have you quoted key leaders in the second and third paragraphs? Have you cleared the quotes with them first? (Remember, who you quote is an organizational decision.)

_____ Have you listed your organization's name several times?

_____ Are all names, titles, and organizations spelled correctly?

_____ Is each sheet marked with an abbreviated headline? (Try to keep your release to two pages. One is fine.)

_____ Did you put "-30-" or "# # # #" to indicate the end of the release? (Why? Because "they" say so.)

© Midwest Academy

28 E. Jackson Blvd. #605, Chicago, IL 60604

(312) 427-2304   mwacademy1@aol.com   www.midwestacademy.com

Checklist for Media Events

_____ Have the date, time, and place been cleared with all the speakers?

_____ Are there other media conflicts (e.g., another major event or press conference)?

_____ Is the room large enough?

_____ Will you need a public address system?

_____ Have volunteers been recruited to set up and clean up the room before and after the press conference?

_____ Do you plan to serve refreshments? If so, have people been asked to bring them?

_____ Who is sending the media advisory?

_____ Who is making follow-up phone calls?

_____ Is a script available for those making follow-up phone calls to the media?

_____ Are visuals, charts, or graphs needed at the press conference?

_____ Who is writing each person's presentation? Are there good quotable sound bites?

_____ Do you need translators?

_____ Is someone drafting a question-and-answer sheet for anticipated questions at the press conference?

_____ Is a time set for speakers to rehearse their presentations and answers to the anticipated questions?

_____ Are materials being prepared for the press kit?

_____ Press release
  _____ Background information on speakers
  _____ Fact sheet
  _____ Organizational background
  _____ Copies of speakers' statements

_____ Will your organization's name be projected well through signs, posters, buttons, and so forth?

_____ Is someone assigned to hang a banner? This can take a while.

_____ Is there a podium sign?

_____ Who will greet the media and staff the sign-in table?

_____ Is someone in your group going to take photos and videos?

_____ Who is assigned to assist the speakers with details at the press conference?

_____ Who will send releases to those who don't attend the press conference?

_____ Who will call reporters who don't attend but will need the information immediately in order to use it? Are volunteers assigned to watch for stories in various media?

_____ Will thank-you notes be sent to all spokespersons and volunteers?

© Midwest Academy

28 E. Jackson Blvd. #605, Chicago, IL 60604

(312) 427-2304   mwacademy1@aol.com   www.midwestacademy.com

Fun tactics, and winning on issues, help keep people involved for the long haul.

15

So you've been called on to lead a workshop. Well, that should be easy; everyone has been to a workshop and knows just what it is. It's about twenty people sitting all day in the most uncomfortable chairs. The workshop leader gets up and says, "For the next seven hours I will speak about international woolen garment shipments." Or else someone says, "Let's break down into groups of three and spend the next seven hours really getting in touch with our feelings about international woolen garment shipments." Whichever style is chosen, the result is the same. Little comes of it, and given what Freud said about woolens, one should never get in touch with them in public.

A workshop can be great or it can be dreadful. If your organization has a reputation for conducting good workshops, people will come, and they will develop into stronger leaders, candidates for office, or coalition partners. If you are known as a good workshop leader, you will get requests to conduct workshops all the time.

The starting point for a great workshop is understanding the strengths and weaknesses of the workshop format as a tool for educating people. By workshop, we mean a group of ten to thirty people meeting for several hours, a day, or at most, a weekend. Unfortunately, you will be

Advance Planning

Preparing the Workshop Program

Conducting the Workshop

Designing and Leading a Workshop

asked all too often to lead a one-hour workshop. Little can be accomplished in this short period. Urge groups to set aside longer periods of time for workshops; three hours is preferable.

A workshop is very good for accomplishing five objectives.

1. *Giving People a General Orientation, Conception, or Overview of the Subject.* For example: "This is how the campaign for public financing of elections will work." "This is how you set up an election day operation." "This is how a group chooses an issue." People can work out the details of their own specific situations later.

2. *Teaching People to Do One Thing Well.* For example: "This is how to talk to your legislator about state aid to education." "This is how to hold a press event about state aid to education."

3. *Creating a Common Language, Attitude, or Approach.* By doing exercises and planning strategy together, people learn a system for analyzing and solving problems. They come out of the workshop better able to communicate and work with each other because they are speaking a common language.

4. *Creating Enthusiasm and Momentum.* If passing the bill in the legislature requires forming a committee in each of nine legislative districts,

for example, hold a workshop. Bring in people from the nine districts and discuss how to set up the committees. They will go home far more committed to the idea and to each other than if you met with them one district at a time. Bringing people together from several districts, cities, or states shows how big and exciting the whole plan is. It helps to convince people that if they each do their part, it will really happen.

5. *Building Confidence.* Most people lack self-confidence, at least when it comes to acting politically. Role-playing a situation gives people confidence in their abilities, especially when the workshop leader and other participants praise and support them. Frequently, people "know" how to do something, but they need the confidence that they know it.

Workshops are bad tools for teaching involved subjects such as nautical navigation, Latin, and solid geometry. Think back to grade school when you learned long division. Yes, you were in a class with other children, but you really learned from a skilled teacher, and there wasn't much the group could have done to help you. Now, contrast learning to *do* long division with learning to *explain* long division to the community. A group can actually do a great deal to help you learn to explain long division. People can brainstorm ways to put across a complex concept in simple terms. Some can role-play community members while others practice explaining long division. You can improve your own technique by listening to others practice theirs. Watching videotapes of people explaining long division to the community might also be helpful.

OK, here comes the point! *Workshops are best for subjects where group participation aids the learning process.* They work less well when they are a substitute for old-fashioned one-on-one teaching. So, plan your workshop to make the best use of the group. Use methods in which the group is a necessary part of the learning process. Avoid methods in which a group is actually a hindrance. If people want to learn nautical navigation, send them to the Coast Guard.

Advance Planning

Leading a good workshop takes time for preparation, as well as skill in leading. The "safest" workshop is usually a presentation followed by a discussion, but it is also the least interesting. Think creatively about the main points you are trying to convey. Find ways to convey the material that will help people better grapple with or absorb the material.

The danger in trying to design an innovative workshop is that it may become cutesy and/or cluttered ("We will now skip rope to demonstrate the relationship between economic growth and full employment"). Ask several people for their feedback on the workshop design. Does it make sense to them? If so, try it. If what you designed doesn't work, revise it for next time. In this section we present some of the basic elements you should take into consideration in planning a workshop.

What Are Your Goals?

Clarify your specific goals, taking into account the areas in which workshops are most helpful. Consider the overall concept with which you want people to leave. Then, identify no more than three ideas or skills that you want people to learn at the workshop. Think about developing a common language and enthusiasm for the issue or project.

Often, the main goal is to build up the confidence of the group members so that they are able to understand, talk about, or try out some new idea. A confidence-building workshop with role-playing and videotaping presentations is going to require a different design from an information workshop.

The workshop must reflect the overall goals and strategy of the sponsoring organization. There is no such thing as just teaching skills independent of an organizational context. Perhaps if the topic were "How to eat a good breakfast," you could discuss it without any organizational considerations. But the moment the topic becomes "Eating a good breakfast at your desk," you must put it in an organizational context.

Who Should Come?

The selection of participants greatly affects the success of the workshop. Even if you are leading a program for another group, make it clear that you want to be consulted about who is invited. Not all workshops are appropriate for everyone.

For example, a tenants' group sponsored a workshop on organizing through direct action methods. The group's leaders debated inviting people from other housing organizations. The workshop leader urged them not to, knowing that a frank discussion of their own group's problems would be impossible with others present. The leaders also considered whether to invite only board members or all active members. It was decided that because expanding the board was a major organizational goal, they would invite the most active members. But some board members objected, saying that the portion of the workshop on strategy was so specific that it was really making policy, which was the board's function. It was then decided to hold a formal board meeting shortly after the workshop to ratify the plans. Details like these have to be considered and will make a difference in the success of the workshop. Here are two guidelines for who should come.

Participants Should Have Similar Backgrounds or Levels of Experience. Unless the workshop is on intergroup relations, the more homogeneous the participants, the better it will be. Without even meaning to, college-educated people tend to push others out of a discussion. Younger people often race ahead of seniors. Native-born people use slang words that foreign-born people don't understand. People with a lot of experience use jargon and acronyms that make inexperienced people feel dumb. If such differences exist within your group, you can hold a workshop for board members and another for new members. You can hold one workshop in the afternoon when mostly seniors will come and another in the evening for working people.

Participants Should Have the Same Relationship to the Organization. Discussions with leaders, staff, members, allies, or people off the street are going to be different. Members may be more interested in discussing an issue, while staff will be more interested in the details of strategy. Leaders will be called on to accomplish one set of things, allies another. Not every discussion is appropriate for everyone. The more types of people who attend, the more difficult it becomes for you to establish a perspective from which to speak and the more disjointed the discussion.

What Are the Participants' Backgrounds?

What do people already know? Have they received previous training or had experience in the subject of the workshop? What are their ages and backgrounds? Is everyone literate? Are there particular problems or issues people want addressed in the workshop? If no one can answer these questions for you, mail the participants a short questionnaire or application form ahead of time. Use the answers to these questions in designing both the content and the style of the workshop.

What Is the Organization?

If the sponsoring group is not your own, learn as much as you can about it before designing the workshop. Learn its history, style, and program by looking over its literature, newsletters, and press clippings and by talking with officers or staff. If the group's leaders are participating in the workshop, should they have some special function? How free are you to disagree with them? Be sure that your goals for the workshop and the organization's are the same. Does the leadership have particular problems it is trying to solve by holding the workshop? Are there major divisions in the organization over the problem? Will they be brought out at the workshop?

Preparing the Workshop Program

Adults learn best by "doing." So, seek hands-on "doing" opportunities. The second-best way adults learn is by both seeing and hearing. If you can supplement presentations with visual aids, they will retain more information. The goal is to present each major piece of information in at least five different ways. You can say it; write it on the chart; ask a question about it; include it in a role-play, quiz, or written exercise; tell a story that makes the point; and summarize it again at the end. (In the language of workshop experts, these are called "non-repetitive redundancies.")

The worst way for people to learn is just by listening to a presentation. Few of us are so interesting that people want to listen for much longer than twenty minutes. Most really good workshops are a combination of presentation, exercise, role-playing, and discussion. The form of a workshop and how material is presented are as important as the actual content. Develop an outline of time use for each section of the workshop. Start by estimating the time slots. Then write a separate content outline that includes exactly what you will say, what the group will do, and what points will be made. Now go back and see if it all fits into your original time estimate. The time outline for a workshop on writing a press release might look like this:

Press Release	_3 Hours_
Introductions	15 minutes
Presentation	20 minutes
Discussion	10 minutes
Exercise	30 minutes
Debriefing	60 minutes
Wrap-up	15 minutes
Evaluations	10 minutes
Extra time	20 minutes

The assumption here is that you have fifteen people in the workshop. The exercise will consist of each person writing a short press release from a longer background paper that you will give them. In the debriefing, each person's release will be read to the group and commented on. The evaluation is a short form that people fill out. This is a tight schedule, but an extra 20 minutes is built in.

Using Exercises and Role-Plays

Both exercises and role-plays are effective ways of teaching workshop participants.

Exercises. Exercises can be practical, such as actually designing a newsletter or making a one-minute speech. They can also be more conceptual.

A problem-solving exercise is usually done in small groups. Participants are given the factual background of a problem and are asked to devise a solution, plan, or strategy. This provides opportunities to reinforce the principles and guidelines you've explained in the presentation part of the workshop and helps people grapple with the crux of the material. Sometimes exercises are used to demonstrate how much people already know, which builds confidence.

The key to success is to keep the exercise simple and make its problem true to life. The more it is based on actual situations in which you were involved, the more real it will sound and the better able you will be to lead the discussion. Don't use situations with which some members of the group have actually had experience. These members will short-circuit the reasoning process by stating what actually happened and then argue with people who have a different idea. The goal is not to have people reconstruct the original circumstances but to learn a method for finding a workable solution.

Role-Plays. Like exercises, role-plays can be more practical or more conceptual. A role-play is a way of recreating a bit of outside reality within a workshop. An exercise is really the first step in a role-play. After solving the problem on paper, the group acts out the solution as a way of testing it. If you are using the workshop to prepare people to sell raffle tickets, for example, they can write a short sales pitch on paper. Role-playing the sales pitch shows who mumbles, looks at the floor, and plays with his ears—problems that you wouldn't spot from the writing.

In shorter workshops, usually only short one-on-one role-plays are used. Larger team role-plays, where the goal is to develop a strategy and reproduce an event such as an action or accountability session, take a great deal of time to prepare, produce, and debrief. Two and a half to three hours are required. If people are being prepared for a specific meeting with certain elected officials, then use a role-play to simulate the meeting, even if it takes up a lot of time. Nothing else will better prepare people.

Most adults complain about having to do role-plays but really enjoy them once they get going. Their main concern is that they don't want to embarrass themselves in front of others. The purpose of a role-play is not to demonstrate how ignorant someone is. Role-plays done well give people experience and build their confidence. Make sure that everyone is given adequate information and that they understand the frame of reference of the role-play. For example, after a role-play dealing with a trade union problem, several members of the group asked the trainer exactly what a union was.

All materials to be handed out in connection with exercises and role-plays should be color coded. It is the only way to make sure that everyone is looking at the right sheet of paper and that one team isn't walking off with another team's background information.

With team role-plays, assign major parts to strong people who will make the role-play work well. Listen to the teams prepare. Prompt if necessary, but be sure to be impartial and give the same information to both teams.

Role-plays should always be debriefed. Begin by asking people who played key roles what their strategy was and how they felt they did. Explain to people what was done well and what could be improved upon. With few exceptions, as long as your comments are generally encouraging and supportive, people are eager to hear about what they could do better. It is very bad form to set up a role-play that doesn't work so that you can sound smart when you debrief it. If you do that, we will publicly deny that you read this book. Also avoid the temptation to give characters in role-plays silly names like Ms. Ima Floozy and Mr. John. It makes people act silly and diverts them from the main point.

Handouts

Workshop participants love receiving handouts. Use them to provide the details and backup information that would otherwise make your presentation long or boring. Also, be sure to provide detailed information in handouts about how to get a more in-depth knowledge about the subject material. An annotated reading list and guide to Web sites is always helpful.

If you are copying someone else's materials, such as this manual, be sure to get permission and give appropriate credit.

Conducting the Workshop

Atmosphere

People care about how things look and feel. They appreciate rooms that are comfortable and attractive. The setting in a room will greatly affect the tone and outcome of a workshop.

Tables are essential. Put them in a big square or horseshoe with chairs around the outside so that the participants can see one another and the charts, videos, or overheads. If the tables are unattractive, cover them with tablecloths or sheets to improve the setting. Remove unneeded chairs.

Clean up a room before you begin any session. Make sure that coffee cups or napkins from previous groups have been cleared away. You might put a hard candy or piece of fruit at every participant's spot to welcome people to the workshop. As the workshop progresses, keep removing previously used charts and posters from the walls in order to avoid visual overload.

A bouquet of flowers adds a touch of class to any workshop. Set the bouquet in a vase near the podium or table for the workshop leader.

Adjust the temperature before you begin the workshop. It should be a bit cool before everyone enters the room. If there is noise from adjacent rooms, try to have it stopped or muffled.

If you are working alone, recruit someone to assist you in setting up for the workshop. That person can serve as the "staff" during the workshop and assist you in handling logistical difficulties and equipment.

An Academy staffer once led a workshop in a large hall where a second group was meeting on the other side of a movable partition. The other group turned out to be the Eastern States Ferret Convention, which brought dozens of these furry little relatives of the skunk. As the fumes came through the partition, people's eyes began to run and there were choking noises. Now, ferrets are fine in moderation, but the point of the story is that if you didn't anticipate the unexpected or can't do anything about it, end early!

Making Introductions

Unless the workshop is very large, take a few minutes to get to know people's names and backgrounds. People are more comfortable in a room if they know others or something about them.

Ask participants to answer a question that gets them talking and that provides you with useful information about their experience. For example, if your workshop is about press releases, ask how their organizations use press releases or if they have ever written one. Avoid icebreakers that don't relate to the workshop's content, such as asking everyone to dance like the flower of their choice.

You may choose to use your introduction period as a way of getting into the material. For example, in a workshop on how to lobby elected officials, you might ask participants to explain when they feel that they are being good lobbyists and when they feel uncomfortable about lobbying. Then use that information to develop a profile about when all of us feel good about lobbying (when we're knowledgeable, prepared, have numbers of people and power) and when we are uncomfortable (when we don't have answers and we don't have power). The key point is that the introduction period should be used to gather information and not just to get names from people.

During this time, draw a rough diagram of the room and put people's names on your drawing in the approximate spot where they are sitting. This map will help you call people by their names. Another suggestion for getting names is to hand out stiff 8.5-by-11-inch paper and ask people to fold it in half and make name tents to place on the table in front of them. The most popular 2-by-3-inch nametags are readable only when shaking hands.

Your Presentation

Even though adults learn least well from just listening to a presentation, some presentation can't be avoided. Use the presentation time to lay out principles, steps, or guidelines to your subject materials. (Sometimes good films or slide shows are available that can be substituted for your presentation. If you can use them, participants will learn from both seeing and hearing.)

Use whatever outline, notes, or script makes you feel most comfortable. If you like having every sentence written out, do it and then practice giving the presentation without appearing that you are reading it.

You may want to write an additional sheet of notes for the discussion period with questions you will ask in order to start the discussion or keep it going. Put down additional points to make or statistics for people who request them.

Most inexperienced presenters tend to provide too much detail and information on a subject. After you have written your first draft of a presentation, go back and cut out the extraneous material. Add in examples and stories that illustrate your main points. Keep it lively and entertaining. Frequent jokes or funny stories are helpful in keeping people's interest. Don't just stand there rattling off statistics.

Feedback during the Workshop

Workshop leaders are always wondering, "Is anyone getting this?" Exercises and role-plays will give you a clue. Check with other staff or officers frequently during the session. Ask the group questions that will help you figure out what people have learned.

One tool that Midwest Academy trainers use is a written one-page multiple-choice or fill-in-the-blanks quiz distributed during the session. Names are not put on the quiz. The quiz is really more a test of the workshop leader's communication skills and the structure of the workshop than of the participants' comprehension skills. For example, if most people missed two particular questions, then the material related to those questions wasn't presented clearly or wasn't presented in a manner that helped people retain it.

Note Taking by Participants

With one exception, which we shall discuss, encourage note taking during presentations. When you put key ideas on a board or newsprint, you get the triple effect of the participants hearing the words, seeing them, and writing them—a great memory boost (non-repetitive redundancies!). Note taking can be encouraged by handing out paper or pads.

There are two options for displaying key ideas. You can write them as you speak, which has the disadvantage of slowing you down and placing your back to the group much of the time. It also leaves you at the mercy of spelling fanatics. If you choose this method, a good trick is to prepare all the notes beforehand, writing them in light pencil on flip charts. They can be read by you but will be invisible to the group until you trace them with your marker. The second way is to prepare the notes beforehand, either on flip charts or overhead projector transparencies. The disadvantage is that as soon as they are displayed, the group will start to copy them without waiting for your explanation. There is no ideal method.

College graduates and professionals instinctively take notes. Those with very little education will do the same, particularly if they see others taking notes. Unfortunately, for very poorly educated people, writing may be sufficiently difficult that it distracts them from what you are saying. With such groups consider discouraging note taking. One method is to hand out a bare-bones outline of your presentation. Tell people to follow along with it and then take it home and that they don't need to take notes unless they want to.

Audiovisuals

Audiovisuals are used in a workshop to support a presentation. Slides or overheads are relatively easy to make and use, especially with computers. While 35 mm slides are often clearer than overheads, they are more expensive and have the disadvantage of placing you in the back of the room with the lights out. Overheads allow you to stand up front with the lights only dimmed. Films also work well but are rapidly being replaced by videos. These are fine, but very few places are equipped with the superlarge screens needed for groups over fifteen people. A four-dollar beam splitter and some cable from Radio Shack will let you quickly connect two or three TV sets to the same VCR and place them around the room. The most frequent problem encountered by Midwest Academy staff is rooms that cannot be darkened. Inquire about this well in advance.

Increasingly, as more people have access to laptop computers they are making presentations with programs such as Microsoft PowerPoint or Corel Presentations, which are shown on large-screen TVs or projected. Most hotels rent the equipment for an outrageous sum, or you may be able to borrow it from a university or union. No doubt time and experience will improve the technique and lower the cost, but from what we have seen so far, something always seems to go wrong.

In fact, Murphy's Law, "If anything can go wrong, it will," certainly applies to all audiovisual equipment. Set up and check all equipment ahead of time. Arrange equipment in the right position so that time is not wasted during the workshop. Have extra bulbs, batteries, fuses, extension cords, and three-prong adapters available.

In general, don't show slides or films and let it go at that. No matter how good the material is, the greater value is in the discussion. As with exercises and role-plays, audiovisuals give people an immediate common experience to which they can react. Sometimes it is the only thing a group has in common, so use the opportunity well. Plan the points to be made in the discussion. Ask questions to see if everyone has the same reaction to the material. Are there patterns in people's reactions that can be traced back to differences in their organizations, issues, jobs, or experiences that can lead to a deeper discussion?

Do not try to substitute a film for an exercise or a role-play. It is not the same. A film does not engage people like a role-play. A film may present material better than a speaker might, but it is still a one-way communication. The group could have shown the film without you.

Discussion

Discussion in a workshop can be exciting and involving, but it needs to be focused on particular topics and facilitated by the workshop leader. Too often, workshop leaders use group discussion as a way to fill up time when they haven't really prepared well. We've all been a part of group discussions that are a collective sharing of ignorance.

Clarify in your mind the purpose and direction of any group discussion. Prepare the key points you want stressed and then design questions for the group that will elicit responses around those points. Don't say: "Has anyone anything to say?" "How did you like the movie?" "What would you like to talk about?" "Are you getting anything out of this?" Instead ask: "What was it that gave the group in the movie the courage to go on?" "What might have discouraged them?" "What power did they have?" "What leadership roles could you identify?"

When you set aside time for discussion, facilitate well. If not, one or two people will dominate most of the discussion. Groups appreciate strong facilitators who encourage broad participation while keeping them to the subject at hand.

Style

Your style is part of your personality. Therefore, some aspects of your style are difficult to change. However, almost every good workshop leader conveys humor, enthusiasm, optimism, knowledge balanced with modesty, and structure. (If none of these are part of your personality, we suggest a long period of reflection.) Good workshop leaders are entertaining. They don't have to be able to tell jokes, but they do have to find ways of laughing at themselves or breaking the tension in a group, particularly with serious material.

Good workshop leaders are enthusiastic about their material. You must convey energy (particularly if your workshop is scheduled right after lunch)! Watch yourself on video sometime. If you are less expressive than you thought, practice being a bit more dramatic in expressing your points. It's often just a matter of raising your voice and speaking more distinctly.

Good workshop leaders are optimistic. Workshop participants want to know that they can do things. Workshops that focus on the negative aspects of a subject are debilitating. Workshop leaders must be realistic but optimistic and must find ways to convey that optimism in workshops. A good workshop leader praises the efforts of workshop participants and maintains the group's energy and spirit.

Good workshop leaders are knowledgeable about their subject material yet modest. If the participants are not familiar with your background and "expertise" on a subject, it is important to share why you were asked to lead the workshop. Giving yourself credentials for leading a workshop is similar to the legitimizing that one does to recruit people. Simply introduce yourself, sharing a bit about why you are equipped to lead the workshop. Don't claim to know everything about the subject.

Good workshop leaders provide structure. If you've followed the outline suggestions made earlier in the chapter, you will have a good structure.

Evaluation

Without fail, prepare an evaluation sheet for participants to fill out at the end of the session. It can be as simple as asking people to list what they found more useful and less useful, or it can go over the workshop section by section for more detailed responses. Some leaders encourage oral evaluations. Others don't. In any event, the evaluation lets you improve your workshop method in the future. It also protects you when the one person who didn't like the workshop goes around saying that no one liked it.

No workshop is ever perfect; things can always be changed or added to make it more effective. Think of your workshops as artistic products in process.

Obviously, the best measure of success is when a participant puts the workshop messages to use or acts on particular insights. Nothing is better evidence of achieving goals than having someone try something you suggested and having it turn out well. As we always say at the Academy, our goal is organizing, not training.

16

At the most fundamental level, an organization needs a board of directors in order to incorporate as a tax-exempt organization. Legally, you must have a board. But organizations need boards for other reasons as well. Boards are needed to help manage the organization effectively, help deal with administrative and financial questions, and build accountability and feedback for the Director. This chapter deals with membership-based community organization boards. The fundamentals of board functioning differ greatly with state or national boards, coalition boards, and the boards of unions, churches, or service agencies.

A community organization board considers itself based in and representative of a community. Community boards fulfill the same legal and administrative functions as agency boards, but they also set the overall direction on programs and policies and provide leadership, vision, and energy in the community itself. The community board is the embodiment of and training ground for an organization's leadership, representing its diversity and strengths. In short, community organization boards are the heart and soul of community organizations.

Responsibilities of Community Organization Boards

Community Organization Board Composition and Structure

Executive Directors and Community Organization Boards

Typical Problems of Community Organization Boards

Working with Community Organization Boards

Responsibilities of Community Organization Boards

Program and Policy Directions

Community organization boards decide the overall program and policy directions of the organization. Their responsibilities include the following:

Set Goals and Policies. All boards approve the organization's annual goals and set its general policies or positions. The extent to which the board is involved and the level of detail with which the board members participate in these activities vary greatly.

Oversee Budget. The board must set or approve the organization's overall budget. All boards are involved in budget work at some level. Community boards should make the political decisions reflected in a budget but should not focus too much on the details. A budget is the best reflection of an organization's priorities. No matter what an organization's goals or the promotional materials say, the real priorities are set forth in the budget by the way money is spent. A board thus sets the overall priorities of the organization by setting or approving the budget.

One good way to approach a budget discussion is to review an annual report, which helps the board reflect on last year's work, set goals for the coming year, and then look at the finances and the budget. New boards may agonize over every budget category, but this should be outgrown as the board and organization develop.

Analyze Power. Community boards must develop their ability to analyze power. How much power does the organization currently have? How much is needed to win on the issues of interest to the community? How can it develop more power? The amount of power the organization has or can build determines the kind of issues it can win.

Choose Issues. Community boards must be actively involved in selecting issues on which the organization will work. Most boards find it useful to develop a set of criteria, similar to those discussed in chapter 3, for selecting issues. Once the criteria are developed, board members must carefully analyze each issue, as well as the overall package of issues on which the organization works.

Develop Strategies. Most community boards are involved in developing strategies for winning on the issues selected. Sometimes strategy development is handled by board committees, sometimes by issue committees chaired by board members but involving non-board members, and sometimes by the full board. It is important that the board is involved at some level and that the full board reviews the strategies because all of its members will be asked to participate in tactics developed to implement the strategies.

Administrative Review

Community organization boards have the same kinds of administrative responsibilities as agency boards or other kinds of boards. They must work with the Director to see that the organization is managed effectively.

Personnel. The board of directors is responsible for hiring, firing (if need be), and evaluating the Director of the organization. The Director, in turn, is responsible for hiring, firing, and evaluating other staff. If the board is involved in interviewing candidates other than the Director, it should be clearly understood that the board's role is only "advisory" to the Director.

Whenever boards become involved in supervising staff members other than the director, there are problems. The board must trust the director to deal with other personnel. If there are unresolved personnel problems, the board should work with the director, get training for the director, or hire a new director.

The statement above appeared in the first (1991) edition of this manual. Since that time, failure to follow this policy has been the biggest single non-financial impediment to organizing. It cannot be stressed enough.

The board must ensure that the organization has a personnel policy and that it is implemented fairly (applied equally to all staff). Without this, employees are unclear about expectations and benefits,

and the organization can be subject to legal suits from disgruntled employees. Many suits in non-profit organizations are filed by the hardworking, conscientious, longtime employees who see a suit as the only means for addressing unfairness in personnel matters. Don't think it can't happen to your group. Frequently, a committee of the board is designated in the personnel policy to work out staff grievances with the Director.

The board of directors needs to assess not only whether a policy is fair but whether it is just. For many non-profits, a key question is the healthcare benefits offered. Until our nation has universal health coverage, employers, including non-profit community organizations, must seek to provide full family healthcare coverage for employees. If an organization expects its staff to stay around for more than a few years, it also needs to consider staff pensions or retirement benefits. Sometimes, it takes an outside group of people, like a board, to think of what's best in the long run for staff. The National Organizers Alliance (NOA) pension program is an option for small non-profits. For more information, contact the NOA Retirement Pension Plan at 202-543-9530 or 800-NOA-PENS.

Financial Management. Because the board is legally responsible for safeguarding the organization's resources, it must ensure that money is handled properly. Wherever there is money, there can be problems. The board needs to know that the accounting systems are in good shape in order to ensure good management and to prevent theft. It is not enough to say that things are fine because Susie handles the books and Susie is trustworthy. Many boards insist on an annual audit in order to get an outside appraisal of the soundness of the organization's financial systems. (See chapter 24.)

A part of financial management is monitoring the organization's income and expenses and altering the budget as needed. The board may need to assist the organization in preparing for cash flow shortages. Staff should have some flexibility on budget categories (i.e., how much can be altered without board approval) but not too much. The amount of flexibility depends on the overall size of the budget, the experience of the staff, and the trusting relations between the Director and the board. Boards should review financial statements at least four times a year. If, for some reason, a financial report repeatedly cannot be made available, the board should be concerned. Routinely not getting reports is a sign that something is wrong.

Legal Matters. A board of directors must make sure that the organization follows all relevant laws, paying special attention to Internal Revenue Service and Federal Election Commission regulations. Board members can be personally liable for an organization's problems, such as failing to deposit federal payroll withholding taxes within three working days. (See chapter 24.)

Tone, Vision, and Community Leadership

Community board members set the tone, vision, and leadership for the community. They provide these at board meetings, at community meetings, and in their overall involvement in the community. In this capacity, they are responsible for the following:

Representing the Public's (Community's) Needs. All boards, at least on some level, are responsible for representing the public's needs and interests to the organization. This is especially true with community boards because the board members are also members of the community.

Representing the Organization. Board members are expected to represent their organization to the general public. This includes speaking with the media in public situations and, very often,

fundraising. Thus, many organizations try to recruit people with fundraising or public relations expertise to serve on their boards. Because community organizations may choose to limit their board members to those who are also part of the organization's direct constituency, they may need to develop the fundraising and public relations skills of their board members.

All community board members should be involved in fundraising. It is not appropriate to lay the full burden of fundraising upon staff people, especially with community boards. Board members should be well situated to approach other community residents, agencies, congregations, and businesses about supporting the work of the organization.

Developing Relationships. Although it is helpful if community board members have expertise in particular issues or in financial or legal matters, it is essential that they be leaders in the community. As was discussed in chapter 11, board members do not become community leaders by virtue of serving on the board. Rather, they become leaders by having or developing relationships so that people will "follow" them.

How do you know if a board member has a following in the community? See how many people that person can turn out for meetings or how many volunteer when asked by the board member.

Leading Activities. Community board members are actively involved in implementing issue strategies by leading activities. They are the spokespersons at events, the people interviewed by the press or quoted in press releases, and the leaders in community meetings. Community board members are involved in doing, not just directing others to do.

Tone and Vision. Most staff members focus on the details of their work and the problems they face (as they should). Board members must help set the positive, activist tone for the organization and provide vision for the future.

Community organizations are not just about winning on particular issues. They help bring grassroots democracy to the community.

Community Organization Board Composition and Structure

Who is on your board matters. Most boards have a nominating committee that oversees the process for nominating its members. (Some board analysts believe that the nominating committee is the board's most important committee because it helps determine who else will serve on the board and thus who will serve on every other committee.) The ideal attributes of community board members are listed below.

Commitment. Members must be committed to the goals of the organization and the principles of direct action organizing.

Objectivity about Staff. Most organizations have found that problems arise when board and staff members are close relatives. Some organizations have guidelines saying that no person can be hired for a staff position if he or she is a relative of someone on the board.

Experience. Organizing and grassroots fundraising experience are of particular importance for board members. A mix of people skilled in administration, finance, personnel, research, and public relations is useful as well.

Leadership. Community board members should have extensive relationships with people in the community. These relationships must be built upon trust and respect.

Willingness and Ability to Work. Community boards need workers: people who are willing and able to commit time. Community boards don't usually seek "big names" who might lend prestige to the organization but are not willing or able to work for it.

Choosing the Board

Be sure that your bylaws clarify how someone gets on the board. Is an annual election held? Is there a nominations committee? If there is an election, who gets to vote? Even though a formal process may seem unnecessary at first, it is important to build in community accountability by having a clear and democratic process for getting on the board. Your bylaws should also spell out how and for what reasons a board member can be removed from the board. Hopefully you won't have to do this, but if it happens you will need clear provisions in the bylaws.

The actual number of members on a board varies a great deal, although everyone should be able and willing to contribute to the growth of the organization. A small board is able to discuss items thoroughly and work in a collegial fashion. Larger boards are able to draw in more diverse perspectives and reach more people in the community, but more decisions tend to be delegated to an executive committee. The size of community boards most commonly ranges from twelve to eighteen members. The terms of office (i.e., the length of time for which someone is to serve on the board) vary as well. Unfortunately, many community groups do not have clear terms of office, so people can stay on the board forever with no automatically occurring review of their status.

Develop a reasonable term of office, usually two or three years, and write it into your bylaws. Coalition boards are exceptions because member groups choose their delegate to the board and can send whom they like for as long as they like. Some boards develop standards for board participation, including how many board meetings (excused or unexcused) can be missed before the person is dropped from the board. Others require board members to volunteer a certain number of hours per month and to keep careful track of their hours. Usually, those on the board elect the officers, although sometimes the community or membership at large elects the officers. All community organizations have a president, secretary, and treasurer. Most state laws require these three positions. Additional leadership positions should be added as needed.

Committees

Almost every community board has an executive committee. It is composed of the board officers (and sometimes others) and frequently also functions as the personnel committee. Additional committees that are common for community boards include

- Budget and finance committee
- Fundraising committee
- Program committee
- Nominating committee
- Annual meeting committee
- Various issue committees

The board can decide about expanding issue committees to involve community residents who do not serve on the board. Do not establish a standing bylaws committee or else you will deal with bylaws forever. Temporary ad hoc committees should deal with bylaws, as well as special events and problems.

Executive Directors and Community Organization Boards

Sometimes Executive Directors wait for their boards to provide the program and policy directions, administrative review, and tone, vision, and community leadership described above. If board members have worked together for a long time and are well trained, they will. If not, they won't.

One of the key jobs of any Executive Director is to "organize" the board. Most board members are eager to be helpful to the organization and to the Director but need guidance and training.

The first thing the Executive Director must do is to develop a personal relationship with each member on the board. The Director must understand each person's self-interest, as well as his or her skills and characteristics. The Director must help each board member participate as fully as desired and must assist the person in developing leadership skills.

It is essential that the board president and the Director develop a good working relationship. Without a healthy relationship between these two positions, conflicts will emerge. They should be friendly but not best friends because the board president needs to be able to represent the concerns of the board as a whole and not be perceived as the defender of the Director.

Most board members need training on their roles and periodic workshops to analyze the board's structure. The Executive Director should work with the board president to assure that this training is provided. Outside trainers can provide assistance in this board training.

The Director must work to involve every board member in the life of the organization. If someone on the board is not functioning well at meetings or not participating at all, the Executive Director should discuss the problem with the board president. Between them, they should develop a plan for approaching the person about the problem.

Part of working with board members, especially when they are new to the board, is helping them grasp the vision and excitement of the organization. Even though providing vision and tone is part of the board's responsibility, it is also the Director's job to help the board develop and understand the broader vision. This is primarily done through one-on-one meetings and through the development of board members as leaders.

Typical Problems of Community Organization Boards

No institution involving human beings is without its problems and conflicts. Community boards are no exception. Below are some of the typical problems that community boards, as well as many agency and coalition boards, encounter.

Clarifying Staff and Board Roles

Every community organization has to clarify what jobs are done by staff and what jobs are done by board members and other volunteers. This is especially problematic when a former board member or volunteer in the community becomes a paid staff person. Questions almost inevitably arise about "why is she getting paid?" It is less a problem when organizations hire an experienced organizer from outside the community who is perceived as bringing in the necessary organizing skills.

Community boards and their staffs need to approach policy conflicts and strategy questions between board members and staff in an open manner. Don't assume they will go away. They probably won't. Schedule an open discussion at a board meeting, drawing on an outside facilitator if needed.

Hasty Budget Decisions

Especially in times of crisis, community boards can make hasty, shortsighted budget decisions unless they are properly trained and well informed about the options available to them. Board members should listen carefully to the Director and knowledgeable staff on budget matters but recognize that they too may panic.

Another budget problem is that boards will allocate money for new projects without regard to where the money will come from. Community boards must learn that for every additional expense, there must be an additional source of income or money must be cut in another budget category. If board members are actively involved in fundraising, they will be less likely to allocate money they don't have. The board must also consider the source of money they do have before reallocating it in the budget. Some income is designated for specific purposes and can't be moved around just because there is a need elsewhere.

As an organization's budget grows, board members may be overwhelmed by the budget, especially new board members. Sometimes board members will focus on a relatively insignificant part of the budget because it is a part that they understand. Boards need to be encouraged to focus on the large financial items that are the organization's priorities and not allow themselves to be diverted into less important, more easily understood budget categories. It has been observed that board members tend to spend the most time discussing the smallest budget items. This is because most people cannot really conceptualize amounts of money that are much larger than their usual household expenses. ("Tell me again, is that millions or billions?")

Board Interference in Personnel Matters

As noted above, the most effective structure that organizations have found for handling personnel matters is for the board of directors to hire an Executive Director, who is then responsible for hiring, firing, and supervising the work of other staff. The board's role is to set the personnel policy and ensure that it is followed. Beyond that, the board must allow the Director to deal with staff. Intervening in personnel matters, such as trying to supervise other staff, only creates conflicts and difficulties. It is unfair for a staff person to have more than one boss. More serious still, when more than one person supervises a staff member, then no one is really in charge and the staff person actually has more independence than if there were a single supervisor.

The other common difficulty is that when a staff member is reprimanded by a Director, he or she may complain to a sympathetic board member. The board member may be flattered by the attention or may see it as a way of increasing power by taking staff loyalty away from the Director. The next step is that the staff person, who is being protected by a board member, ends up spending time on that member's pet projects. This is not a healthy process. If there are legitimate questions about how the staff person was dealt with, they should be raised with the Director in accord with a grievance procedure and then appealed to the board personnel committee if necessary.

Lack of Clarity on Issues before the Board

Many community boards deal with extraneous issues because the real issues that need decisions or discussion are not clearly stated or adequately prepared. It is important for board members to receive materials ahead of time and have agendas that clarify what needs to be accomplished at meetings. The Director and board president must work together to ensure that agendas are clear, background materials are adequate, and meetings are chaired well.

Restricting Staff Attendance at Board Meetings

Many community boards restrict staff presence at board meetings. Sometimes these boards become unnecessarily rigid on the issue and rule that no staff member, except the Director, can attend or speak at board meetings. This may be a backlash from situations in which staff members dominated board meetings. Regardless of the origin of this problem, community boards should develop a sensible approach to staff at board meetings. Staff members should attend parts of board meetings that make sense and should be able to speak if called on by the Director or the board. Directors should ensure that staff provide solid background information but don't dominate discussions. During personnel discussions about the Director or salaries, all staff should be asked to leave the room.

Reluctance to Make Choices

Sometimes community boards are reluctant to make the important "hard" decisions. It may seem easier to foist the decision off to staff, but ultimately the board will resent whatever decision the staff makes.

Most community boards face difficult choices. The organization cannot take on all the important issues in the community. It must choose issues on which to work and strategies to pursue. If you find your board fudging on these kinds of decisions and throwing them back to the staff, you need to stop and regroup. (One reason to pay for professional staff is to have someone to force the board to make hard choices.)

Poor Handling of Director Evaluation

An annual evaluation of the Director is a board responsibility; however, if it is not handled delicately, the Director will leave, even if the board thinks the Director is doing a terrific job. The president of the board or a small committee should do the bulk of the work on an evaluation. A summary, leaving out gory details, should then be presented to the board. The entire evaluation process must be conducted confidentially. The evaluation must always be approached as a means for supporting and developing a Director.

If the Director needs improvement in some areas (and most people need improvement in some areas), the board president or personnel committee should talk with the Director and find ways to advance the Director's development in those areas. The growth areas should be raised only in the context of overall positive leadership.

If there are major problems that suggest that the Director should be removed, the board must bite the bullet and get rid of the Director. It is better to deal with firing a Director than to watch a potentially strong organization stagnate or deteriorate. Be sure to review some literature on how to handle getting rid of a Director, both legally and humanely. (A few references are suggested in the bibliographical section on supervision.)

Board Members Are Unclear about Roles and Responsibilities

Many new community board members are unclear about their roles and thus hesitate to take on responsibilities or speak up at meetings. Every community board should write down the expectations it has of all board members and its specific expectations for officers and committee chairs.

In addition, every new board member should receive an orientation. This should include background materials to read about the organization as well as information about board participation. The Director and/or board president should arrange to meet with new board members to explain more about what is expected of them and to answer questions.

Most community boards find it useful to bring in outside trainers to assist in board development. The issues of roles and responsibilities are usually covered in most board training sessions; however, the board should identify its questions as clearly as possible prior to connecting with a trainer.

Board Members Who Function Like Administrators, Not Community Leaders

Sometimes, community board members view themselves as "experts" or "advisors to staff" instead of community leaders. Community boards must build power in the community. This requires each board member to become a leader by developing strong relationships in the community. A community board cannot simply address the legal and management issues facing the organization. It must also organize. It must analyze power, choose issues, develop strategies, and lead in tactics.

Most community boards of directors are vibrant organisms. They grow and develop, but not without some conflicts and pain. Nurturing and developing your community board is not merely another job. It is essential to a community organization because the board is the embodiment of the organization in the community. A strong board is one characteristic that distinguishes a community organization from an agency located in the community.

Community organization boards provide program and policy direction, administrative review, tone, vision, and community leadership. These boards build and lead strong democratic community organizations that can control or influence decisions affecting the community. Effective community boards serve as a training ground for all those who serve on the board and demonstrate models for decision making and community control to government bodies. Community boards are a key component of citizen action and citizen control in a democracy.

17

Religious organizations are some of the most powerful institutions in many communities. They also offer moral leadership to both their members and much of the community at large. Organizers who are active members of religious denominations find it perfectly natural to work with religious organizations. Others with more secular backgrounds have concerns and questions.

Long before there were community action organizations, congregations played that role. In more recent years, religious and non-religious activists have functioned in separate worlds, although many of their concerns are the same. As organizers, we need to bridge these worlds and help the religious and progressive communities work together more closely.

Why Work Together?

Mutual Self-Interests

It is in the mutual self-interests of religious and non-religious groups to work together. Why do community organizations, unions, and statewide citizen organizations want to work with religious groups?

People. Lots of people are affiliated with religious groups. In fact, 42 percent of the U.S.

Working with Religious Organizations

population attends church at least once a week. Fifty percent of the Jewish community consider themselves "religious." Muslim, Hindu, and Buddhist communities are growing rapidly.

Organized Institution. Religious organizations are organized. They have volunteers and structures that can be mobilized for social justice.

Resources. Religious institutions have lots of material resources in addition to their human ones. They have money, buildings, buses, office equipment, and many other financial and in-kind resources that are needed in organizing work. The largest recipients of donor dollars are religious institutions, and almost half of those funds are used on charitable activities and community service.

Respect/Credibility. Few institutions bring as much respect and credibility as religious groups. Many organizing campaigns need respect and credibility, especially at the beginning stages.

Values. Religious institutions provide leadership on issues of moral concern and provide arenas in which large numbers of people discuss their fundamental values.

Racial Diversity. The religious community as a whole, and some national denominations in particular, cross racial lines. Very few other national institutions reach all sectors of U.S. society. By working with religious organizations, progressive organizations increase their opportunities for working cross-culturally and building multicultural organizations and coalitions.

Why do religious groups want to work with citizen organizations and unions?

Ministry. The most fundamental reason why religious groups want to work with community and state organizations is that they share values and by working together can help religious organizations meet their goals of ministry. Most religious denominations and faith bodies believe that part of their ministry is to be a witness in the world. Justice is a fundamental theme for most denominations and faith bodies. And yet at the local level, congregations are confused about how to act effectively on their concerns and values. State and community social action groups as well as Labor groups can provide concrete strategies for putting their faith into action.

Congregational Development. Local congregations are concerned about their own growth and development. Working with community groups helps them make the surrounding area a more desirable place to live. In addition, many congregations have found that social action and community involvement revitalize their congregations and encourage more people to join.

Leadership Development. Congregations, like most institutions, are concerned about training and developing their leaders. Organizing provides opportunities for leaders to be trained and develop new skills.

Recognition/Visibility. Like most institutions, congregations want to receive recognition for the work that they do. If a congregation is active on a particular issue, it will want the visibility that results from participating in a larger coalition or organization.

If you understand a congregation's self-interest, you are better equipped to address how your organization's work can assist the congregation. By all means, stress the moral aspects of your endeavor, but don't forget to mention the direct benefits to the congregation.

Involvement in Issues

At the turn of the millennium, President Bill Clinton and Congress finally agreed to some modest debt relief for the most indebted countries. There is no question that this occurred because of a national campaign launched by the major faith groups in the United States based upon the "Jubilee" themes of the Old Testament, which call for releasing people from debt (and servitude) every fifty years. Thousands of people of faith met with their members of Congress. They encircled the International Monetary Fund headquarters and prayed. They held a 3,000-person prayer service during the World Trade Organization meetings in Seattle, Washington, and generated thousands of calls and letters in support of debt relief.

Several states in the 1990s saw significant low-income housing campaigns to secure additional

funds to create a Housing Trust Fund. All of the successful campaigns had programs that reached out and mobilized the religious community. Key tactics included placing inserts in church bulletins, congregational letter writing, prayer services, and forums with legislators in congregations.

In 1999, San Jose, California, passed the nation's highest living wage bill. A key component to the passage of the bill was the pressure put on city legislators by members of the religious community. Over Labor Day weekend, 5,000 postcards supporting the living wage bill were sent to legislators from congregation members.

At a Jobs with Justice action at the headquarters of Kentucky Fried Chicken (KFC) in Louisville, Kentucky, the involvement of the religious community provided a useful tactic. Hundreds of worker justice activists attending the annual Jobs with Justice Conference in Louisville were asked to hold a rally outside the KFC headquarters. A small delegation of thirty people, including ten or so religious leaders, was sent inside to find the person in charge and get him to come out to talk with the group. Unfortunately, the man in charge was found long before all the buses of demonstrators were unloaded. The religious leaders were asked to delay things. They began a prayer and then another prayer and yet another, keeping the KFC executive well occupied until the group had all assembled and was ready for the meeting to start.

Concerns/Possible Problem Areas

Working with religious organizations is not necessarily easy. Indeed, there are problem areas that you should prepare for and concerns that you will want to consider. However, most of these can be addressed or avoided.

Separation of Church and State. One of the first questions you will hear raised when you try to involve religious organizations in social justice issues and organizing efforts is "Well, what about the separation of church and state?" (You will hear this issue more in White churches than in African-American churches or synagogues.) This phrase is highly misunderstood and misused. The proper response for an organizer to this issue is what is true: "Yes, we fully support the separation of church and state." You do not want the church controlling the state, nor do you want the state controlling religious groups. We support Article I of the U.S. Constitution, which says, "Congress shall make no law respecting an establishment of religion."

The "separation of church and state" phrase is sometimes raised to justify not getting involved in organizing or social justice issues, but no denomination except perhaps the Jehovah's Witnesses is consistent on this matter. Religious folks vote and take their faith with them into the ballot box. Churches, mosques, temples, and synagogues are involved in a whole range of "political" issues, ranging from offtrack betting to abortion to peace. The real issue is not whether religious groups are involved in political issues but rather how they're involved and on what issues.

Divisions within the Congregation. Frequently, the real reason why congregations won't get involved in social justice issues is that people within the congregation disagree on the issue. A small segment of the congregation may work on the issue, like a peace committee, but the entire congregation doesn't because of the fear of splitting the congregation. Where there are major divisions on an issue in a congregation, it is unlikely that it will become involved. Congregational leaders cannot involve congregations in issues that will divide the congregation.

On the other hand, dozens of progressive issues are not controversial for congregations,

especially if presented properly. Most individual congregations are both racially and economically segregated. The more homogeneous they are, the more likely that the whole congregation would agree or disagree on a particular issue. Thus, there are clearly congregations that will want to work with you and congregations that won't. Go with those that do want to work with you.

Differences on Other Issues. A number of progressive organizers hesitate to involve congregations in organizing campaigns because they disagree with the congregations' positions on other issues, such as abortion or gay rights, or they maintain inaccurate stereotypes about religious people. Stick to the issues at hand and don't feel obligated to share your personal opinions on other issues unless they actually are organizational positions. It is very unlikely that you will be asked about non-germane issues; however, if you are, simply respond that the organization does not have a position on that issue (assuming it doesn't).

You do not have to agree with everyone on every issue in order to work together on issues of mutual concern. Find the areas of commonality and move on. Avoid requiring litmus tests before you work with people.

Tax Concerns. Some congregations are concerned that by becoming involved or supporting an action organization, they will lose their 501(c)(3) tax status. If the organization is a 501(c)(3) or a 501(c)(4), it is almost inconceivable that there could be a problem. A congregation would have to devote more than 20 percent of its resources to lobbying before there would be a problem. There are some legitimate concerns about partisan electoral work, although non-partisan electoral work is fine (such as non-partisan voter registration). Tax-deductible funds, such as congregations receive, are not to be used for partisan electoral work. (See chapter 24.)

Style. Frequently, the biggest barrier to involving religious congregations is not a matter of substance but of style. All groups have their own language, dress, and appropriate mode of behavior. Religious organizations are no exception. Talk with people active in the religious organization and get advice on how best to approach the denomination or congregation.

Stealing Leaders. Congregations may be concerned that your group wants to steal their active leadership. Find ways to support and develop the congregations' leaders. Help them involve and draw the entire congregation into your organization's activities in ways that build and unify the congregation.

Overworked Staff. Many small urban congregations are struggling for survival. Their pastoral staff and key lay leadership are overwhelmed. They may not be able to consider another issue, no matter how worthy, unless you can suggest simple ways the congregation can be involved that don't rely upon already overworked personnel.

Segregation. Even though the religious community as a whole is racially diverse, individual congregations are not. They tend to reflect the segregation of the community. If you seek racial diversity, you will need to select congregations and denominations carefully.

Steps to Take toward Working with Religious Organizations

Assessing Your Community

If you want to involve religious groups in your organizing work, you will need to assess which denominations or faith groups are likely constituents (or allies) and which you want to approach first. You can either try to involve those

most important politically and numerically or those most likely to become involved. Most groups do a combination of the two.

The easiest way to find out which denominations are numerically strongest in your community is to count the number of listings in the Yellow Pages under "churches." (Synagogues, mosques, and temples are usually listed there as well.) If the community you are trying to organize is the state, call the State Council of Churches (sometimes called the Conference of Churches or the Interfaith Council). Most counties are heavily dominated by one or two denominations, reflecting historical settlement and migration patterns.

Unfortunately, the most prominent denomination in an area is not always the easiest to get involved. The leaders tend to be the most closely tied into the region's power structures and consequently are reluctant to challenge the status quo. When a denomination is smaller in numbers (less powerful), the leaders tend to be more open to coalitional work.

Some denominations have strong positions on social justice issues and good internal networks for activating congregations. These are likely to be the easiest denominations to involve. Try to identify the more active ones and approach their leaders on your issues either at the regional or local level.

Even though some denominations may be the most likely to get involved, there are always congregations that are far more active and progressive than their denominations might suggest. Don't write off any congregation just because the denomination tends to be a more conservative one.

It is also critically important to seek out religious centers and congregations that serve immigrant communities. Islamic mosques and Buddhist and Hindu temples may be the best places to reach many Asian, Middle Eastern, and African immigrant communities.

Most communities have a council of the religious leaders in the community. In fact, there are usually a number of these bodies. A standard set of councils is the Interfaith Council (primarily mainline Protestants, Catholics, and Jews), the Black Ministerial Alliance, and the Evangelical Ministers Association. Larger cities are likely to have a Rabbinical Council and an Islamic Council as well.

If you are in a small town, none of these councils will have staff; thus, the appropriate person to meet with is the president of the council. In large towns, some of the larger councils or associations will have staff. Staff people can give you a good assessment of the denominations and faith groups in the area and which to contact for your issue.

If you want to talk with the entire council, ask to attend one of its meetings (which are usually held monthly). Do not have high expectations for what you can achieve by meeting with these councils. They tend to be more networking groups for the clergy than agencies with programs. Appropriate things to ask for include endorsements, contacts within local congregations, and the names of ministers who would like to become involved. The councils themselves seldom "organize." Nor do they give money. Consider passing a sheet around the room during your presentation asking people to sign their names if they want you to meet with them and others in the congregation about the issue or the organization. Be sure to highlight any resources that are geared for congregations, like bulletin inserts or adult study programs.

Making the Right Request of the Right Person

Each denomination or faith group has its own regional structure, congregational decision-making body, style of worship, and committees for social action. The best way to learn about them is simply to ask people within each denomination. Ministers, in particular, like to talk about their denominations.

In general, most denominations or faith bodies have a regional structure. For some, it is a state; for others, it is a metropolitan area. For example, there is the Illinois Baptist Association for the Baptists and the Archdiocese of Chicago for the Roman Catholics. Other names for the regional levels are synod (Lutheran), presbytery (Presbyterian), and conference (Methodist). (See the charts at the end of the chapter for an introduction to terms.) At this regional level, many denominations have a staff person assigned to peace and justice, social action, community concerns, or some such category. In addition, there may be a regional committee within the denomination, like the African Methodist Episcopal Conference Social Action Committee. Such committees will be composed of lay and clergy members from across the region. Their members are usually some of the most active leaders within the denominations. When you meet with regional social action staff or committees, ask about the following:

- *Mailings.* Most regional groupings send out mailings to portions of their membership. Ask them to include information about your group or issue in one of their mailings.
- *Money.* Regional denominations may have small amounts of money for local projects. Consider asking for money to cover the costs of involving their members or designing materials especially for religious groups.
- *Key People/Congregations.* Regional leaders can put you in touch with the people and

congregations that would be most concerned and active.

- *Speaking Opportunities*. Find out if the group has any regional gatherings. If so, see if you can be on the program to present your issue.
- *Articles*. Ask if the denomination has a regional publication. If so, ask if it can arrange to publish an article on your issue.

At the local congregational level, you almost always want to talk first with the minister, priest, imam, or rabbi. Frequently, these are not the people who will be the most active in your organization, but you need their "blessing" to talk with others in the congregation. When you meet with these members of the clergy, find out about the general direction and programs of the congregation. Also ask for the following:

- *Introductions*. Ask the pastor to introduce you to the key people in the congregation. Ask for suggestions on ways to involve the entire congregation. Find out about social action committees, women's committees, and other active groups.
- *Prayer/Speaking*. Most members of the clergy like to speak in public. They are good people to open meetings (with a prayer), close meetings (with a prayer), or speak about the moral implications of an issue. You might also want them to participate in a press conference or press event.
- *Notices in Bulletins*. Ask if you can place announcements in the congregation's bulletin or newsletter. Find out to whom the notices should be sent.
- *Other Contacts*. Ministers know other ministers. Get the names of other religious leaders concerned about these issues.

Occasionally the clergy are good organizers, but more often, they are simply too busy. Get the

clergy's support, but work more closely with lay leadership within the congregation. Sometimes the social action committee (also called Church and Society or the peace and justice committee) members are the best people with whom to work. In other congregations, the social action people are perceived as unrepresentative of the congregation. In this situation, you may be more effective working with the women's committee, the parish board, or the adult education committee. Seek out the most powerful committees. Below are the kinds of things you can ask for from the lay committee members:

- *Announcements*. Congregations have various means for getting the word out to members about upcoming activities. Some means include bulletins, newsletters, announcement boards, telephone trees, and "minutes for mission" (a short time during a service in which community announcements and congregational missions are mentioned).
- *Material Support*. A congregation can support your organization or work in many ways. Some committees will have small pots of money for which they are responsible. Others have the authorization to request funds from the congregation decision-making body (board, vestry, council). Even if no money is available, you can usually get some in-kind contributions. The dollar value of these can be enormous. Items in this category include buses, meeting space, photocopying/printing, supplies, refreshments, and donated goods for grassroots fundraising events.
- *Meetings*. In addition to asking for meeting space, ask for groups of people to talk with about your issue. Appropriate forums might be adult education classes, Lenten studies, family night suppers, women's meetings, and special forums. In some congregations, you or another member of your group might be asked

to deliver a message (sermon, homily) in the regular service. If so, ask for additional time after the service to meet with people who have questions. This way you will know who really cares about your issue and will be able to answer questions they might have.

- *Letters/Calls.* There are a number of different ways to get congregations to write letters or make phone calls to elected officials. Standard techniques include letter-writing tables in the vestibule or during coffee hour, times set aside for letter writing during committee meetings, activation of prayer chains for letters, "offerings of letters" during services, or requests for letters and calls in bulletins and newsletters.

- *Turnout.* If a congregation is really concerned about and involved in an issue, the leaders can help turn out people for community meetings and events.

Reaching Diverse Communities

The United States religious community is becoming much more pluralistic, and thus it is important in many communities for organizers to learn more about Islam, Hinduism, Buddhism, and other faiths the growth of which reflects increased immigration.

Islam is one of the fastest growing religions in America, with an estimated six to eight million Muslims in the United States with approximately 3,000 mosques. Although no one has exact figures, it is estimated that 25 to 50 percent of the Muslims in the United States are African Americans and the balance are Middle Eastern, African, or Asian immigrants. All major cities have active mosques that should be approached about getting involved in social justice issues. Large cities have an Islamic Council that includes leaders from many mosques. The Islamic community does not have denominations and movements like the Christian and Jewish communities do, so it is best

to work directly with mosques and their clergy and lay leadership.

In many Asian communities, Buddhist and Hindu temples are important gathering places. They often do not have structured worship services in quite the same ways that the Christian, Jewish, and Muslim religions do, but they are important centers nonetheless.

Guidelines for Working with the Religious Community

Develop an Ongoing Relationship. Don't approach religious leaders or congregations only at a point of crisis. Develop a relationship with them. Get religious leaders on your board or other appropriate bodies.

Involve the Religious Community in Your Organizational Planning and Strategies. The religious community likes to help plan how to mobilize itself. Refrain from developing organizing campaigns for congregations without involving them in the planning. It is also important to develop special materials and organizing strategies for working with congregations. You can't realistically expect a congregation to adopt your resources if they are not designed with congregations in mind.

Recognize Past Involvement. If you know of a congregation's or denomination's past involvement, acknowledge it. If you know of statements it has made on social issues that support your concerns, mention them; however, don't wait until you know this information to contact the congregations.

Be Aware of Religious Holidays. Purim, Passover, Rosh Hashanah, Yom Kippur, Hanukkah, and Sukkot are important to the Jewish community. Note that the Jewish Sabbath begins Friday evening at sundown and runs to

Saturday evening at sundown. Ash Wednesday, Palm Sunday, Maundy Thursday, Good Friday, Easter, and Christmas are important to the Christian community. Many congregations also have special events and services around Mother's Day and Thanksgiving. The Feast of the Epiphany or Three Kings is important in the Latino community, as is Ramadan and Eid in the Muslim community.

Avoid Non-germane Issues. Do not raise issues of controversy within the religious community unless you are working on those issues. Do not discuss the Middle East in synagogues or abortion in churches.

Ask about the Order of Service and Appropriate Dress If You Are Speaking to a Congregation. Go through all the details of what you might need to know, such as where to stand, appropriate things to begin and close with, usual length of time, and special procedures for entering and exiting.

Stress Basic Religious Themes. Don't try to pass yourself off as a Bible or Torah or Quran expert; however, do stress basic themes of justice, charity, stewardship, and concern for the well-being of the whole being (both spiritual and physical).

Avoid Theological Issues. Avoid complex theological concepts such as sanctification, predestination, and any other big-word concept! Don't quote theologians unless you are sure they are acceptable (e.g., Martin Luther to Lutherans or John Wesley to Methodists).

Understand Scriptural Context. Too often, organizers unfamiliar with religious texts pull material and quote it totally out of context. Be sure to check with a member of the clergy if you have questions about a particular passage.

Avoid Saying or Implying that "God Is on Our Side." Organizers hope God is on their side, but avoid claiming it, particularly in matters of public policy. Implementation of God's will is tough for mere mortals to assess, although groups certainly want the religious community's prayers and faithful guidance.

Pray at Appropriate Times. If religious people are involved in your activities, arrange to have prayers led at appropriate times, such as at the beginning or end of meetings or before meals. Avoid clapping at the end of the prayer, no matter how moving and inspirational. It is inappropriate.

Involve Key Jewish Organizations. In addition to synagogues and denominational structures, try including the following:

- National Council of Jewish Women, 53 W. 23rd Street, New York, NY 10010, (212) 645-4048. The Council operates programs in social and legislative action. Contact the local chapter in your community.
- Jewish Federations. There are approximately 200 Jewish Federations in the United States and Canada. All major metropolitan areas have Jewish Federations that coordinate programs for the community. Some are more socially active than others. Frequently, the Women's Divisions of the Federations contain some of the most socially active people.
- Jewish Fund for Justice, 260 Fifth Avenue, New York, NY 10010, (212) 213-2113. The Fund supports organizing and social justice efforts, particularly ones that link Jewish communities with Black and Hispanic communities.

Involve Key Christian Organizations. In addition to the denominations, there are "parachurch" organizations. Some of them are quite active and can put you in touch with activist-oriented church leaders.

- Church Women United, 475 Riverside Drive, Room 500, New York, NY 10115, (212) 870-2347. Church Women United is a laywomen's group with approximately 1,200 chapters across the country. This is one of the more racially integrated organizations among churches. It is a good source for active churchwomen.
- Call to Action, 4419 N. Kedzie, Chicago, IL 60625, (312) 604-0400. Laypeople, religious, and clergy working together to foster peace and justice. The group sponsors a large annual conference linking small faith communities and church renewal organizations.
- Evangelicals for Social Action, 10 Lancaster Avenue, Winnewood, PA 19096, (610) 645-9390. This small organization is a good entree for finding evangelicals who are concerned about social action. There are local chapters across the country.
- Sojourners, 2401 15th Street, N.W., Washington, DC 20009, (800) 714-7474. Begun as a magazine, Sojourners is now a network of people putting their faith into action.
- Pax Christi, 532 West 8th Street, Erie, PA 16502, (814) 453-4955. Pax Christi is a Catholic social action group that works on peace and justice concerns. There are 250 local chapters.

Involve Key Islamic Organizations. The following are good resources for understanding and working with the Islamic community:
- American Muslim Council, 1212 New York Avenue, NW, Suite 400, Washington, DC 20015, (202) 789-2262. The American Muslim Council works with the Islamic Councils all over the United States. The American Muslim Council publishes many documents, including a simple brochure on the fundamentals of Islam that is particularly helpful.
- Council on American-Islamic Relations, 1050 17th Street, N.W., Suite 490, Washington, DC 20036, (202) 659-CAIR (2247). This organization publishes an excellent document, "An Employer's Guide to Islamic Religious Practices," that helps introduce people to key Islamic religious practices. It's good for organizers as well as employers.

Religious organizations are institutions, complete with bureaucracies, strengths, and weaknesses. They may not always be as easy to involve as you would like, but they are important in most communities and can greatly strengthen your work. Some will support you. Others won't. Do your best to find the support. Identify the mutual self-interests between your organization and the religious institutions. Work with the congregations to put their members' faith into action. The fundamental values of justice and compassion are the ones we strive for in our world. Call on the religious institutions to join you in "loosing the bands of wickedness, undoing the heavy burdens, letting the oppressed go free, breaking every yoke, and giving bread to the hungry, shelter to the homeless, and clothes to the naked" (Isaiah 58:6–7).

Selected Forms of Address

Category	Written Form of Address and Salutation	In Person
Archbishop (Roman Catholic)	The Most Reverend John Smith Archbishop of _____ Your Excellency:	Bishop Smith
Bishop (Episcopal)	The Right Reverend John Smith Bishop of _____ Dear Bishop Smith:	Bishop Smith
Bishop (Methodist)	The Reverend Jane Smith Bishop of_____ Dear Bishop Smith:	Bishop Smith
Bishop (Roman Catholic)	The Most Reverend John Smith Bishop of _____ Dear Bishop Smith:	Bishop Smith
Cardinal (Roman Catholic)	His Eminence John Cardinal Smith Your Eminence:	Cardinal Smith
Clergy (most Protestants)	The Reverend Jane Smith Dear Ms. Smith:	Reverend Smith
Deacon (some Protestant)	Deacon Jane Smith Dear Deacon Smith	Deacon Smith
Dean of a Cathedral (Episcopal)	The Very Reverend John Smith Dean of _____ Dear Dean Smith:	Reverend Smith
Elder (some Protestants)	Elder Jane Smith Dear Elder Smith:	Ms. Smith
Imam (Muslims)	Imam Khalil Muhammad Dear Imam Muhammad	Imam Muhammad
Monsignor (Roman Catholic)	The Right Reverend Monsignor John Smith Dear Monsignor Smith:	Monsignor Smith
Priest (Episcopal)	The Reverend Jane Smith Dear Ms. Smith:	Reverend Smith
Priest (Roman Catholic)	The Reverend John Smith Dear Father Smith:	Father Smith
Rabbi	Rabbi John Smith Dear Rabbi Smith:	Rabbi Smith
Sister (Roman Catholic)	Sister Jane Smith Dear Sister Jane:	Sister Jane

© Midwest Academy
28 E. Jackson Blvd. #605, Chicago, IL 60604
(312) 427-2304   mwacademy1@aol.com   www.midwestacademy.com

Selected Denominational Terms

Denomination	National	Regional	Local	Hired Leader
African Methodist Episcopal Church	General Conference (President & Senior Bishop)	District (Bishop)	Church, Congregation	Minister
American Baptist Churches in the USA	Biennial Convention (President & General Secretary)	Association (Executive Minister)	Church, Congregation	Minister
Christian Church (Disciples of Christ)	General Assembly (General Minister & President)	Regional Office (Regional Minister)	Church, Congregation	Minister
Episcopal Church	General Convention (Presiding Bishop & Primate)	Diocese (Bishop) Deanery (Dean)	Church, Parish	Priest
Evangelical Lutheran Church in America	Churchwide Assembly (Bishop)	Region Synod (Bishop)	Church, Congregation	Minister
Presbyterian Church (USA)	General Assembly (Moderator & Stated Clerk)	Synod (Synod Executive), Presbytery (Presbytery Executive)	Church, Congregation	Minister
Progressive National Baptist Convention, Inc.	Annual Session (President & General Secretary)	Regional (Regional President), State Convention (State President)	Church, Congregation	Pastor, Minister
Roman Catholic	National Conference of Catholic Bishops (canonical), U.S. Catholic Conference (civil)	Archdiocese Diocese (Bishop)	Parish	Pastor, Priest
Southern Baptist Convention	Annual Convention (President)	State Convention (Executive Director), Association (executive Director)	Church	Minister, Preacher, Pastor
Union of American Hebrew Congregations	National Office (President)	Region (Director)	Temple, Synagogue, Congregation	Rabbi
United Church of Christ	General Synod (President)	Region Conference (Conference Minister)	Church, Congregation	Minister
United Methodist Church	General Conference	Annual Conference (Bishop), District (District Superintendent)	Church, Congregation	Minister

Please note: These are not parallel structures. The size, power, and structures vary greatly between denominations.

© Midwest Academy

28 E. Jackson Blvd. #605, Chicago, IL 60604

(312) 427-2304   mwacademy1@aol.com   www.midwestacademy.com

18

Unions are valuable partners in many community, statewide, and national coalitions. In order to improve the quality of people's lives, both unions and citizen organizations seek to build citizen power by building unity. Unions often have the members, resources, political contacts, and power that can be essential to winning citizens' issues. Community and citizen organizations not only share with unions an interest in many issues but can also lend valued support to Labor's battles, both in the legislature and in the workplace. The chapter that follows this one addresses the nuts and bolts of partnerships between community and Labor groups from a community point of view. This chapter, written for citizen organizers by a Labor Organizing Director and a Mobilization Director, is designed to help community groups understand how labor unions are structured, the recent changes in Labor, and how community groups and unions work together from a union point of view.

Finding Common Ground

Increasingly, we find we are working together, we are winning together, and we are forging long-term alliances that are changing the

Working with Local Unions, Central Labor Councils, and Building and Construction Trades Councils

country. Citizen groups and unions often have common agendas and a shared history of struggle. Citizen groups recognize that many unions have been in the forefront on civil rights, pay equity, childcare, and parental leave, as well as right-to-know legislation. Unions pioneered many tactics years ago that are now tactics we all use to advance our causes. Tent cities, boycotts, sit-ins, sit-downs, civil disobedience, non-violent action, and strikes are all part of union history and the history of citizen groups.

In recent years, unions have faced assaults from all sides. Employers and the government have worked to weaken Labor. As a result, there has been a dramatic decline in the percentage of the workforce represented by unions. Direct consequences of this have been stagnating and declining wages combined with a growing disparity in wealth.

Starting with the election of AFL-CIO leaders John Sweeney, Rich Trumka, and Linda Chavez Thompson, there has been a renewed vigor and excitement in the Labor movement on the local and national levels. Unions are on the offensive and re-examining strategies and tactics needed to win in organizing and bargaining campaigns. Local and national coalitions and alliances with community, religious, and other organizations are becoming central to Labor's attempts to rebuild its membership, power, and the lives of working families.

There is a unique opportunity to work with a newly reinvigorated Labor movement. It is aggressively expanding its organizing, mobilization, political, and coalition-building efforts. In 1998, 450,000 new workers were organized and union membership grew for the first time in recent years. Community groups and building trades unions have worked together to defend prevailing-wage laws that ensure good-paying construction jobs and the highest quality construction of public projects.

The goals of Labor and citizen organizations overlap more often as we face common enemies and issues. The struggles to protect public services against tax cuts for the wealthy and to stop the privatization of public employee jobs are the same struggle. Environmentalists and unions have found themselves allied on issues where workers and the community are threatened by toxic chemicals used without proper protections. Unions and groups advocating for better patient care are working together to challenge the managed-care industry. There is a direct relationship between union membership, Labor's political mobilization, and the ability to elect progressive candidates.

A combination of the booming economy, increasing distrust of the corporate agenda, pent-up frustration over stagnant wages, and a growing disparity in wealth have set the stage for increased activism. Labor is embracing allies and agendas that it previously held at arm's length. Labor has enormous resources in terms of members and is a key part of successful coalition and community work. It is critical that we find common ground. We need to work together in coalitions that serve a mutual goal, such as saving social security, and we need to support each other's struggles. At no time in recent history has there been more of a need and opportunity for Labor and citizen organizations to work together.

Examples of Joint Union-Community Activities

Union Cities

Over 100 communities across the United States, through their Central Labor Councils, have signed on to Union Cities, a framework developed by activists at the grassroots level to build a progressive movement in communities. It includes eight steps to organize new workers into unions, mobilize 1 percent of unions' existing membership base and allies into Street Heat mobilization teams, change the face of union leadership to reflect union diversity, and build coalitions to support community issues. These strategies have been met with great enthusiasm to revitalize Labor's base.

Campaign against Prop. 226

When the Labor movement is focused and unified and working with community allies, everyone wins. This happened in 1998 in California where allies and the Labor movement at the national, state, and local levels came together to defeat a state ballot initiative that sought to destroy working families. The work done on Proposition 226 helped lay the groundwork for Gray Davis winning the race for Governor and a whole series of progressive candidates winning elections in California.

Justice for Janitors

Increasingly, unions have focused on organizing low-wage and immigrant workers. Justice for Janitors successfully organized tens of thousands of janitors, winning union contracts and higher wages by making the campaign both a union organizing campaign and an important community campaign. The campaign exposed the relationship between tax breaks and subsidies for the real estate industry, non-union cleaning contractors, low wages, and impoverishment of minority communities.

The campaign has used non-violent civil disobedience to bring attention to the plight of "invisible" workers such as janitors. In Washington, D.C., hundreds of people were arrested for blocking streets and the 14th Street Bridge, bringing the city to a standstill. In 1998, after a ten-year campaign, the Service Employees International Union (SEIU) won a first-ever citywide contract for 5,000 janitors, proving that low-wage, part-time immigrant workers can organize even when opposed by powerful political and real estate interests.

From Union Summer to Student Sit-Ins

The AFL-CIO started Union Summer as a way to introduce students to the new Labor movement over summer break. This program is paying off in unexpected ways. Recently, campuses have been swept by sit-ins and campaigns protesting the sale of "official" school-logo garments that are produced in sweatshops.

Voice@Work: The Freedom to Choose a Union

Unions and community and religious groups are launching Freedom to Choose a Union, a national campaign to protect workers' freedom to choose a union. The campaign will expose violations of workers' rights and target both employers and their political allies who interfere with organizing campaigns. This will offer an opportunity for Labor and the community to work together to demand that politicians, companies, and private citizens support workers' freedom to choose a union.

Trade, Jobs, and the Environment

A broad coalition of organizations joined together at the World Trade Organization meeting in Seattle and again in Washington, D.C., to demand that the needs of workers, the environment, and good paying jobs be on the agenda as a critical part of the discussion of trade.

Religion and Labor

Interfaith committees to support workers' rights have been formed on national and local levels. In Las Vegas, Nevada, the Interfaith Committee played an active role in supporting the organizing of the Hotel Employees–Restaurant Employees (HERE), SEIU, and the building and construction trades. Las Vegas has seen tens of thousands of workers organized into unions, proving that unions can win a decent standard of living for service, immigrant, and low-wage workers in a right-to-work state. Religion and Labor committees are expanding their work across the country with Central Labor Councils through their Labor in the Pulpits program.

Understanding Labor's Structure

The first step toward working successfully with unions on the local level is to understand

---

AMERICAN UNION STRUCTURE

Individual Union	AFL-CIO
National Level	
International union (e.g., Auto Workers, Machinists, AFSCME, SEIU, CWA).	AFL/CIO. The Federation of unions at the national level.
The members are individual workers who join through local unions.	The members are international unions. Each is an independent organization.
State or Regional Level	
The state or regional body of the international union (e.g., Region 9, United Auto Workers).	State labor federations which belong to the AFL-CIO. Called "State Feds."
The members are local unions of the international union.	The members are local unions and central labor councils in the state.
City, Town, or County Level	
Local unions, district councils, and joint boards (e.g., Local 101, Brown County School Employees; DC 37, AFSCME; Local 2804, YXZ Steel Co., US Steel Workers).	Central labor councils of the AFL-CIO.
The members are individual workers.	The members are local unions in the area.

Labor's structure, or more correctly, structures. Two main structures run parallel to each other from the national to the local level. The first is the structure of any given union, such as the International Association of Machinists or the Communication Workers of America (CWA). The second is the structure of the American Federation of Labor–Congress of Industrial Organizations. The AFL-CIO is not a union. It is a federation of unions that is organized as a federation down to the local level. The two structures are depicted in the box on this page.

Labor at the National Level

Through its convention and executive council, the AFL-CIO makes policy for Labor and carries out a wide variety of functions in the political arena.

As of June 1999, seventy-eight national and international unions were affiliated with the AFL-CIO. (The word "international" means a national union. It is used because most unions have affiliates in Canada or Puerto Rico, such as the International Association of Machinists.)

In addition to belonging to the AFL-CIO as a whole, individual unions are affiliated with trade and industrial departments within the AFL-CIO structure. These departments serve the needs of particular groups of unions such as building trades or transportation trades unions. The AFL-CIO both supports and is supported by State Labor Federations in all fifty states and Puerto Rico. At the community level are over six hundred Central Labor Councils, which are themselves federations of local unions in a city, county, or region of a state.

It is unlikely that organizers learning about unions for the first time from this manual will have contact with the national leadership of either the AFL-CIO or its member unions. Most organizers will instead encounter international unions at the regional, state, or local levels and the AFL-CIO at the State Federation or Central Labor Council levels.

State Labor Federations

State Labor Federations are voluntarily supported by local unions. Commonly called "State Feds," these federations coordinate Labor's legislative and political work. They also support strikes, assist their affiliates in organizing, and do public relations activities.

Regional State Structures

International unions may also have a state or regional structure, although many unions do not. A distinction should be made between state, regional, or district structures, which are largely for administrative or political purposes, and district councils or joint boards, which are amalgams of local unions that are often too small to support their own individual staffs or facilities.

Local Unions

Local unions usually operate in a specific city or geographic area and have a "jurisdiction," that is, a type of worker they represent (telephone workers, social workers, teachers, janitors, or carpenters). Local unions vary dramatically in size, resources, and community involvement. Some have a few hundred members and no full-time staff. Others have thousands of members, their own buildings, printing facilities, and many staff.

Joint boards and district councils are organizations of smaller local unions within the same international union. By pooling resources, locals that could not otherwise afford staff can share resources. These bodies have their own structure of officers. The individual locals within them also have officers, who may be unpaid. The members of local unions are all usually in the same industry if not the same company. Joint board or District Council members, on the other hand, can come from different companies and different industries. Local unions elect their own officers. They have an executive board, committees, and a steward system at each work site. A steward is an appointed or elected union representative at the workplace, sometimes called a delegate.

A local union officer has a huge number of tasks to work on, from handling hundreds of workplace grievances, negotiating contracts, organizing to bring in more members, involving the local in political and legislative and community campaigns, and paying bills to implementing the international union's agenda. The first responsibility of a local union officer is to ensure that the day-to-day business of the local is completed. If that isn't done, the local will decline and the officer will be voted out.

Central Labor Councils

Local unions in cities and counties affiliate with an AFL-CIO Central Labor Council in order to work together on political, legislative, and community issues. Labor Councils can unify the Labor movement and mobilize members to support union and community campaigns.

The mission of the Central Labor Council is to organize in the community to promote social justice for all working people. Local unions send delegates to their council's monthly meetings to share information about what is happening in their locals, support other unions' campaigns, and work together in committees to carry out the goals of the council. Central Labor Councils are funded primarily by dues from their local union affiliates. They must meet their own expenses.

As is the case with State Labor Federations, there is no rule saying that a local must belong. An individual international union might have a rule that its locals must belong to central Labor bodies, but the council itself can't make such a rule. They have no authority over the local unions in their areas.

Most officers of Central Labor Councils are volunteers. Outside of large cities, few councils have paid organizing staff. Some councils have a building, while others operate out of their presidents' homes. A Central Labor Council president can often give you information about unions in the community.

Some Labor Councils have signed on to the Union Cities strategy, whereby its local unions plan ways to build political, economic, and community power for working families in their communities around an eight-step process.

Building and Construction Trades Department, State Councils, and Local Building Trades Councils

Most building trades' locals are affiliated with State Federations, Central Labor Councils, and building and construction trades councils that are focused on issues of construction workers and their unions. The fifteen construction unions in the Building and Construction Trades Department (BCTD), AFL-CIO, have statewide councils and building and construction trades councils in most communities. They coordinate electoral, legislative, organizing, and other activities to protect and improve job opportunities and standards for construction workers. In recent years there has been a significant increase in the mobilizing and organizing activities of construction unions.

Understanding Unions' Motivations

Political Interests

Labor organizations are highly political in two senses of the word. First, many play a very active role in local electoral politics: they endorse candidates and actively work in campaigns. Citizen organizers should know the history here. Usually, elected officials who are strong supporters of Labor also have good records on other citizen issues and vice versa, but this is not necessarily the case. If your group has opposed or pressured a politician supported by local unions, it is very important to be aware of this when asking them to help you. It is also a problem when you ask unions to target elected officials whom they consider allies on working-family issues. Of course, this is true of any group, including your own; only the issues are different.

The second sense in which unions can be political is that some have a very active internal political life. Some factions vie for control of the organization through the election of officers. Stay clear of Labor's internal politics. When approaching Labor for cooperation on a local, district, or state level, go straight to the elected officers or top staff. Don't have dealings with people who want to involve you in intrigue. Someone wins and someone loses every union election. You should be able to keep on good terms with the union no matter who wins. Whether you are working with a local, State Fed, or Labor Council officer, being on good terms also means respecting the leaders' agenda and realizing that they have responsibilities that must come ahead of work with outside groups.

Local Union Self-Interest

Certain things will make your job easier in approaching local union officers to cooperate with a citizens' organization. First, if your issue is one that higher bodies of the union or AFL-CIO have already endorsed and asked the local unions to work on, then the door is partly open. Often, local officers will be trying to find a way to squeeze another hour into the day for this issue. If you come with a plan that is very specific and requires the union to do a set and limited amount, you will be welcomed. On the other hand, if you announce that you have come to "coordinate their efforts" and then propose several interminable meetings with people who don't know what to do, your reception may be less than enthusiastic.

Second, it helps if your issue is one that will materially benefit the union's members. It is easier all around if the officers can present it as an additional thing the union does to better the members' lives. Remember that, unlike community groups that may get money from grants,

canvassing, or even government agencies, every cent a local union has comes from the members' dues. (Dues are often several hundred dollars a year, depending on the member's pay scale.)

The members join unions primarily to win benefits on the job. Everything else is extra. If they feel that job-related issues are not being taken care of, or if they don't agree about your issue, they will be reluctant to see their dues money being spent to support it. Citizen organizations are often ambivalent about this point. On the one hand, they want union leaders to be accountable to the members. On the other hand, when the members disagree with the citizen group's issues, the group wants the union leaders to go ahead and support it anyway.

Third, you can help to promote a close working relationship with a local union if your issue is one on which Labor-backed candidates can later campaign or one that Labor can use to attack opponents for not supporting. Many unions are becoming increasingly involved with the type of issue campaigns that some citizen groups conduct. To local unions, "political action" used to mean electoral campaigns, but this is beginning to change. However, if you are in a position to talk with them about elections, you are immediately speaking the same language; other types of campaigns take some explanation. Unions do not work under the restrictions that apply to tax-exempt citizen groups. They are, however, prevented by law from spending dues money on electoral campaigns. Campaign work is done through political action committees, which they must fund separately. This money is contributed almost entirely by the members.

The key to working with local unions and Central Labor Councils is thus the same as working with any other organization. *Understand their self-interests.* This means understanding the personal self-interests of the officers and staff, understanding the organizational self-interest of the union, and understanding its political self-interest as well.

As with other groups, whoever asks for help and gets it incurs a debt. Thus, you may be expected to help the union sometime in the future.

Approaching a Local Union

Here is a checklist of things to find out before approaching a local union. Having this information will help you to figure out the degree of interest any particular local union will have in your issue and what it can do to help. Ask friends in Labor. A little research will give you a better idea of what the local can gain by working with you and how you can adjust your program to help the union's members. Local officers will be impressed if you know some of this.

- Number of members?
- Type of members?
  - occupation
  - income
  - sex/race
- Neighborhoods where members live?
- Location of work sites?
- Government or private-sector workers?
- Growing or declining membership?
- Size of staff? (Paid officers count as staff.)
  - Ongoing organizing campaigns?
  - Active in politics or in the community?
  - Around what issues?
  - Facilities?
- Who really runs the union? (It is usually the highest ranking paid elected officer. If, for example, there is an unpaid president and a paid elected business agent, the business agent is probably the person you would approach first. If no one is paid, then it is usually the principal officer.)

Approaching a Central Labor Council

Central Labor Councils reflect the political complexion of the unions in their area. Often community organizations will have relations with those local unions that are most socially active. At the Labor Council you will meet the whole Labor family, from the most progressive to those closer toward the center.

While Central Labor Councils also have intense internal politics, usually the unions in them have figured out how to work together on a common electoral and legislative program. Unlike local unions, Labor Councils are voluntary coalitions, and there are many lessons about coalition building to be learned from them. In developing a relationship with the Central Labor Council, the first questions to ask are, Who are the officers and what local unions do they come from? Is there a paid officer on the council? Are the top council officers also the officers of their own locals? Because you want to talk to the person who can actually commit the resources of the organization, find out who really has the power. Find out if the largest locals in the council are public employee, building trades, manufacturing, or service unions. This will, to some degree, influence the type of issues the council will be interested in, and you will be better able to analyze its self-interest.

Approaching Building and Construction Trades Councils

Construction is a hypercompetitive industry in which good-paying union jobs are threatened every day by lower-paying non-union contractors. Working with building trades councils offers the opportunity to jointly press for spending on important public works projects that benefit the community and create high-paying jobs. For such a coalition to work, the community group must be ready to stand firm on the principle that the work be done by union labor.

Several building and construction councils are working with community groups to increase access of People of Color to the trades. This is an important area in which community groups can help.

Assistance Labor Can Offer

Labor organizations, especially those with which you have an ongoing relationship, may be able to offer citizen organizations the following types of resources and assistance:
- Phone banks
- Meeting rooms, auditorium
- Printing
- Access to members
- Article in newsletter
- Political contacts
- Volunteers
- Officers to participate in press events
- Members with experience in activities, e.g., coordinating rallies or designing leaflets
- Community services liaisons
- Members with specific expertise, e.g., teachers who know the school system
- Training and job opportunities through union apprenticeship programs
- Street Heat (turnout)

The Midwest Academy thanks Marilyn Sneiderman and Stephen Lerner for contributing this chapter. Marilyn has had many years of experience in Labor education, Labor-community coalitions, and union work and is currently the National Director of Field Mobilization for the AFL-CIO. Stephen has been a union organizer for twenty-five years, directed the Justice for Janitors campaign, and is currently the Organizing Director for the Building and Construction Trades Department.

Ask the union about other ways in which it can help. As with any successful coalition, the focus on the specific issues must reflect the self-interest of the organizations. Understanding a union's self-interest and the demands that the organization is facing, its specific resources, its accomplishments, and its experience will produce a more positive relationship. Both unions and citizen organizations seek power through unity.

Glossary of Labor Terms

AFL-CIO (American Federation of Labor and Congress of Industrial Organizations). A federation of international unions in the United States, formed by the 1955 merger of the AFL (which consisted largely of craft or occupational unions) and the CIO (which consisted of industrial unions).

AFL-CIO Central Labor Council. In local areas, local unions may form Central Labor Councils. These are active in city and county politics as well as at the state legislative and congressional district levels. They are often directly involved in mobilizing support for affiliate and community campaigns.

AFL-CIO Committee on Political Education (COPE). The political action arm of the AFL-CIO, COPE is primarily involved in electoral politics and political education among AFL-CIO members. COPE makes campaign contributions and coordinates the support of member unions for endorsed candidates. Many individual unions also have their own political action committees, as do some large locals. It is not legal in the United States to use union dues for electoral campaigns. All electoral money is contributed by union members voluntarily and separately from their dues payments.

Agency Shop. A provision in a union contract that requires all non-union-member employees in a bargaining unit, as a condition of employment, to pay the union a fixed amount, usually the same as dues, for services rendered by the union. Such provisions are rare. Where they exist, they greatly strengthen the union and ensure its financial base. An agency shop means that the members don't have to subsidize services for non-members. Unions are required by law to provide the same services to non-members in a bargaining unit as they provide to members.

Agreement (Contract). A written agreement between an employer and an employee organization, usually for a definite term, defining conditions of employment, rights of employees and the employee organization, and procedures for settling disputes.

Arbitration. Usually the final step of a grievance procedure in which a dispute between a union and an employer is taken to an outside professional arbitrator for decision. In some contracts, the arbitrator's decision is binding; in others it is advisory.

Authorization Card (Cards, Card Drive). The process of petitioning for an election of a bargaining representative is begun when the employees sign cards designating a particular union as their representative. When a majority of the bargaining unit has signed cards, the National Labor Relations Board will, if asked, put the election procedure into motion.

Bargaining Agent. The union designated by a government agency, such as the National Labor Relations Board, or recognized voluntarily by the employer as the exclusive representative of all employees in the bargaining unit for purposes of collective bargaining.

Bargaining Unit (Negotiating Unit). A group of workers who bargain collectively with the employer. The unit may include all the workers in a single plant or in a number of plants, or it may include only the workers in a single craft or department. The final unit is determined by the NLRB or agreed to jointly by the union and the employer.

Business Agent (B.A.; Union Representative). A full-time staff member of a local union whose job is to represent workers in the local.

Card Check Recognition. A procedure whereby signed authorization cards are checked against a list of employees in a prospective bargaining unit to determine if the union has majority status. The employer may recognize the union on the basis of this check without the necessity of a formal election. The negotiation with an employer for card check recognition is often conducted by an outside party, such as a respected member of the community. Increasingly, unions are pressuring employers to follow card check recognition procedures instead of the expensive and lengthy delays of an election conducted by the NLRB.

Certification Election. An election usually conducted by the National Labor Relations Board, or a state board, in which employees vote for or against union representation. Often several unions compete against each other in the election. "No representation" is automatically listed as an option on the ballot. Voting is secret.

Check-Off. A contract clause authorizing the employer to deduct union dues from paychecks of those members who authorize dues deduction. The employer then transfers the dues to the unions.

Closed Shop. A union security provision in a contract that requires the employer to hire and retain only union members. This provision is unlawful under national and state legislation and should not be confused with a Union Shop, which requires employees in a bargaining unit to pay dues to the union as a condition of employment.

Collective Bargaining. A process, usually regulated by law, in which a group of employees and their employer negotiate issues of wages, hours, and other conditions of the employer-employee relationship for the purpose of reaching a mutually acceptable agreement and the execution of a written contract incorporating that agreement.

Concerted Activity. The rights, protected by the National Labor Relations Act (NLRA), of two or more employees to act in concert to effect their wages, hours of work or working conditions, to form, join or assist Labor organizations.

Constitution and Bylaws. Legal documents governing the administration of local and international unions. Adopted by union conventions or by membership vote, these rules generally cover elections and duties of officers, conventions, committees, and dues.

Cost-of-Living Clause/Escalator Clause. A section of a contract providing that workers will receive an automatic raise in pay when the Consumer Price Index of the Labor Department goes up. The raise is based on a formula of so many tenths of a percent for each point's rise of the index.

Contract. A written agreement reached through collective bargaining that sets forth wages, hours, and other conditions of employment. The contract is normally set for a term as short as one year or as long as three; at the end of such a term, a new contract is negotiated.

Davis-Bacon Laws. Laws that require the prevailing wage be paid on federally financed construction projects. Many states have "little Davis-Bacon" laws that require projects financed by state monies to pay prevailing wages.

Decertification. Withdrawal by a government agency, such as the NLRB, of a union's official recognition as the exclusive bargaining representative. The NLRB will withdraw certification if a majority of employees vote against their union representative in a decertification election.

District Council. Several local unions of the same international in a given geographic area may form a District Council as a way of sharing staff and reducing overhead costs. The council coordinates bargaining and provides services to the members. Council leadership is elected by members of the locals.

ESOP (Employee Stock Ownership Plan). A plan whereby a block of company stock is transferred to employees. In some ESOPs, unions or employee organizations buy a controlling interest in a company and become the management. Other ESOPs are established by the existing management to protect itself from corporate raiders, to secure tax benefits, or to avoid commitments to pensioners. The number of employees in ESOPs is growing very rapidly.

Excelsior List. Established in the case of *Excelsior Underwear*, the list of names and addresses of employees eligible to vote in a union election. It is normally provided by the employer to the union within ten days after the election date has been set or agreed upon at the NLRB.

Fact Finder. An individual or group appointed to receive facts in an employment dispute and make recommendations for settlement. Fact finders are usually chosen by the parties to the dispute; they may be appointed by a court or in the case of a public employee dispute, by a Mayor or Governor.

Federal Mediation and Conciliation Service. A service provided by the government to help deadlocked negotiators reach a settlement. This agency is less concerned with the merits of the issues that are brought before it and more concerned with avoiding or ending strikes.

Grievance. A formal complaint by an employee that charges that management has violated some aspect of the union contract.

Grievance Procedure. A formal procedure specified in a union contract that provides for the adjustment of grievances through discussion at progressively higher levels of authority in management and the union, which could lead to arbitration by a neutral party.

International Representative. A staff member of an international union, often an organizer. International reps report directly to someone in the union's national headquarters, unlike business agents and other staff on local payrolls.

International Union. A national union is called "international" because it represents workers in Canada and/or Puerto Rico. It is the parent body of local unions and an affiliate of the AFL-CIO (although a very few unions are independent). The jurisdiction of an international union is usually industrial or craft in character, although in the last decade the lines have blurred. Today, many unions will organize any type of employee if the opportunity arises.

Joint Board. A structure very much like a District Council wherein the executive boards of several local unions of the same international will amalgamate themselves into a joint board for a certain geographic area or a trade.

Jurisdiction. The specific industry, craft, or geographical area a local union is chartered to organize or represent.

L-M Report. The annual financial statement of income and expenses, including salaries of union officers and staff, that unions are required to file with the Labor Management (LM) Division of the U.S. Labor Department.

Local Representative. The staff member of a local union. People with this title perform a wide range of duties usually related to servicing contracts. Unlike a business agent, this is rarely an elected title. In unions where officers are often staff, there is a major distinction of power and standing between people elected to paid positions and those merely hired.

Local Union. A group of organized employees holding a charter from a national or international Labor organization. A local may be confined to union members in one company or one specific locality, or it may cover multiple contracts with various employers.

Lockout. A denial of employment by the employer for the purpose of forcing workers to settle on the employer's terms.

Master Contract. A union contract covering several companies in one industry.

Mediation (Conciliation). An attempt by a third party to help in negotiations or the settlement of a labor dispute through suggestions, advice, or other ways of stimulating an agreement, short of dictating its provisions.

National Labor Relations Board (NLRB). An agency of the U.S. government that enforces the Wagner and Taft-Hartley Acts. It conducts most private-sector certification elections. The NLRB's function is to define appropriate bargaining units, hold elections, determine majority status for voluntary card check recognition, certify unions to represent employees, interpret and apply the law's provisions prohibiting employer and union unfair labor practices, and otherwise enforce the provisions of U.S. labor laws.

Negotiating Committee. A committee composed of members of a union that meets with company negotiators to negotiate a contract. Often the committee is a large body that has the responsibility of deciding the union's bargaining position. A smaller group of leaders of the committee may form the negotiating team, which participates in the actual meetings with management.

Neutrality Agreement. An agreement between a union and employer requiring the employer not to oppose efforts of its workers to organize a union.

Occupational Health and Safety Administration (OSHA). The federal agency responsible for setting and maintaining health standards in the workplace, particularly related to toxic chemicals, noise, and air quality, as well as machine safety. OSHA has been rendered highly ineffective by reductions in the number of its inspectors. As a result, many unions are now establishing health and safety committees.

Open Shop. A workplace in which employees do not have to belong to the union or pay dues to secure or retain employment with a company, even though there may be a collective bargaining agreement. The union is obligated by law to represent members and non-members equally, regardless of whether the workplace is an open shop or a union shop.

Organizer (or Union or Labor Organizer). An employee of a union or federation (usually paid but sometimes a volunteer) whose duties include recruiting new members for the union, assisting in forming unions in non-union companies, leading campaigns for recognition, and so forth.

Organizing Committee. The employees in a non-union shop who are designated to represent their co-workers during the representation campaign. Organizing committee members, among other things, usually sign up their co-workers on authorization cards or petitions, hand out leaflets, attend meetings, and visit workers at home in support of the union effort.

Permanent Replacements. Under current labor law, when employees engage in an economic strike, the employer has the right to hire permanent replacements. After the strike has ended, if no back-to-work agreement is reached between the union and the employer, employees replaced during the strike are put on a preferential hiring list and must wait for openings to occur.

Piecework. Pay by the number of units completed. The theory is that the faster you work, the more you get paid. Many workers have learned that once they exceed a certain speed, the rate gets cut.

Project Labor Agreements. Agreements between a public entity and construction unions that set wages, benefits, and other working conditions on construction projects. They require all contractors working on the job, union or non-union, to pay union wages, provide health insurance and other benefits, and hire workers through union hiring halls. Project Labor Agreements are designed to protect construction workers while providing the highest quality construction for local communities by setting standards that protect communities from contractors that have low wages, unsafe conditions, and limited training opportunities.

Rank and File. The members of a union as distinct from the officers.

Ratification Election. When a negotiating committee reaches a tentative agreement, it must then by law, and usually the union's constitution, submit the agreement to the whole membership for a vote.

Regions. Like joint boards or District Councils, regions are another form of intermediate organization between a local union and the international union. Joint boards and councils are usually composed of small locals and their service members. Regions more often have administrative and legislative functions and are bodies through which the services of the international are delivered to the locals. Regions have staff and their officers are usually elected.

Representation Election. An election conducted to determine by a majority vote of the employees in an appropriate bargaining unit which, if any, union is desired as their representative. These elections are usually conducted by the National Labor Relations Board or by a State Labor Relations Board.

Recognition. When an employer agrees to recognize a union as the bargaining agent for the employees.

"Right-to-Work" Laws. An anti-union term coined to describe state laws that make it illegal for a collective bargaining agreement to contain clauses requiring union membership as a condition of employment.

Scab. A derogatory term used for a person who crosses a picket line in order to work at a place whose employees are on strike. Also used as a verb, as in "Don't scab."

Seniority. A worker's length of service with an employer. Under a union contract, seniority often determines promotions, layoffs, recalls, or transfers.

Shop Steward (Representative or Delegate). A worker, typically elected, who officially represents other workers on the job, enforces the contract, and helps people with grievances.

Speed-Up or Stretch-Out. An increase in the amount of work an employee is expected to do without an increase in pay. The speed of the machines may be increased (speed-up), or the worker may be required to tend a greater number of machines (stretch-out).

State Labor Federation (State Fed, State Labor Council). A body of the AFL-CIO organized on the state level. State Feds exist in all fifty states and are composed of local unions and local Labor Councils. They function mainly as Labor's political and legislative arm. Their officers are elected at a convention.

Stipulation by Consent Agreement (Stip). An agreement between an employer and the union, sanctioned by the NLRB, that establishes the terms of the election and the scope of the bargaining unit.

Street Heat. A multi-union rapid response team, developed through Central Labor Councils, made up of 1 percent of union members and community allies in an area that can mobilize support for union and community campaigns.

Taft-Hartley Act. A major piece of legislation regulating collective bargaining today. Passed in 1947 over the veto of President Harry Truman, the Act was referred to by the legendary John L. Lewis of the United Mine Workers of America as "the first ugly, savage thrust of Fascism in America." The act repealed many of the rights given to Labor by the Wagner Act and the Norris-LaGuardia Act. Among many other things, it re-instituted injunctions against strikes and allowed for court-ordered "cooling-off" periods and bans on mass picketing. It permitted employers to sue unions for "unfair labor practices," abolished the closed shop, prohibited secondary boycotts, encouraged the passage of "right-to-work" laws, prohibited unions from making political campaign contributions, and required all union officers on every level to sign a non-communist affidavit.

Trusteeship (Receivership). In extreme circumstances, usually associated with corruption, a local union can lose its right to govern its own affairs, and a trustee will be designated by the international to supervise the local. Trustees are sometimes designated by a court of law. On rare occasions, trusteeship has been used against dissident members who are trying to reform the international leadership.

Unfair Labor Practice. A charge filed with a court or regulatory agency stating that an action by either an employer or an employee organization violates provisions of a national or state labor law.

Unfair Labor Practice Strike. A strike caused at least in part by an employer's unfair labor practices. By law, during such a strike, management may only hire temporary replacements who are supposed to be let go at the end of the strike.

Union Label or Bug. A stamp or tag on a product, or a card in a store, to show that the work is done by union labor. The bug is the printer's symbol. (The small number near the bug usually indicates the shop in which the material was printed. Union bugs have been known to be counterfeited, particularly on a candidate's campaign literature.)

Union Local. A branch of an international or national union. Locals are the one part of the Labor structure that members actually join and that represent them vis-à-vis their employers. Union members are local members first and are members of national unions and of the AFL-CIO by virtue of being local members. A local's jurisdiction, or "turf," may be one plant, office, or shop. It may be one company. It may be geographic, covering a city or part of a state. On rare occasions, locals are nationally chartered (e.g., Local 925 of the Service Employees Union and, in its early history, Local 1199 of the Retail Drug Union).

Union Cities. Framework for Central Labor Councils to build political, economic, and social power for working families in their communities.

Union Density. The portion of the workforce organized by unions. Higher density is an important factor in unions' power to drive higher wages and benefits and better working conditions for a workforce.

Union Security. Protection of a union's status by provisions in a contract (e.g., sole representation, union shop, agency shop, maintenance-of-membership, check-off).

Union Shop. Form of union security provided in the collective bargaining agreement that requires employees to belong to or pay dues to the union as a condition of employment.

Voice@Work. The Freedom to Choose a Union is a campaign to protect workers' rights to join a union free from employer interference in organizing campaigns.

Volunteer Organizing Committee. Term sometimes used to describe union members who volunteer for the union during organizing campaigns. Volunteers may donate their time or be compensated for lost wages while they assist the campaign by visiting workers at their homes, leafleting, and attending meetings.

Wagner Act (National Labor Relations Act). The main legislation regulating collective bargaining. In 1933, a year in which over 900,000 workers struck for union recognition, Congress passed the National Industrial Recovery Act (NIRA), of which section 7(a) guaranteed, for the first time in American history, that workers have the right to organize unions. After 1,500,000 workers struck for recognition in 1934 and 1,150,000 struck the next year, the Supreme Court invalidated the NIRA in May 1935. In July 1935, the Wagner Act was passed, again giving workers the right to organize and bargain collectively. The Act established the National Labor Relations Board to administer private-sector bargaining and hold representation elections.

The Midwest Academy thanks Jim H. Williams for his help with this glossary.

19

What is new about Labor-community partnerships is that for the first time in many decades, the problems of low wages and exploitation on the job are being addressed by community organizations in cooperation with unions.

Community groups have long understood that problems such as housing, education, crime, or healthcare come about because people have inadequate income. Instead of trying to increase income at the workplace level, community organizations have pressured government to supplement income either by giving people money or by providing services. Some community organizations have supported wage legislation or the wage demands of public employees such as teachers, but beyond this it hasn't been considered possible for community groups to pressure private-sector employers to raise wages. When every member of the community group works for a different employer, there is no common target.

This was not always the situation. In the early decades of the twentieth century, large immigrant communities developed right around one particular factory or industry—the Lowell textile workers, the Pittsburgh steelworkers, and the New York garment workers, for example. Then, community organizing, union organizing, and

Building Labor-Community Partnerships

political organizing were very closely related. That era ended when the plants closed and the communities dispersed.

In recent years, new opportunities have arisen to directly challenge low wages through Labor-community alliances. The change is happening for five reasons:

- There is a renewed interest on the part of unions in organizing low-wage service and production workers.
- The economic boom has brought increasing numbers of people from low-income communities into the workforce.
- Long-overlooked possibilities for Labor, religious, and community organization cooperation are at last being recognized.
- The demographics are changing. As the income gap widens between rich and poor and as the middle class moves out of certain areas, greater geographic concentrations of the working poor are taking place.
- Immigration is bringing in new groups of workers who often settle in the same communities and then help each other to find work in the same industries. Consequently, there is a greater likelihood now that the members of any particular community or religious organization will have common employers or

employers who are linked through a common industry association.

While far from the situation in the early 1900s, when the population of a whole town might be working in the same mine or mill, these changes have put wages and union organization on the agenda of many non-Labor organizations.

At the beginning of this millennium, conditions for many workers look bleak. Just a few of the facts confirm what community groups have experienced at the local level.

- Over two-thirds of new jobs don't support families with wages that can pay for the basics of food, shelter, schooling, and transportation. Consequently, many parents work two or three jobs to make ends meet.
- Most low-wage jobs don't provide affordable health insurance.
- Pensions and other old-age security measures are virtually unheard of for low-wage workers, those who are least financially prepared for retirement.
- Part-time, contingent jobs are growing by leaps and bounds, offering no security for workers and keeping many without benefits.
- Thousands of workplaces routinely violate the basic labor laws, illegally denying workers

overtime, cheating workers of hours, and using child labor. Labor abuses of immigrant workers are particularly egregious because these workers are unaware of their rights and fearful of deportation.

- Welfare "reform" has added many new workers to the low-wage workforce without challenging the inadequate societal support for workers, especially those with families, who fill the low-wage jobs in society.
- The increasing economic disparity between wage earners is the Achilles heel of the economy. The pie is increasing, but not everyone is benefiting. (See chapter 26 for more details.)

While community groups have observed the deterioration of their members' working conditions, the Labor movement has been in a time of transition. From 1973 until the mid-1990s, the Labor movement was clearly losing ground. The percentage of organized workers declined from 36 percent to 16 percent. The Labor movement

recognized that if the trend didn't change, unions soon would be irrelevant. Labor leaders have challenged themselves to start reaching out to traditionally unorganized parts of the workforce, aggressively organizing the unorganized, improving conditions in organized shops, and building partnerships with community and religious allies.

Because Labor-community partnerships are emerging so rapidly and their impact is so potentially significant, the year 2001 edition of this manual includes this new chapter on developing such partnerships.

In Delaware, a reverend was hired to coordinate the Sussex County Ministry and to involve the Episcopal religious community of the county in issues of justice. Delaware is the headquarters for Perdue Chicken, Case Farms Chicken, and Townsend Chicken. As he began meeting with members of the community, the reverend learned of the problems faced by the people who work for the poultry industry, including those who

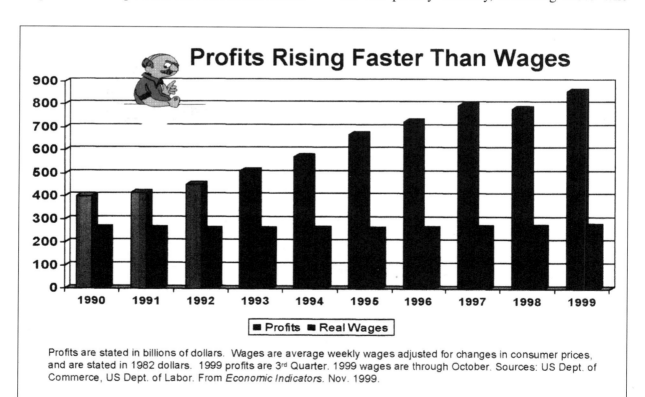

Profits are stated in billions of dollars. Wages are average weekly wages adjusted for changes in consumer prices, and are stated in 1982 dollars. 1999 profits are 3rd Quarter. 1999 wages are through October. Sources: US Dept. of Commerce, US Dept. of Labor. From *Economic Indicators*. Nov. 1999.

Organizing for Social Change

process chicken, catch the chickens, and grow the chickens. It became clear that while there were many services that religious institutions could perform for their members, few were as important as improving wages and working conditions at major employers in the area. The reverend drew together an alliance, which included religious leaders across denominational lines, the United Food and Commercial Workers (UFCW)—which represented process workers in half the poultry plants in the region—chicken growers, and catchers. After the first year, the alliance expanded to include environmentalists and the Humane Society. All parties had a direct self-interest in ending corporate abuse of people, animals, and the environment. United, they could begin to challenge "Big Chicken."

In the late nineties, an Omaha-based organizer with the Industrial Areas Foundation (IAF) began building a church-based community organization. In the first two years of base building, he met with members of congregations, including hundreds of meat-packing workers. When he talked with congregants about their lives and priorities, it was clear that meat-packing workers needed a stronger union in the plants and that the unions needed broader community support to challenge the packing companies to improve wages, benefits, and working conditions. Building a community-Labor partnership wasn't an "add-on" to the work of community organizing through churches; it was absolutely integral to people's lives and the survival of the basic community institutions.

In New Orleans, Wade Rathke, founder of ACORN (Association of Community Organizations for Reform Now) and the Secretary-Treasurer of the New Orleans Central Labor Council, realized that conditions for many of the low-wage workers among ACORN's members were unlikely to improve without a major organizing campaign in the city's hotels. A hotel organizing campaign couldn't succeed without broad-based community support, and another community-Labor partnership was formed.

In San Jose, the Central Labor Council President and one of her staff recruited religious leaders to organize the Interfaith Council on Race, Religion, Economic, and Social Justice. Together, the Central Labor Council and the Interfaith Council built support for passage of the nation's highest living wage bill, which raised the minimum wage that an employer in the area must pay to be eligible to get contracts from local government.

Why Labor-Community Alliances Are Needed

Breaking the Law Is Common

Sweatshops are generally defined as "routine violators of wage and hour laws." Under that definition, thousands of U.S. workplaces are sweatshops. In various Department of Labor studies, 60 percent of poultry plants were found to be violating wage and hour laws, 90 percent of farms employing farm labor, 30 percent of nursing homes, and 50 percent of restaurants. In every community across the nation, workers are routinely being denied their basic wages, overtime compensation, and basic health and safety protections.

The Right to Organize Is Being Lost

When workers want to band together collectively in the workplace to improve wages, benefits, and working conditions, they do so by forming a union. The right to do so was first guaranteed by an act of Congress in 1935.

Unfortunately, U.S. workers face a very hostile climate for organizing unions. Workers who choose to organize for a collective voice on the job are often viewed as disloyal troublemakers. This is true even in non-profit and religious institutions that claim to protect workers' rights to organize. In a recent survey, 44 percent of all working Americans who are not currently represented by unions would vote to join a union if they had the opportunity to do so without risking their jobs. Workers are afraid.

This hostile environment toward unions is created both by weak labor protections in the law and by an aggressive union-busting industry. No industrialized nation has weaker laws or such a vibrant union-busting industry.

U.S. labor law is dominated by the National Labor Relations Act and the Taft-Hartley amendments. The original National Labor Relations Act of 1935 was passed to improve workers' living standards by increasing the power of unions. Over the course of the next sixty-five years, the intent of the law has been changed via amendments to the act and various judicial and administrative decisions that weaken the right to organize. The Taft-Hartley amendments to the NLRA, passed in 1947, strengthened managers' abilities to oppose unions. The amendments permitted employers to campaign against union representation as long as there was "no threat of reprisal or force or promise of benefit."

The weak laws alone would be bad enough for workers who choose to organize. But a sophisticated, $500-million-a-year industry has developed to consult and advise employers on how to oppose unions. Over 80 percent of companies faced with union organizing efforts wage anti-union campaigns.

What happens to workers who attempt to organize?

- Most workers are required by their employers (91 percent) to attend mandatory meetings on company time explaining to workers why unions are bad and why they should vote against a union.

- Union organizers are generally denied access to the workplace and are prevented from speaking to workers.
- Over 10,000 workers are illegally fired each year for exercising their "right to organize."
- Half of private-sector employers threaten to eliminate all the workers' jobs if they join together in a union.

Most of this anti-union activity occurs after the workers have signed cards indicating they want to be represented by a union and before the official Labor Board–supervised election. If the point of an election is to determine what workers really want, then it would seem that both sides—the union and management—should be able to present their cases fairly. But given the laws, the anti-union campaigns, and the control that employers have over workers' lives, the cases are not presented evenly.

The company can control the flow of information when workers are forced to attend anti-union meetings, while the union is unable to even obtain a complete mailing list of employees. One of the functions of a community-Labor alliance is to somewhat balance the scales. It is essential to a free choice that community and religious groups reflect, amplify, and legitimize the union's message. In addition, corporations can sometimes be made more cautious about their illegal or immoral anti-union tactics if they know that a community-Labor alliance will spotlight and publicize such actions.

If the union wins the election and gets official recognition as the bargaining agent for the workers, then the really hard part of the process begins. The union and the company must negotiate a contract, which sets wages, benefits, and working conditions and clarifies basic values and expectations. The contract is where the different perspectives between employers and employees get resolved into something everyone can agree to.

According to the law, all parties must bargain "in good faith." But the law doesn't require that a contract be reached, and the company can stall for months and even years. There are cases in which companies have stalled negotiations for so long that the rules allowed another election to be called and another attempt was made to oust the union. Meanwhile, the workers saw no gains, and pro-union people were fired or intimidated. Although it is difficult to prove legally that someone isn't bargaining in good faith, experience has shown that if everyone really wants to negotiate a contract, it can be done in a relatively short period of time.

If a union and management cannot come to some agreement over a contract, union members can vote to go on strike. Although much publicized, strikes occur in only a small percentage of contract negotiations. Most workers are reluctant to strike and use it only as a last resort. In a strike, workers withhold their labor for a certain period of time in order to put pressure on the company to negotiate a contract. During a strike, workers lose their wages and are ineligible for public benefits, such as unemployment insurance or food stamps (unless they were previously eligible).

Under U.S. labor law, even though workers have the "right to strike," if the workers go out, they can be permanently replaced. This right to strike and lose your job is one of the oddities of U.S. labor law. No other industrialized nation allows companies to permanently replace striking workers. Though it is technically legal in the United States, permanent replacement of striking workers is not ethical. Most religious bodies in the United States have publicly condemned the practice of permanently replacing striking workers because it upsets the balance of power between employees and employers. The passage of national legislation prohibiting striker replacement would be a major step toward making the right to organize a reality. Community-Labor alliances can monitor the progress of contract negotiations, and if the company is "image conscious" (not all companies are), this may hasten a settlement.

Equally despicable is the uniquely U.S. corporate practice of locking out workers before a contract can be settled. In a few situations, when workers attempt to negotiate a contract, the corporate management decides that things aren't going well and it simply locks the doors and refuses to let the existing workers in. Replacement workers are hired to take the jobs of the locked-out workers. This practice, called a "lockout," has received little public attention but is thoroughly outside the ethical principles outlined by the various faith traditions. Once a contract is agreed upon, it customarily prohibits both strikes and lockouts during the time it is in effect. This is also uniquely American. In Europe and much of the world, workers frequently conduct strikes as short as a few hours as a way to settle day-to-day grievances. The ability to strike over working conditions—a shop safety violation, for example—greatly enhances worker power and dignity as well as the relevance of the union.

Building Partnerships

Building partnerships between Labor and community groups is based on mutual self-interest. It is not community folks helping Labor folks just to be nice or the other way around. Both Labor organizations and community groups benefit when workers are organized in the workplace to advocate for family wages, benefits, and working conditions. And community and Labor organizations can grow with strong support from the other. This statement, however, is too general to be the foundation of a working alliance. Self-interest is specific as well as general. Workers at a specific company may live in this neighborhood but not that one. They may belong to one congregation but not another. The situation may call for the support of a community group that speaks English or of one that speaks Chinese. While effective partnerships are based on mutual self-interest, unions and religious and community groups will know the others' self-interests if they talk together and listen to each other.

What Kind of Partnership Do You Want?

Chapter 9 discusses building alliances. All the guidelines in that chapter apply to building Labor community and religion partnerships.

Initially, you should have some sense of what sort of partnership you want. Do you want to form a coalition, an organization of organizations? Or do you want an informal alliance that forms around particular issues? There is no "right" model, but it is helpful to know what you want to build because how you get there varies. A variety of community-Labor partnerships exist around the country. Below is a brief description of some of the various formations and their models.

USAction and Other Statewide Citizen Action Organizations

The organizations with the longest history of uniting Labor and community groups are the statewide citizen action organizations that began in the eighties and nineties as coalitions of community groups and unions. They work jointly on legislative and public policies that unite everyone, such as universal healthcare, environmental policies, or insurance reform. In some states, they work on issues of direct concern to Labor groups such as workers compensation, living wage, or education. The groups mentioned above, and many others, are members of the

recently formed national organization USAction. The SEIU, the American Federation of State, County and Municipal Employees (AFSCME), and the CWA also sit on the board of USAction. Other unions are likely to join.

Religion-Labor Groups

In fifty cities across the country, interfaith religion-Labor groups have formed to build partnerships between the religious community and the Labor community. Interfaith groups are structured in many different ways. Some groups, such as the New York City Labor-Religion Coalition, involve both religious and Labor leaders. Although called coalitions, they are usually not formal coalitions of organizations but rather informal collections of active leaders from both the religious and Labor communities.

Some groups, such as the Las Vegas Interfaith Council for Worker Justice, are coalitions of congregations, with a structured relationship with the Labor leadership. Other groups, such as the Chicago Interfaith Committee on Worker Issues and Clergy and Laity United for Economic Justice in Los Angeles, are composed primarily of concerned religious leaders from a diversity of denominations and faiths but with a formal liaison to the Central Labor Council. For the most up-to-date list of these groups, see the Web site of the National Interfaith Committee for Worker Justice at www.nicwj.org.

Jobs with Justice Groups

Jobs with Justice is a coalition of Labor, religious, and community groups that work to support worker issues. There are over thirty Jobs with Justice local coalitions around the country. When Jobs with Justice was formed, it focused primarily on building support within and across individual unions. In recent years, a great deal of attention has been devoted to building stronger ties with the religious community and local neighborhood organizations.

Jobs with Justice spearheaded the development of Workers Rights Boards. These boards formally and publicly hear workers' cases. Although the boards have no legal authority, they do hold moral authority and have helped improve conditions for many workers. For more information about forming a board, contact Jobs with Justice, (202) 434-1106.

ACORN

ACORN is a national membership organization of people in lower income communities. ACORN groups have developed ties with the SEIU because ACORN found many of its community members working in low-wage service jobs and recognized that to truly help its members, many of their workplaces needed to be unionized. Consequently, ACORN affiliates around the nation tend to have connections with SEIU locals organizing home-care workers, hotel workers, nursing home workers, or other low-wage service workers.

ACORN has played leadership roles in about half of the living wage campaigns, which have been terrific tools for building broad-based partnerships between Labor, religious, and community organizations.

Industrial Areas Foundation

BUILD, the IAF affiliate in Baltimore, has developed one of the strongest religion-Labor partnerships in the country. BUILD was formed as an organization of congregations in Baltimore working together to improve conditions for the congregation's members. After many years of organizing primarily within the religious community, the organization embarked on the nation's first living wage campaign, which inspired dozens of communities to follow suit in organizing similar campaigns. The campaign strengthened the organization's ties with the Labor community.

Following the successful living wage campaign, BUILD constructed a partnership with AFSCME to address welfare reform issues and other low-wage worker issues.

Other IAF affiliate organizations are building partnerships with unions, recruiting them as members, and seeking to replicate BUILD's success in working with unions in ways that build the organization, build the unions, and strengthen the community at large.

Immigrant Workers Centers

A couple dozen immigrant workers centers around the country help workers understand their rights as workers and organize against abusive employers. Most of these workers centers have developed strong ties with the unions that organize in workplaces employing lots of immigrant workers.

As U.S. society becomes increasingly diverse, unions are challenged to organize and serve workers who speak many different languages and bring many different cultural attitudes toward unions. Immigrant workers centers have provided a bridge between the workers and the unions, helping both to understand one another.

The best list of immigrant workers centers is distributed by the Phoenix Fund for Workers and Communities, c/o The New World Foundation, 100 East 85th Street, New York, NY 10028, (212) 249-1023.

Guidelines for Building Labor-Community Partnerships

Build Relationships Now. Don't wait until there is a crisis and you need a community-Labor partnership. Get to know people now. Figure out who in the community and who in Labor is interested in working together.

Seek Broad Religious Diversity. All religions support justice. All faith traditions believe workers should be treated with respect and dignity. But few religious leaders have direct experience working with unions and intervening for justice in the workplace. Recruit Catholics, Protestants, Jews, Muslims, Buddhists, Evangelicals, and anyone else with a large presence in your community. Do not allow stereotypes about various groups to hinder your broad outreach. Workers need the active involvement of all denominations and faiths.

Seek Broad Union Involvement. Some unions have a great deal more experience working in partnerships than others. Work with those who are willing and able, but invite all the unions in the community to be involved.

Seek Broad Community Organization Involvement. A range of community organizations, including organizing, advocacy, and more mainstream social service agencies, may be interested in worker issues.

Seek Broad Racial Diversity. As Dr. Martin Luther King Jr. said, "Sunday morning is the most segregated hour of the week." Indeed, the religious community is even more divided by race than by denomination. It is important to involve a broad diversity of people from the beginning. (Unions, interestingly, are now among the most diverse organizations in America.)

Not Everyone Needs to Be Involved. Not all unions, community organizations, or religious groups are ready to work in partnerships. Don't wait for them indefinitely. Work with those who are able and willing.

Work Closely with Existing Labor Structures. Regardless of the structure of your organization, it is important to communicate directly with the official local elected Labor leadership, not just rank-and-file groups or individual members who

ask you to become involved. Contact the President of the local union or District Council involved, as well as the head of the Central Labor Council or the State Federation of Labor. If you do not communicate initially with the official leadership, some suspicions and concerns may be raised that could have been avoided.

Focus on Action, Not Structure. Organizations that come together around concrete needs of workers and concrete educational programs are better off than those that focus lots of energy on internal structure. Although it is important to understand your basic structure and to have some leadership structures, don't spend too much time on formal items, such as bylaws. Spend the bulk of your time and energy focusing on action and education.

Wait to Formalize Leaders. If you plan to have a formal coalition with elected officers, consider waiting to confirm all the leaders until you have a broad diversity of leaders from which to choose and until you are sure who is really committed to the work.

Respect the Different Cultures and Internal Processes. Cultures are widely different between unions and most religious or community organizations. For example, community and religious groups think in terms of what is good for the community as a whole or for working people as a whole, but before taking into account such broader considerations, unions are required (by law) to represent the immediate financial interests of the specific individuals who are their dues-paying members. You don't have to fully understand all the differences, but recognize that they exist and must be respected.

Many union staff and leaders come to community-Labor partnerships very distrustful of "outsiders." This may be the result of past experience or because cooperating in an alliance adds a whole new element to some union staff person's workload. For many years, unions operated in isolation from community groups and even found themselves publicly attacked and criticized. Such words sound strange in light of recent antiglobalization and sweatshop campaigns, which continue to unite unions with so many different groups. However, older trade unionists and members of progressive organizations still remember when they were occasionally divided, and unions were divided from each other, on issues regarding race, foreign policy, and the environment, among others. Your group may have to prove itself before you get much cooperation from Labor. And if you have concerns or questions about Labor, do not air them publicly. Unions, like citizen organizations, are rightly unwilling to work with people who publicly criticize them.

Holding the First Meeting

The first meeting is important in setting the right tone and direction. Sometimes groups decide to have a daylong community-Religion-Labor workshop on "Shared Values" as a means of getting started and identifying interest. Others decide to begin with an organizational and mission focus. Either way, the first meeting is critical. The first meeting should model your values and commitments. It should

- Involve diverse faith groups, community groups, and unions.
- Be racially diverse.
- Involve the central Labor leadership.
- Start with prayer or a unifying reading.
- Involve everyone in discussions and plans.
- Avoid getting bogged down in boring matters.
- Have a tight agenda with a good chair or moderator.

- Give everyone something concrete to do before the next meeting.

A Good First Project

Sometimes a community-Labor group is formed because of a pending Labor problem. In such cases, it is obvious what the first project should be. In other situations, it is important to select some initial projects that build relationships between the religious and Labor communities and broaden the base of involvement.

One good first project is to host a *Labor in the Pulpits* program. This program recruits and trains union people to speak in congregations over Labor Day weekend. Good materials are available to help you with this project from the National Interfaith Committee for Worker Justice. Usually, the Central Labor Council takes responsibility for recruiting the Labor speakers, and the religious community recruits the congregations and trains the speakers. In 1998, over thirty cities hosted Labor in the Pulpits programs. Non-religious organizations can invite union speakers to their annual meetings and other events.

Living wage campaigns have jump-started many community-Labor partnerships. The best background on living wage campaigns is available from www.livingwagecampaign.org.

Many groups are seeking ways to *clean up U.S. sweatshops*. In addition to being informed consumers, groups may want to work with the local Department of Labor to develop or distribute complaint forms and hold workshops in congregations informing workers of their rights in the workplace.

Many groups *develop programs to help workers understand their rights*. The Chicago Interfaith Committee on Worker Issues developed a Worker

Rights Manual explaining workers rights and how to complain to appropriate agencies. Both Department of Labor staff and union staff help lead the workshops so workers understand their legal options and their organizing options. The manual is available in English, Spanish, and Polish. Workshops are being conducted by Labor leaders in congregations to inform workers of their rights. For a copy of the manual or information on workshops, send $3 to the Chicago Interfaith Committee, 1020 W. Bryn Mawr, Chicago, IL 60660-4627.

One good way to involve religious and community leaders in particularly difficult worker issues is to *form a fact-finding delegation*. The delegation, composed of religious and community leaders, meets with workers and hears their concerns. Usually, the delegation attempts to meet with management. Sometimes they do meet, and occasionally, the meeting in itself helps resolve problems. More often, the delegation is denied a meeting with management. Whether or not there is a meeting, if there seems to be no commitment on the company's side to addressing the workers' concerns, the delegation then writes a report of its findings and recommendations. The report is then released publicly.

Whatever else citizen and religious organizations may achieve, it is hard to imagine developing a more just society without creating more just economic relationships in the workplace. Community-Labor partnerships are critical for the twenty-first century.

20

The essence of direct action organizing is to find the other side's weakest point and to focus all your strength on it. Tactical investigation is a key approach to locating weak points. Although exposing tactical weaknesses doesn't in itself change the balance of power, it does open an avenue of attack as part of a larger strategy to change power relations. If a particular weakness is large enough to change the relationship of power, it is a strategic weakness, not a tactical weakness. But a number of tactical weaknesses can add up to a strategic weakness.

Tactical weaknesses take many forms. An opponent who breaks the law or flouts regulations

Not Research but Political-Economic Intelligence

Tips for Investigators

Organizing Your Research

Finding Information in Print and Online

Guide to Information Sources

Many people contributed to this chapter. The current version was written by Jane Hunter and is partly adapted from the Service Employees International Union's forthcoming research manual, for which she is one of the principal writers. This revised chapter builds on previous editions prepared by the SEIU Assistant Research Director Steve Askin, Barbara Sampson, a former researcher for New Jersey Citizen Action and the Communication Workers of America, and Barry Greever of the Midwest Academy. This chapter is based on the 1972 pamphlet "Tactical Investigations for People Struggles" by Barry Greever, which appeared in previous editions of the Midwest Academy manual. The dean of tactical investigations, Greever has inspired a whole generation of organizers, researchers, and investigators.

Tactical Investigations

incurs a tactical weakness that can be exploited. Having a conflict of interest or lying in public does the same thing, as does acting inconsistently with an expected role. An elected official who takes a vacation trip paid for by a corporation has acted inconsistently with an expected role, even without further evidence of wrongdoing. These are the things that tactical investigators look for. We will stress over and over that nothing automatically happens when an investigator uncovers a tactical weakness. It is only an avenue. Organization is required to utilize it.

Not Research but Political-Economic Intelligence

Research: A careful systematic study and investigation in some field of knowledge.
—Webster's Dictionary

Intelligence: Intelligence deals with all the things which should be known in advance of initiating a course of action.
—Britannica

Many organizers, particularly those who are college graduates, call the process of locating information "research." But the word "research" often implies knowledge divorced from action. In the academic world, one is expected to approach a research project with an open mind, free of preconceived ideas or values.

"Intelligence," on the other hand, is about finding the strengths and weaknesses of an opponent. The distinction cannot be overemphasized: research requires one mind-set and intelligence quite a different one.

The following definition of intelligence, taken from a military training manual, makes the distinction clearer.

> [Intelligence is] the product resulting from the collection, evaluation, analysis, integration, and interpretation of all available information [that] is immediately or potentially significant to planning.

Intelligence, therefore, is oriented toward action. It has little to do with knowledge for the sake of knowledge. It involves gathering pieces of information, large and small, working with them until a pattern emerges, and then using that information tactically against an opponent. It would be self-defeating to do research for a citizen organization with the view that you are simply studying some field of knowledge. If you are working for a tenant organization, you must have the attitude that you are investigating the landlord, not studying housing. If you are working in an election campaign, you are investigating an opponent and looking for illegal campaign practices. Some examples will illustrate this point. In Louisville, Kentucky, the aldermen appointed a "Mayor's Advisory Committee" to study a new housing code that had been proposed by a tenant organization. Tactical investigation revealed the following:

- Nine of the twelve advisory committee members owned property.
- Five of the nine were landlords.
- The value of the property being rented out by landlords on the committee was nearly half a million dollars, high by local standards at the time.
- One committee member owned rental property jointly with the alderman who appointed him to the committee.

This information was used to alert community organizations and to discredit the committee when it proposed a housing code biased against tenants. There was obviously a major conflict of interest here.

In New Jersey, landlords claimed that rent control increased property taxes for non-renting homeowners. Tactical investigation challenged this by comparing the rate of property tax increases in communities with and without rent control. The information was sent to legislators. It was used to get press and was presented in testimony before City Councils considering rent control. It showed council members the landlord's organization could not be trusted to present accurate information to public bodies.

When insurance companies tried to justify rate hikes by claiming that they were losing money on their *policies*, citizen investigators revealed how much profit they were getting from investing the *premiums*. This changed the whole nature of the debate. Elected officials had to be more cautious about supporting the insurance industry that had deceived them.

A state government claimed that it was saving money by contracting out work, but union investigators demonstrated that contracting out was actually more expensive. This information was used in union contract negotiations when the state argued that union employees should take pay cuts to bring costs down to the private-sector level.

In Massachusetts, an organization was working to get a toxic dumpsite cleaned up. The group traced ownership of the land to a local bank but couldn't force the bank to act. Further investigation showed that a nearby YMCA had substantial deposits in the bank. The organization pressured the "Y" to pressure the bank, and the cleanup soon began. It was not the expected role of the "Y" to be supporting a polluter. In this situation, the "Y" and other bank customers become secondary targets.

It should be clear from these examples that tactical investigation is essential to many successful campaigns. It is not a luxury, and organizations must budget money for it. A citizens' organization should hire an investigator or train its own staff members in investigative skills. (Where such a position exists, it is usually called "researcher" or "policy analyst." Although the names imply a somewhat different concept of the job, people with those titles should think of themselves as investigators.)

In issue and electoral campaigns or coalitions, the organization with the best information often takes the leadership and media spotlight. No matter how strong they are in other ways, groups that must rely on others for investigative and issue research will often be somewhat marginal. Information gives you control over the issue, access to the press, and the ability to direct the debate. We have often seen large coalitions of citizen organizations, unions, and other groups that revolve around a small public interest research organization in which a single investigator/researcher provides the information and thus has great power.

Tips for Investigators

A military manual made this comment that is striking in its applicability to investigative research by citizen organizations:

> The collection of information is made difficult by the fact that the enemy makes every practicable effort to defeat collection attempts. Accordingly, strengths, dispositions, and movements are concealed. Censorship and communications security measures are enforced; false information is disseminated and tactical measures designated to deceive are adopted.

This section will help you to overcome such difficulties.

Start with a Plan as Part of an Organizing Strategy

You don't have to be an expert. Investigations aren't the same as giving legal advice or prescribing medicine, so don't be afraid to jump in and get started. But first, have a plan. The importance of the plan is that it tells you specifically what to look for. Without it, many investigators, particularly beginners, will try to substitute quantity for quality.

The investigation plan is determined by the overall strategy of the campaign. Often an organization leader will say, "Let's do some research and see what comes up; then we can develop a strategy." This is an invitation to an open-ended investigative project that produces mush. The strategy comes first. Being told to look for some environmental official on whom to put pressure is an unfocused assignment. Being told to find accurate information that will expose the misdeeds of the state environmental commissioner is more specific. In fact, you pretty much know what will achieve the goal: finding out that the person

- Lied.
- Failed to enforce the law.
- Had a major conflict of interest.
- Misspent money.
- Issued inaccurate reports.

Finding any of this information is still a big job, but at least you know where to start. The organization must also understand that simply finding such evidence will not be sufficient. What is critical is how the information is used and orchestrated and what kind of campaign is mobilized around it.

The plan should include the following:

- What are you trying to accomplish? That is, what real-world result will occur if you find the information that you are looking for? Investigation can be an endless process unless it is focused on a clear, expected result. The result is not the same as the information you are seeking. It is what the information will be used to achieve.
- What information are you looking for?
- Where can you find it?
- What is the timeline for each phase of the investigation?

Keep in Mind the Two Cardinal Rules of Investigation

Rule #1. You Can Always Get the Information You Need. This is an essential frame of mind. It is true. If you don't believe it, get a different job. Lack of tenacity plagues starting investigators. After one or two unsuccessful attempts to locate information, they quit, concluding that the information can't be found. This is precisely what government agencies, corporations, and individuals with power want you to think. In reality, there are very few situations in which the needed information can't be found—one way or another.

Corollary #1. Someone Already Did It. We live in the most overstudied society in the world. There are few things that you will ever want to know that someone hasn't already found out. The first step in any investigative assignment is to figure out who has already done it.

Corollary #2. Someone Will. Look for a college professor who will assign the problem to students. Check with friendly journalists (although you risk losing control of the information). Talk with people at policy institutes, large service agencies, and even foundations. Someone wants to research this. Larger city libraries even have reference librarians who look up information for you. Staff in regional offices of the Labor Department's Bureau of Labor Statistics and the Census Bureau will look up facts from their standard reports and give you information over the phone, or you can download it from the Web.

Rule #2. It's Your Right! This too is a required attitude and frame of mind. It is also true (most of the time). It is easy for the inexperienced investigator to be cowed by public agencies and corporations. You are morally entitled to 100 percent and legally entitled to 95 percent of the information you are seeking (as long as it doesn't violate someone's legitimate personal privacy).

People who refuse to give it to you can be rightfully and publicly asked, "What are you trying to hide?"

Look for Patterns in Bits and Pieces of Information

An investigation rarely produces a big scoop or a spectacular story. Usually you find bits of information that must be assembled into a pattern before they are useful.

Suppose you find, by checking through the motor vehicle bureau, that your state representative buys a very expensive new car every two years. This information doesn't tell you much by itself. But add the fact that his personal financial disclosure statement, filed with the Secretary of State, says that he has no outside business interests, no large amount of wealth, and no spouse. Add that he has campaigned on being a full-time legislator. Now add his statement that legislators need a pay raise and he is thinking of leaving politics because he can't live on his salary. A strong suspicion of an undisclosed source of income starts to emerge from all of this. Documenting that income source will expose a tactical weakness for the elected official because it is illegal to lie in a disclosure statement. A direction for the next tactical move is now established. Some embarrassing questions can be put to the representative in a public forum. There is also a direction for further investigation.

Learn to Use Computers

Some organizers are still "technopeasants." But look what a computer can do:

- A computer can take you onto the Internet, increasingly the cheapest and easiest place to do research (not to mention connecting with allies). The basic skills needed for Internet surfing will equip you to use online research services and the CD-ROMs that are replacing many library reference works.

- A computer can zip through repetitive tasks, such as creating/using form letters to request documents.
- Taking notes and keeping records on a computer cuts down on paper clutter and makes it a snap to find key details.
- More sophisticated (but not all that complicated) computer applications include spreadsheets and databases for analyzing the data you find. These programs will generate charts that dramatically display your research findings.

One investigator made a database of all the contributions she could find from major corporations in her state to the Republican Party. She included contributions from various partners, officers, and directors of the companies as well as their families. Not only did she list money given to individual campaign committees but to county committees, the state committee, the Governor's ball, and so on. The computer added up all the various contributions, produced a grand total from each company, and ranked the companies by amount contributed.

Next, the investigator made a separate database of all the companies that got non-bid state contracts (that is, contracts that were given without competitive bidding). Then she had the computer cross check the two databases. Guess who got many of the non-bid state contracts?

Her study resulted in two months of legislative hearings. It was of great value to the state employees' union that was fighting the practice of contracting out state work to private companies. The Governor had claimed contracting out would get the politics out of service delivery and make the work more efficient. Instead it added even more political graft.

Could she have done the same thing with a pack of index cards instead of a computer? Yes. But then why not use a wax tablet and a sharp stick? It all depends on how you want to spend your time.

Make Bureaucracy Work for You

Dealing with public officials can be both frustrating and rewarding. Usually they see their role as protecting themselves and those higher up. They, like community organizers, have long understood that in government and politics, information is a route to power.

On the other hand, many regulatory agencies have staff who sincerely care about the agencies' missions and are frustrated by their superiors' inaction. These are the most valuable people to find. They can act as both guides and sources.

Many more staff people have no strong private opinions and simply work to make a living. They will respond to you on the basis of things that have nothing at all to do with the issue at hand. In government, sometimes the most difficult people to deal with are the lowest level clerks who have been there twenty years. Often, their job is to fend off people like you, and they are good at it. But these people can also be very helpful. It is always best to be polite and friendly. Over time, develop helpful relationships. Remember people's names when you greet them. Acting arrogant or making threats will do you no good at all; neither will insisting on your legal right to the information. The issue of rights will be decided higher up and much later.

It is often easier and faster for a college student to get information for a term paper than for a citizen organization to get the same data. The student doesn't put the bureaucracy on guard. However, the student won't be able to develop the ongoing relationships with agency staff that come with being direct about the organization you are representing and what you are trying to do. Each time you talk with someone, ask who else in the department knows about the subject and then contact that person. Eventually you will develop a road map of the internal structure of the department and learn who is helpful.

Figure out the best time to visit the agency. Early morning is frequently a good time—but not first thing in the morning when the staff are still hanging up their coats. Don't come at lunchtime when a single worker may cover the office. Don't drop by late in the day when the staff are getting ready to close up. Ask the clerks if some days are busier than others.

Use Freedom of Information Laws

Freedom of information, open government, or sunshine laws spell out your rights to obtain government records—including many records that public agencies collect on private organizations and companies. The federal Freedom of Information Act (FOIA) covers records held by federal agencies; state and local laws govern access to the records of state and local agencies.

Although freedom of information laws are meant to ensure access to government documents, officials often use them to frustrate citizens' records requests. You can avoid frustration by taking a little time to learn to use the laws to your advantage. First, find out the public records laws in your area. Both state and local laws might cover some agencies. Then, understand the basics of what these public records laws do and don't cover.

In general, you *cannot* get records containing private data on individuals (personnel or arrest records, for example), criminal investigations, and proprietary information (trade secrets). Some of these off-limits items may be found in court case files (see "Court Records," below). On the other hand, most agency reports, studies, budgets, minutes, and regulatory files are accessible. Indeed, many agencies issue annual reports similar to corporate annual reports in order to justify their budgets. Agency correspondence and internal memoranda may or may not be available.

While you cannot "foia" (shorthand for requesting records from any government agency, pronounced "foya") documents from private corporations or non-profit groups, you can often find revealing records on these entities in government agencies' files. In investigation, as in organizing, a key principle is *Look first for the point of regulation*—the government agency that oversees your research target. Then think creatively about where additional records might be. Is the private organization getting government grants, contracts, or corporate welfare? Is it applying for permits or variances? Check each agency with which you think the organization might be interacting.

Always look for a publicly funded entity's involvement with the private-sector group you're researching. A newspaper fruitlessly sought documents on a "private" policy discussion group comprised of corporate and elected officials—until someone realized that public university brass participated in the group. Reluctant educators turned over memos that revealed the group's focus on implementing policy rather than discussing it.

It's never a mistake to request records that you suspect may be exempt from disclosure or "classified." The better your knowledge of the sunshine law governing an agency's documents, the better the case you'll be able to make for their release. As a matter of policy, some agencies routinely ignore all freedom of information requests until the threat of legal action prods them into compliance.

Correctly citing the law that justifies your request is the best way to keep officials from stonewalling you on the pretext that your request letter is not in conformance with the law. For example, if the law under which you're requesting records says officials must respond in ten days, say in your letter "I'm anticipating your response by April 20th, the maximum time allowed by Section 31.B of the Public Records Law." Similarly, if the law you're using permits public inspection of records "on demand," try walking into the agency and asking to look at the records. But bring a written request to hand officials who try to show you the door!

Fortunately, you don't need to detour through law school to draft airtight requests. There are many sources of free help with public records requests. Sample request letters are widely available, from books such as those cited below and from activist FOI (freedom of information) organizations. In some states, every public agency is required to have someone who acts as the freedom of information officer. Many federal agencies also have FOI officers.

You can find a comprehensive listing of links to FOI resources on the Internet at www.nfoic.org, the home page of the National Freedom of Information Coalition. For an automatically generated information request letter to a federal agency, point your browser to www.rcfp.org/foi_lett.html. For a similar, fill-in-the-blanks letter to a state or local agency, go to www.splc.org/ltr_sample.html.

An important guiding principle for records requests is specificity: you have to know specifically what you want. In other words, to find it, you must already know (or at least suspect) that it exists. You can't just say, "Give me everything you have on toxics." Agencies don't keep library-style card catalogues of the papers in their files. On the other hand, agencies usually can comply with a request for "all correspondence with and about Poisons-'r-us Inc."

It's helpful to have a guide to an agency's holdings, either an agency staff member or a friendly clerk; an elected official or a college professor might also help you. Another way of gaining insight into an agency's recordkeeping is to request—under the relevant public records law—a list of the forms it uses, with a sample of each.

Often information released to the public will lead to additional information that has not been released. An official might say in a newspaper interview, "A study done by my department shows that there is no problem of toxic dumping in this community." Don't take at face value what the official says the study shows. Go and ask for it. The data often can be interpreted differently. Sometimes published material will footnote other sources such as "Unpublished study by Department of Transportation, 2000." Again, this gives you a specific item to request.

Play One Set of Records against Another

Companies, particularly still-regulated utilities, whose rates are based in part on the value of their physical plant, often like to show regulatory agencies that their property is worth a great deal. To the tax collector, however, they maintain that it's worth less. Some companies keep multiple sets of books for different purposes. Often the documents they file with different agencies will have conflicting data.

Organize for Information

When other methods fail to produce the information you want, you can begin a long process of demanding it under sunshine laws, but often it is faster and better to engage in direct action to get the information. Involve the press and take dramatic steps. If you know a friendly reporter, first try having her request the information. You might get it that way, and if not you may have gained an ally. Asking an elected official to request the information also works, and putting pressure on the official to make the request builds the organization.

Often agencies charge stiff fees for documents. These might include a "lookup fee" or an "expedition fee," as well as a photocopying fee, which might be a dollar or more a page, even for a hundred-page study. Your organization can go public with the story that an agency is using exorbitant fees to limit public access to information and demand that fees be waived. Mention that your group is a non-profit public interest organization and ask, "What are they trying to hide?" In general, organizing for information allows you to seize the moral high ground. It usually results in a victory for you and a mess for the other side.

Obviously, these methods are of much less use against private corporations, over which you have very little power. Instead, pressure government regulatory agencies to request the corporate information for you. As always, *look for the point of regulation.*

Keep Careful Records

Being able to document the source of information can be as important as the information itself. It can also save hours later, when you have to answer questions. Keep records and dates of everything you do and of every conversation. Make sure to mark all the documents you collect with the date of issue and the date you got them. When photocopying books and documents, always copy the title page. Keep the names of people, even clerks, who give you documents and information. This can be useful later if, for example, someone failed to give you the most recent version of a report and then his agency criticizes you for having old data.

Record investigative paths that led nowhere as well as those that were helpful. In later years, you or someone else may have to go over the same ground. A complete record of your methodology will save weeks of work.

Organizing Your Research

Timing

It is never too early to start compiling information on individuals and organizations your group will need to pressure. When community groups monitor the local real estate market, they may be able to intervene strategically before a notorious developer buys into the neighborhood. When trade unionists monitor changes in a company's leadership or ownership, they equip themselves to take effective action when the new management is most vulnerable to pressure. Major investors read the business press *every day* to find out what's happening to the companies whose shares they own. Activists must do no less.

It is also never too late to start. If you know where to look *and how to look,* you may be able to pull together the key financial and business facts on an individual or company with a few days of library research or a few hours at a computer keyboard. While you can't reclaim missed opportunities for strategic action, you can quickly bring your information up to date. Use the home pages of Internet access providers and some search engines that supply you with daily news and allow you to customize your news requests.

Finding Information in Print and Online

Literally thousands of print and computerized information sources can help you understand companies, non-profit organizations, and government agencies. Although some types of organizations are harder to investigate than others, there is rarely a shortage of detailed information waiting to be found when you know where to look.

In most cases, your biggest problem will be information overload, not lack of data.

Space will not allow us to list every data source useful to your organization, so we will intersperse this chapter with references to other, more detailed guides that provide addresses and phone numbers for government disclosure offices or give you further advice on specific types of research. *Three books are so important that they should occupy a prominent spot on every activist researcher's shelf:*

Dennis King, *Get the Facts on Anyone*, Arco Publications, 3rd edition, 1999 ($15, paperback). The best simple guide to techniques for investigating people; also has strong sections on court and property records.

Matthew Lesko, *Lesko's Info-Power III*, Visible Ink Press, Detroit, 1997 ($39.95, paperback). A massive, well-indexed, 1,500+ page guide to public information sources. (CompuServe subscribers can access some of its information by typing GO LESKO.)

Steve Weinberg, *The Reporter's Handbook: An Investigator's Guide to Documents and Techniques,* St. Martin's Press, New York. The best broad guide to techniques for investigating businesses and non-profit organizations. The third edition, published in 1996, is available from Investigative Reporters and Editors, 26A Walter Williams Hall, UMC School of Journalism, Columbia, MO 65211.

Before the electronic information age, researchers knew that they had to walk into a large public or university library, find the business reference books, and dig in. Or they could go to the right government or private agency and ask for the appropriate public documents. For example, one might ask the Securities and Exchange Commission for reports from publicly traded corporations, the Occupational Safety and Health Administration for reports on workplace injuries, or The Foundation Center for information on donors to a non-profit employer.

Today, the Internet and online information vendors make it possible for you to do most of the research with your computer. The "information superhighway" offers the fastest route to most of the data you need; an hour of online research may save you days of library work or help you find dozens of valuable sources otherwise not available in your local community. However, it's possible to get lost on the information superhighway. On the Internet, this will just cost you the time you spend surfing around. But if you make a wrong turn while using some premium online services, the tolls can be steep; the same database search that costs $10 if you do it the right way could cost $100, even $1,000, if you do it the wrong way.

Dozens of service providers offer thousands of computerized information sources, both on the Internet and through stand-alone services. In almost all cases it makes sense to start with the Internet's vast, free resources, then proceed to low-cost services, and only then, if you can't find what you need, move on to expensive and specialized online databases. This chapter will give you enough information to get started using free and low-cost data sources; it will also help you determine when to use costlier services.

Internet and online research has one major limitation: organizations seldom computerize reports and records predating their online debut. In general, you'll find little information on the Internet predating 1990 and little that's earlier than 1983 on premium online services.

We've used three symbols throughout this chapter to designate three categories of data sources: free, lower cost, and higher cost. Within each category, we use **boldface** type to mark sources and information most useful to activist researchers.

A square box (❑) directs you toward sources (print and electronic) that are free or very inexpensive. Use these first whenever you can. They include traditional resources like your local public library and the Internet.

The ¢¢¢ symbol marks resources that your organization can use without too much fear of breaking the budget. This price bracket includes the online services CompuServe and America Online, which you or your fellow activists may already use at home as Internet service providers. Of the two, CompuServe (now merged with AOL) offers a much greater selection of databases; America Online's research offerings are limited. We strongly recommend subscribing to CompuServe, even if you don't want its Internet service.

The $$$ symbol identifies costly, business-oriented, premium online services. These services may contain the most useful information, but they can cost you many times what you'll pay for information obtained elsewhere. And much (although not all) of the information they offer can also be found on CompuServe, if you know where to look.

Occasionally we will use a mixed symbol, $/¢, to mark moderately expensive services that offer good value for the price.

New and inexperienced users should confine their online research to the lowest-cost services.

If you do need to use the high-end services, Dialog and Lexis-Nexis, it may be more cost-effective to hire a professional researcher like the DataCenter in Oakland, California (510-835-4692), than to pay for a month's subscription and the inevitable learning curve. Alternatively, in many communities, the local library (or the county law library) will search one of these services for you at cost or at a modest surcharge. Most lawyers use Lexis-Nexis, so you may also

be able to arrange for searches through your organization's legal counsel.

Prices and available databases change constantly, so don't assume that this chapter is complete or up to date. We've included price information to give you an idea of the relative cost of various information sources; actual charges will change over time.

You will constantly face tradeoffs between time and money. For example, let's say that your target is a midsize industrial company operating a hazardous, waste-burning cement kiln in your community. You want to find every significant mention of the company over the past three years in two different daily newspapers and the local weekly business paper. You expect that this will mean looking at the titles of 200 articles that mentioned the company and making copies of the 25 most important ones. You'd also like to find a list of stories about the company in national business publications. You can

❑ Spend a day or more in the library searching through microfilmed back issues of the local papers and the various indexes of business periodicals.

Probable cost: $5–$10 for copying.

Tradeoffs: Cost is very low, but unless the local papers publish comprehensive indexes, you will waste lots of time and miss many key articles.

¢¢¢ Spend a couple of hours searching the same publications in CompuServe databases or through Internet vendors.

Probable cost: Expect to pay between $2 and $4 per story, for a total cost of, at most, $100.

❑ Spend several hours surfing the Internet, checking to see if any of the news reports you're seeking are posted on the newspaper's own or some other Web site.

Tradeoffs: You'll spend more money,

but with online searches, you'll find every reference to the company, no matter how deep in a story it's buried. And you may get lucky and find, with a small investment of time, that the local papers you want to search make their archives available on the Internet for free or at a modest cost. (The box entitled "What You Need to Know to Be an Online Ace" explains how to find newspapers on the Internet.)

$$$ Carefully plan your research and subscribe for a short time to either Dialog or Lexis-Nexis, the premium online services. You'll still have to plan carefully since, in addition to subscribing, you'll have to pay for each item retrieved. The search may take half an hour or less.

Probable cost: several hundred dollars.

Tradeoffs: Expensive, but allows you to scan multiple news sources in a single search and may have publications no other service offers. Additionally, you can then search Lexis-Nexis for court cases, property records, and corporate filings on your target company. For your money, you get to refine your searches very precisely to focus on only aspects of the company you need to research: particular product lines, divisions, or personalities. Sometimes these services offer the only route to the data you need.

Guide to Information Sources

News and Information Sources Covering All Types of Organizations

Every activist group should identify and subscribe to—or read regularly on the Internet—a few of the trade and business publications that most often run stories about its areas of interest. *Do this now! Don't wait until you face a crisis.* Alternatively, you can set up an electronic "clipping file" of current news about the company of interest from many different sources. (See "Online Clipping Services," below)

You may be able to subscribe to Internet editions of some publications; some subscriptions, such as *Business Week*, may include access to online editions. What sources you need to read depends on the organizations and topics you are monitoring.

For multinationals or major publicly traded U.S. companies, national business publications will be the best source of "big picture" information on issues affecting the company as a whole. Because it is a daily newspaper, *The Wall Street Journal* contains more information than any other general business publication. General business magazines like *Business Week, Forbes,* or *Fortune* contain fewer corporate details and cover fewer companies but publish in-depth articles that provide more analysis and explanation of trends affecting companies and industries. These general publications are most useful if you want to understand the national and global competitive situation for major industries.

Every industry, no matter how small, has its own specialized trade journals or newsletters. There are thousands of them. Reading one or two of these publications regularly will foster familiarity with the major issues and trends affecting the target company. It will help you identify vulnerabilities and develop strategies long before the campaign begins.

The following selected titles will give you an idea of the diversity of the business press:

American Machinist, Bank Management, Beverage World, Boating Industry, Defense Cleanup, Engineering and

A Note on Terminology: "Public" and "Private" Companies

Activist researchers need to understand the difference between "public" (or publicly traded) and "private" (or closely held corporations.

"Public" does not mean that the company exists to benefit the public as a whole. Rather, it means that shares in the business are traded in a market (one of the Stock Exchanges or the "over-the-counter" market) where any member of the public can buy or sell them. The Securities and Exchange Commission requires public corporations to make financial statements and other information to the public. In general, you know that a company is "publicly traded" if you find it listed in the stock tables of any daily newspaper that covers the major stock exchanges and the "over-the-counter" stock market.

A "private" corporation is generally owned by one or a small group of individuals. It does not offer shares to the general public and is thus exempt from many disclosure requirements. However, some industries—including broadcasting, health care, and insurance—have their own special disclosure requirements that make it possible to obtain detailed financial data on "private" as well as "public" corporations in these industries.

Mining Journal, Electronic Materials Technology News, Energy Daily, Food Engineering International, Footwear News, Grocery Marketing, Modern Paint and Coatings, National Petroleum News, Nursing Homes, Oil and Gas Journal, Packaging Digest, Pesticide and Toxic Chemical News, Playthings, Pulp and Paper International, Retail Banker International, Semiconductor Industry and Business Survey, Telephony, Water Technology News.

There are, additionally, hundreds of special-ized publications covering specialized areas of government and non-profit activity.

For all "target" organizations except the very smallest, the major wire services (increasingly called "news agencies") are also a great source of information. Until recently, you had to own a media organization to read the wires. Today, anyone can read the major wire services on the Internet, including some of their archives. You can also use "electronic clipping services" to collect current news agency stories about your company. For background on the company, back issues of your local newspaper can also be very useful.

❏ Almost all daily newspapers maintain detailed clipping files on local companies; a sympathetic reporter might let you take a look at the file. Or check with the newspaper's librarian: some papers allow public access to their clipping files, although they often charge a fee. Many public and university libraries also maintain good clipping files on local issues. A few newspapers maintain some or all of their back issues on the Internet and don't charge for searching and reading them.

¢¢¢ Back issues of all the trade periodicals listed above, and hundreds more, are available in CompuServe's Business Database Plus. *Cost:* $1 per article to obtain full text copies. Some information vendors on the Internet offer similar databases for $2 or $3 per article. (See the "Online Vendors" box.)

$$$ If you can't find the right industry journals and newsletters through a modestly priced service, you can turn to Lexis-Nexis or Dialog.

What You Need to Know to Be an Online Ace

Challenge	How it works	How/when you use it
Do I need to know what all that alphabet soup means?	You need to know only these few basics: URL: a term often used instead of "Internet address." It stands for Uniform Resource Locator. www: World Wide Web, a major element of the ad hoc network of computers that make up the Internet. http: often seen at the beginning of a URL, short for hypertext transfer protocol. The text that follows usually identifies the owner or location of a site—the computer where the data or service is located. html (or htm): seen at the end of a URL, short for hypertext markup language, the most common Internet text and graphics format.	If you ever need to discuss an Internet address.
Use a search engine	Search engines locate pages or "sites" on the World Wide Web containing "keywords" (names or phrases) that you type in. An engine displays its search results on your screen with active links, which you can click with a mouse to open. Almost every page on the Internet has a little search engine, but some of the "name brand" engines (www.altavista.com, www.lycos.com, www.yahoo.com) conduct more extensive searches. However, search engines cover only a small fraction of the millions of Web sites. Meta-engines (such as www.askjeeves.com and www.dogpile.com) search multiple search engines.	Get proficient with a few search engines by carefully reading their "hints" or "tips," which will tell you how to write your keywords. When you find a page that you'd like to return to, "bookmark" it (if your browser is Netscape) or save it as a "favorite" (if you're using Internet Explorer).

Challenge	How it works	How/when you use it
Find a company's Web site	Seeking the company's name with a search engine might turn up three hundred pages, one of which might be the company's home page. The better way is to use sites that do this for you.	Click on either of these pages for a wide variety of company home pages: www.companiesonline.com or http://businessdirectory.dowjones.com/. If you know the target company is privately held, try www.corporate-information.com. For a Forbes 500 company, go to www.forbes.com/forbes/120296/500intro.htm. Another site to try is www.hoovers.com.
Find free news on the Internet	You can now read all the nation's major dailies (except *The Wall Street Journal)* for free. Most smaller papers and many magazines also post their text on the Internet. Find publications' URLs on their paper versions or through the sites in the next column. These sites, however, give you mostly current news. One notable exception is www.justquotes.com, which gives you a list of news stories (and other data) about a target company.	These sites will take you to lists of links for newspapers around the United States and the world: www.newspaperlinks.com or www.yahoo.com:80/News/Newspapers/. For local business weeklies on the Web, see www.amcity.com/. You can also get titles, dates, and in some cases, summaries of articles by databases that charge only for downloads. (These are identified with an * in the Online Vendors box.)
Find telephone numbers and addresses	Phone directories have proliferated on the Internet. The good ones have both White and Yellow Pages and separate look-ups for e-mail addresses.	Some of the best are www.info-space.com, www.switchboard.com, and www.555-1212.com.
Tap into scuttlebut about a company	Disaffected employees and burned consumers are increasingly trading information (and venting) on the World Wide Web through news groups or mailing lists called "list servers" (e.g., Listserv), which facilitate group discussions via e-mail.	To find news groups, use the specialized search engine www.dejanews.com. You may well learn of a list server from reading news group postings. If not, you can try finding one at www.onelist.com.

Online Clipping Services

You can set up your own clipping electronic file to gather news reports containing one or more "keywords" that you choose. The numerous clipping services search different sets of publications and store articles for up to two weeks. When it comes to clipping services, money doesn't always get you higher-quality data. Indeed, as they compete to lure readers to their Web sites, many media and "portal" companies are offering excellent free clipping services. (Even more companies offer to set up a free "stock portfolio," which you might find handy for tracking the performance of a publicly traded company.)

❏ Excite's free NewsTracker searches dozens of publications, both first-string and obscure, and keeps them several days or more. (Go to www.excite.com, and after you register, look near the bottom of the page for NewsTracker.)

$/¢ CompuServe's Executive News Service (ENS), which costs $15 an hour to use, gathers stories from AP, Reuters, UPI, Dow Jones, and DPA. It also clips from BusinessWire and PRNewsWire, which carry organizations' news releases. Through Comtex, ENS searches dozens of international news sources.

¢¢¢ America Online has a free clipping service, called "News Profiles." Though it's limited to AP, BusinessWire, and PRNewsWire, you'll get each story as a separate e-mail message. (To set up your keywords, go to "My AOL" in the "Members" menu, then choose "Personalize.")

Note: Depending on the type of subscription you have, you may also run up hourly usage fees on CompuServe and AOL.

$$$ If the clipping services above don't have the sources you need, you might consider the richer service that Dow Jones Interactive offers its subscribers. Each clipping "folder" (that is, each subject) costs about $10 per month, plus you'll pay $2 and up for each report you download. Additionally, you'll need to buy an annual subscription ($69 at press time), which will get you full access to the online *Wall Street Journal* and unlimited searches through an extensive collection of databases, but there's an additional charge for each item you retrieve.

General Reference Works Covering All Types of Businesses

We live in an age of mergers, acquisitions, and diversification, of corporate concentration and global integration. To understand a business or a non-profit organization, you need not only to follow the news but also to map the often unreported changes in corporate structures and external relationships. The reference books listed in this section will help you map a company's internal and external power relationships.

The references listed in this section cover both publicly traded companies (approximately 11,000 mostly larger firms that sell their shares to the public and must satisfy special reporting requirements) and smaller "private" firms.

Most of the works in this section are available from one or more online services. You'll find print versions in the reference or business section of a medium-size public library or university library. Libraries may also have these references on CD-ROMs, which offer the advantage of searching by keywords and, perhaps, copying onto a floppy disk.

Funk and Scott's Index of Corporations and Industries (commonly referred to as F&S)

Online Vendors

Vendor	Description	Contact information
$/¢ CompuServe	The best way for activist researchers to access top-quality databases; can also be used as Internet service provider.	www.compuserve.com or (800) 848-8990
KnowX	The best site for public records, mentioned often in this chapter.	www.knowx.com
$/¢ Northern Light	*Most articles cost $2 to $4, and you get warned if an article is very short, plus you get a money-back guarantee. Moreover, searches often retrieve stories and Web pages for which there is no charge.*	www.northernlight.com/search.html
$/¢ Financial Times' Global Archive	Searches thousands of publications, including many European and Asian sources.	www.ft.com
$/¢ Electric Library Business Edition	A wide variety of publications and business information, available for a blanket monthly subscription of $14.95 or $89.95 annually.	http://business.elibrary.com
$/¢ Dow Jones Interactive	A wide variety of news sources, government and company documents, each at a surcharge above the yearly subscription; includes *The Wall Street Journal*. Prices of news stories are competitive with other providers'.	http://nrstg1s.djnr.com
$$$ Dialog	Premium online database vendor; subscription plus download charges.	www.dialog.com
$$$ Lexis-Nexis	Premium online database vendor.	www.lexis-nexis.com

is one of the best guides for current information on companies and industries. Updated monthly, it indexes most periodicals, newspapers, etc. Funk and Scott also publishes a quarterly Index of Corporate Change, which covers recent mergers and acquisitions.

$$$ Computer-searchable for 1980–present on Dialog.

Standard and Poor's (S&P) Register of Corporations, Directors, and Executives includes two volumes. Volume I lists approximately 37,000 public and private companies and the titles of over 400,000 corporate officials. Company information includes financial data, SIC (Standard Industrial Classification) number, products and services, and number of employees. Volume II lists 75,000 biographies of directors and executives. This guide, unlike others, often lists home addresses.

¢¢¢ CompuServe has some S&P materials available for $2 an item.

$$$ Both volumes (and other S&P materials) are available on Dialog. Cost: $1.40/minute plus per item surcharges.

❏ Your library has the print version and may have access to an electronic version.

Credit profiles are the business equivalent of your credit bureau report. Unlike personal reports—which are confidential information—credit bureaus can and do sell reports on businesses. These reports will tell you the magnitude of a company's trade debts, the speed with which it pays its bills, and what classes of payments (if any) it may be delaying. If you think the company is headed into financial troubles, credit profiles can provide a valuable early warning.

$$$ **TRW** (Experian) business profiles may include credit histories, financial information and ratios, information on liens, judgments, and bankruptcies, and basic

company information. Available on CompuServe, for $39 each. (Type **go trwrep** or **experian**.)

$$$ **Experian** on the Internet, at www.experian.com, markets the same information sold through CompuServe in separate segments. Its credit "snapshot" report costs $14.95, to cite one example.

Dun and Bradstreet (D&B) directories are the first place to turn for data on millions of small and medium-size companies. The company's print publications include *D&B's Million Dollar Directory* for basic officer, ownership, line of business, and sales data on 161,000 companies with more than $25 million/year in sales, 250+ employees, or a net worth over $500,000. The *D&B's Middle Market Directory* covers smaller companies. *D&B's Healthcare Reference Book* covers hospitals, nursing homes, and other healthcare institutions. *The Reference Book of Corporate Management* covers presidents, directors, vice presidents, and officers of public and private U.S. companies. Arranged by company, information includes titles, occupational history, education, outside corporate affiliations, date of birth, and marital status.

D&B—Dun's Market Identifiers offers some, though less-detailed, personnel and financial information on more than 7.5 million U.S. businesses. *D&B—Dun's Electronic Business Directory* covers 8.9 million U.S. businesses and professional people. Another electronic version, *Dun's Financial Records Plus* provides in-depth information on about 750,000 firms.

$$$ D&B directories are available online through CompuServe, Dialog, Dow Jones, KnowX (www.knowx.com), and other major electronic information providers in varying formats. Dialog offers the most comprehensive versions, but it's more expensive. CompuServe,

KnowX, and other vendors may offer better value for inexperienced users because their charges, though high, are based on the amount of information read or retrieved, not the time spent finding it.

$$$ CompuServe (typically $10 to search and retrieve each group of five company names plus $25 to $80 per report) offers easy access for occasional users but will actually prove more costly than the premium vendors if you use D&B directories regularly.

❏ Some libraries will have database as well as print versions of D&B directories. For a free copy of *Dun's Online Code Guide*, which will help you interpret the information found in D&B publications, and for current information on where to find D&B products online, call (800) 223-1026.

Directory of Corporate Affiliations (Who Owns Whom) is a valuable annual guide to 4,000 parent companies and 46,000 divisions, subsidiaries, and affiliates of publicly traded corporations with considerable assets. Some private companies are included.

❏ Available only in print version.

The Thomas Register of American Manufacturers and **Thomas Register Catalog File** offer, for some companies, more detailed data than most of the S&P reference works. But they cover a more limited range of several hundred thousand companies.

❏ At press time the publisher was making its registers available free at www.thomasregister.com.

$/¢ Thomas Register Online is also available through CompuServe at $5 for each group of five company names and $5 for a list-ing selected from one of the displayed names, as well as on Dialog for a comparable amount.

$/¢ State secretaries of state and UCC (Uniform Commercial Code) offices charge widely varying fees for copies of corporate records. *Lesko's Info-Power III* contains a complete directory of state corporate records and UCC offices, including information on walk-in, telephone, and—for at least 20 states—online electronic access to some or all of the information. Fees for access to documents vary widely.

KnowX has corporate records and UCC filings for many states. If you can't find the information you want there, try the Public Record Research Library's listing of public records vendors (www.brbpub.com/pubrecsites.htm).

$$$ Lexis-Nexis provides recent property assessment and sales data for most states, as well as corporation, partnership, or professional licensing records from many states.

Government Files Covering All Types of Businesses

The federal government collects vast amounts of data on publicly traded companies and has very detailed files on some types of smaller firms, ranging from broadcasters to banks to non-profit organizations.

But to access the broadest repositories of public information—covering millions of businesses of all types and sizes—you must turn to records maintained at the local level, primarily by state and local agencies. These agencies are usually the best sources of information on operational details of small companies and, in many cases, individual plants within larger firms. Many states have laws that open almost all their data for public inspection. (See "Use Freedom of Information Laws," above.)

Since every state has its own data collection and disclosure systems, we can't tell you exactly what you'll need to do to get the right information in your state. Fortunately, many data systems are similar from state to state, and some states now pool industry information on a regional basis. Best of all, information is increasingly available online, either posted on the Internet by state and local governments or offered for sale by information vendors. You'll find specific recommendations for obtaining each type of record discussed in this section. Here are some general guidelines:

$$$ For "one-stop shopping," when you need to look electronically at several states at once, nothing beats Lexis-Nexis, but charges will be very high.

❏ Since so much is available on the Internet and state and local paper files are available very inexpensively, activists working on a tight budget should view Lexis-Nexis as a last resort.

$/¢ A sensible time-money compromise is often KnowX (www.knowx.com), which sells many of the government records discussed in this section for an average price of $15.

In most communities, you'll find government officials to be accessible and quite helpful. Developing good relationships with certain key officials can be an enormous asset in your research.

The first step in using state and local information is finding the agencies and officials who have the data you need.

- Most states have designated a specific office as the single point of contact for leading you to business and financial information. For a list of these offices, turn to *The Reporter's Handbook*.
- Use the *State Executive Directory* (published by Carroll Publishing Company, Washington, D.C.) or the *Government Phone Book USA* (Omnigraphics, Detroit), or obtain the appropriate state, county, or municipal government directory, which should list various departments and personnel.
- Call the state capital library (virtually all states have one) for help in finding the right document or official.

State and Local Business Records

You probably won't need any directory if you're looking for the three most basic types of business records: **corporate registrations**, **UCC filings**, and **real estate records**. In most states, these records are organized as follows:

Corporation and partnership records are usually available from the corporation division in the office of the Secretary of State. A company's **Articles of Incorporation** detail the place of business, date of incorporation, nature of business, names and addresses of directors, officers, and incorporators, names and addresses of agents, and capitalization. Other documents that may be available include amendments to the Articles of Incorporation, notices of consolidation and mergers, and changes of names. Most states require some kind of annual report to be filed, and these often contain some financial information.

Uniform Commercial Code filings are also usually found in the Secretary of State's office. Records stored here will tell you if the company has borrowed against assets other than real estate. (Information on mortgages will be in a separate office, described below.) UCC filings normally give the name and address of the debtor and creditor, a description of the property used as collateral, and the maturity date of the loan. UCCs are an indispensable source of information on creditor relationships. If you don't know the name of a partnership (or suspect it may be operating under another name), look in the **index of "fictitious business names."** If the corporate division at the Secretary of State's office does not keep this index, you will be told which office does. County offices, most typically recorders of deeds, keep countywide indexes of fictitious business names.

Real property records in almost all states are maintained at the city or county level. They are essential for the corporate investigator. Real property records may show you that company-owned property is being undertaxed—a great campaigning issue for generating sympathy among local homeowners. Property-ownership records may reveal conflicts of interest involving corporate officers or board members involved in "sweet-heart" real estate transactions with the company. However, they are easily misunderstood. To avoid embarrassing yourself and your organization, make sure you really understand the documents before using them in your campaign.

- **Ownership information** will usually be found in the office of the **recorder** or **registrar of deeds**, which frequently falls under the city or county clerk. Whatever this office may be called, it is the place to locate real estate transaction records (**mortgages** and **deeds**) and records of **liens** (including tax liens) against property. These records also identify mortgage lenders and, in many cases, building or renovation contractors. Additionally, these documents will sometimes reveal the terms of purchase of a privately held company or, for a public company, the

terms of industrial revenue bonds designed to create a "healthy business climate" for the company. You will usually find these records indexed by the names of buyer and seller, borrower and lender, etc., in a series of "grantee/grantor" volumes. In some jurisdictions, the indexes may be wholly or partly computerized. In any event, be sure to look at both indexes.

Property tax records, usually found in the **assessor's** office, will give you information about the assessed value and tax payments on a property. Finding the right record is normally a three-step process:

First, find the addresses of properties owned by the target company or individual; second, look up the "lot and square" designations for those properties; third, look up the assessment record for each lot/square designation. Note that assessed value is less than market value in some jurisdictions, so find out about local practices before charging that company (or company official's) property has been "under-assessed."

While at the assessor's office, also check tax abatement roles and tax exemption roles. These records may give a hint that your research target has received an unfair advantage or is misusing a charitable or religious exemption.

Here are examples of how an organization used the tax assessor's records.

A local teacher's union wanted to increase the city's education budget. Volunteers were trained to search the assessor's records, looking for recent sales of commercial property. Having obtained the old valuation and the new selling price, the association challenged any assessments that were artificially low, demanding more accurate assessments and thus raising taxes on these commercial buildings. Without this, it might have taken years before the assessor routinely got around to reassessing the properties.

The same method was applied in a tactical way in another city when the tax assessor himself was made the target of a campaign. Researchers found a few big examples of underassessed commercial property and then demanded that the assessor conduct a thorough reexamination of his records. (The targets, chosen for their inability to move out of the community, included a bank and a racetrack.)

- **Building departments, planning departments**, or **zoning boards** maintain files on the processing of applications for zoning variances, building permits, and the like. Their files may reveal that a company has built new facilities, made alterations without proper permission, or committed other zoning or licensing violations.

❑ Many jurisdictions have computerized their property tax records. You may be able to conduct a free computer search for all properties held by a particular owner within the jurisdiction.

In some communities, current assessment data (and occasionally other property records) can also be found at major public libraries.

Public Record Research Library maintains a Web page of links to free state and local government sites, some offering property records, some corporate records, and some UCC filings: www.brbpub.com/pubrecsites.htm.

Locating the right records can be difficult. For a more detailed overview of property records research, including specialized topics such as federal real estate transactions, interstate land sales, and local zoning/planning regulations, turn to *The Reporter's Handbook.*

Court Records

Court records include criminal and civil cases filed by and against individuals, groups, companies, and government bodies. Cases that may provide especially useful information include bankruptcies, complaints about a company from customers or consumers, claims by one company against another, government prosecution of an individual or company for illegal acts or practices, and divorces.

Most court records are available for public inspection. Others may be temporarily or permanently "sealed." In addition to the federal court system, each state runs its own judicial system. Typically, local courts within those systems don't even cross-index each other's records. That makes searching for court records tedious and time-consuming. Often, however, they can yield a wealth of information and for private companies can be one of the most comprehensive sources of data. A researcher refused access to administrative files on police discipline found one problem officer's divorce case file and learned that he'd been allowed to keep his pension.

Locating court records involves two steps: finding the court and finding the case. Sometimes a researcher will discover a case through news stories or other records and will need to determine in which court it was filed. Alternatively, a thorough researcher will want to search for cases in all the courts in the districts and counties in which a company or individuals are active.

❑ The government section of a telephone directory is the best source for locating courts at all levels of government. On the Internet, find federal courts at www.uscourts.gov and the courthouses in a state system via the "government" link on www.yahoo.com.

In both the federal and state court systems, records are kept and accessed through the court clerk's office. Expect that every clerk's office will have its own system for indexing, examining, and photocopying cases. Savvy researchers entering a clerk's office for the first time will ask how to look up a case number and request the case; when they get the file, they will ask the clerk to show them how to mark the pages they want copied. Whether the clerk or the researcher searches for cases on the computer terminal most courts now use, it is crucial to search for the names of the corporation or individual as *both plaintiff and defendant* (sometimes identified as *respondent*). If the clerk's office indexes civil and criminal cases separately, search both indexes. (Family, traffic, and probate cases may be in yet other indexes.)

❑ *Get the Facts on Anyone* contains the best available simple overview of the various types of court records and techniques for accessing them.

❑ Courts are increasingly putting some of their records online. You will seldom find the text of court filings, but often you'll find listings of cases, the parties involved, and the chronology of actions on a case, known as a docket. These are some URLs to try: www.brbpub.com/pubrecsites.htm, www.ncsc.dni.us, www.law.indiana. edu/law/v-lib/lawindex.html.

¢¢¢ PACER, an online service coordinated by the administration office of the federal courts, offers direct online access to dockets, opinion texts, and court calendars from most federal district and appeals courts. Terms of access and information availability vary, depending on the court. Some files are accessible free of charge; others cost up to $0.60/minute. Call (800) 676-6856 for information and the required advance registration. A free Internet version of PACER, RACER, was just starting at press time. Check its progress at www.brbpub.com/pubrecsites.htm.

$/¢ KnowX charges $1 to search for lawsuits and from $7 to $15 to retrieve the search's results (which will not be the full text of pleadings).

$$$ Lexis gives you electronic access to state and federal appeals, district court decisions, and some lower-level cases. *You can access the Lexis case libraries on CompuServe.* A competing service, Westlaw, offers similar databases. These services will lead you to important or precedent-setting cases—major suits over environmental or labor law violations, for example—but probably won't help you track down most of the mundane monetary and personal disputes that are settled in the lower courts.

State and Local Economic Development Offices

Many states, counties, and cities have procedures by which companies can seek tax abatements, industrial revenue bonds (IRBs), or other financial benefits. In most cases, companies must submit detailed applications to obtain such benefits. In some jurisdictions, the application forms (which can be a gold mine of financial data) are available for public inspection.

❑ *Lesko's Info-Power III* contains a lengthy listing (pp. 720–749, 1997 edition) of state and local business development agencies. Check with the appropriate agency to find out what files on your target company are publicly accessible.

General References Covering Publicly Traded Companies

As we've already seen, commercial directories and databases contain a wealth of information on millions of companies of all sizes.

You can find even more information if your target is one of the 11,000 "public" companies, which annually pour a wealth of data into the files of the U.S. Securities and Exchange Commission. (Publicly owned banks file disclosures with other agencies; see "Obtaining Data on Banks and Financial Institutions," below.)

Ultimately, you will want to look at the full text of the SEC documents. However, if you're new to corporate research, or if you need to see how your company is doing in comparison to others, it will be easier to start with some of the business reference books and databases that compile management and financial summaries based on SEC documents, news reports, and other sources. These publications include:

Standard and Poor's Publications and Databases

S&P Register of Corporations, Directors, and Executives, described above, gives history, basic financial data, capital structure information, lines of business, subsidiaries, lists of officers and directors, and additional information on thousands of publicly traded companies. Related S&P services provide current news and short financial/management information summaries on these companies.

❏ Printed editions are widely available in libraries, which may also have the works on CD-ROMs.

$/¢ The lowest-cost electronic version of these publications is on CompuServe, which charges between $2 and $15 an item.

$$$ Available on Dialog.

Moody's Industrial Manual and Other Publications

An annual financial and historical report on selected publicly traded industrial corporations that includes a twenty-year record of sales, profits, assets, dividends, equity, and other financial essentials. The directory lists banking agents for each bond or stock issue and also includes information about the company's record of acquisitions and mergers. Moody's also publishes a *Public Utilities Manual*, a *Transportation Manual*, and a *Bank and Finance Manual*, which give the same information for companies in those industries.

❏ Available in print.

$$$ Available on CompuServe and on Dialog.

❏ **Corporate data on the Internet** is also available. A multitude of investor-oriented Internet operations offer information on publicly traded companies. Some offer bare-bones information for free and more in-depth data to subscribers. Two good ones are Hoover's Online, at www.hoovers.com, and the Wall Street Research Network, at www.wsrn.com/home/companyResearch.html.

Securities and Exchange Commission Documents from Publicly Traded Companies

All SEC filings are available to the public and, as the accompanying box shows, can be obtained in several ways.

What You'll Find in the SEC Files

For a full explanation of Securities and Exchange Commission filings and their contents, request a copy of "A User's Guide to the Facilities of the Public Reference Room," available from the U.S. Securities and Exchange Commission, Office of Filings, Information and

How to Get SEC-Required Documents on Publicly Traded Companies

Full text of documents filed electronically after May 1996*

*The SEC does not accept all forms electronically. The agency began phasing in electronic filing in 1994, so some filings are available for that year and 1995.

All SEC filings

❑ Many services provide SEC filings for free on the Internet. Some have EDGAR (acronym for "Electronic Data Gathering and Retrieval") as part of their name. One of the best, Free EDGAR, www.freedgar.com, lets you search for companies and their major shareholders and retrieve the full text of documents. Free EDGAR will also track your target company, e-mailing you an alert whenever the firm files a disclosure with the SEC. The SEC's own site, www.sec.gov/edaux/searches.htm, is capable of more powerful searches but is slightly more complicated. This site posts filings within forty-eight hours of their submission.

¢¢¢ You can examine filings for free and buy photocopies at the SEC's three public reference rooms:
- Washington, DC: 450 5th Street, NW, Room 1024, Washington, DC 20549, (202) 942-8090
- Chicago: 500 W. Madison Street, Suite 1400, Chicago, IL 60661, (312) 353-7390
- New York: 7 World Trade Center Suite 1300, New York, N.Y. 10048, (212) 748-8000

¢¢¢ Order copies from the Washington reference room, listed above.

¢¢¢ Examine and copy filings at depository libraries, which collect federal government documents. (Your local public library can tell you the location of the nearest depository library.)

$$$ Use a document retrieval service. Contact Disclosure, Inc., which operates the SEC reference rooms, at (800) 638-8241, or one of the private services listed in the section entitled "Information on Any Company" in *Lesko's Info-Power III* (p. 645, 1997 edition). Your costs will run from $18 up.

Documents from the company

❑ Companies will generally send copies of their annual report and some other documents on request.

¢¢¢ If you buy a share of the company's stock, you'll automatically receive the annual report, proxy statement, and notice of the annual meeting. Shareholders can also get, on request, copies of the company's 10-K form and other SEC filings.

SEC extracts from online vendors

$/¢ The Disclosure SEC database offers a standardized summary of the major SEC filings, including data extracted from proxy statements, annual reports, registration statements, and 10-K, 20-F, 10-Q and 8-K forms. CompuServe lets you buy individual elements of these summaries for as little as $3 or $4. The full package for a company costs $23. Lexis-Nexis and Dialog offer the same database.

These extracts can be more useful than the full documents when you need basic information fast or you want it in a standardized format that lets you easily compare several different companies. To assist in your analysis, ask Disclosure (mentioned above) for a copy of its free publication: *A Guide to Database Elements.*

Consumer Services, Washington, DC 20549. Alternatively, explore the topics on the SEC's home page, www.sec.gov. The following brief descriptions will stress the elements most useful to activists.

Annual Report to Shareholder. This is the principal document companies use to communicate directly with shareholders. It offers the company's view of itself, as presented by incumbent management. It generally begins with a letter to shareholders designed to present management in the best possible light. Annual reports normally offer some current history and general descriptions of current activities, along with an audited balance sheet, income statement, and cash flow statement.

The letter to shareholders may prove especially useful in constructing contract demands, since it usually emphasizes the firm's financial successes. The audited financial statements (and especially the footnotes that follow) will provide a useful, but not complete, picture of the company's financial performance.

Learn to read between the lines: A description of a new plant, product line, or subsidiary may suggest fertile ground for organizing or show you how the company is diversifying away from products or services produced at unionized facilities. **Companies distribute annual reports and proxy statements to all shareholders,** so buying a share of stock is an easy way to make sure that you receive these important documents as soon as they are released. Virtually all public companies have an investor relations department that will send the annual report, upon request, to anyone who requests one, shareholder or not.

Note that the SEC does not accept electronically filed annual reports, so you can't get them on the Internet through the SEC's EDGAR database. However, much of the same information appears *(minus the gloss of the annual report) in the Form 10-K (see below), which is filed electronically.*

Proxy Statement or Notice of Annual Meeting. The proxy statement is the official notice mailed to every shareholder on matters to be brought before a company's annual meeting. It contains a wealth of information available nowhere else. It is especially helpful in preparing profiles of officers and directors because it contains information on their fees, salaries, benefits and stock options, stock holdings in the company, principal outside business connections, and any business dealings between them and the company. It will also discuss any proposed merger, consolidation, or acquisition that requires shareholder approval. In this era of corporate consolidations, companies increasingly create plans (known on Wall Street as "shark repellent" or "poison pills") designed to discourage hostile takeovers. The appearance of such proposals—which may include staggered terms for directors, authority to issue extra stock, or other provisions giving directors broad discretion to restructure the company—may indicate that management fears a takeover bid. Like the annual report, this document is distributed to all shareholders.

Form 10-K. The most comprehensive SEC required document, Form 10-K filed by all public companies with more than 500 shareholders and $3 million in assets. Because the SEC precisely specifies the information that must be included and the form of presentation, companies find it hard to hide or obscure unfavorable information. This form will provide information on

- State of incorporation.
- Address and telephone number for the principal executive offices.
- Title, number of shares, and exchange where traded for each class of stock.
- Aggregate market value of voting stock held by non-affiliates of the company.

- Details on principal products and services produced, the markets where they are sold, and the methods of distribution.
- Details on significant income-producing assets including plants, mines, patents, trademarks, licenses, and franchises.
- Details on conditions and activities that "materially" affect current or potential future income, including the competitive environment, research activities, and pending legal proceedings.
- Segment data: if the company has multiple subsidiaries or lines of business, three years of total sales and net income data for each segment that provides more than 10 percent of total sales or pretax income.
- Ownership data: the identity of any investor owning 10 percent or more of any class of securities and the amount owned.
- Details on all securities held by officers and directors.
- Stock market data, including dividend payments and high and low stock prices for the past two years, plus a discussion of future dividend projections.
- Selected financial data including five years of figures on
  - net sales
  - operating revenue
  - income or loss from continuing operations
  - total assets
  - long-term debt and other obligations
  - cash dividends per common share of stock
- Management's discussion and analysis of financial condition and results of operation, including:
  - liquidity
  - capital resources
  - results of operations
  - favorable and unfavorable trends
  - significant sources of future uncertainty

  - explanation of any "material" changes in financial performance as a whole
  - some data (though rarely as much as you will want) on subsidiary operations
  - a discussion of the effects of inflation and changing prices
- Financial statements and supplementary data including two years of audited balance sheets and three years of audited income and cash flow statements.
- Personal data on directors and executive officers, including name, office, term of office, and a very brief biography.
- Pay, bonus, and benefits data for directors and the highest-paid officers.
- Exhibits, financial statements, schedules and reports from Form 8-K (see below), including complete audited financial information and a list of exhibits filed. Also, information on any unscheduled material events or corporate changes that occurred during the year (see discussion of Form 8-K below).

Researchers often fail to use this part of the 10-K (which can run to hundreds or thousands of pages) to the fullest advantage. You should examine it carefully for data on the company, its subsidiaries, assets, loan agreements, and banking relationships.

Form 10-Q. This quarterly update of the 10-K is less reliable because it is unaudited. It is important nonetheless because it will report new lawsuits and any material changes in operations, including long-term contracts, new financing, and mergers or acquisitions.

Form 8-K. This report must be filed within 15 days after any significant change in ownership or financing. It will contain the financial statements of any business bought or sold by the company and will report changes in control of the company, acquisition or disposition of significant assets, bankruptcy or receivership, a change in auditors, resignation of directors, and other "material" events. **Because 8-Ks provide the first notice of any major change in operations, they should be watched closely throughout your campaign since they contain highly significant information that may dramatically affect strategic choices. The corporate investigator should be especially careful to watch for these reports.**

❏ Since the timing of 8-Ks cannot be predicted in advance, **you may find it useful during a campaign to subscribe to Free EDGAR's automatic notification service**, which will alert you by e-mail when your target company makes SEC filings. Sign up (for free, naturally) at www.freedgar.com.

$$$ If you prefer, you can buy the same service from a company known as Disclosure (see box). Reports will automatically be mailed to you upon receipt at a cost of $37 per report. (Disclosure also provides similar subscription services covering other SEC documents.)

Forms 3, 4, and 5. These forms document shareholdings by directors, officers, and owners of more than 10 percent of any class of equity securities. Form 3 is the initial filing, Form 4 reports changes in holdings, and Form 5 offers an annual summary.

Form 13-F. This form is a quarterly report on the shareholdings of institutional investment managers including banks, insurance companies, investment advisers, investment companies, foundations, and pension funds that manage more than $100 million in equity securities. When used in conjunction with the *Money Market Directory* (see "Sources of Information on Pension Funds"), these documents can tell which shareholders/managers also manage funds for unions, public pension funds, church groups, and other groups of investors who might be open to your group's appeals for support.

Forms 13-D, 13-E3, 13-G, 14-D1, and 14-D9. These forms document various aspects of an attempted takeover of a company including share purchases by investors seeking a controlling interest, management responses to takeover attempts, and moves by any publicly traded company to "go private."

Form 20-F. Filed by approximately 500 foreign companies that raise capital in the United States, Form 20-F provides a more limited version of the information U.S.-based public companies disclose in their 10-K forms.

Registration Statements for Stock Offerings (Forms S1–S3, S6–S18, N1, and N2). These forms must be filed by a company before it may offer shares to the public. They contain much useful data, including

• Detailed information about the share issue, including marketing agreements, distribution methods, issuance agreements, company relationships with any "experts" named in the registration, unregistered or "special" sales of shares, and the use to which stock sale proceeds will be put.

• Information about the company's subsidiaries, franchises, and concessions.

• Financial statements and related exhibits. Registration of new securities may indicate that the company plans an expansion that will require large sums of money.

Registration Statements for Stock Trading (Forms 8-A, 8-B, and 10). These forms are required when a company has 500 or more shareholders and $5 million or more in assets or intends to have its shares trade on a national exchange. They offer an initial disclosure of financial and business information and establish the public file into which some of the other forms discussed above (such as the 8-K, 10-K, and 10-Q) will ultimately be deposited.

Official Summary of Security Transactions and Holdings. This is a monthly SEC compilation of "insider" stock transactions covering all public companies. Reviewing it over time will help you discover who are the most active buyers and sellers of substantial blocks of shares.

$/¢   This publication is available for $23 from the Government Printing Office, as are subscriptions for $115 a year. (Phone (202) 512-1800 and ask for ISN #746-001-00000-2.)

Obtaining Financial Data on Non-Profit Organizations

Because non-profit organizations are exempt from federal and many state and local taxes, they must publicly disclose details of their operations—some of which can be quite valuable to researchers. One set of these disclosures helped a community group expose how a Right Wing religious group used its government-funded childcare contracts to pay its officers big six-figure salaries and to pay inflated fees for services to officers' relatives and the husband of a County Commissioner. That took the steam out of the group's efforts to take on additional social-service contracts.

How to Obtain the Documents Non-Profits Must File with the IRS

Every tax-exempt organization must annually file **Form 990**, a public disclosure tax return, with the Internal Revenue Service. Schedule A, attached to the Form 990, contains useful details on compensation for executives, leading contractors, and highly paid employees. Form 1023, an organization's application for tax-exempt status, contains its stated charitable or educational purpose and other revealing details. These valuable documents can be obtained from three sources:

- The organization itself
- The IRS
- State authorities

The Filing Organization. The only *sure* way to obtain Form 990s (along with some important related documents that may not be available from state disclosure offices) is to go directly to the main office of your target institution. Under federal law, non-profits must make copies of the most recent three years of their Form 990s and of their Form 1023 for anyone who walks in and requests them. Make sure you include in all requests that you want Schedule A, a critically important part of Form 990. The organization must make the copies the same day, unless it is unusually busy, in which case it must make the copies within five days. (If you arrive late in the day, it can delay making copies until the following day.) It must also let you inspect the documents and, if you wish, make copies on your own portable equipment. The organization may charge you for making copies but no more than the IRS charges (currently $1.00 for the first page and $0.15 for each additional page).

Since many institutions profess ignorance regarding their legal obligations in this area, you should carry a memo explaining the law. (If you plan to take notes by hand, bring several blank forms so you can quickly copy the numbers into the appropriate spaces. You can obtain copies of all forms from the IRS or its Web page, www.irs. ustreas.gov/prod/forms_pubs/forms.html.

Non-profits must provide copies of three years of their Form 990s and their Form 1023 within thirty days of receiving a written request. They may request payment of the copying fee and postage in advance.

Note that organizations that post their Forms 990 and 1023 on the Internet can legally refuse requests for copies. But the organization must tell you its URL.

The IRS. The IRS says it can respond to requests for copies of Form 990s within thirty days and provide most of the copies within that time frame. Fax your requests to (801) 775-8803, the IRS Exempt Organization office in Ogden, Utah. State clearly the forms you want, the years for which you want them, and the organization's exact address or employer identification number (EIN). The IRS will bill you when it ships your copies.

The States. State disclosure offices usually respond much more quickly, but their files do not cover all charities. In most cases, state filing requirements are based on public fundraising within the state, not physical location of the charity. (See *Annual Survey of State Laws Regulating Charitable Solicitations*, updated each year by the American Association of Fund-Raising Counsel, (212) 354-5799, for a state-by-state description of current disclosure requirements. You can also find your state's practices by going to the home pages of the national associations of attorneys general and secretaries of state: www.naag.org/aglinks.htm and www.sos.state.md.us/sos/charity/html/otstates.html.) Thus, some groups file nowhere, while others file in many states. Some states require that charities note the availability of public filings in their fundraising mailings. In some state capitals, among them Albany (New York) and Sacramento (California), you can make an appointment to review charity registration files on the premises. In some cases, these files will contain revealing correspondence between regulators and the charity, as well as other documents that may prove far more valuable than the Form 990s themselves.

Whenever you request charitable disclosures from a state, you should specify that you need "the last three years of (insert name of state report) and the federal Form 990 including Schedule A for (insert full name and address of target organization) and all of its affiliates."

A Brief Note on Form 990-PF. Grant-giving private foundations (ranging from Ford and Rockefeller to thousands of smaller organizations) must file annual 990-PF forms that list the beneficiaries of their largess. Microfiche copies of virtually *all* 990-PFs are available for public inspection at libraries maintained in many cities around the United States by The Foundation Center. (Call the Washington, D.C., Foundation Center, (202) 331-1400, for information on the location nearest you.) Even more useful, The Foundation Center has also compiled a number of print publications and databases giving information by *grant recipient*. These will let you find out, for example, which major donors have contributed to a particular hospital or university. You can find the center's publications at many libraries; its databases are available on Dialog and other online services. (There's more information on private foundations in the section below on investigating individuals.)

How to Read Form 990 and Related Documents

Useful items to look at in the federal charitable disclosures include the following:

1. **Form 990**

    Part I: Revenue, Expenses, and Changes in Net Assets

    Line 1, "Total contributions, gifts, grants, etc." Tells you how much money an organization receives as charitable donations and government grants. This information can help you locate government agencies and private funders that may have influence over the organization.

Line 2, "Program service revenue." Total revenue from all sources. Examining changes in this figure (and the detailed breakdowns) over a three-year period will help you understand funding trends. Additional detail will be found in Part VII.

(The community group mentioned above found the total of the Right Wing group's income in Lines 1 and 2.)

Line 18, "Excess (or deficit) for the year." Equivalent to "net profit" in the private sector. A high profit rate can be used to document the organization's wealth and, in extreme cases, to challenge its non-profit status.

Line 21, "Net assets or fund balances at end of year." Equivalent to "retained earnings" in the private sector. Rapid growth in the fund balance may suggest that the institution is more interested in accumulating wealth than using its resources to serve the community.

Part II: Statement of Functional Expenses

Line 43, "Other Expenses." Sometimes will give you evidence of spending inappropriate to a charity.

Part III: Statement of Program Service Accomplishments

This section will give you valuable information on spending for specific segments of the employer's activity.

Part V: List of Officers, Directors, and Key Employees

This is often the most valuable portion of a Form 990 because it contains details on officers' salaries and benefits. In some cases it will show that the director and other officers are grossly overpaid and that they are receiving much larger annual percentage increases than they pay their workers. This turned out to be the case with a Right Wing group, which paid its executives over $200,000 and its program workers $5 an hour.

To find out if executive pay is out of line with other organizations, check the figures against compensation surveys published annually in *The Chronicle of Philanthropy, Modern Healthcare*, or other trade publications covering non-profits.

Part VI: Other Information

Answers to questions in this section may provide evidence of conflicts of interest or other irregularities. Conversely, if the statements made by the organization here contradict what you know about its operations, you may have grounds for questioning its tax exemption. Note especially Line 78 (and the related, more detailed disclosures in Part IX).

Part IX: Information Regarding Taxable Subsidiaries

The information found here regarding for-profit affiliates can have important implications at the state level because some states are more restrictive than the federal government on some tax exemption-related issues. In particular, use of the non-profit institution's buildings by a for-profit subsidiary could trigger a partial loss of real estate tax exemption. In some cases, it may be useful to contact the appropriate county, city, or town authorities to find out if real estate taxes are being paid and to protest any improper failure to pay.

2. Form 990, Schedule A

This critically important document gives you pay and benefits data for the five highest-paid non-officer employees (usually the senior administrators) and the five highest-paid professional service providers. It also provides information on lobbying expenditures (if any) and transactions with non-charitable organizations. The activists examining the rightist group's Schedule A found that the group paid a generous rental to the County Commissioner's husband, a huge legal retainer to one of the officer's brothers, and exorbitant amounts to suppliers with family links to other officers.

It's easy to understand why organizations often try to omit this form from their disclosures to state agencies and individual requesters. Make sure that this schedule is included with any Form 990s provided to you.

3. Form 1023

This is the original application to the IRS for tax exemption. It is available from the institution or the IRS but may not be available from state authorities. Make sure you specifically request "all schedules and supporting documents or papers filed by the organization when it applied for exemption." Form 1023 includes detailed descriptions of the organization's charitable objectives, its links with other organizations, and various areas of potential conflict of interest.

Schedule C of Form 1023 provides additional information on non-profit hospitals. It describes the hospital's policies on treatment of the indigent, financing of charity care, and provision of subsidized office space to physicians. If claims made in this section are inaccurate (e.g., the hospital is failing to adhere to its stated charity care policies or has spent more than the indicated amount on subsidies for doctors), this may provide a basis for challenging the tax exemption.

Schedule F provides similar information on nursing homes.

As with Part VI of Form 990, discrepancies between statements to the IRS and the actual practices of the exempt organization could provide a basis for challenging its exempt status.

4. IRS Form 990T

This form reports taxable "unrelated business income" (which is taxable) from activities not related to the institution's "charitable purpose." Analysis of taxable activities can be crucial to understanding a non-profit organization.

(Note: This is the one Form 990–related document that the organization may legally withhold; however, organizations unfamiliar with the rules have been known to release this document to requesters when confronted with a request for "Form 990 and all related forms and schedules.")

Obtaining Data on Banks and Financial Institutions

The banking industry has changed dramatically in recent years. Bank mergers have become an increasingly significant phenomenon. Many banks are now owned by holding companies. Legislative changes have allowed banks, brokerage firms, mutual funds, and other financial service companies to compete for each other's traditional customers.

Most larger banks and bank-holding companies are publicly traded and thus must file disclosure documents with their regulatory agencies.

Moreover, banks and other financial institutions must also comply with a number of even more detailed disclosure requirements. Banks face much closer financial scrutiny than most other business entities and have some special legal obligations, most notably under the Community Reinvestment Act (CRA), to serve the public interest. In addition, banks are often especially susceptible to public pressure because they are more concerned than most businesses with their community image.

Basic Reference Books on the Banking Industry

You will find helpful general information in the following:

- ***Moody's Bank and Financial Manual*** is an excellent quick reference on specific banks and for general banking information. You'll find it in most major public libraries.

- **Rand McNally Bank Directory** and ***Thomson Bank Directory*** give the name, financial statements, officers, directors, and branch locations for over 45,000 banks and subsidiaries in the United States and elsewhere.

Banking Records: Comptroller of the Currency

An arm of the U.S. Treasury Department, the Office of the Comptroller of the Currency (OCC), is one of four federal agencies that regulate the banking industry. It collects information on

- Nationally chartered banks (banks with "national" or the abbreviations "N.A." or "N.S.&T." in their titles).
- District of Columbia banks.
- Foreign banks with U.S. branch offices.
- Bank-holding companies.
- Corporations created to hold investments in foreign banks.

Most of the information provided to OCC by national banks is available to the public. The financial data in a bank's *Report of Condition* and *Report of Income* is available on request. *Bank Annual Reports* and *Registration of Securities Statements* are also publicly available, though some sections may be withheld as "proprietary information" at the request of the reporting institution. In addition, certain sections of a branch bank application are always confidential.

Although it has an extensive World Wide Web site (www.occ.treas.gov), the OCC does not make these routine filings available electronically. You can phone the OCC's communications section at (202) 874-4700 for information, but you will probably be told to request the filings in writing from

Communications Section
Comptroller of the Currency
250 E Street, SW
Washington, DC 20219

Banking Records: The Federal Reserve System

The Federal Reserve System (FRS) performs two functions:

- It acts as the nation's central bank and executor of U.S. monetary policy.
- It assists in the regulation of commercial banks.

For the purposes of this manual, we are primarily interested in the regulatory function. Specifically, FRS regulates

- State banks that are members of the Federal Reserve System.
- Bank-holding companies.
- International operating subsidiaries of U.S. banks (known as Edge Act corporations).

Information can be obtained from the FRS through its Web page (www.ffiec.gov/NIC) and two offices.

- The Internet site provides a balance sheet, an income statement, and details on a bank's holdings and liabilities. When you look up an institution, the information includes the bank's regulator.
- The Banking Supervision and Regulation Division maintains the securities registrations and annual reports of publicly held banks. Requests for these documents can be made either in writing or by visiting the offices.
- The Freedom of Information Office provides general assistance in locating individual bank filings or in obtaining more general data gathered by the FRS. Both offices can be contacted at

Federal Reserve System
20th and C Streets, NW
Washington, DC 20551
(202) 452-3684

Reports to the FRS are generally open to the public, although like other bank regulators, FRS lets banks keep some forms partly confidential. The reporting forms are also similar to those provided by the OCC and the Federal Deposit Insurance Corporation (FDIC), but form numbers often differ.

Records Maintained under the Community Reinvestment Act

By law, every bank must maintain a CRA file that is open to public inspection. CRA data includes detailed information on lending to low-income and minority borrowers. When a bank discriminates against the poor or minority group members, CRA records can provide a very powerful source of evidence.

Additionally, the CRA solicits community input—both to the bank and to the Comptroller of the Currency's Community and Consumer Policy office, at the above address. For more information, phone (202) 874-4428 or go to www.occ.treas.gov.

Federal Deposit Insurance Corporation

The FDIC was set up in 1933 in response to Depression-induced bank failures. It insures the customers of member banks for up to $100,000 and regulates the activities of state-chartered banks that are not members of the Federal Reserve System (see below). In fulfilling its responsibilities, the FDIC conducts periodic examinations of member banks and requires them to provide periodic reports of condition and income. As with the OCC, much of the information gathered by the FDIC is available to the public. Reports of Condition and Reports of Income are available in their entirety. Under the public disclosure rules of the agency, individual member banks may request confidentiality for information that they consider proprietary. However, such requests are infrequently made and even less frequently granted. As with the comptroller, *requests for information must be made in writing*. Note, however, that, if a bank is state-chartered, you may be able to get its information from the state regulator. (See "State Banking Commissions," below.)

Much of the information gathered by the FDIC is similar to the OCC's, but form numbers are slightly different. FDIC information overlaps with that available from the Federal Reserve but is often easier to obtain. At press time, none of the disclosures were available on the agency's Web site, www.fdic.gov.

Requests for details on the forms available from the FDIC and requests for copies of those forms should be addressed to

Federal Deposit Insurance Corporation
Data Request Section
550 17th Street, NW
Washington, DC 20429

Office of Thrift Supervision

The Office of Thrift Supervision (OTS) is responsible for regulating savings and loan associations (S&Ls) and other home mortgage lenders. State S&Ls are chartered by their respective state agencies but also have the option of joining the Federal Home Loan Bank System, a related agency.

S&Ls that issue stock must supply proxy information to the OTS. Like other bank regulatory agencies, the OTS (www.ots.treas.gov) requires that savings and loans file semiannual reports on member institutions' income and condition. In addition to basic financial data like that provided in reports filed with the OCC and the FDIC, these reports also show consultant and legal fees, advertising expenses, and reimbursements.

To request access to OTS filings, contact
Office of Thrift Supervision
U.S. Department of the Treasury
1700 G Street, NW
Washington, DC 20552

Home Mortgage Disclosure Act (HMDA)

A bank must make available a form detailing the number of its mortgage and home improvement loans, their amounts, and the geographic locations in which they were made. Together with the CRA statements, these documents can be used to determine whether a bank has illegally discriminated against certain residents of a particular community on the basis of race, income, or neighborhood (a practice often known as "redlining"). Evidence of redlining can be used to challenge bank applications for new branch licenses.

State Banking Commissions

State-chartered banks are regulated by state banking commissions. Laws vary from state to state, but most commissions collect detailed reports on bank income and condition. State banking commissions may also collect information on consumer complaints and stock transactions and are almost always located in the state capital. For a list of state banking commissions and a summary of their data disclosure policies, see pp. 437–440 of *Lesko's Info-Power III* (1997 edition). Find your state commission's Web site (if any) through the government option on www.yahoo.com.

Finding Information on Government Contractors

Few business activities produce a more detailed public record than sales of goods or services to the government. At the federal level, the *Commerce Business Daily* publishes listings of all U.S. government contracts and subcontracts, civilian and military, worth more than $25,000. Whether the contract is at the federal, state, or local level, a transaction with the government will result in creation of the following documents, most or all of which are available to the public:

- Lists of government contracts, dollar values, and products provided.
- Bid specifications, detailing the goods or services to be provided and the exact conditions of delivery.
- The actual bids and the government agencies' evaluations of same. (Bid documents may

contain details on company operations and plant capacity designed to show that the company is capable of producing the required product.)

- Government audits of the contracting company. (At the federal level, the General Accounting Office has broad authority to audit activities of any government agency and its contractors. Call (202) 512-6000 or search the agency's Web site (www.gao.gov) to find out if your target company's government business activities have ever been examined. In addition, virtually all federal agencies have an inspector general whose audit reports—or summaries thereof—are usually available to the public.

You can get lists of companies that, because of bad behavior, have been barred from government contracting.

- The U.S. Department of Labor's Office of Federal Contract Compliance Programs publishes a list of contractors ineligible for federal contracts. Phone (202) 219-9475.
- The General Services Administration issues a monthly *Consolidated List of Debarred, Suspended and Ineligible Contractors.* Order it from the Government Printing Office, listed at the end of this section.

  ❏ *Lesko's Info-Power III* (pp. 823–833, 1997 edition) offers valuable information on contracting, plus a list of state procurement offices. Contact the office in any state with which your company has contracts for details on public access to contract documents.

  ❏ You can search *Commerce Business Daily* back to 1995 free at www.govcon.com. All you must do is register at the site.

  ¢¢¢ The last 90 days of contract announcements can be searched electronically on

CompuServe. (Type GO CBD.) Cost: $1/search plus $2/full listing.

$$$ Nexis and Dialog offer *Commerce Business Daily* online for 1982 to the present. You can also arrange for Dialog to send you an electronic alert each time the publication mentions a particular company.

$$$ If you must have paper, you can subscribe to *Commerce Business Daily* for $208 a year. Order from

Superintendent of Documents
U.S. Government Printing Office
Washington, DC 20402
(202) 512-1800

Researching Foreign Investment and International Trade

Increasingly, activists find themselves in disputes involving foreign companies and multinationals that have "globalized" their operations so thoroughly that they are literally stateless.

Profiling such companies poses special problems, since U.S. reference sources may have only limited information on foreign parent, subsidiary, or affiliate companies. Yet understanding their operations around the world is crucial because it may help your organization build broader coalitions, find overseas points of vulnerability, or even challenge a company's legal right to conduct certain operations.

  ❏ The Internet has made researching overseas companies much easier than it once was. Almost every Internet service provider offers links and directories to sites in other countries. **A marvelous place to start your research is** www.corporateinformation.com, **which has links to business-oriented sites in dozens of countries.**

$/¢ CompuServe offers extensive links to European business resources. So does the *Financial Times'* Internet operation, www.ft.com.

Annual Reports

Global Research Company (1502 South Big Bend Blvd., St. Louis, MO 63117, phone (314) 647-0081, fax (314) 647-4001) maintains an extensive library of foreign corporate annual reports and other documents and will search for overseas reports and documents not in their files.

Directories

Directory of Foreign Firm Operations in the United States. Published by the World Trade Academy Press in New York, this is a useful reference source. This multivolume set can be found in larger public or university libraries.

D&B—Dun's European Market Identifiers and *International Market Identifiers.* This series of electronic directories offers basic information (company name, address, phone number, sales, number of employees, executives' names) for at least 2.4 million European, Asian, African, Canadian, and Latin American companies.

$$$ Available on Dialog and CompuServe. Regular users of this service should note that the Dialog version is less expensive and offers a wider range of search options.

Government Experts and Information Sources

The Department of Commerce maintains a vast information gathering and dissemination network that includes district offices in the United States, country and product experts in Washington, and business specialists stationed abroad. For many of these experts, giving out information is an important part of their official responsibilities. U.S. businesses use this network constantly to get up-to-date information on prospects for buying, selling, or investing abroad; foreign firms tap into the network to get data on U.S. markets and investment potential. But these experts work for all Americans—not just the corporations—and most of them are more than willing to share their knowledge with your organization. Although some of the information they receive is "classified" or "proprietary," most of it is available to the public.

You can call these experts for advice on determining where a U.S. company sells its products abroad, information on the size, structure, and other investments of a foreign-owned employer, and much more. If you know the other countries in which your target company operates, you can contact the U.S. "Overseas Commercial Counselor" in that country for information.

The broadest business expert network is maintained by the U.S. Department of Commerce. But the government also maintains a staff of specialized trade experts in areas including mining (U.S. Bureau of Mines), agricultural trade (U.S. Department of Agriculture), and oil and gas (U.S. Department of Energy). Most states also maintain international trade offices, which can be useful in helping you track overseas investments by companies headquartered in the state or foreign investors operating in the state.

❏ Phone an expert and ask for the information you need! Experts are used to talking with information seekers and may answer your questions on the phone or direct you to a useful reference publication. You'll find a detailed list of international trade experts in *Lesko's Info-Power III* (pp. 843–860, 1997 edition). Or phone the public affairs office of the Commerce Department's International Trade Administration at (202) 482-0543.

❏ Check out the Internet offerings of relevant government agencies. Find an exhaustive list of links to federal agencies at www.lib.lsu.edu/gov/fedgov.html.

$/¢ If you don't find anything helpful there, go to FedWorld, www.fedworld.gov, a collection of databases from the National Technical Information Service (NTIS), an agency of the Commerce Department. You can access many of the same NTIS databases on CompuServe or Dialog.

❏ More than 1,400 university and public libraries across the country serve as federal depository libraries. You can visit any one of them to examine a wide range of trade-related (and other) U.S. government publications. (Even a university that restricts public use of its general collection is required to provide free access to depository materials.)

Other Information Sources

The International Labor Rights Education and Research Fund (110 Maryland Avenue, NE, Washington, DC 20002, phone (202) 544-7198) works closely with the Labor movement and has produced many publications on labor rights violations around the world. Its publications and expert staff members may be able to help you identify and analyze labor rights violations by foreign affiliates of your target company. They can also explain how the labor rights provisions in some international trade laws and treaties may sometimes be used to challenge imports of products produced abroad under unfair labor conditions.

❏ *Peacenet* carries a wide range of international news services, with special emphasis on the developing world. It maintains online news and discussion areas specifically focusing on international labor rights. Some (but not all) of these news sources are organized as electronically searchable databases that you can use to find information on the overseas activities of your target company. Its URL is www.igc.org.

Sources for Investigating Individuals

Many of the same sources recommended above for researching companies are useful for investigating individuals. This section will discuss some individual-specific uses for those sources and then introduce some resources expressly for researching individuals.

Property Records

Note the history of the individual's real estate transactions—any partnerships, trusts, or unexplained shifts of ownership. Is the person's property heavily mortgaged? Are there liens on it? Does the individual owe back taxes? Is the property worth a surprising amount?

In some cases, you may want to check property owned by the individual's relatives. In other cases, you may want to look beyond the obvious—the individual's home turf—for recent property acquisitions. In *The Reporter's Handbook* (p. 431), Steven Weinberg recounts some clever ways local politicians and bureaucrats can take payoffs, among them real estate transactions near the home base of out-of-town developers.

Courthouse Records

When you're researching an individual's legal history, you'll do best to let your tactical objective guide you.

If you've heard rumors that school board member Jones has a substance abuse problem, you might check local courts to see if she's had DUI (driving under the influence) convictions. A good way to get an idea of an individual's assets is to find a divorce, probate, or bankruptcy case, although almost any case could contain references to property. Adversarial parties in cases you turn up might be eager to give you additional information.

If you're looking for evidence of a person's shady past, you might need to look for old cases—fraud prosecutions or lawsuits—where he used to live. For example, when a pro-landlord faction attempted to take over a tenant organization, an investigation of the faction's candidate for the board revealed that he was a disbarred lawyer who had gone to jail for cheating a client. When leaflets with this information were put under doors, he withdrew from the election. The investigator did not just start an open-ended search of court records. Someone remembered the story and the investigator documented it.

We must add to this story that the event raised a serious ethical question and split the organization. Many people felt that it was improper to distribute such information under doors in a person's own home, and they felt badly for his family. Consider this carefully.

$/¢ You can find many records on individuals on KnowX, www.KnowX.com.

Other Courthouse Records

Often, especially in rural counties, you'll be able to find all the above records in the county courthouse. In more urban counties, you'll probably have to visit several buildings. As you go, check the following records for information on the individual you're investigating.

Other Records of Personal Property. These records differ widely from state to state. In some places, lists of automobiles are kept; in others, financial assets are also listed.

Voter Registration Records. A surprising amount of information can be found here. In New York City, for example, a registration record available to the public will show a person's address, apartment number, home phone number, employer at date of registration, age, previous address, citizenship status, mailing address if different from home address, date of registration, and party enrollment, as well as the person's signature. The reason for cancellation of registration is also noted (e.g., criminal conviction). There is also a list of all the elections in which the person voted.

Such information could enhance many types of investigations. Electoral candidates have used voter registration data to show that opponents actually lived outside the district, previously belonged to another party, or hadn't bothered to vote in major races.

Directories

There are directories for virtually everything. "Who's Who" type directories have become a big business. The books are produced to be sold not only to libraries but also to all the people listed. Reference librarians are often happy to advise and help you find material in these books. Many can also be found on the Internet, using a search engine or your local library's home page.

Kline's Guide to American Directories. This is a very useful list of about 5,000 other directories. It tells you what to look for in the library. You will never actually consult most of these directories, which include obscure listings such as companies that preshrink textiles.

City Directories. These are published for many medium-sized cities. Polks and Coles are two of many companies that publish them. They list addresses, phone numbers, businesses, spouses, and other household members.

Who's Who. Biographical information volunteered by the person listed is found in this famous book. The information usually includes spouses and family members, occupation, married names of children and their spouses, education, club membership, military service, honors, and religious affiliation. The major publisher is Marquis (much of the Marquis series is available on the Dialog database and on CompuServe, as part of its larger biographical database, reached by typing GO BIOGRAPHY), but there are many others. Among the many volumes are

- *Who's Who in America*
- *Who's Who in the East (West, South, Southwest, Midwest)*
- *Who's Who of American Judges*
- *Who's Who in World Jewry*
- *Who's Who of American Women*
- *Who's Who in Commerce*
- *Who's Who in Banking*
- *Who's Who in American Politics*
- *Who's Who in Insurance*
- *Who's Who in American College and University Administration*

Lawyers: *Martindale and Hubbell Law Directory*. This directory is organized by state and county and lists lawyers by name and by firm. It also sometimes lists representative clients of the firm. (Before the laws were liberalized in some states, this was the only form of advertising lawyers had.)

This directory can be useful for tracking down judges' previous connections, although back issues rarely remain on library shelves. It also helps identify conflicts of interest of lawyers running for office or appointed to public bodies. In most states, the majority of the legislators are lawyers, and it is often helpful to know what firm a person comes from and who the other partners are.

❏ Martindale-Hubbell's Web site, www.martindale.com, gives some information on lawyers for free. Your state's bar association probably has at least some information on the Internet; phone and ask for the URL.

Social Registers and Blue Books. These contain information on rich people.

Foundation Directories: *National Data Book of Foundations, Foundation Directory, Foundation Reports*. The *Data Book* lists all 27,000 U.S. foundations. The *Directory*, a listing of nearly 7,000 of the largest U.S. foundations, contains an index of their directors, as well as descriptions of each organization's purpose and financial situation. It also contains an index of their directors. In addition, many foundations produce annual reports telling to whom grants were given.

A non-profit organization, The Foundation Center, operates 123 cooperative collections of foundation material located in the United States, Canada, Mexico, and other parts of the world. The collections include copies of Internal Revenue Service Form 990-PF (see below). In addition, they contain information on area foundations. Some have a complete collection of materials on all foundations. For the collection nearest you, call (800) 424-9836, or write

The Foundation Center
79 5th Ave.
New York, NY 10003

Citizen organizations usually use the *Foundation Directory* to write grant applications, but the index of directors is also good for tactical investigations. It sometimes leads to discovering conflicts of interest. Foundations with large assets but small grant outlays, for example, may be giving a hint that corporate money is being hidden from the tax collector, especially if they are family controlled.

When opponents release a harmful study to the press, the article may indicate that it was paid for by a particular foundation grant. You will want to know who is behind that foundation. Foundation reports are helpful when you suspect that a corporation or industry group is financing a "public interest" organization that lobbies against you. All of this is helpful in locating secondary targets.

IRS Form 990-PF. All non-profits must file annually. Form 990-PF lists officers, trustees, grants, and assets.

J.R. Taft Publications: *Foundation Reporter, Trustees of Wealth*, and *Corporate Reporter* provide additional information on foundations.

Hometown Newspapers

Small-town papers are the ideal sources of information on individuals who aren't rich or famous. (They can also be unbeatable sources on small local companies.)

For example, a nationwide strike had received the support of the leaders of many major religious denominations. A committee aiding the strikers was arranging phone calls from the religious leaders to company board members of the same denomination. When they were unable to find a religious affiliation listed for one board member, they checked his name through his hometown newspaper and came up with a news story on his father's funeral. From that report, they were able to trace the family's religious background.

Even if a small paper has gone online (which you can find out at www.newspaperlinks.com), its archives are seldom indexed and almost never included in online databases. If you need old news stories, the best place to get them is from the paper itself. All papers maintain indexed files of all their articles. They are under no obligation to allow you to use them, however. Relations with a friendly reporter can help a great deal if the newspaper isn't forthcoming.

Small-Town Libraries

Many small libraries keep "vertical files" of newspaper clippings on local people, businesses, and issues that affect the community. If they don't have a file on your research target, they will have high stacks of the local papers for you to search the old-fashioned way—page by page.

Other Specialized Research Topics

At both state and federal levels, a wide range of regulatory agencies monitor company performance and maintain files on companies that violate laws and guidelines. Space does not permit us to list all these agencies in detail.

Consumer Protection

A number of state and federal agencies maintain records about companies or products that have engendered consumer complaints. When available, they can be very useful in building public support against the target company by helping you document patterns of consumer abuse.

❏ For a list of State Consumer Protection agencies and details on data availability, see *Lesko's Info-Power III* (pp. 108–116, 1997 edition). Good starting points for Internet research are Consumer's Union (www.consumersunion.org), Consumer Action (www.consumeraction.org), the Better Business Bureau (www.bbb.org), and the home pages of your state attorney general and county district attorney.

Environmental Protection

Environmental impact studies are often required before companies may build or expand manufacturing facilities. These studies will contain information about water supply and quality, air quality, type of discharges, records of complaints, violations, and enforcement actions. They can often be used to generate opposition from community groups and citizens to a proposed facility. Court and regulatory findings regarding environmental violations can also provide organizing leverage. Environmental monitoring agencies gather vast amounts of potentially useful information. This brief list will merely scratch the surface.

❏ The U.S. Nuclear Regulatory Commission's NUDOCs system offers free online access to inspection reports, violation notices, and other records covering organizations that use radioactive material, including 110 nuclear power plants and 23,000 hospitals, universities, and other NRC licensees. It also contains a wide range of congressional materials, hearing transcripts, and scientific data. For an access password, contact the Office of Information and Resource Management, U.S. Nuclear Regulatory Commission, MNBB 6219, Washington, DC 20555.

❏ The U.S. Department of Energy's TRANSET database provides access to shipment and accident records, from 1991 to the present, for nuclear waste and other radioactive materials. For free access, contact Division 6321, Sandia National Laboratories, Box 5800, Albuquerque, NM 87185.

❏ Peacenet and its sister system, Econet (www.igc.org), offer more than a dozen news services and discussion "conferences" on environmental issues, with a strong emphasis on monitoring and reporting corporate abuses. Additionally, Econet has an archive of older material.

❏ Toxnet, a set of nine databases that comprise the Toxicology Data Network, is available through Medlars (www.cisti. nrc.ca/cisti/eps/medlar_e.html). Within Toxnet, you will find valuable research tools such as the Toxic Release Inventory—a record of toxic chemical releases since 1987—organized by company, location, and year.

Occupational Safety and Health

Several services now offer electronic access to the past five years of Occupational Safety and Health Administration violation records.

❏ Medlars, the National Library of Medicine's system of more than 30 medical databases, at www.cisti.nrc.ca/cisti/eps/medlar_e.html.

❏ You can do a quick search for violations by entering a target company's name at OSHA's "library": www.osha.gov/readingroom.html.

$/¢ For background, CompuServe's Health Database Plus (GO HLTDB) has dozens of publications, including some specializing in occupational safety and health, which you can search for free. You pay $1 each for articles you read or retrieve.

$$$ A more extensive collection of health-related journals can be found on Paperchase (GO PAPERCHASE), which, on CompuServe, costs $12 an hour, plus $18 and up per article. Dialog, Lexis-Nexis, and Westlaw all offer some access to OSHA files.

Conclusion

Tactical investigation provides the ammunition for direct action organizing. The concept of tactical weakness and the skill in finding it need to be learned by all organizers and leaders in citizen organizations. Often an organization will have one person who does the investigative work. This is a lost opportunity because many can actually participate in it and, in doing so, build leadership. In fact, investigative work isn't limited to people with formal education. In a Chicago public housing project, tenants gathered up paint chips from their apartments, labeled them in little plastic bags, and took them to a meeting of the Chicago Housing Authority. There they demanded that the chips be tested for lead paint. This was a tactical investigation in every sense of the word. Evidence was collected, and a public agency was forced to analyze it. It was also a fine tactic that resulted in the apartments being painted for the first time in many years. The integration of tactical investigation and direct action has proven to be a particularly powerful combination for building citizen power.

Metro Seniors in Action members raise money with a Rock-a-Thon in the Daley Plaza, Chicago.

PART III
Support for Organization

21

The grassroots fundraising that your members do in their own communities is an integral part of building an organization. Not only is it a source of money that comes virtually without restrictions on its use, but grassroots fundraising gives people a sense of their own power. Leaders develop when they raise funds to support their own organization. Members and leaders feel a great deal more power when they raise $10,000 through events than when one person writes a grant proposal and a foundation contributes $10,000, although that is also welcome.

Funding Sources

Raising funds for your organization can be done in many ways, including proposal writing, large-donor solicitation, direct-mail appeals, canvassing, government and foundation grants, and grassroots fundraising. Most organizations find that they need a diversified funding base to sustain them over a period of time. As the following discussion shows, it is risky to depend too heavily on any one type of fundraising, except grassroots fundraising.

Funding Sources

The Fundamentals of Grassroots Fundraising

Grassroots Fundraising Ideas

Grassroots Fundraising

Government or Foundation Fundraising

In the early 1980s, Richard Viguerie, the New Right direct-mail guru, claimed that the number-one priority of the New Right was to defund the "Left." First, the Reagan Administration and then the Gingrich Congress slashed budgets for programs that provided funds for community organizations such as VISTA, Community Action Programs, legal services, and social service outreach programs. Some groups that depended primarily upon these funds had to close their doors. Others were severely crippled. The days in which groups could depend upon government funds are long past.

Many organizations receive another form of government money. They attempt to combine organizing or advocacy with providing a direct service, such as a health education program, for which they have a local government contract. There are two reasons why this almost always turns out to be a bad idea. The first is that you can't organize against your funders. Groups quickly find that their contracts are held hostage to their good behavior in politics. The second reason is that once an organization becomes skilled at providing services and negotiating contracts, that becomes the easiest way to ensure that the budget is covered. Getting money for organizing is much harder.

Over a few years, what started out as a direct action organization develops a staff and a management that sees service as its primary activity. The organizers get shunted off to the side and are viewed by the rest of the staff as troublemakers who threaten their funding and jobs.

Although foundation grants have supported most of the important work of community organizations and state and national coalitions, it is essential that organizations not become solely dependent upon just a few foundation sources. Some foundations are faddish in their giving, funding campaign finance reform this year and "capacity building" the next. It's great if your issue happens to be "in," but remember, it will soon be "out." The other enormously frustrating aspect of foundation giving is that the foundations constantly seek "new" projects and give "seed" money rather than providing ongoing general support. Even if you have a great program, after two or three years you usually have to figure out ways to describe it as something "new," or you have to shift funds to new (possibly less significant) programs.

Too many groups find themselves "funder-driven," chasing foundation dollars by continually changing programs. Worse, as fads change in the foundation world, new groups are constantly created that compete with the older organizations for staff, members, and funding of all kinds. In recent years, social change foundations have become increasingly directive, very often taking on an issue, deciding both the policy objectives and strategy, and then doing what amounts to hiring citizen groups to carry out the foundation's plan. There have also been an increasing number of quasi foundations that basically organize money. Having no endowments of their own, they get the support of several large foundations to carry out a specific issue campaign and then act as brokers, funding citizen groups with the other foundations' money while calling the shots on policy. Some foundations, although they fund public interest advocacy, have conservative boards that foster pro-corporate measures. In spite of all of this, foundation fundraising remains a major part of every organization's budget.

Grassroots Fundraising

According to the American Association of Fund-Raising Counsel, in a typical year, about 81 percent of U.S. charitable contributions comes from individuals, 7 percent from bequests, and only 7 percent from foundations and 5 percent from corporations. Thus, 88 percent comes from individuals. Not only does most money come from people, but 85 percent of all money given comes from people with incomes of $50,000 or less. Of course, charitable contributions and social change contributions are not exactly the same thing, but these statistics help to explain how it is possible that so many of our groups have successfully built a grassroots funding program based on low to moderate income families. However little income people may have, they still try to give to what they think is important. (There is a Jewish tradition that when you give someone charity, you must include enough so that the person can, in turn, give to someone else. In this view, giving creates dignity and the feeling of being a part of the community, the loss of which is as harmful as going without food.)

Ideally, your organization should seek as much money as possible directly from its membership in dues, contributions, and grassroots fundraising events. Realistically, most organizations find that they must develop additional outside sources, such as foundations and large donor giving. For assistance and information on a variety of fundraising approaches, visit one of the reference collections or cooperating collections of The Foundation Center, headquartered at 79 Fifth Avenue, New York, NY 10003. These collections are located in over 100 cities, with at least one in each state. To check on locations and current information, call (800) 424-9836.

The Fundamentals of Grassroots Fundraising

Set a Goal

Work with your leaders to develop an annual budget. Often the budget categories suggested by accountants are not the most useful for giving leaders the kind of financial picture that will motivate them to raise money. They need to see the precise relationship between the program they want and the fundraising they must do.

Put up chart paper and start with the basics, such as rent, electricity, and training. (Yes, training!) Then, add in the salaries of non-program staff like clerical staff or the bookkeeper if you are fortunate enough to have such people.

After these basic expenses, make your budget into a campaign budget so that leaders can see the actual cost of the issue work they want the organization to do. List each of the issue campaigns or issue committees of the organization, and put down the costs in such a way that all of the remaining organizational expenses are allocated to an issue campaign. For each campaign include

- The total staff cost of the campaign. If there are three campaigns, you might say that each includes one-fifth of the Director's time and one-third of the organizer's time. Put down the total dollar amount for each campaign.
- Postage, mailing, and duplicating for the campaign.
- Travel and other special costs, such as committee meetings. Add in one-third of the cost of Lobby Day or the annual convention to the cost of the campaign.
- The phone bill, allocated between the campaigns.
- If you get free stuff, such as meeting space at the library, the cost if you had to rent it.

If the organization is planning to start an additional campaign, cost out that one as well, so the leaders can see how much they will need.

On a second sheet, put down all the organization's income. Include the cash value of in-kind contributions, such as office space or free meeting space. Then, list foundation grants, dues, contributions, proceeds from fundraisers, etc. If the group is deeply in debt, mention it, but budget only the amount that will have to be paid in the current year. Most organizations will find that there is a manageable shortfall on the income side, much of which can be made up with grassroots fundraising. The leaders will be rightfully impressed with the size of the total budget and with how much they have already raised. More important, they can now see the relationship between fundraising and issue campaigns in a way that people don't usually get from a typical treasurer's report.

Make a Fundraising Calendar

One of the benefits of grassroots fundraising is that you can control the timing of when you raise the funds. For many groups, the end of the summer is a tight financial time. If you know this, you can plan your grassroots fundraisers accordingly. You can also schedule special fundraising events at times of the year that are less hectic programmatically, although you may find that you raise the most money during your peak programmatic months.

Make a calendar of the coming year. Fill in regularly scheduled events, timing on grants and special appeals, holidays, heavy programmatic periods, and other relevant information. You can also plan fundraising events for times when your constituency has the most money. For example, the end-of-the-year events are difficult for most poor and working people because they are buying holiday gifts. (On the other hand, upper management types may have just received their year-end bonuses and be flush with cash.) Decide when you need money the most and the best times for your organization to hold grassroots fundraising events. By planning well in advance, you can recruit a solid core of people to serve on your fundraising committee(s).

Observe the Following Guidelines

Aim for Worthwhile Amounts. Sometimes when groups talk about grassroots fundraising, they think about small garage sales or bake sales. Grassroots fundraising certainly includes these, but it does not necessarily have to raise small amounts of money. Work with your leaders to raise $10,000 instead of $1,000, especially if it will take comparable amounts of effort. If a member will give one hour to raise money, what would you rather have that member do in the hour: bake cookies, sell $25 ads for the ad book, or sell one $1 raffle ticket? Of course, it doesn't quite work this way. Some people who are happy to bake would just die if they had to sell ads, and some will do all three things, so there does need to be a mix of activities. But often people raise small amounts because you ask them to do small things when, with the same effort, they could raise more.

Raise More Money Than You Spend! Just because another group made money on a certain project, don't assume that your group can. Carefully analyze why and how the other group made the money. For example, one senior organization annually brings in a large portion of its budget through a phone-a-thon. Active members call other seniors on their list and ask for contributions. Would this work for your group? It might very well work, but analyze the particulars. The seniors have sufficient volunteer callers; they can call during the day and reach other seniors who are home during the day. Will your members have to call in the evening when everyone is trying to get dinner on the table and help with the kids' homework, and will you be competing with all the professional telemarketing calls that come at the same hour? This is not to discourage phone-a-thons. They are a great way to raise money. It is just to say don't borrow any method from other organizations unless you really understand why it worked for them.

Study the Economics and Sociology of Selling Stuff. One of the biggest traps is assuming that groups can sell inexpensive items, such as candy, and make money. Groups that make big money selling things almost always have large numbers of willing sellers, usually children, whose parents buy much of the merchandise. Unless you have dozens of sellers, you may have trouble. On the other hand, many groups have made money from such activities. The key again is careful analysis. How many people will have to sell how many items each day to pay the basic costs and then reach a certain goal? Do you have one hundred members who can each sell two cookbooks a day for fourteen days? It means that each person will have to see at least twenty-eight potential customers, but since some of those will say no, the number of customers is closer to forty. The members of your group need to make an honest assessment of their own contacts.

When it comes to fundraising, a community or a workplace is like a little economy, a little village, all its own. Most community-minded people are raising money for their church, school, and organization all during the year. In every neighborhood, factory, and office, people are approaching their friends to buy something. The unwritten rule is that if you sell your organization's cookbook to a friend or co-worker for three dollars, you are obligated to buy something of comparable cost when your friend is raising money. If you sell eighty-four dollars worth of cookbooks at three dollars a book, that's like going into debt for three dollars to everyone you know (twenty-eight people). Each of the cookbook buyers will come around later to sell you their three dollars worth of school candy or raffle tickets. It would seem, therefore, to be much less trouble if you simply gave your organization the eighty-four dollars and didn't sell anything. But there is a problem with that. Friends from other groups would still come to you to sell you their stuff, and you would still buy it because that's the nice thing to do. If you have nothing to sell to them in return, then you have no way to "recover" the money that you give to them.

If you can sell the cookbooks to strangers on the street or sell ads to businesses, that would result in true income because you wouldn't have to return the favor by buying something later.

Otherwise, what you are really doing is participating in a big rotating pool of money that moves around the community or workplace from organization to organization depending on who is doing fundraising that week. While the cookbook money appears to be coming to your group from other people, it is in reality your own members' money. This is a fine and necessary part of community life. It means, however, that the amount of money your organization can raise by having members sell things to their friends is limited, in the long run, by how much your members can afford to give away themselves. It also shows the importance of raising money from strangers. A Chicago community group, for example, holds an annual street festival that draws huge crowds of people whom no one knows. This is perfect.

Avoid Events That Require a Large Up-Front Investment. Lots of groups have lost money on concerts in which they had to pay for a hall and a performer. The performer was good but not well enough known to draw the numbers needed to make money. Many groups have had cartons of T-shirts left over because someone overestimated the market. A raffle will rarely make more money because you purchase an expensive prize than it will if you give smaller prizes donated by local merchants. How much you make is determined more by the number of ticket sellers and less by the prize. (There are exceptions, such as the time that a Chicago group raffled off a Rolls Royce. But even here, the group almost lost its shirt by not having enough ticket sellers.) Once a project proves its ability to raise funds, you may be willing to invest more.

Raise Money for Your Issue, Not for Your Overhead. It is much easier to raise money to support a campaign to eliminate a tax on food or to defend social security than to raise money to pay the organization's debt or phone bill. In other words, don't have a rent party; have a party to raise money to send buses to the Capitol. By raising money around your program, you also publicize the issue and potentially recruit new volunteers. A New York City organization holding a rally on a popular community issue discovered that it could sell sponsorships. People, particularly local elected officials, each paid twenty-five dollars to be listed as a sponsor on the rally leaflet, of which several thousand were distributed. In fact, the leaflet had to be reprinted to include additional sponsors.

Have Fun. Lots of projects will raise money. Let people use their own creativity. If the members of the fundraising committee have fun planning and implementing their event, they are likely to get involved again and to draw others to work with them.

Build on Past Successful Events. Don't skip from project to project. Once you identify a fundraising idea that works, repeat it annually. Not only do you learn how to run it more efficiently, but your group becomes identified with that annual event, making it easier to promote.

It seems that groups take several years to learn how to tap their true market. Most groups find that their fundraising income increases dramatically for a few years and then tends to level off. Typically, a small organization that raises $5,000 the first year can raise $10,000 the second year and even $20,000 the third year. After that, the amount of money tends not to increase much. A good example of this process is the typical ad book campaign. In the first year, selling ads to neighborhood merchants is difficult because the members don't have the experience and there is no book to show. (You can make up a few sample pages on a computer.) In the second year, sellers can go back to the merchants, show them their own ads in the book, and ask them to renew. This is a much easier sell, and the base of ads on which to build becomes larger each year. Here's another example: Members of an organization in Nebraska decided to hold an art auction. They also invited their coalition partners to contribute art for a share of the proceeds. The first year, no one quite understood the project, but the auction itself was a fun event in the upstairs room of a local restaurant, and by the second year it had begun to be something people looked forward to.

In order to facilitate increasing funds from year to year, it is important to keep careful records of all expenses, contacts, vendors, and so forth. Immediately after an event, the planning committee should evaluate it and write down suggestions for the following year. These notes should be kept for use by the next year's committee.

Maintain High Ethical Standards. It is essential that your organization remain both rigorously honest in all of its fundraising and accountable to its constituents. If not, the group's image could be tarnished and its overall political effectiveness diminished. It is better to raise money steadily and develop a solid reputation than to lurch forward, leaving ethical questions in people's minds.

Build Leaders. Grassroots fundraising should not only raise money, it should also develop leaders. Joan Flanagan, author of *The Grass Roots Fundraising Book* (see the bibliography for more information), suggests selecting co-chairs for your fundraising committee. Have each co-chair recruit four or five people. Keep careful, measurable records on each person's contribution, such as who sells the most tickets or recruits the most participants. The co-chair whose group raises the most money should be given greater responsibilities, perhaps added to the board of directors, or given another important leadership role. The person who does the best among the group members should be asked to be the co-chair for the next year. Thus, you build in succession from year to

year and ensure that the best fundraisers are in leadership roles.

Budget Money to Raise Money. It is quite difficult to raise money without beginning with some. Budget some money. It not only is more realistic, but it also conveys to committee members how much you value and respect their work if you entrust them with funds.

Devote Organizational Time to Fundraising. All too often, groups treat fundraising like the ugly duckling, assuming no one will want to do it (at least no one in their right mind). Fundraising is discussed almost last on the agenda, after we've discussed all the "important" matters, again conveying that it is not valued as much as other contributions. Grassroots fundraising requires excellent leadership skills. Give fundraising and those who lead the efforts their due respect.

Follow the Religious Congregations

Without question, the religious congregations do the best grassroots fundraising. They follow many of the guidelines described above. Religious congregations have learned how to do the following:

Ask Frequently. Most religious congregations ask for money at least fifty-two times per year, and no one gets upset. Figure out ways to structure regular giving from your membership or constituency. Make sure that people are asked to contribute every time you have a public meeting. Most people can and will give regularly if asked.

Ask Volunteers. Religious congregations understand that their most active members will be their most active givers. Unfortunately, too many organizers want to separate volunteers from givers. Don't accept anyone saying "We can't ask our volunteers. They already give so much time." Volunteers who give time will also give money. The more volunteers you have, the more sources of regular givers you have as well. One very active member of a New York group couldn't stand the organization's office and kept urging a change. When the group finally found a new space, she appeared and paid for the moving van.

Instill the Expectation of Giving. Everyone who joins a religious congregation expects to contribute to it: The value of giving is instilled in membership. From the very beginning, try to instill this value in your members. Don't shy away from discussing funds. Talk about the topic openly and ask members to support the organization openly and regularly.

Ask Personally and Publicly. Many congregations have a committee of people who meet with each member and discuss what that person will "pledge" for the next year. Members are encouraged to tithe (set aside a tenth of their income) for the work of the congregation. Your group may not feel it can ask for a tithe, but consider asking for 1 percent or X dollars per week. Consider setting up a committee to visit all your members and ask them personally to contribute for the next year. Volunteer committees can do this in organizations with small memberships. Larger statewide organizations use professional phone canvassers to personally ask for support.

Not only should members be asked personally to provide support, they should also be recognized publicly. In some churches people are asked to bring their contributions to the front of the congregation. This "public" request is effectively used by politicians as well, though it is rarely seen in citizen organizations. In church and temple building campaigns, one frequently sees an outdoor "thermometer" measuring the congregation's progress toward reaching the fundraising goal. Similarly, we need to make our needs visibly known to the community.

Grassroots Fundraising Ideas

Ask at Every Opportunity. This is the easiest idea. Ask for money at every meeting.

Raffles. As long as your raffle prizes are donated or very cheap, it is hard to lose money. Consider holding a raffle in conjunction with other events, banquets, or programs as an extra moneymaker. (Please note that most states and some cities have laws regulating raffles.)

Food Tastings. Many community groups organize food tasting events in conjunction with neighborhood restaurants. People pay to try small samples of food. It's fun for community people and good promotion for the restaurants. This is particularly successful if your community has different ethnic restaurants. The food tasting events can be run in several ways. Your group can provide the space and charge a space fee to the restaurants that sell their samples. Other groups sell tickets and divide the proceeds with the restaurants. Either way, it's hard to lose money. A side benefit is that you develop good relationships with area restaurants.

You might also consider a special kind of food tasting, such as desserts or wines. A state representative in Seattle held "The Chocolate Challenge." Friends were asked to donate their favorite chocolate dessert, and the chocolate tasting affair was held at the home of another friend. Fancy chocolate truffles and champagne were purchased to supplement the donated chocolates. Guests were asked to donate $50 to the campaign. The invitations, designed like a candy bar, were printed on brown paper with silver lettering and wrapped in foil. The affair, both easy and fun, grossed about $3,000 and netted about $2,400. Such events should be scheduled later in the evening, around 8:00 P.M., in order to attract the "after-dinner crowd."

An organization in Iowa turned an annual wine tasting fundraiser into a weekend wine festival that now attracts people from neighboring cities and states and covers a large portion of the organization's budget.

Songs. Consider asking a community or congregational choir to volunteer to individually sing songs to people for Valentine's Day. Songs by phone can be sold for $15 each. In addition to the singers, you need a few good coordinators to publicize the "last-minute Valentine gift" and to organize who will call whom. Choir members will need to rehearse "My Funny Valentine" and other classics.

Phone-a-thons. Phone-a-thons directed to your membership base are an excellent way to raise funds. Expenses are low when volunteers call from donated phones. Many organizations have found that regular solicitation of their memberships by phone is their best source of membership fundraising.

Benefit Concerts and Performances. If the performers and the hall are donated, benefit performances are usually good fundraisers. If your benefit performance meets the guidelines suggested above (primarily, it doesn't require lots of up-front money), you should not have difficulties. Be sure to use some of the program time to promote your organization and provide visible leadership roles. To minimize your risks and maximize your profits, get a copy of *Note by Note: A Guide to Concert Productions.*

Dinners. Many organizations hold fundraising dinners because they are enjoyable as well as good sources of money. Unless the food is donated, in order to make a significant amount of money, you will have to charge a good deal more than the actual cost of the dinner. Most organizations try to sell whole tables (eight or ten seats) to allied organizations, corporations, unions, or neighborhood businesses. These contributors do not always fill their tables and will often allow you to use their seats to give discounted tickets to people who might have trouble affording the dinner. In addition to selling tables, most groups use a raffle or ad book to boost the overall income of the event. The usual way to get institutional contributors is to honor someone with institutional connections whose professional colleagues will then attend the dinner.

Organizations in which members are of low to moderate income often ask if dinner tickets should be priced so that the members can actually afford them. With the type of dinner held in a hotel or banquet hall, it is not expected that the profit from ticket sales will come primarily from the organization's own members. Rather, it must come from institutional supporters and businesses. Price the tickets high. You can always discount them for your members.

Many organizations are finding that they can get all of the financial and political benefits of a dinner without actually serving a meal. People will happily come for a cocktail party and hors d'oeuvres. You can give the same awards and hear the same speeches as at a dinner *and* get everyone home earlier, something people will greatly appreciate. Because the cost to you is substantially less than for a full dinner, the profit margin is usually higher.

Ads/Ad Books. Individuals like to see their names in print, and organizations and businesses have community relations and advertising budgets. Because of this, you can produce a successful ad book to be distributed at a dinner or other organizational function. Indeed, some money cannot be gotten any other way. Some local corporate managers have discretion over advertising budgets but are not allowed to simply give away money. Purchasing advertising from you is perfectly acceptable, while making a donation would raise questions.

The Connecticut Citizen Action Group (CCAG) has produced ad books for years and has raised up to $20,000 from its annual ad book. Leaders in local chapters across the state sell the ads. The book includes one-page descriptions of each chapter or region, one-page descriptions on each CCAG issue campaign, and the ads themselves. The ads are placed in three categories: (1) local businesses patronized by CCAG staff and leaders place ads ranging from $50 to $1,000; (2) organizational allies, such as unions, and politicians place ads in the same price range; and (3) CCAG leaders, members, friends, and even former staff place their names for fees of $10 to $25 per person. Approximately 2,000 books are printed and distributed at major CCAG events. Printing the books costs the organization approximately $3,000, but in recent years local unions have donated printing. CCAG discovered that more politicians will buy ads if the book is produced right before election time. The centerfold is sold at a premium price, as is the back cover. Some organizations will include specially priced gold or silver pages. Although it adds to the cost, all printing by progressive organizations should include the union label as a matter of principle.

Flowers. Consider selling flowers around holidays, such as lilies around Easter, poinsettias around Christmas, or potted plants for Mother's Day.

Rummage Sales. It's hard to lose money on a rummage sale because there are usually no overhead costs unless you set up an ongoing thrift store. A key factor in most rummage sales is the weather. If it's a nice day and you can display items outside, you will make more money than inside. Be sure, however, to analyze the use of your staff and volunteer time. If the rummage sale requires lots of time and earns small amounts of money, it may not be worth it. The real skill in running a rummage sale, which comes only with experience, is knowing when to start cutting prices. The goal is to end the sale with no rummage left over. For example, by the end of the day, used clothing that was going for a dollar an item is sold for a dollar a bag. Combine the sale with a raffle and a food table. You can get the food donated. Have "Toss the Beanbag" type games for children that offer a prize worth a few cents. (Goldfish die on the way home.) If the children are diverted, their parents are more likely to buy. Try to arrange for free entertainment; you can even treat the sale as a talent show. The idea is that the longer people stay, the more they will spend.

Baby Contests. The Baltimore NAACP chapter has raised large amounts of money on an annual baby contest, called the "Human Dolls on Parade for Freedom." (Children are eligible up to five years old.) At one time the organization grossed $60,000 and cleared approximately $50,000. Not bad for a baby contest! Most babies are sponsored by a church or organization. A few babies are entered as "independents." Votes are sold at $.25 per vote or $5.00 per book of votes. The baby who gets the most votes wins a fancy cup with an inscription, a $500 savings bond, and his or her picture on a billboard (which is donated by a local company). The baby winner's church gets a special plaque. All "serious candidates" (those who bring in over $200 worth of votes) get their pictures published, with their parents, in *The Baltimore Afro-American*. The space is donated by the paper, but the NAACP covers the cost of the photographs. This Freedom Baby contest is an annual event, and the church plaque has become prestigious for a congregation to receive.

Bingo. Depending on your area, bingo may be a potential source of funds for your group. Some groups run their own bingo games, while others band together to run them. After you have reviewed the potential market, check your state laws. Bingo is tightly monitored by the state government. For years, the Midwest Academy bingo games helped underwrite the cost of low-income participants at training sessions. In order to make the program work effectively, you must find a dedicated core of volunteers who love bingo.

House Parties, Coffees, and Similar Events. The idea for all of these comes from the basic Tupperware Party. Someone volunteers their home and, either alone or with two or three friends, invites relatives, friends, and acquaintances to come and hear a short talk about your group's issue. The invitation also explains that the event is to raise money. "Bring your checkbook. I know that when you hear how serious a problem this is, you will want to contribute to the solution." As with all events, invitations should be mailed and followed up with phone calls. The program usually consists of a short talk, a discussion, letter writing or petition signing, an appeal for funds, and an appeal for people to host

similar parties. The fund appeal should be made by the host or hostess. An allied state representative or member of the City Council may appreciate a chance to speak and will draw more people. Longtime fundraiser Judy Maslen of the Connecticut Citizen Action Group observes that some people will give money at functions similar to this who haven't given in other ways. It seems they just like the social aspect. She has found that once such people's names are added to a donor list, they will give again in response to a mail or phone appeal. We don't usually think of house parties as list builders, but they can be.

Conclusion

The above list of suggestions is not meant to be comprehensive. There are many other ways to raise funds from your constituency that will be fun, effective, and leadership building. Following the guidelines, choose a project that people want to develop and try it. If it works, keep doing it!

22

O rganizers need to be strong in four
areas:

- Envisioning a future that they want to help
  shape
- People skills
- Strategy and the ability to develop strong
  organizing plans
- Basic administration

To be successful, good organizers can't lose
track of details. They have to call people back
when they say they will. They have to remember
to thank people. They have to find papers from
six months ago. Basically, organizers have to get
control of their work.

This chapter is devoted to administrative systems for organizers. If you have a system that
works, keep it; but if not, consider trying some of
these suggestions.

Keeping Track of Tasks

One of the most frustrating aspects of an organizer's work is the need to keep track of millions
of detailed tasks as well as the "big picture" strategy and plan. The following system should help.
The system combines three time tracking tools—

Controlling Your Work:
Administrative Systems

a timeline, calendar, and "To Do" list—into one overall method.

1. *Project Timeline.* This usually takes the form of the huge wall calendar that shows several months or the whole year. Small routine items should not go on the timeline, but major projects should. Put down all major events and then work backwards through the stages of preparation so, for example, you would write "Prepare agenda for planning meeting" about a week before the meeting and a week after the mailing goes out. Preparing the agenda includes all the subtasks of talking it over with the leadership, perhaps having a smaller meeting about it, writing it, duplicating it, etc. You don't need to put the small tasks on the timeline, you are just blocking out the time in which to do them. In this way, you can assess when you can add other work and when you cannot. A timeline also helps an organizer work with others in terms of what work can be added and what dropped.

2. *Your Calendar.* Your calendar is different from the timeline. The timeline includes general categories of things that need to be done within a week, such as "get out a mailing" or "do promotional work." The calendar, of course, notes particular meetings or people you are supposed to call back on a certain day at a certain time. It is also your main tool for scheduling. An ever-increasing number of calendars, schedulers, and personal organizers are on the market. Any will do. The best ones allow you a full page with hours for each day plus a monthly summary. The main point is that you have just *one*. Too often an organizer will have a desk calendar, a pocket calendar, an electronic organizer that was a birthday present, and a scheduler on the computer. This is a potential disaster. You will inevitably put down a meeting in one place and then look in another. Throw out all but one. Avoid those generic calendars that don't come with printed dates and you have to write them in. Even Julius Caesar got it wrong some of the time.

3. *Daily "To Do" List.* Your daily or weekly "To Do" list is compiled by consulting the above two items. It is the basic guide to your day. Keep it where you can see it all day. Go through your calendar in the morning or the night before, and mark down the specific meetings or calls that need to be made. Review your campaign timeline and put down the specific tasks that need to be done that day. Include all the routine responsibilities

Sample Timeline

This is a timeline for a community organizer working on a large community event to be held in the first week of February. The organizer is holding organizing/recruitment meetings with block clubs and large building committees in the community.

Week of Jan. 1

Arrange for agenda planning committee.

Call people for turnout/recruitment committee.

Staff meeting—Wednesday.

Set dates for organizing meetings and committees for next four weeks.

Week of Jan. 8

Hold agenda planning committee meeting.

Hold turnout/recruitment meeting.

Draft revised brochure.

Board meeting—Thursday.

Hold two organizing meetings.

Week of Jan. 15

Do follow-up to meetings.

Do prep work for next round of meetings.

Staff meeting—Wednesday.

Hold three organizing meetings.

Week of Jan. 22

Hold next agenda planning committee meeting.

Hold next turnout/recruitment meeting.

Send press advisory for event.

Recruit volunteers to bring refreshments.

Set dates for next week's organizing meetings.

Week of Jan. 29

Hold final turnout/recruitment and agenda meetings.

Make press follow-up calls.

Review presentations with leaders.

Staff meeting—Wednesday.

Prepare materials for board meeting.

Hold two organizing meetings.

Week of Feb. 5

Do last-minute details for event.

Hold event.

Do follow-up to event, including thank you notes to leaders.

Staff meeting—Wednesday.

Call all senior clubs and congregations in area.

---

that require time. Write down addresses, phone numbers, amounts of money, and materials you will need for the tasks and any notes about who to see and what to say. Carry over undone tasks from previous "To Do" lists. If you have too much to do, figure out with your supervisor what should be cut or postponed. Behind the "To Do" list, keep lists of the various items you want to talk about with people. This way, you're not constantly interrupting people with numerous phone calls, nor will you forget to tell them things.

Make sure that when you accomplish a task on your "To Do" list, you cross it out to get a feeling of accomplishment. In order to have the satisfaction of crossing out items, some organizers have been known to write down things that weren't originally on their "To Do" list but that they did anyway.

Computer Programs

Many new programs are available for organizing time and projects. They will even flash a reminder and ring a bell. Some people swear by them; others swear at them. Some think it is best to use a paper system that won't break down and have to be sent off for repairs. Those who use computer schedulers and electronic organizers learn really fast that they only work if you keep a backup. They will crash—it is only a matter of time—and the longer it takes for the first crash, the bigger the problem you will have. Back them up!

Steve Max has been known to use the ultimate low-tech solution: a clothesline strung above his desk with notes attached with clothespins. Post-its may be the modern "high-tech" equivalent. If you don't know what a clothespin is, ask your grandparents. [I now have a Post-it program in my computer. S.M.]

Keeping Track of Paper

Most people need some sort of filing system. If you can find paper quickly, then your system is probably working. If you can't, then you need to find a new system or use the system you established. The purpose of any filing system is to *retrieve* items, not to file them. Three types of file systems are used by organizers: tickler files, issue/project files, and daily files.

Tickler Files

A tickler file in arranged in chronological order. It can be weekly or monthly or whatever works for you. People place information in the file to remind them of activities that need to be done by a certain date. At the start of each week or each month, look in the file to see what matters need to be attended to at that time.

For example, your lobbyist registration report form or the application for a sound permit go in the tickler file. So do the forms for foundation reports or, when there is no form, a note telling you that a certain report is due in two weeks. Some groups have separate foundation tickler files, which include grant applications as well as reports. Tickler files only work if you check them at the appropriate times. You will even wish that you had stuck that birthday card for your spouse in the file. Of course, if you could remember to do that, you wouldn't need the file in the first place. If you use a good combination of the calendar, timeline, and "To Do" lists, you probably don't need a tickler file system at all.

Issue/Project Files

Organizers develop dozens of files on particular issues and projects. It is usually easier to find items if you can divide your files into basic categories. For example, if you have a four-drawer file cabinet, you might put everything related to a specific organizing campaign in one drawer, organizational/office items in another (budgets, personnel policies, and internal memos), material from and about organizations that you work with in a third drawer, and background on general issues and elected officials in the last drawer. In each drawer, most file items should be in alphabetical order and then in chronological order. So, information regarding your campaign on school financing goes under "S," and within that folder add new information in the front and throw out old information from the back. If you hold lots of meetings or training sessions, you might want a series of files in chronological order. By making groupings of files, you can get to the right file drawer quickly. It almost doesn't matter what system you use as long as you have a system.

Two-thirds of the stuff you save will never be used again, and of that, most will never even be seen again. It will simply be tossed. It is always better to know who can give you current information on issues and programs, than to save stuff. There are a few exceptions.

- When you get the first glimmer of interest in an issue, start a newspaper-clipping file. These are a great source of newsletter material, quotations, and the correct spelling of names, and they can help locate allies, targets, and additional sources of information.
- File anything that appears on local elected officials, including all their campaign literature. You can use it to remind them of past commitments.
- Keep every scrap of paper, including all correspondence that comes *out* of your office and pertains to any issue campaign. File it by campaign. This is partly a defensive measure as questions may later be raised about how funding was used, what your spokesperson actually said on a certain date, whether you were within IRS guidelines, and so forth. These files can also be helpful for orienting new staff, writing articles about the campaign, and getting a degree if you go back to school. Some organizations get a very large three-ring notebook for each campaign and keep everything in that.
- If local papers print election returns by district, file those results. You can always get them from the Board of Elections, but if you are looking for the vulnerabilities of a target or a place to do voter registration, it is more convenient to have the material on file.

What about the computer as a filing system? After all, so much information is available online. Still, if you do heavy-duty writing of articles, reports, testimony or legislation, there is still nothing like being able to spread all the source material out on your desk (or the floor) where you can look it all over. For that reason, it actually makes sense to print out computer files and put them in with the rest of the paper. (Some people will consider this to be counterrevolutionary.)

As the number of useful Internet addresses (URLs) grows, filing these takes some thought. Offices with older computers tend to have older versions of Web browsers, which simply store URLs in a "Favorites" list with no subdivisions. If that is what you have, replace it. New versions can usually be downloaded free. Because URLs take up relatively little space and the Web is less than instantaneous, save addresses in order to avoid visiting more pages than you have to on the way to what you need. For example, don't file just the address for the home page of your legislature. Also file the address of the committee that deals with your issue and the address of the page that has the text of the bill in which you are interested. Go directly to what you want rather than viewing many layers of a Web site. If you do store lots of addresses, be sure to delete ones that are no longer needed, or move them to a catchall file, as the lists can easily get too large to be useful.

Take full advantage of your e-mail program's ability to file the messages you receive. Folders and subfolders can be set up for campaigns, issues, and individuals just as in a conventional file drawer, but a surprisingly small number of people use this function. As with paper, the tendency is to put everything into the In Box until it is too full to be useful.

Remember that your computer has its own idea of what to file and is probably keeping a copy of all the Web pages that you visit and all the artwork that appeared on them. If you are a heavy-duty Web user, this stuff can crowd your hard drive and needs to be cleaned out from time to time. It can be limited to a predetermined quantity depending on your operating system.

Daily Files
Some organizers keep a desk file called a "daily" file. Material is placed in it daily until it fills up. Then it is stuck in the file drawer and a

new one started. A copy of every letter sent and records of phone calls are kept in it in chronological order, with the most recent items going in the front of the file. For important items, a double filing system is used in which one copy is filed in the issue file and the other in the daily file.

A daily file is excellent if you talk with lots of different people or need to access information quickly. If you have forgotten whom you talked with last week about a certain issue, flip back a week through your daily file and find the record of the call or letter.

Managing Your Files

One of the biggest problems with organizers is not their filing system itself but not using the filing system. Even with the best of systems, one has to file. Identify the time of day in which you are least productive and use it to file. Learn to file at least weekly, if not as you go along.

Do your own filing. You can rarely find things that other people file. Don't have volunteers or interns do it for you unless you write on every piece of paper exactly where you want it put. The categories that you create and what you save are part of your outlook on life. This is illustrated by the story of the previous occupant of an office who left behind two boxes crammed full of bits of string. One was neatly marked "String for Later Use." The other was marked "String to Be Thrown Out." This person's decision to save the string to be thrown out reflects deep emotions toward string, perhaps the result of growing up during the Great Depression of the 1930s.

Before you change jobs, clean your files. Throw most things away, except financial information and the basic summaries and outlines of what happened. In general, people don't use other people's files. They should, perhaps, but they don't. Most organizations accumulate mounds of unused, unread paper. A new staff member is much more likely to read and use twenty files from a previous staff person than two hundred. If two hundred files are turned over, the new person probably won't go through any of the files. Of course, you must keep all legal files, such as financial records and board minutes.

If you can't bear to part with documents and you think they might have some historic value, send them to the Historical Society. When the Midwest Academy moved into new office space with less storage room, dozens of boxes of documents were sent to the Historical Society. The Society will sort and store the information.

Keeping Track of People, Calls, and Meetings

Because organizers deal with so many people over the course of a year, they just can't remember everything they would like. Thus, it is important to develop systems to keep track of people, what you say to them, and meetings you have with them. Devise your systems assuming that you will forget everything. The following systems are popular.

Leadership Records

Organizers must keep track of the key leaders and people with whom they work. These records are set up according to how you organize. If you work by state legislative districts, the records are organized by district. If you work by buildings in a community, then the records are organized by buildings. These records always have the contact person's name, address, phone and fax numbers, and e-mail address. They frequently include information such as the best times to reach the person, interest or skill areas, languages spoken, spouse's and children's names, committee participation, date of last conversation, and significant contacts. In the past, organizers kept these records in card files. Currently, most of this information is kept in computer databases so that it can also be used to generate address labels (for meeting notices) and phone lists.

Call Sheets

If you spend a lot of time on the phone, make a "record of phone call" form to jot down the date you talked, the essential points in the conversation, and the items to which you agreed. You may think you can remember each phone call, but you probably cannot. Kim Bobo uses goldenrod-colored phone sheets that stand out from other paper on her desk. The categories needed on your phone sheets will vary but should probably be similar to those shown on the example form at the end of this chapter. Please note the follow-up section on the form. This is critical for organizers because it is so easy to forget to do things we promised over the phone. The phone sheet should not be filed until each item on the follow-up section is dated, indicating when the follow-up task was completed.

For new organizers, these call sheets are a good tool for reviewing work and problems. A new staff member and his or her supervisor can discuss the calls using the information on the call sheets. The sheets can also make it easier to delegate follow-up tasks.

Calling Logbook

Some organizers keep a log of all calls in one notebook. The date is put at the top of the page or at the beginning of the day's calls. The person's name, phone number, and a brief summary of the call are listed for each call.

Computerized Records of Calls

Some organizers keep a word-processing file or database on each person talked with regularly.

This is appropriate only if you have a computer at your desk. A headset is essential so your hands are free to use a keyboard. An organizer who used this method for years, while supervising a staff of five, comments that it is a most useful system for calls that you initiate but works much less well when people are calling you. If the computer is off it takes time to start it and to get to the right file. By the time you are ready to start making notes the call can be over. The second disadvantage is that you have to go looking for your follow-up "To Do" notes instead of having them in a pile on the desk. The big advantage is that as long as you associate the information you enter with a name, a date, an issue, or some other identifying word, the FIND function of your software program will locate it for you, so your entries can be less structured. A couple of keystrokes will neatly date everything you enter.

Meeting Records

Especially in situations where someone else may have to organize based on your work, it is useful to have good records of meetings with people. A simple form can be developed that can be used for meetings with one person or with a group of people. Make sure to keep the form simple or it will become a burden and no one will complete it.

Postcards/Thank-You Notes

It is very important to communicate with people, especially to thank them. Steve Max keeps a pile of postcards in his desk and drops people little thoughts as they come to him, such as "You did a good job leading that meeting last week." Kim Bobo keeps a pile of thank-you notes in her desk and a list of thank-yous to send in a separate column on her "To Do" list. Jackie Kendall carries cards with her on trips to write in her spare time. You may also want to keep extra get well and birthday cards.

Keeping Track of Time

This manual does not need to devote much space to time management because there are dozens of excellent books on the subject. A few basic guidelines are in order, however.

Know Your Energy Cycle

Some kinds of work are easier to do during certain parts of the day. For example, some people write best at the beginning of the day. Consequently, they should do all writing at the beginning of the day and save calls until the afternoon.

Don't Let the Phones Dictate Your Life

Just because someone has a quarter doesn't mean that they have the right to make a bell ring in your ear. As organizers, we spend a lot of time on the phone. However, we also need time to think, write, and plan without interruptions. Don't take calls all the time—unplug your phone if necessary. If you are meeting with someone, don't take phone calls. It is disrespectful to the person and makes the meetings last twice as long. Voice mail is wonderful for our work.

Use Phones for Short Meetings

Talking on the phone is not the best way to build personal relationships, but phone meetings are usually shorter than personal meetings. Use phones to "meet" when you are conducting business and don't need to build a strong relationship or when you already have one.

Stay Away from the Web Unless You Really Need It

Younger organizers who grew up with the Web sometimes don't recognize that looking up information on the Web can be more time-consuming than using a phone book or calling 411. Often making a phone call or consulting a reference manual is the fastest method.

Remember the "Deal with Paper Once" Rule

Even though it is not always possible to deal with paper only once, keeping the rule in your head can save you lots of time. Many items can be dealt with by immediately tossing them, scribbling a note on the top, or sending a thank-you note quickly. Avoid reading and rereading documents. If you find yourself constantly shuttling paper from one pile to another, file or toss it.

Advocate for Laborsaving Equipment and Systems

Most non-profit organizations are short on money, and thus it is hard to budget money for equipment that seems costly in the short run, even though it clearly makes sense in terms of long-term labor savings. Nonetheless, groups must budget for laborsaving devices because their most valuable asset is staff and volunteer time. Laborsaving devices include good copy machines that collate and staple, fax and scanning machines, folding machines, and postage machines that seal envelopes. Calculate the amount of staff and volunteer time that could be saved by investing in additional equipment and begin advocating within your organization for adequate support to enhance your productivity—but don't be a nudge when money is tight. Remember also that you don't really want to eliminate all the work that volunteers come into the office to do. Those jobs are also organization builders.

Keep Track of Your Time

Most organizations have a timesheet that must be completed on a regular basis. Even if you do not fill out timesheets, keep careful records of your time in order to calculate vacation time and to answer questions that might arise about your hours (either too few or too many). Organizers tend to work many nights and weekends, and thus it is important to keep track of your time to ensure that you don't burn yourself out. Working too many hours over an extended period of time is as bad as working too few. The easiest way to keep records on your hours is just to write the total number of hours on your calendar each day.

If you feel that your time is out of control but you're not sure what the problems are, keep track of how you spend your time in fifteen-minute blocks over a two-week period. Put down *everything* you did during the day. At the end of the two weeks, analyze the timesheets and assess ways to work more efficiently.

If you want a better record of your work to meet funding requirements or for legal reasons, consider developing a timesheet that reflects the various parts of your job. You may need to separate out tax-exempt educational activities from grassroots lobbying. You can complete the regular timesheet for accounting purposes and keep a more detailed record for your own use.

Asking for Supervision

Although an entire chapter of this manual is devoted to supervision, a few comments are appropriate here as well, particularly for the person needing more supervision. No matter how good your administrative systems are and how efficiently you approach tasks, your work must meet the goals of the organization. The best person to consult about your work meeting the organization's goals is your supervisor.

Too many organizers receive inadequate supervision. They know it, but they do nothing about it. Think of one of your jobs as being to organize your supervisor so that he or she gives you the supervision you need. Don't wait for your supervisor to give you the kind of supervision you want. Go to him or her and explain precisely what you would like done. Don't demand hours, but suggest, for example: "Let's meet once a week for one hour. I will review my updated campaign timeline and my last week's 'to do' sheet and my current 'to do' sheet." Suggesting specific kinds of supervision is helpful to your supervisor. Most supervisors want to be good at their jobs, but they don't know how, especially given all the demands on their time.

Do your best to come to an agreement with your supervisor upon goals and objectives that are realistic and achievable. Use the administrative tools suggested above to monitor the progress of your work.

Surviving for the Long Haul

The struggle for social justice is a long-term commitment. You must develop work habits and lifestyles that can be maintained over a long period of years. Chapter 25, "Working for the Long Haul," suggests a number of ways to survive and not "burn out," but one part of surviving for the long haul is to develop strong administrative systems. By developing better systems or controlling your time and work habits, you will be better equipped to plan realistically. This, in turn, will allow you to use resources (especially time) well and also to win on issues without killing yourself in the process. Seeing success in your work will sustain you for future work.

Record of Call

Name: _____   Phone: _____

Organization: _____   Date: _____

Summary of Conversation:

Follow-up needed:

23

What Makes a Good Supervisor?

Do unto Others

There are many similarities between being a good supervisor and being a good leader. The similarity is not a coincidence: to be a good supervisor is to be a good leader.

One of the best ways to judge whether or not you are a good supervisor is to picture the kind of supervisor you would like to have and then consider whether or not you match that picture. Generally speaking, if we treat people as we would like to be treated, we will be well on the way to being good supervisors.

As with leadership, it's helpful to differentiate between skills and qualities. The qualities all good supervisors need include honesty, self-assurance, enthusiasm, a positive attitude, commitment to the organization, a willingness to work hard, and the ability to enjoy helping others to succeed. Although sometimes these attitudes can be developed, they are not "learned" in quite the same ways skills are. The qualities reflect who you are as a person.

All supervisors must also develop strong skills in setting priorities, planning work, making wise decisions, delegating responsibility, providing constructive and supportive feedback, using

Supervision

time efficiently, and training staff. If you supervise organizers, you must learn to teach organizing skills to your staff as well. Most important, a supervisor needs to carry around a mental blueprint for the overall development of the organization and to be able to see how any given activity either fits or doesn't fit the plan.

In addition, most supervisory jobs require other special skills, such as public speaking or budgeting. As a supervisor, you must evaluate your job, assess what skills are essential, and develop your weaker skills. Build to your strengths. That is, hire people around you who are stronger in your weaker areas so that you can both learn from them and have a stronger team. It is a sign of insecurity when a manager hires only people who know less than he or she does.

Balance Personnel and Program Supervision

A good supervisor provides both solid *personnel* and *program* supervision. Good personnel supervision is helping each person to become the best worker possible and to develop his or her skills. It includes helping the staff work together as a whole. Good program supervision means building the organization, raising money, winning on issues, and developing the volunteer leadership of the organization.

Personnel and Program Supervision

PERSONNEL	PROGRAM
Teach Specific Skills	Win Issues
Encourage Taking Responsibility	Build Membership
Instill Self-Confidence	Increase Coalition Partners
Raise Political Understanding	Raise Money
Develop Teamwork	Develop Electoral Capability
Raise Performance Standards	Expand Leadership
Build Morale	Gain Media Visibility
Resolve Disputes	Extend Issue Expertise

These two types of supervision must always be balanced. Your organization can't have a strong program for long unless you are also developing its personnel—helping staff members to grow, learn new skills, and feel good about themselves. On the other hand, a supervisor's main goal is not to win popularity contests. While you should always get along with the staff and seek their respect, your purpose is to build the organization. Frequently you may have to challenge your staff, hold them accountable, or ask them to do jobs they don't like.

Knowing when to emphasize personnel leadership over program leadership is complicated by the fact that staff often do not know what type of leadership they really need and don't always ask for the right thing. For example, a common complaint heard at some time in virtually every organization is that there is "insufficient communication." On the face of things, it would appear that more communication, that is, more personnel leadership, is needed to correct this problem. It may be that the supervisor is not meeting individually with staff members on a weekly basis, that staff meetings are not held frequently enough, or that staff based away from the main office are out of the loop. On the other hand, there have been many situations in which meetings and communication have been increased but the staff continue to complain that they don't get enough information. In this case, the staff are probably asking for something else that they can't put into words. Such complaints are often an indication that the staff do not have a clear enough sense of overall program direction, campaign strategy, or issue priority. They are not asking for more details; they are asking for the big picture. Staff members may not be clear about how their individual projects fit into the overall structure. In other words, the need is for neither more nor longer meetings. Rather, specific gaps in the staff's knowledge must be filled. Probably the supervisor had not sufficiently thought through these matters either. Most of the time, a staff meeting focused on the strategy for a specific campaign is worth three meetings on improving interpersonal communication.

Many supervisors find it helpful to set organizational goals with their staff and then to make an overall timeline for the year so that everyone has a good sense of the big picture. Then, the supervisor should work with each individual staff member to make sure that his or her work fits in with the overall goals and that his or her timeline is realistic and includes the established organizational priorities. You may also want all those you supervise to share their plans with one another in order to encourage mutual support. Save the materials from the goal-setting meeting and review it at the end of the year, if not sooner.

As supervisors in social change organizations, we are also called upon to share a vision of a more just society with those whom we supervise. We can help people see how their work contributes to the broader goals of the organization and to the vision of creating a different world. The political development of the staff should include receiving suggested reading lists, discussing current events, hearing invited speakers at staff meetings, or attending major events held by other groups. Supervisors can play a part in transforming people and raising them to new levels of social consciousness. In doing so, both the person and the organization will grow. In addition to following all the above guidelines, we must convey enthusiasm and commitment toward the mission of the organization.

Principles of Supervision

One straightforward and commonsense approach to administration was developed in 1916 by Henri Fayol, the chief executive officer of a French mining corporation. He developed a list of what he considered essential principles of management. While written with for-profit companies in mind, these principles are just as applicable to non-profits. Unfortunately, many non-profits often seem to be trying to do just the opposite.

Fayol's principles are as follows:

1. Work should be divided into portions so that each person (or group of people) will know what job they are supposed to perform and what the expectations are for their performance.

2. Managers must have the authority to give orders and instructions, but they must also accept responsibility for whether or not the work is done right.

3. Managers are responsible for building morale within the workforce and for enforcing discipline of the workforce. Managers must be true to their word.

4. An individual should have only one boss. Fayol called this "unity of command." It is often also called a "chain of command."

   (This point cannot be stressed enough. We have seen many organizations in which organizing staff and even volunteer leaders are considered to be at the bottom of the chain, and they receive simultaneous and often conflicting instructions or priorities from everyone above them.)

5. Every organization should have only one master plan, one set of overriding goals that establishes a unity of direction.

6. Everyone, but especially managers, must place their interests second to those of the total organization.

7. Pay and rewards should reflect each person's efforts and each person's contribution to the organization's goal, not what the worker's personal relationship is to management.

   (The point is to avoid favoritism, not to ignore principles such as seniority or uniform pay scales.)

8. Orders and instructions should flow down a chain of command from a higher manager to a lower one. Communications and complaints should move upward through the same channel.

9. Materials and technology should be in their proper place. Routine procedures should be established and maintained to minimize effort and waste.

10. Workers should be encouraged to exercise initiative.

11. Workers should be treated equally and fairly.

Undoubtedly, Fayol meant that workers should be treated equally to each other, not to management. This poses a problem for social change organizations because we believe in social equality. It is best to frankly acknowledge that according to the bylaws, an organization belongs to its board, which has the legal responsibility. The board hires a Director and the staff is subordinate. This causes resentment only if a pretense of equality is made while power is exercised in a less than open fashion. If an organization wishes to practice true staff equality, it must be constituted so that if all staff members have an equal voice, they are also equally liable for matters such as debts, lawsuits, or IRS violations.

Establish Fair Personnel Procedures

Every organization should have a written personnel policy and an evaluation process that everyone knows about. The personnel policy should clarify all benefits including holidays, vacations, disability, sick days, leaves, and compensatory time. It should cover hours of work, office procedures, expense reimbursement, dress code, and sexual harassment and discrimination policies. It should explain the basic process for evaluations, probations, firing, and grievances.

If you find your organization lacks a personnel policy, urge that a process be established to draft one immediately. The board will then need to approve the policy. Sometimes a personnel committee of the board will draft the policy, which must be updated regularly as new policy and legal issues arise.

Every personnel policy should contain a grievance procedure. Careful consideration should be given to the level to which the final appeal is addressed. In some groups, the final appeal is to the Executive Director. This tends to discourage employees from using the procedure because they assume that the decision that they are appealing was made on the Director's authority in the first place. The personnel committee of the board is regarded as a more neutral body to hear appeals. In many situations, a Director would rather settle a grievance than let it get to the board level. The board committee, on the other hand, is often reluctant to overrule its Director. These two tendencies probably balance each other out from the employees' point of view, making the board committee the best choice. Some large organizations send unresolved grievances to a professional mediator as the final step after the Director's decision. This is the fairest method, but it can be very expensive, and often mediators don't understand what social change organizations do or how they work. A sample grievance procedure is included at the end of this chapter. Note that a grievance procedure is a method for interpreting and applying the organization's personnel policies. It is only as good as the policies on which it is based.

Avoid Surprises

Make sure people have written job descriptions that accurately reflect the work they are expected to do. If people do not have realistic job descriptions, you are in a poor position to question someone's work. (See the bibliography for references on writing personnel policies and job descriptions.)

Evaluations. It's important for staff to receive regular evaluations. New organizing staff should receive a formal evaluation after their first three to six months. An annual evaluation is fine for everyone else. Do not do evaluations only when there is a problem. That kind of random behavior makes people dread evaluations. Be sure to clarify desired improvement goals in people's evaluations.

Regular Feedback. Talk with staff regularly about their strengths and growth areas. Nothing on an evaluation should be a surprise.

Probation. There should be no surprise firings. They are unjust, are demoralizing to other staff, and make the organization vulnerable to lawsuits. If someone's work is not adequate, identify the criteria for improvement and support. Put the concerns in writing, give a copy to the person, and put one in the person's personnel file. If the matter is quite serious, place the person on probation. Again, make sure you have a written record. Then if the improvements are not made by a specified date, the person can be fired.

Job Changes. Major office changes, work reassignments, or job changes should not be a surprise. If changes need to be made, prepare people as much as possible. Talk individually with everyone about the upcoming changes and how each person will be affected.

Layoffs. All too often in the world of social change organizing, money runs out and layoffs are required. There is no good way to handle this. Ideally, some objective system such as seniority should be followed, but ongoing foundation grants are often tied to specific programs that involve staff who are not interchangeable. There are also problems of maintaining racial and gender balance, which defy any neat solutions. The best advice is to keep everyone's unemployment insurance benefits paid up and to allow the staff an opportunity to suggest fundraising and cost-cutting suggestions before layoffs are implemented. Staff should be kept apprised of the financial health of the organization and should be warned, when hired, if funding for the position is not long term. There is always a temptation to withhold bad news as long as possible out of fear that it will cause a panic that makes everything worse. But be fair. It is no fun to lay off anyone, let alone someone who just got married, is pregnant, or bought a house a week before they got laid off.

Maintain Confidentiality on Personnel Matters

Reprimanding or putting someone on probation must be done with the utmost confidentiality. It is totally improper to discuss confidential personnel matters with other staff who do not need to know by virtue of their jobs. Only those who must know (Personnel Director and/or your supervisor) should be told. If people complain to you about a person's work and it seems legitimate, thank them and tell them you'll take care of the situation. Do not give details on how you will do it.

Lock personnel files that contain evaluations, references, and/or letters requiring work improvements. Staff should not be tempted by unlocked records.

Make a Decision Rather Than Wallow in Indecision

It is not fun to make difficult decisions, especially when people care deeply about their work. However, once input has been given and the options have been discussed, a decision must be made. Unless new information can be secured that is likely to affect the outcome of a decision, go ahead and make the decision, even if it's not perfect. Obviously, you want to make good decisions, but at a certain point, any decision is better than none.

Ask yourself if you are making the decision your replacement would make. New Directors are sometimes able to view programs and performance evaluations more objectively than those who have been around for a while, and thus it's useful to challenge yourself to view things as your replacement would.

Do not dump a difficult decision onto others unless it is their area of responsibility and they want to make the decision. Be willing to make the difficult decisions, but do so humbly. Be willing to admit, up-front, that it's a hard decision and you could be wrong, but your judgment is such and such, and the job calls for you to make this decision. Later, if you find you were wrong, admit it.

Involve People in Important Decisions and Recommendations That Directly Affect Them

Organizations run better if there is participatory decision making. This is not consensus decision making; it is involving people in the important decisions (or important staff recommendations to the board) and the decisions that directly affect them.

The decisions or recommendations to the board that all members should be involved in (even if they don't want to be) include overall budget priorities and organizational or departmental goals. In addition, people want to be a part of decisions that directly affect them, such as moving their desks (although they don't care if you move someone else's desk and it doesn't affect them). Sometimes it is difficult to figure out what recommendations or decisions people want to be involved in and what ones they don't. We can't have the luxury of involving everyone in every decision or every recommendation. That would be a waste of time. If you are unclear about what decisions people want to be a part of, ask them.

In general, when you are having a department or organizational meeting, it is helpful to clarify who is making the decision on a subject being discussed. Is the group going to decide? Are you going to decide? It is not good for you to approach a meeting thinking that if the group's view is the same as yours, then the group makes the decision, but if they differ, you make the decision. People will catch on quickly and feel taken advantage of. It's better to be up-front about seeking input and saying that you will make the decision if that's the case. In addition, because many decisions arise on a regular basis, they should be "routinized." Everyone should understand who makes these regular decisions so that this need not be gone over each time.

Some groups prefer consensus decision making. According to *Building United Judgment: A Handbook for Consensus Decision-Making,* there are some "prerequisite" group conditions that are important for successfully using consensus decision making. Members of the group should have a unity of purpose, equal access to power, willingness to change attitudes, and eagerness to learn skills. In addition, the group should have plenty of time for making decisions. Because many social change groups cannot meet these conditions, they are unable to use consensus decision making.

Try to Keep your Ego Out of Supervision: "Pride Goeth Before Destruction and a Haughty Spirit Before a Fall"

All supervisors should struggle against letting their own egos enter into supervisory relationships. Here are a number of things you can do in this respect:

- Encourage recognition of your staff from outside the organization or department. Don't take all the credit yourself.

- If there are any perks (special trips, speaking, training, dinners), share them.
- If you've made a decision that everyone hates (and it's not really an important one), don't stick to it out of pride. Apologize and change it.
- Build in feedback opportunities for your staff. Take criticism seriously and try to grow from it. Share personal growth goals with staff and ask for their help.
- Avoid saying "I" when it should be "we," or "my" when it should be "ours." (But also avoid saying "we" when you really do mean "I.")
- Because something is crystal clear in your own mind, don't assume it is clear to others. If staff do not seem to grasp what you want done, assume that it is your fault, not theirs. Try putting your thoughts on paper. Set aside specific times to discuss assignments so that directions are not given "on the run."

Approach Supervision in a Positive, Problem-Solving Mode

The tone with which you approach personnel and program problems will be noted by the staff, and they will act accordingly. Don't ignore problems, but always approach them in a problem-solving fashion, as opposed to a complaining way. Every time someone complains about a problem, help him or her think through how it can be addressed. It is usually best to reduce problems to a few smaller changeable specifics rather than to enlarge upon them. ("The overall trouble with this organization is . . ." or "You always do this sort of thing . . . .") Problems cannot be solved at that level of generality. In the same vein, if you have a "feeling" about someone but can't back it up with specific examples, don't mention it. Criticism should be focused on specific work-related problems and not on feelings. Always assume the best about staff, particularly their desire to do a good job. Don't ever let anyone hear you speaking badly about any staff member or leader. In fact, avoid speaking badly of any other citizen organization. By personal example, you can help to avoid an atmosphere filled with griping, complaining, and gossiping. If people want to gripe, encourage them to discuss sports or food instead.

Strive to Be the Best Supervisor, Not the Best Friend

One of the hardest things to learn as a supervisor is that sometimes you have to make decisions or suggest things that make people mad at you. You cannot be a best friend to people. In fact, friendship, in the personal sense of the word, does not enter into a supervisory relationship. Yours is a professional relationship, part of which involves enforcing performance standards that you would never dream of applying to your personal friends. However, if you do a good job so that the people whom you supervise are successful at theirs, then you will be on good terms with most of the staff most of the time. Face it, as long as you hold the final say over someone's job, you will never be "one of the gang." The last thing you ever want to hear is "And I thought you were my friend."

You will be a better supervisor if you understand what those you supervise want out of their jobs. Do they want to learn certain skills? Do they want a steady job? Do they want items to add to their resume? As in all organizing, we will work better with people if we understand their self-interest and find ways to meet or enhance it.

Offer Specific, Immediate Feedback

People's work deserves immediate and specific feedback, both complimentary and constructive. Tell people what you like and also what would strengthen their work performance. Don't ignore small problems if specific improvements could be made. There is a tension, however, between not wanting to micromanage a project in preparation and still having final check-off when it is finished. Try to avoid telling staff that a finished project is inadequate and needs to be done over. Ask to see early drafts and strategy charts, or talk over initial plans. At the risk of meddling, it is better to offer suggestions while the work is still in progress. Unless something is a true disaster, your attitude should be "If it's finished, I love it." Not everything we do needs to be perfect. We don't have time for perfection. When you hear a staff person bragging about being a perfectionist, try to indicate that perfection in all matters is not a goal. Perfectionists tend to drive themselves and others crazy. We need high-quality work on the important matters, but on unimportant matters, it is better to just get the work done.

Putting the emphasis on getting the job done means that you stress achievement more than efforts. Effort counts for something but not as much as achievement. We're here to build our organizations and we need to reward (for example, by publicly recognizing achievers or giving them additional responsibilities) people who help build the organization and not just those who try hard and/or get along with everyone.

When staff are under a great deal of strain, such as when making an important public presentation or conducting a large conference, they do not need to hear negative comments at that moment. Save them until later. If you are mad at someone, you should wait to discuss a problem until you are not upset and can present your concerns calmly. We all like positive feedback. Don't worry about giving too much. Always take the extra time to write positive comments on people's written work and to personally and publicly thank and praise them.

Supervise Directly Only Five or Six People

You can supervise more people but only for a short period of time. If you have many more people, you will need to develop another level of supervisors within your staff. Give the stronger staff members the opportunity to learn parts of your job that they are interested in and able to do. It is especially important that people develop supervisory skills. Because these are best learned by doing, allow some of your stronger people to train and supervise other staff. The mark of a good supervisor is that when she or he leaves, things go on smoothly. Making yourself irreplaceable is a sign of insecurity, not leadership.

Delegate, Don't Abdicate

You cannot make all the decisions and be directly responsible for everything in your department or agency. Even if you could, you wouldn't want to because it wouldn't develop staff.

How you delegate work responsibilities depends on the maturity and skills of the staff involved. The approach to delegation is a judgment call that you must make. Simply delegating without taking into account the staff you are delegating to is not good supervision. It is abdicating responsibility. As in developing a strategy, there can be many ways to approach a problem and many will be equally good. Be willing to have someone approach a problem somewhat differently than you if it still accomplishes the same goal.

Paul Hersey and Ken Blanchard have developed some useful theories on "situational leadership" in supervising staff. They suggest that different levels of task and relationship supervision are needed, based on people's skill and maturity. Below are categories they suggest. (For further details, see *Management of Organizational Behavior: Utilizing Human Resources*, listed in the bibliography.)

- *For skilled, mature staff:* You should indicate the project you want accomplished and the general parameters, such as time frame and budget. Ask the staff if they have questions. Then tell them that you trust their ability to do the job and urge them to go ahead. Set up some review dates with you along the way. Sometimes people may hesitate, but if you really think they are capable, then it is important to encourage them to take responsibility. If people feel confident about doing a job and you give too much direction, they will be insulted.

- *For skilled but not mature staff:* If you know staff can do the job but they tend to be lazy or inefficient with their use of time or money, you need to be much more directive about the parameters: "I want to see your first draft by next Monday."

- *For mature but not skilled staff:* Spend a fair amount of time outlining the job. Talk through the basic approaches with the staff member. Set a general timeline for the work with which the person feels comfortable. Urge the person to talk with you at any time about problems and approaches.

- *For immature and unskilled staff:* In general, if you have staff who are both immature and unskilled, you should get rid of them, unless your organization's purpose is to train them. However, if you feel you must work with someone who is both immature and unskilled, you will need to spend a lot of time providing strong instructions, intense supervision, and extensive training.

Solicit and Use Ideas

Especially on important matters, it is good to solicit ideas from staff. More heads thinking on difficult program matters can come up with better approaches. Do not approach personnel matters this way because they need to be kept confidential. When an idea is good, use it and give credit to its originator.

Manage Your Own Time Well

Time management is critical for all supervisors. There is never enough time to do everything you want or are expected to do. Thus, you need to take control of your time and set priorities. Review the guidelines in chapter 22 on administrative systems and check out some books from your public library on time management. Many good books are available on this subject. Be sure to

- *Establish Administrative Systems That Work for You.* These include good file systems and daily "To Do" lists.
- *Assure Certain Periods of Uninterrupted Work Time.* This can be done in numerous ways: set aside quiet hours in which no one can interrupt you and you don't take calls, arrive at work before everyone else does or stay later, work at home one morning a week, or whatever works for you. Every supervisor needs uninterrupted time to think, plan, and write.
- *Keep Lists of Things to Talk about with People.* Don't interrupt your staff regularly and they won't interrupt you. Keep a running list of things about which you want to talk with people so that your meeting time is used efficiently and you remember all the important items they need to know. Staff are not very understanding about supervisors forgetting to tell them key pieces of information.
- *If Your Time Seems out of Control, Keep Track of It.* Track your time in fifteen-minute blocks for two weeks, then assess your timesheets. Many professionals use this time management tool annually. This is also a good way to get control of what a staff person is doing if you are unclear about it. It's easier to request this of your staff if you have done it too.

- *Drop or Scale Back Work.* We can't do everything. As a supervisor, you have to help people in this area, including yourself.
- *Get Advice from Staff.* When you are feeling most stressed, it is useful to talk through problems with your staff. Get their advice and assistance.

Build to Your Strengths

Each of us has strengths and weaknesses that we bring to our jobs. Identify the program strengths you bring to your particular position. Find helpful ways to offer those strengths to your staff. Strive to become solid in your weaker areas and to get assistance from others in your department/organization who are stronger in your weaker areas. Ask your supervisor, or the board president or chair of the personnel committee if you are the Executive Director, to give you an annual review in order to get objective input on your goals, accomplishments, strengths, and weaknesses. Urge the person conducting the review to get feedback from your staff on specific ways you could improve your supervision.

Supervising Organizers

Supervising an organizer usually means that you, the supervisor, are really the organizer working with someone else who is in an apprentice relationship to you. This situation occurs because, unfortunately, in many organizations the role of organizer is seen as an entry-level position. The lowest paid, least experienced people are hired as organizers and when at last they reach a level of competence, they are either promoted out of the position or they leave for a better-paying job elsewhere.

The most difficult aspect of supervising organizers is learning how to evaluate the information you get from your organizing staff. Only rarely will you have the opportunity to see their work firsthand or to meet the people with whom they are dealing day to day.

What Are You Building?

Successful supervision depends on both you and the organizer you are supervising being completely clear about the structure of what is being *built*. This is not the same as what is being won, and it is not the same as the function of what is being built. If you were to say, "We are building an organization to protect children's health," then protecting health is the function, but it is not the structure. Are you building an individual membership organization or a coalition? Is it a membership-run organization or a staff-run public interest organization? Is this a campaign of your organization that also involves other people or groups? If it is, then what is the relationship of the leaders of the campaign to the leaders of your organization? These are basically organizing model questions. What is being built must first be clear in your mind. Every decision, no matter how small, depends on the nature of the overall structural conception, even what is put on the organizer's business card.

Often a group will receive funding or a contract for a new organizing venture that doesn't exactly fit within its structure. For example, a state citizens coalition got funding to hold workshops for victims of sexual harassment. It might seem to you, the supervisor, that there is no need to raise complicated structural questions about such a project because the answers will probably not matter in practice. However, the organizer needs to be able to clearly explain to people whether they are being asked to become members of your organization or to be its clients. Are the harassment victims going to join, work with, affiliate with, attend, or be serviced by your organization? Do they relate to your organization directly or through a separate project, activity, support group, coalition, campaign, or function? What are they expected to build? If your organization is a statewide coalition of 115 groups, none of which has anything to do with sexual harassment, where does this activity fit? Without clarity on these matters, the organizer can't easily describe the project, much less recruit victims of sexual harassment to it and build it. Knowing what the project *does* is not a substitute for knowing what it *is*.

Have a Long-Term Plan

The organizer is busy with the day-to-day details and, except for the most experienced, will not be planning a year or two years ahead. Only an organizer who has been through several campaigns from start to finish will know how what is done today will affect what happens a year from now. Often the supervisor will have to make up for the organizer's lack of experience and provide the long-term vision. How will this campaign set us up for the next campaign? Is there a way to win the issue so that it has an impact on the next election? Are there leaders who might be political candidates in the future? What will be introduced in the next session of the City Council to which we will have to respond? How can we overcome the reluctance of a key organization to ally with us? What person or activity will open the doors to the Labor community or the religious community? How do we avoid being typed as a single-issue group during our first campaign? What will help develop a local funding base? What might frighten away potential funders? The supervisor is always making current decisions with an eye to future developments. Organizers eventually learn to do this, but it takes time.

Always, Always Work from a Strategy Chart

The first step in establishing the supervisory relationship is asking the organizer to make a strategy chart of the campaign or of their specific part in it. Don't assist at first, as the process of making the chart highlights gaps in the organizer's knowledge of the area, the issue, and many other facets of the campaign. Typically, problems lie not in the Goals or Targets columns, which have probably already been established, or with the first part of the Organizational Considerations column, the resources, which have also been decided. Focus on the second part of Organizational Considerations: exactly how is the campaign going to build the organization? Then, look at the Constituency, which will probably be too limited, and at Tactics, which may not involve enough of the constituents or bring about face-to-face meetings with the target. Remember that with a working strategy chart you don't put words such as "seniors" in the Constituency column. You list all the senior groups by name, with a contact person and phone number. Making the chart can take most of a day. When the chart is in satisfactory form (it is never final), have the organizer make a timeline. The chart and the timeline provide the basis for supervising the organizer's work.

Establish What Needs to Be Checked Off with You and When

Decide what written materials you need to approve before they can go out in the name of the organization, and put your list in writing. At the start of a supervisory relationship, ask to see just about everything. Later, as you learn the organizer's strengths, you can shorten the list. If the organizer is weak in writing press releases or designing leaflets, make your suggestions orally and ask for a new draft. It might be faster for you to just fix it yourself, but if you do, the organizer won't learn.

Establish a procedure for a weekly written report from every organizer. It should contain a brief account of all organizational contacts made in the past week, and a "To Do" list for the coming week. This report, along with the strategy chart and timeline, is the basis for your weekly supervisory conversation. Organizers seem to have a great deal of difficulty completing these reports and probably resent them, but they are necessary. When an organizer falls weeks behind in reporting, it is a sure sign of trouble in either program or morale.

One purpose of these reports is to track the organizer's progress in building the campaign by recruiting individual members or groups. Are enough contacts being made, and how are people responding? You may need to set numerical goals for contacting the groups from the Constituency column of the strategy chart. Beware of organizers who are too easily reached by phone (other than cell phones). Organizers should not be in the office, and when they are, they should be talking on the phone, not waiting for it to ring. Organizers who stay in the office producing paper are not organizing. People, not paper, win campaigns. If contacts are being made but the response is weak, then do some troubleshooting. Ask the organizer to call you or come in person to role-play a recruitment conversation. Is the problem in the organizer's presentation, or is the problem with the issue itself? Is the organizer addressing the self-interest of the person or group being recruited? Is the organizer talking to a person who can actually commit the group? (This is often a problem with recruiting unions.) Are there better known local leaders who can make an introductory phone call for the organizer? Is there a structural barrier to joining with you?

("Here is a wonderful opportunity for your group to join my organization and totally lose your identity. Now, this is what I need you to do . . . .")

The Organizer Is Your Eyes and Ears

The organizer, not you, needs to have the primary relationship with the members, leaders, allies, and media contacts associated with the campaign. Even if these people are accessible to you, it is wise to stay away most of the time. If you are often on the scene, they will start calling you instead of the organizer because everyone wants to speak with the top person. Don't stay away totally. You need to form your own impression of the people, places, targets, and activities involved, but generally let the organizer be your eyes, ears, and even your voice. For this to work, however, you first need to learn what meaning lies behind the words that the organizer uses to communicate with you.

"How did your steering committee meeting go?"
"It was good."
"How many people?"
"A lot."
"Any new people?"
"Yes, Mary."
"Who is Mary?"
"She is with a union."
"What union?"
"The AFL-CIO."

What makes a meeting good in the organizer's mind? Was it that it started on time, everyone spoke, it adopted a program, or something else? Keep probing. Go over the agenda and get a point-by-point report. Do this until both you and the organizer have a common understanding of what constitutes a good meeting. How many is a lot of people for this kind of meeting, five or fifteen? How many were expected and how many came? Always ask for specific numbers; it reinforces that in organizing, quantity matters. Why doesn't Mary have a last name? This might be a danger sign. Did the organizer not get properly introduced, was the name forgotten, or is it just that everyone knows Mary, and the organizer thinks that you must know her as well? What union she is from matters. Unless the organizer means to say that she is from the State Labor Federation, then AFL-CIO is the wrong answer. There is a specific union out there, and she has a specific position in it. She might be a union member not officially representing the union at all; she might be a staff member or the president. From a supervisory perspective, this is a significant part of the conversation because it points to a possible weakness that needs to be corrected. (A useful device is to supply your staff with business cards and insist that they hand one to every new person they meet. Often they will get a card in return, which tells them the person's organization and title.) After you have been working with the organizer for some time, you will know how to decode the conversation.

Supervising Is Knowing What Questions to Ask

It is amazing what the staff you supervise believe that you already know, don't need to know, forgot to tell you, or think is inconsequential. You will never get the information you need without asking the right questions. Here is a true story. A supervisor in a distant office should have asked the following questions. As a result of not asking, he didn't get important information until a month later. The questions were these:

Did the dry cleaning plant downstairs from the office blow up just as the field canvass was heading toward the van? Were the canvassers sprayed with cleaning chemicals, and did the Fire Department have to come and hose them down in the parking lot?

When you have your weekly check-in with your organizer, ask both open-ended and specific questions: "How do you feel?" "Is everyone on staff OK?" "Anything unusual happen in the last week?" "Is Fred (the chair of the committee) over the flu?" (Fred could be in the hospital with pneumonia, but you'll never be told unless you ask.) "Did you talk to anyone on the committee?" (Why not?) "Was there anything about us or the issue in the papers?" "What groups did you visit last week, who did you talk to, what did they say?"

At the start of a supervisory relationship, ask to see everything the staff person does. Give standing instructions that you want copies of all letters, memos, reports, agendas, press clips on the issue, and even brochures and newsletters from allied organizations in the area where the organizer is working. (One of the most valuable documents sent to a supervisor was a program book the organizer picked up at the annual Jefferson-Jackson Day Dinner of the county Democratic Party. The advertising and greeting pages were a veritable Who's Who of all the politically connected individuals, organizations, law firms, companies, unions, and potential donors in the county.) In addition to giving you a better feel for the organizing environment, all of these will suggest questions that you need to ask. You don't have to read absolutely everything, but request it.

If you are located in a different city or neighborhood, keep maps of the area where the organizer is working, and look at them during conversations. Ask for the maps with political district boundaries as well as street maps. Know the election results and voting records of area officials. Maps tell you a lot and suggest things that conversations don't. Are the organizer's recruitment visits concentrated in too small an area to produce the needed political clout to move the bill, or are they diffused over too wide an area? Do the people being recruited live in the district of a state Rep. who already supports you, or worse, one you can never move? Are groups likely to be of one ethnicity or one religion based on the neighborhood? Is there public transportation to City Hall? Is a neighborhood park a good place to leaflet parents?

It is also helpful to maintain limited communication with a few individuals who have some connection to the area or the campaign. This is tricky because you don't want to intrude, appear to be checking up, or do anything that could be interpreted as a lack of confidence in the organizer. But if there are a few people, perhaps board members, with whom you have a prior relationship, keep up those contacts.

Keep the Chain of Command Clear

An organizer who is supervised by more than one person is supervised by no one. All instructions should come through you, even if they originate elsewhere in the organization. No one really wants to be supervised. Everyone would much rather work independently and will naturally try to find ways to do so. The moment a second supervisor is in the mix, all accountability goes. "Gee, Steve, I know I'm supposed to make those visits, but Melanie told me I had to line up sponsors for the fundraiser." "Gee, Melanie, I know I am supposed to get those sponsors, but Rochelle told me I had to file my lobbyist registration report." "Gee, Rochelle I know the report is important, but Steve told me . . . ."

Conclusion

There are no magic means for becoming a good supervisor. It requires perseverance and hard work, especially with diverse personnel and when there are too few resources to accomplish all we hope to achieve. And yet, supervising staff can be enormously rewarding. You help people grow, you strengthen the organization, and you see concrete results. Your influence on staff not only affects their current performance but can also influence the overall direction of their careers. Nothing can be more rewarding than knowing you strengthened the ranks of committed people working for social justice.

Sample Grievance Procedure

There is no one right way to write a grievance procedure. Every organization has different needs and we do not present this sample as a model. At most, it is a starting point. This procedure is based on one designed by Academy Adjunct Trainer Hetty Rosenstein for New Jersey Citizen Action, a large statewide coalition that presently has over forty staff members located in three offices. The size is important because a smaller organization would have different steps, particularly when the Director is also the supervisor. Remember that a grievance procedure is only as good as the underlying personnel policy. Unclear personnel policies make it difficult to resolve grievances. Clear and comprehensive personnel policies can reduce the number of grievances that the staff will file.

Grievance Procedure of the _____ Organization

I. Purpose:

The purpose of this internal Grievance Procedure is to provide a peaceful, amicable, and fair means of settling disputes that occur between Staff and Management. This procedure is to be used internally only and does not confer upon either Management or Staff any remedies other than those specifically contained herein.

II. Scope and Eligibility:

A. Staff who have passed the Probationary Period may make use of both the Disciplinary and Non-Disciplinary Grievance Procedure. Staff who have not yet passed the Probationary Period may make use of the Non-Disciplinary Grievance Procedure for matters other than Performance Evaluations.

B. Staff may grieve any disciplinary action involving a suspension, demotion, or removal through the third step of the Procedure. Staff grieving such discipline may skip the first step of the Grievance Procedure if they choose to do so.

C. Staff may grieve discipline for minor infractions that do not involve suspension, demotion, or removal through the second step of the Grievance Procedure.

D. Staff may also grieve non-disciplinary matters involving Terms and Conditions of Employment, including Performance Evaluations, Leave Time, Hours of Work, Application of Layoff Procedures, Job Postings, Reimbursement for Expenses, and other matters distinctly addressed in the Policies and Procedures Manual. These grievances may be appealed through the third step as noted in this policy.

E. Prior to filing a Grievance, Staff are encouraged to seek resolution of matters by discussing their concerns with their Supervisor informally.

III. The Grievance Procedure is as follows:

A. First Step in the Non-Disciplinary Grievance Procedure:

1. A Staff Member may fill out a Grievance Form or present his/her Grievance in writing to his/her Immediate Supervisor within 10 working days of the event the Staff Member is grieving. The Grievance shall include a brief but clear description of what issues the Staff Member wants addressed. The Grievance will also include a clear explanation of the remedy the Staff Member is seeking.

Example:

> *Staff Name*: Wanda Worker
> *Date of Grievance*: 4/1/00
> *Grievance*:
> I was approved for only 2 weeks vacation in May. I have accrued 4 weeks vacation and I requested to use 3 weeks in May.

Solution:

Approve me for 3 weeks vacation in May.

2. After the Immediate Supervisor receives the Grievance, (s)he shall meet with the Staff Member to try to resolve the Grievance as soon as is feasible but no later than within 3 working days unless a delay is mutually agreed to.

3. At the meeting, if the Staff Member and the Supervisor resolve the Grievance, both shall sign off on the Grievance as resolved and the matter shall be closed. Grievance resolutions shall not serve as a precedent in any other matter.

4. A copy of the Grievance and its resolution shall be kept in the Supervisor's Grievance file only as a record that the matter was resolved and closed.

5. If the Staff Member and the Supervisor do not resolve the Grievance, the Supervisor shall issue a memo to that effect or respond on the Grievance Form, as soon as is feasible but no later than 48 hours after the first-step meeting, that the Grievance has not been resolved and why.

B. Second Step in Non-Disciplinary Grievances:

1. The Executive Director (ED) shall call a hearing of the Staff Member, the Staff Member's Representative (co-worker), and the Supervisor within 5 days of receipt of the appeal.

2. The Staff Member may represent him/herself or be represented by a co-worker.

3. The Staff Member's spokesperson shall go first, presenting witnesses and submitting written evidence. The Supervisor may cross-examine witnesses.

4. Management may then refute the Staff Member's case by calling witnesses and sub-

mitting written evidence. The Staff Member may cross-examine Management's witnesses.

5. The Staff Member shall have the burden to prove that (s)he has been treated unfairly or not in accordance with the Policies and Procedures Manual.

6. The Executive Director shall issue a decision as soon as feasible but no later than 5 working days. The Executive Director may deny the grievance, provide for the remedy the Staff Member asked for, or order another remedy.

C. Third Step in Non-Disciplinary Matters:

1. Staff may appeal the ED's decision in non-disciplinary matters by submitting a written appeal, within 5 working days of receipt of the second-step decision, to the Board Personnel Committee. This appeal shall be submitted through the Chair of the Board, copied to the Executive Director, and shall include all decisions and documents previously submitted during the Grievance Procedure. No new evidence may be submitted at this level of the appeal.

2. The Chair shall distribute the appeal to the rest of the Personnel Committee and shall confer with the Committee to determine whether or not the Staff Member has proven that (s)he has not been treated in accordance with the Policies and Procedures Manual. After reaching an agreement with the Committee, or by majority vote if a consensus is not reached, the Chair shall issue a final decision on the matter.

D. First Step in a Disciplinary Grievance:

1. A Staff Member may submit a Grievance about a disciplinary matter by filling out a Grievance Form or submitting a memo of appeal within 10 working days of receiving notice that (s)he is being disciplined.

2. After the Immediate Supervisor receives the

Grievance, (s)he shall meet with the Staff Member to try to resolve the Grievance as soon as is feasible but no later than within 3 working days unless a delay is mutually agreed to.

3. At the meeting, if the Staff Member and the Supervisor resolve the Grievance, both shall sign off on the Grievance as resolved and the matter shall be closed. Grievance resolutions shall not serve as a precedent in any other matter. The resolution shall be attached to the original memo or notice of discipline and shall be kept in the Staff Member's personnel file.

4. If the Staff Member and the Supervisor do not resolve the Grievance, the Supervisor shall issue a memo to that effect or respond on the Grievance Form, as soon as is feasible but no later than 2 working days after the first-step meeting, that the Grievance has not been resolved and why.

E. Second Step in Disciplinary Grievances:

1. The Staff Member may appeal the Supervisor's response by submitting an appeal to the Executive Director with a marked Grievance Form or by submitting a memo within 5 working days of receipt of the Supervisor's response.

2. The Executive Director shall call a hearing of the Staff Member, the co-worker the Staff Member has designated as a Representative, and the Management Representative (the Supervisor), as soon as possible but no later that 5 working days of receipt of the appeal.

3. In disciplinary matters, the burden to prove just cause for discipline shall be on the party bringing the discipline (Management). In non-disciplinary matters, the burden of proof shall be on the party bringing the Grievance (Staff Member).

4. Conduct of second-step disciplinary hearings:
   a. The Executive Director shall hear the case.

b. The Management Representative shall present its case first by calling witnesses and submitting all written evidence. (Written statements will not be used as evidence in a hearing where witnesses are available except to supplement the record.) Staff may represent themselves or be represented by a co-worker. The Spokesperson for the Staff Member may cross-examine witnesses.

c. The Staff Member's Representative may then call witnesses and submit written evidence in the Staff Member's defense. Management may cross-examine the Staff Member's witnesses.

d. The Executive Director may ask questions of witnesses to clarify a point or to explore a relevant matter raised during the hearing.

e. Both sides will have an opportunity to rebut each other's case.

f. After hearing from both sides, the Executive Director shall issue a decision as soon as feasible but no later than 5 working days. The decision shall specifically address whether or not Management has met its burden of proof. The Executive Director may sustain the discipline, overturn the discipline, or reduce the penalty.

g. In disciplinary matters involving minor infractions that do not involve suspensions, demotion, or removal, the Executive Director's decision shall be final and not subject to appeal in any other forum.

F. Third Step in Disciplinary Matters involving Suspensions, Demotions, or Removal:

1. Staff may appeal the ED's decision in disciplinary matters by submitting a written appeal, within 5 working days of receipt of the second-step decision, to the Board Personnel Committee. This appeal shall be submitted through the Chair of the Board,

copied to the Executive Director, and shall include all decisions and documents previously submitted during the Grievance procedure. No new evidence may be submitted at this level of the appeal.

2. The Chair shall distribute the appeal to the rest of the Personnel Committee and shall call a hearing within 10 working days.

3. The Executive Director or his/her designee shall present Management's case through witnesses and evidence.

4. The Staff Member may represent him/herself or be represented by a co-worker and may cross-examine witnesses as well as present witnesses in his/her own behalf.

5. The Staff Member may then defend him/herself with witnesses and written evidence, which Management may cross-examine.

6. The Committee may ask questions of witnesses or seek further clarification of written evidence.

7. After hearing from the parties, the Committee shall deliberate and reach a decision by a majority vote.

8. The decision shall be issued by the entire Committee, through the Chair, within 5 working days, and the vote of the Committee shall be kept confidential by the Committee members. The Committee may sustain the discipline, overturn the discipline, or reduce the penalty.

9. The Committee's decision in disciplinary matters shall be final and is not subject to appeal in any other forum.

IV. General Information:

A. If at any point in the Grievance Procedure, the person to whom the Staff Member is to submit his/her appeal is not available, the appeal may be submitted to any Director or to the Board Chair and still be considered to be timely.

B. If at any point in the Grievance Procedure, the Executive Director finds that (s)he will not be available, or believes it best that (s)he recuse him/herself from ruling on the matter, the Executive Director may designate the Board Chair or the Chair's designee to act in his/her stead. Should the Chair substitute for the Executive Director in the second step of the procedure, however, (s)he shall designate someone else to sit in on the third step in the event of an appeal.

C. Discipline shall not be imposed until after a decision at the second step except where there is an indictment for criminal conduct or where the safety of others is a consideration.

D. Conviction of a crime greater than a misdemeanor shall be grounds for immediate termination without a hearing at the discretion of the Executive Director.

E. At any time during the Grievance Procedure, the parties can agree to settle the matter.

24

Operating a non-profit organization is serious business: there are legal and financial matters to which you must attend. This chapter is not meant to substitute for getting sound legal and financial advice. Rather, it is meant to suggest a number of areas to investigate and about which you may need to seek professional advice. Over the long haul, you will also want your organization to develop the internal capacity to handle routine legal and financial matters.

It is best to approach these complicated matters with a positive frame of mind. Think of your budget as an internal management tool and your financial records as painting pictures of your programs. If your accounting procedures are handled properly, then outside reports to funders, the Internal Revenue Service, and other government agencies should be relatively straightforward.

Basic Standards

The basic standards described below are recommended for non-profit organizations. Use them in developing your organization's internal capacity to handle financial and legal matters.

Financial and Legal Matters

Personnel

Adequate Staffing. Even the smallest non-profit organization must ensure that its staff is equipped to handle legal and financial matters. Sometimes a volunteer treasurer on the board does this. As an organization grows, it should hire a competent financial manager and sufficient staff to handle reporting requirements.

Some new organizations use outside experts or technical assistants to administer financial and legal matters. Make sure that they share the information so that your staff and leaders will understand what needs to be done in the future.

Independent Accountant. All but the smallest organizations should acquire consulting assistance from a professional accountant. This is usually done in connection with an audit.

Finance Committee. Every organization should have a finance committee. In some organizations, it is a joint board/staff committee; in others, these committees are separate. The committee is responsible for monitoring the organization's financial position and performance, proposing budgets and revisions to the board of directors, and overseeing the audit engagement.

Personnel Policy. Every organization needs written personnel policies, which are distributed to all staff and board members. The personnel policies should cover procedures for hiring, firing, and setting salaries, as well as matters such as benefits, holidays, office hours, dress codes, reimbursement for expenses, and special staff expectations. Many policies also outline affirmative action plans. Written policies should be consistently adhered to. This will ensure that employees are treated fairly and will protect the organization from being sued.

The organization's hiring practices must comply with federal and state antidiscrimination policy. Whoever interviews candidates for staff positions should be aware of the personnel policies and know how to conduct a proper interview. Certain questions asked in an interview—such as "What does your husband do?" or "How old are you?"—could subject the organization to a discrimination suit. Make sure hiring policies and practices adhere to the Americans with Disabilities Act (ADA), Family Leave Act, and specific state laws.

Budgeting and Reporting Capability

Annual Budget. Seek to have a detailed projection of income and expenses approved at least two months prior to the start of the year, first by the finance committee and then by the board of directors. Minor budget revisions can be made at the beginning of the year to account for year-end actual figures. Larger organizations find it helpful to move toward a two-year budget.

Financial Statements. Every month the Executive Director should review timely and accurate balance sheets and operating statements with budget variances and year-to-date totals. You will also need financial statements for each board meeting and financial committee meeting unless they meet more often than monthly.

Cash-Flow Projections. Seldom does the same amount of money come in every week or every month. Nor are expenses the same weekly or monthly. The organization needs to develop a cash-flow projection in order to anticipate when there will and won't be cash on hand. Each year, you should develop a monthly cash-flow projection, which you then adjust based on actual receipts and disbursements. Some organizations need to do weekly cash-flow projections as well, particularly in tight financial months.

Annual Audit and Internal Control

Annual Audit. Foundations or government agencies may require your organization to have an audit. Check their guidelines carefully. Even if not required, an annual audit can catch errors and discrepancies and is highly recommended. If your budget is over $250,000, your board is likely to insist on an annual audit by a Certified Public Accountant within six months of the close of the fiscal year. Because many foundations ask to see copies of your annual audit, an audit will support your fundraising efforts as well as ensure that your financial records are sound.

Regardless of requirements, it is recommended that you get an outside annual review by a Certified Public Accountant. If an audit is not required, smaller organizations might want to consider a review instead.

Internal Control. Every organization should develop a comprehensive system of internal controls to safeguard the organization's assets, ensure the accuracy of accounting records, and control disbursements. A good system of internal controls requires segregation of duties. You know you have internal controls if employees during the regular course of business discover errors or irregularities, not just the auditors. Your organization should have

- A good budgeting system that allows you to compare budgeted amounts with actual amounts.
- Controls over petty cash.
- Reconciliation on a monthly basis.
- At least two people counting cash.
- Segregated duties.

Government Compliance

Payroll Tax Compliance. Every organization must provide for timely deposits of all federal, state, and local taxes and filing of tax reports. Federal tax deposits must be made within three days after your pay date unless the organization has a very small or very large payroll. State tax deposit regulations vary by state. Consult your accountant for rules that apply. The penalties for late deposits are enormous. Board members and key staff are personally liable for the withheld portion of federal payroll taxes.

Rules governing state taxes vary; check them. If operating in more than one state, make sure you are aware of the regulations and reporting requirements in each state.

Government Reporting Compliance. In addition to paying payroll taxes, non-profit organizations must file the IRS Form 990 Annual Report and comply with state charitable solicitation registration and reporting requirements.

Workers' Compensation. Every organization with employees must pay workers' compensation insurance. Some states have compulsory programs. Most states require that you purchase insurance through an insurance agent.

Disclosure Laws. Affected staff should understand and comply with the relevant items of the disclosure laws. The IRS requires an organization to make its Form 990 readily available to those who ask for it. Each office must have the last three years of its organization's IRS Form 990 on site for public inspection. Organizations with multiple offices are required to have a copy of their Form 990 in each office of thirty or more employees. Certain supplements do not have to be made available. Check with current requirements and consult an attorney familiar with the requirements for non-profit organizations.

A 501(c)(4) organization must disclose in writing, at the time of solicitation, that contributions to it are not tax deductible. A 501(c)(3) organization that sponsors a fundraising event must notify contributors if the event contribution is not fully deductible. For example, if an organization sponsors a fundraising dinner and the actual cost of the dinner is $25 but the ticket price is $100, the contributor must be told that only $75 of the $100 ticket "contribution" is actually tax deductible. (The remaining $25 is a purchase of food, not a contribution.)

The law requires that 501(c)(3) organizations supply adequate receipts of contributions to contributors making donations of $250 or more. Many states also have extensive disclosure laws. See the "State Solicitation Registration" section toward the end of this chapter.

The Lobbying Disclosure Act of 1995 establishes registration and reporting requirements for federal lobbying activity. One confusing aspect of the requirements is the definition of lobbying, which is significantly broader than the Internal Revenue Service definition of lobbying. The Lobbying Disclosure Act bans 501(c)(4) organizations that lobby from receiving any federal funds, including awards, grants, contracts or loans. Review the law carefully to determine if it applies to your organization.

Compliance with the Internal Revenue Service and Federal Election Commission. In order to maintain an organization's tax status, it must comply with regulations. Organizations that are involved in federal electoral activity must comply with the Federal Election Commission regulations, and those involved in state electoral activity must comply with election laws.

Contingency Planning

Contingency Plan. The financial committee should develop a contingency plan to respond to major overspending and/or income shortfalls.

Contingency Fund. Work toward establishing a fund to cover budget shortfalls or cash-flow difficulties. Fifteen percent of your annual budget is a recommended amount for standard cash-flow variations, although more or less may be needed given your organization's particular circumstances.

Generally Accepted Accounting Principles

The accounting profession has developed a body of accounting principles and procedures to provide uniformity in the preparation of financial statements. Uniformity is necessary so that statements can be properly interpreted and compared. This is especially important for non-profit organizations because of their accountability to the public for effective and prudent use of resources to achieve the organization's purposes.

The Financial Accounting Standards Board (FASB) and the American Institute of Certified Public Accountants (AICPA) prescribe accounting principles and reporting practices to be followed by Certified Public Accountants (CPAs) when conducting audits. Collectively these are called "generally accepted accounting principles" (GAAP).

Adherence to GAAP is required of an organization only in preparation of financial statements that will be subject to an independent audit; departures from GAAP would be noted in a review or compilation. Otherwise, using GAAP is a matter of choice depending upon usefulness and practicality. For all but the smallest citizen organizations, however, using the following GAAP is desirable.

Accrual or Cash Basis

What Is It? Financial records can be kept either on an accrual basis or on a cash basis. An accrual system of accounting shows the revenues and expenses in the accounting period in which the revenues were *earned* and expenses were *incurred*. A cash-basis system, in contrast, records revenues when they are *received* and expenses when they are *paid*.

Why Choose One Over the Other? An accrual system generally results in a fairer presentation of an organization's financial position and the results of its operations. Cash-basis accounting can result in an inaccurate and distorted picture if it leaves out bills owed, but not paid, or fees earned, but not received. On the other hand, if an organization pays its bills immediately and has limited sources of income, a cash-basis system may be simpler and an adequate reflection of your financial picture.

Double-Entry Basis

What Is It? The double-entry basis is a method of accounting in which each financial transaction must be recorded on the books with a debit and a credit entry.

Why Use It? This is a self-balancing system that ensures the mathematical accuracy of the bookkeeping entries.

Functional Basis

What Is It? A functional method of accounting enables you to generate year-end financial reports that separate your organization's expenditures into three broad functional categories: Program Services, General Administrative, and Fundraising. Program Services are those activities related directly to the purpose for which your organization was formed. Look at the IRS Form 990 when you set up your accounts in order to make your year-end reporting as simple as possible.

Why Do It? The organization's management, donor constituency, and some government agencies want to know how much of each dollar raised goes to your program and how much goes to support. Some contributors make decisions on the basis of this percentage. Sometimes a high percentage figure in one area is used as a trigger for state audits.

One difficulty here is that these categories are much more clear in a service delivery organization than in an advocacy organization. For example, at a hot lunch program, money spent on food is easily separated from money spent on fundraising. In an advocacy organization that has a phone or door-to-door canvass, part of a canvasser's time may be spent on soliciting money and part on asking the same person to write a letter or send an e-mail to a member of the legislature. The total cost of canvassing must be broken down between program and fundraising.

Consistency

What Is It? Consistency means using the same methods of accounting (e.g., valuation of assets accrual methods) from one period to another.

Why Do It? Consistency ensures that comparable transactions are treated in a similar manner from year to year. Otherwise, one cannot tell if changes in financial statements reflect actual changes in performance and position or result from changes in accounting methods.

Materiality

What Is It? An item is "material" if its disclosure or the method of treating it would be likely to "make a difference" in the judgment and conduct of a reasonable person reading the financial statements.

Why Do It? Materiality provides a standard for making judgments about how to treat questionable items.

Full Disclosure

What Is It? Full disclosure requires disclosure in financial statements, and the notes to the statements, of all financial and other information needed for a fair presentation of the organization's position and performance.

Why Do It? Having full disclosure covers items for which there is no specific disclosure rule to ensure that the reader is not misled by the statements. Full disclosure requires footnotes for material items not apparent in the statements so the reader has information to evaluate them properly.

Incorporation

Why Incorporate?

The main reason to incorporate is to limit the liability of people who are part of the organization—officers, directors, members, employees, etc. Incorporation, with rare exception (e.g., liability to the Internal Revenue Service for withheld taxes), means that only the organization's assets are at risk for its obligations be they routine debts or the result of a lawsuit against the organization, unless those in charge are negligent or corrupt. Board members and directors must recognize that they are morally, legally, and financially responsible for the organization. They cannot escape responsibility by remaining ignorant of their organization's business affairs.

We often hear leaders say that they aren't afraid of slap suits because their organization is incorporated. A slap suit is a lawsuit brought against a citizen organization and its leaders by a corporation. The purpose of the suit is to frighten the leaders and make them spend time and money defending themselves so that they cannot continue their campaign against the corporation. The corporation doesn't care if the suit has any legal merit or if it is eventually throw out of court. Intimidation is the only purpose, and the group's incorporation will not prevent this.

Non-Profit/Not for Profit

The things that distinguish a non-profit (not-for-profit) corporation from a business corporation are its purpose and its actual performance. A business organization's purpose is to realize a net profit for its owners. The non-profit's purpose is described in its founding documents (Articles of Incorporation and bylaws). Its purpose is to meet some socially desirable need of the community, and law prohibits it from operating for the benefit of individuals or businesses.

"Non-profit" does not mean that the organization has to operate at a loss or that it is prohibited from generating a surplus ("profit"). No one can own or get a cut of the surplus, if there is one, and no part of the assets or income can go to its directors or members, except as payment for services. Any "profit" is retained by the organization to further its tax-exempt purpose.

Articles of Incorporation

The Articles of Incorporation is the governing document filed with the Secretary of State at the time of incorporation. The Articles state the organization's name, purposes, powers, limits, classes of membership, incorporators (initial directors), and principal office. This step precedes applying for a federal tax-exempt status from the Internal Revenue Service.

Purposes. The purpose clause of the Articles should limit the group's activities to those allowable in the Internal Revenue Code section under which a tax exemption is sought. Get IRS Form 1023 and Publication 557 for the language the Internal Revenue Service requires in your Articles of Incorporation.

Limits. The powers clause states that activities will be limited according to the Code section under which tax exemption (if any) will be sought; no part of the income or assets will be distributed to officers, directors, members, or other individuals; and if the organization is dissolved, the assets will be disposed of only for tax-exempt purposes.

Bylaws

The bylaws are the internal procedural rules of the organization and generally do not need to be filed with the Secretary of State. The bylaws state how directors and officers are chosen and removed, what decisions they can make, how meetings are called, how voting is conducted, the number for quorums, and so forth. Read some sample bylaws from other non-profits to assist you in developing yours.

In considering a tax-exemption application (or in an audit), the IRS reviews the bylaws to make sure that they are consistent with the Articles and the law and that they provide the organizational structure to carry out the purposes stated in the Articles.

Membership definitions are important for organizations that want to be able to work on federal elections. The Federal Election Commission regulations require certain membership criteria for an organization to be able to communicate its electoral positions to its members. (See the discussion of the Federal Election Campaign Act below.)

Bylaws may not seem important until the organization faces political disagreements. At that point, it matters who is on the board, how you get on the board, and how votes are counted. Make sure from the beginning that organizational control is lodged appropriately.

Tax-Exempt Status

Federal Tax-Exempt Status

In addition to determining an organization's status under state law by incorporating as a non-profit (not-for-profit) corporation, many organizations seek federal tax-exempt status under section 501 of the federal tax code (including sections 501(c)(3) and 501(c)(4)) or section 527 of the code. Organizations that meet the qualifications under one of these sections receive various types of favorable treatment under the tax code, such as exemption from federal tax on the organization's income. However, federal tax-exempt status also comes with restrictions on the organization's activities, particularly lobbying and election-related activities. The general rule is that non-profits that receive greater federal tax advantages are more restricted in their advocacy activities. Groups that want the tax benefits but feel too constrained by the restrictions frequently create a series of connected organizations that allow them to pursue a variety of advocacy strategies.

501(c)(3) Organizations

The most common types of tax-exempt organization are those organized under tax code section 501(c)(3). The activities of these organizations must be almost entirely educational, charitable, or scientific, and thus these organizations include non-profit healthcare providers and other human service organizations, educational institutions, non-partisan policy research organizations, churches and other religious institutions, and foundations and other grantmaking organizations. There are two kinds of 501(c)(3) organization: public charities and private foundations.

Public Charities. In general, public charities are 501(c)(3) organizations that receive support for their activities from the general public, as opposed to a small number of generous benefactors. The law provides extremely favorable treatment for these organizations: 501(c)(3) public charities are exempt from most federal taxes, and most contributions to these organizations are tax deductible. As the general rule suggests, these substantial federal tax advantages mean that 501(c)(3) lobbying and other advocacy activities are limited by federal law. Nonetheless, all 501(c)(3) organizations are permitted to engage in advocacy activities to at least some degree.

Public Support Tests. A variety of tests exist to demonstrate the required public support for a public charity. For example, a 501(c)(3) may demonstrate that a third of its budget comes from public sources—grants and contributions from other public charities, government grants, and individual grants of up to 2 percent of the 501(c)(3)'s budget. (Contributions of greater than 2 percent of the 501(c)(3)'s budget count as "public support" only up to the 2 percent limit.) Alternatively, a public charity may show that it receives at least 10 percent public support and has other ways to demonstrate its connection to the community, such as community board members and a community-driven mission. Groups that receive a substantial portion of their income from admission fees, such as theater groups, may also qualify as public charities under an entirely different test.

Lobbying. 501(c)(3) public charities may lobby. The exact amount of lobbying they may do depends on the size of the organization and which of two sets of rules governing lobbying applies to the organizations.

Of the two possible tests, most public charities will be better off choosing to use the "501(h) Expenditure Test" (named after the section of the tax code that created it), which provides a clear definition of lobbying and limits based on how much money the organization spends on lobbying. In many cases, this test allows a 501(c)(3) to expand its advocacy, either by engaging in activities that fall outside the test's technical definitions of lobbying or by engaging in low- or no-cost lobbying (such as volunteer-based efforts) that stretch the test's expenditure-based limits further. One feature of the 501(h) test may adversely affect very large organizations: The 501(h) test, unlike its alternative, does impose an absolute cap on annual lobbying expenditures of $1 million per year.

	501(c)(3) (Public Charities)	501(c)(4) (Civic Leagues and Social Welfare Organizations)	527 (Political Organizations)
Tax Treatment	Exempt from federal income tax. Donors may claim tax deduction for contributions. Private foundations may award grants with fewer constraints. Donors exempt from federal gift tax. Donors may deduct full value of gifts of appreciated stock without paying federal capital gains tax.	Exempt from federal income tax. Donors may deduct full value of gifts of appreciated stock without paying federal capital gains tax. However, • Contributions *not* tax deductible. • Private foundations may give only restricted grants. • Contributions *not* exempt from gift tax.	Exempt from federal income tax. Donors exempt from federal gift tax. However, • Contributions *not* tax deductible. • Private foundations may *not* give grants. • Donors may owe capital gains tax on gifts of appreciated stock.
Lobbying Activities	Permitted, but limited.	Unlimited.	Technically permitted, but such activities are taxed unless done to support or oppose a candidate.
Election-Related Activities	No intervention in candidate campaigns (activities in support of or in opposition to candidates). Non-partisan voter education, voter registration, etc., permitted.	Partisan activity permitted as a secondary activity of the organization, subject to federal or state election laws (see next section). Partisan activities may be taxed.	Partisan electoral activities limited only by federal or state election laws (see next section).

The alternative system of limits on 501(c)(3) lobbying—the so-called "Insubstantial Part Test"—offers only the vague guidance that a 501(c)(3) public charity may lobby so long as that lobbying is "no substantial part" of its activities. Under this test, lobbying is left undefined and even volunteer activities that require no expenditures by the 501(c)(3) are likely to count against the limits. Many commentators have suggested that a 501(c)(3) using the insubstantial part test would be safe if it limited its lobbying to 5 percent of the organization's activities.

Unless the 501(c)(3) public charity acts, the generally inferior insubstantial part test will be used to measure the organization's lobbying activities. 501(c)(3) public charities must *choose* to have the 501(h) test apply to them by making the one-time 501(h) "election" using Internal Revenue Service Form 5768, an extremely easy-to-complete tax form. However, some types of public charities—notably churches (or similar religious institutions) and their closely connected programs—are not permitted to make the 501(h) election and must do any lobbying under the insubstantial part test.

Under the 501(h) expenditure test, public charities can spend as much as 20 percent of their budget on all lobbying, and they can spend a lesser amount—a quarter of their overall lobbying limit—on grassroots lobbying (activities designed to encourage the general public to directly lobby elected officials). For example, a 501(c)(3) public charity that spends $400,000 per year on its charitable activities may spend $80,000 (20 percent) of those funds on lobbying, including as much as $20,000 (25 percent of $80,000) on grassroots lobbying. As the size of an organization's annual budget increases, the percentage of those expenditures that the organization can spend on lobbying declines.

Direct lobbying (lobbying that isn't grassroots lobbying) occurs when a representative of the organization communicates the organization's view on a specific piece of legislation to an official, such as a member of a City Council or a state or federal legislator (or a staff person for such an official). It is also direct lobbying to urge the public to support or oppose an initiative, referendum, or other ballot measure (under the theory that in voting on a ballot measure the voters are acting as if they were a huge legislature). "Specific legislation" includes not merely proposed legislation that has been introduced but also any specific idea for legislation. For example, "our schools are in trouble" is not a statement about specific legislation, but "we should pay teachers more" makes a specific legislative proposal.

Grassroots lobbying occurs when the organization urges the general public to communicate the organization's position on a piece of specific legislation to these officials. Unless a communication includes a "call to action"—something to encourage the reader or listener to contact a legislator—the communication will generally not be considered lobbying. The regulations specify that a call to action occurs when the organization does any of the following:

- Explicitly urges readers to contact a legislator about the legislation.
- Provides the address, telephone number, or similar information for a legislator.
- Provides a petition, postcard, or similar means for the reader to communicate with a legislator.
- Identifies one or more legislators as being opposed or undecided about the bill or being a member of the relevant committee or subcommittee that will vote on the bill.

Fortunately, an organization's members are treated as a part of the organization, so urging them to contact public officials about legislation is considered direct, not grassroots, lobbying.

Note that both of these definitions exclude certain activities. It is *not* lobbying to bring a lawsuit. It is *not* lobbying to encourage an administrative agency (such as a State Department of Health or Department of Labor) to create or change an administrative rule. It is *not* lobbying to advocate before special purpose bodies such as school boards and zoning boards.

In addition, there are specific exceptions for some activities that otherwise might appear to fit the definition of lobbying under the 501(h) rules. For example, it is *not* lobbying to prepare and distribute a "non-partisan analysis" that provides a complete enough discussion of a legislative proposal to allow a reader to make up his or her own mind about the proposal (even if the analysis comes to a conclusion on the merits of that proposal). Nor is it lobbying to respond to a written request for assistance from a legislative committee to help the committee with a legislative proposal, such as a letter from a committee chair inviting the organization to testify before the committee.

The organization is required to track expenditures in a way sufficient to show that it hasn't exceeded its lobbying limits. Some of the types of expenditures that could count toward the lobbying limit are

- Paid staff time spent meeting legislators, preparing testimony, or encouraging others to testify.
- Printing, copying, or mailing expenses to get the organization's message to legislators.
- Prorated cost of any newsletter article urging the organization's members to speak out on legislation (prorating based on the space the lobbying message takes in the newsletter).

- Prorated share of rented space used in support of lobbying (a good way to handle this is to prorate the cost based on the percentage of staff time spent lobbying).

Election-Related Activities. 501(c)(3) public charities are more limited in their election-related activities. While 501(c)(3)s may engage in non-partisan voter education and voter participation activities, they are absolutely prohibited from any activity that tends to support or oppose any candidate for public office.

501(c)(3) public charities may not endorse candidates, rate candidates, contribute to candidates, or do anything else that could seem to help or hurt a candidate. The Internal Revenue Service will examine an activity based on all the surrounding "facts and circumstances" to determine whether a 501(c)(3)'s activities violate this rule. For example, a 501(c)(3) organization may criticize a legislator for failing to support an important piece of legislation during the legislative session, but if the 501(c)(3) runs a similar criticism during the legislator's campaign for reelection, the IRS might find it to be an impermissible campaign intervention.

The IRS has provided a limited amount of guidance on permissible 501(c)(3) activities during an election season. 501(c)(3)s may do the following:

- Publish non-partisan voter guides that print the results of a questionnaire asking each candidate his or her position on a broad range of issues.
- Sponsor non-partisan debates or forums in which all candidates are questioned on a broad range of issues.
- Encourage citizens to register to vote, and get registered voters to go to the polls on election day (but 501(c)(3)s may *not* encourage voters

to support or oppose a particular candidate, even by encouraging the use of a particular policy issue as a litmus test).

- Brief all candidates who respond to the 501(c)(3)'s invitation to learn the 501(c)(3)'s stance on key policy issues.

Other types of non-partisan activities are also permitted, but because the rules in this area are so strict, 501(c)(3)s would be wise to get more information from a knowledgeable source before launching an election-related activity.

Private Foundations. Private foundations are 501(c)(3)s that fail to meet the public support requirements that would qualify them as public charities. Typically, private foundations give grants to other organizations for charitable activities.

The rules for private foundations are substantially stricter than those for public charities. Private foundations are not allowed to lobby themselves nor are they allowed to "earmark" grants for lobbying. However, private foundations *may* give a public charity a grant for the general support of its operations, and the public charity may choose to spend that grant, in whole or in part, on lobbying. Similarly, a private foundation *may* give a public charity a grant for a specific project, even if that project includes some lobbying, as long as the amount that the foundation gives does not exceed the non-lobbying portion of the project's budget. Foundations should be careful, however, not to include language in their grant agreements that forbid use of their funds for lobbying. This unnecessary language can impose additional contractual restrictions on grantees that exceed the limits on public charity lobbying under law.

Private foundations may support the non-partisan election-related activities of public charities, but special rules apply when a foundation seeks to earmark a grant for a non-partisan voter registration or get-out-the-vote effort. Private foundations seeking to make such a grant or public charities that hope to receive such a grant should consult with a knowledgeable lawyer.

Private foundations may give grants to organizations that are not public charities, but, in general, they will have to restrict the use of these grants through a system known as "expenditure responsibility." Expenditure responsibility generally requires that the grantee not spend any of the grant funds for lobbying or partisan election-related activity and that the grantee file sufficient documentation with the private foundation to prove that the grant was spent for the intended charitable purposes. Many foundations are reluctant to make these grants to non-public charities, perhaps out of the mistaken belief that the rules are more burdensome than they, in fact, are.

501(c)(4) Organizations

A 501(c)(4) is a "social welfare organization" or "civic league" that may pursue educational, lobbying, and political activities. A 501(c)(4)'s "primary" activities must be those to benefit the public, including any activity in which a 501(c)(3) organization may legally engage. 501(c)(4)s are exempt from most federal taxes, but contributions to a 501(c)(4) are not tax deductible. Again following the general rule, 501(c)(4)s receive fewer benefits under the federal tax code but face fewer restrictions on their advocacy activities.

Lobbying. 501(c)(4)s may do an unlimited amount of lobbying, including working for the passage of legislation and ballot measures.

Election-Related Activity. Unlike a 501(c)(3), a 501(c)(4) may carry out some partisan political activities without jeopardizing its tax-exempt status as long as such activities do not become the *primary* activity of the organization. 501(c)(4)s should watch out for tax consequences of political activity, however. The law requires 501(c)(4)s to pay tax on either the amount the organization spends on political activity or the amount the organization receives in annual investment income (such as income earned through mutual funds), whichever is less. (Note that this means that a 501(c)(4) with no investment income for the year will not owe tax on any expenditures for political activity.) 501(c)(4)s may also engage in an unlimited amount of *non-partisan* election-related activity without fear of taxation.

In addition to these requirements imposed by federal tax law, 501(c)(4)s must also comply with relevant federal or state election laws that may impose restrictions on their activities. These rules are described below. (In general, election laws have little impact on 501(c)(3)s because the federal tax rules governing their electoral activity are so strict.)

527 Organizations

Section 527 is the section of the tax code for many different types of political organizations. Political parties and campaigns are organized under Section 527, as are various types of non-candidate political committees. This discussion focused on so-called "political action committees" (PACs) designed with the primary purpose of supporting or opposing candidates for office.

A PAC is generally exempt from federal taxation to the extent that it spends its funds on partisan political activities and related expenses. PACs can contribute to candidates' campaigns (up to state and federal election law limits on campaign contributions), make independent expenditures for or against candidates, and distribute materials to the general public that are skewed to support or oppose particular candidates. While tax law obligations for PACs are few, most PACs are required to report contributions and expenditures under federal or state election laws (see the discussion of election law below).

In general, PACs are subject to federal tax on any funds they spend on lobbying or other non-electoral activities. In most cases, a 501(c)(4) or even a 501(c)(3) is a better choice to fund a lobbying effort because of the possible tax consequences for the PAC. However, the IRS has in recent years approved the creation of organizations under Section 527 that engage in lobbying activities or other activities that seem unrelated to an election if the organization can show an electoral purpose for the activity. For example, one of these organizations might oppose a piece of legislation in order to hurt the re-election chances of a legislator who is closely associated with the bill.

For a brief period, these so-called "soft PACs" or "stealth PACs," unlike other types of PACs, were not required to disclose their contributors or expenditures because their apparently non-electoral activities did not trigger federal election law reporting requirements. However, Congress has now required these new 527 organizations to file reports with the IRS that are substantially similar to those that more traditional PACs must file with the Federal Election Commission.

Integrated Strategies Using 501(c)(3)s, 501(c)(4)s, and PACs

Meaningful social change is generally accomplished through a coordinated set of strategies. For example, the fight for civil rights in this country has been waged in the courts, the legislatures, the polling booths, and the streets. Pursuing multiple strategies to address social problems often requires the participation of several types of tax-exempt organization with diverse skills and capacities. Frequently 501(c)(3)s, 501(c)(4)s, and PACs will be working on the same general issue, with each engaged in activities particularly appropriate for that type or organization. In many cases, these organizations are formally affiliated. For example, a 501(c)(3) may create a 501(c)(4) when an issue demands more lobbying than the amount permitted under the 501(c)(3)'s lobbying limits. Foundations are often reluctant to fund 501(c)(4)s, so a 501(c)(4) might create a 501(c)(3) to seek foundation funds to do policy research and education related to the organizations' general area of concern. Or a 501(c)(4) might create a connected PAC to create change at the ballot box when the 501(c)(4)'s legislative efforts fail.

The key to dealing with these relationships between organizations is to maintain appropriate separation between them. The basic idea is to keep the organizations' finances and decision making independent. Specifically, the organizations should separate their

- Bank accounts. Related 501(c)(3)s and 501(c)(4)s must maintain separate bank accounts. This is important to ensure that a 501(c)(3) never inadvertently subsidizes 501(c)(4) activities such as partisan electoral activity.
- Activities. While the organizations may be working on the same general issue, each must have its own program. Every activity of a tax-exempt organization must have a purpose consistent with the organization's tax status. For example, a 501(c)(3) could do a research report on toxic waste sites in a community, and its related 501(c)(4) could use that report to criticize candidates for office who failed to act against polluters. However, a 501(c)(3) could *not* do this research with the sole purpose providing the information to the 501(c)(4) for electoral work.

- Boards. While it is possible for some or all of the members of the 501(c)(3) and 501(c)(4) boards of directors to overlap, organizations should hold separate board meetings for each organization. Having different board officers for each organization and fewer members who serve on both boards can help to demonstrate the necessary separation between the two organizations—particularly valuable if the 501(c)(4) plans to engage in any partisan election-related activity.
- Staff. Related organizations can share staff, but each organization must pay its fair portion of staff salaries and benefits. The best way to do this is for staff members to complete timesheets documenting the time they spend working for each organization. Shared staff members typically receive a paycheck from one of the organizations, and that organization is then reimbursed by the other organization for its share of the staff member's time.
- Rent and other overhead expenses. Rent for shared office space and similar overhead expenses must also be apportioned between the organizations in some reasonable way. One method is to prorate rent according to the percentage of hours the staff spend working for each organization.
- Office equipment. Copiers, computers, and other office equipment can also be a shared expense. Organizations that can precisely track use (for example, by requiring staff to input codes for copier use) can apportion costs directly. Otherwise, the cost of office equipment can be shared using any other reasonable method.

Because of the strict limit on partisan political activities by 501(c)(3) organizations, it is particularly important to maintain a clear separation between a 501(c)(3) and an affiliated 501(c)(4) that is engaged in political activities, either itself or through its connected PAC.

Election Laws

In addition to federal tax law, federal and state (and sometimes even local) election laws govern the election-related activity of tax-exempt, non-profit corporations just as these laws regulate for-profit corporations. In practice, these laws rarely affect 501(c)(3) organizations because of the strict ban on partisan activities under federal tax law. However, these laws frequently affect other types of non-profit organizations.

Federal Election Campaign Act

The Federal Election Campaign Act (FECA) governs the activities related to elections to federal offices—President, Vice President, U.S. Senator, and Member of the U.S. House of Representatives. FECA restricts the election-related activities of corporations, but non-profit corporations can engage in extensive electoral advocacy in certain areas. In addition, PACs are generally not incorporated, and so they may more directly support or oppose candidates.

In general, no corporation, including incorporated 501(c)(4)s, may directly support or oppose a candidate under FECA. Corporations may not

- Make cash or in-kind contributions to candidates. In-kind contributions include donated office space, staff support, or services.
- Engage in communications or activities "coordinated" with a candidate, campaign, or party. An activity or communication is coordinated when the candidate, campaign, or party exercises some control over how the activity or communication is carried out or what it consists of.
- Spend any money in support of communications containing "express advocacy." Express

advocacy is a communication that clearly identifies a candidate for office and includes words that specifically encourage the audience to support or oppose the candidate, such as "elect," "vote for," "support," "defeat," "re-elect," or "oppose." (These types of words and phrases are sometimes referred to as the "magic words.")

In practice, these restrictions allow a huge range of electoral activity, such as "issue advocacy." Corporations are free to make independent expenditures for communications or activities that are *not* coordinated with a candidate and that do *not* contain the magic words of express advocacy. For example, a 501(c)(4) organization may criticize a candidate's previous support of bad legislation or run advertisements contrasting two candidates' views on an issue of importance to the organization.

In addition to this issue advocacy, 501(c)(4)s and other non-profit corporations may also engage in partisan electoral communications that expressly support or oppose candidates by taking advantage of one of several key exceptions to the general ban on express advocacy:

- A corporation may send an express advocacy message in communication directed to *members* of the corporation (or shareholders, certain staff members, and their families).
- A corporation may *endorse* a candidate to its members and announce that endorsement through its usual press channels (such as the same press list to which it sends other press announcements).
- Certain non-profit corporations that meet special requirements may send express advocacy messages to the general public. To qualify under this exception, these corporations may receive no support from any for-profit corporation or labor union. However, the rules for

this exception are complex, and any corporation seeking to use this exception should consult a lawyer first.

For advocates who want even greater flexibility in electoral communications, a PAC may be the answer. Because PACs are typically not incorporated, they are not subject to the express advocacy limits under FECA.

Under FECA, PACs may be independent entities or connected to a corporation—including a non-profit corporation. A 501(c)(4) may establish such a connected PAC (called a "Separate Segregated Fund" or "SSF"), but a 501(c)(3) may not because of the bar on 501(c)(3) participation in political activities. A corporation that creates a connected PAC may pay all the administrative and fundraising costs associated with that PAC, but the PAC may solicit contributions only from members (or shareholders) of the corporation or certain members of the corporation's staff (or their families). Independent PACs, on the other hand, must pay all their administrative and fundraising expenses but may solicit contributions from anyone.

The rules for the two types of PACs are otherwise quite similar. PACs may make direct contributions to candidates, subject to limits under FECA (currently $1,000 per candidate per election, except for "multicandidate" PACs, which may make contributions of $5,000 per candidate per election). These contributions may take the form of in-kind contributions to campaigns, such as paying the salary of employees from the connected 501(c)(4) who work for the campaign. In addition, PACs may make independent expenditures for communications that include express advocacy messages supporting or opposing candidates. (However, if these communications are coordinated with a candidate, they will become contributions to that candidate.)

PACs have extensive reporting obligations concerning both the sources of their funds and their expenditures. People who run PACs should get whatever help they need to learn and comply with these rules.

State Election Laws

State elections are governed not by FECA but by state (and sometimes local) election laws. These laws vary a great deal from state to state, and a complete discussion of them would be impossible here in this short space. Some election laws mirror the FECA, prohibiting most election-related activity by corporations. Others are much more permissive—in many states corporations may make direct contributions of money or other assistance to candidates and campaigns. Check your state office of elections for more details.

One key point is that state election laws often govern advocacy for or against ballot measures. While the federal tax law treats this activity as lobbying, most states regulate it as an election-related activity. As a result, non-profit corporations that engage in this type of activity—*including 501(c)(3)s*—should check their state and local laws.

Lobbyist Registration and Reporting Laws

Every state, as well as the federal government, has some law that regulates legislative lobbying. None of these laws place any restrictions on the *amount* of lobbying that an organization may do, but most require lobbyists or the organizations for which they work to register as a lobbyist and report their lobbying activities.

The federal law is the Lobbying Disclosure Act, and information on its requirements is available from the Office of the Clerk of the House of

Representatives. Information on most state laws is available either from the state legislature or from the state ethics office.

It is important to understand that the definition of "lobbying" under these laws may vary substantially from the IRS definition of lobbying that applies to 501(c)(3) organizations under the 501(h) expenditure test. For example, the 501(h) test excludes administrative advocacy from the definition of lobbying, but many states require non-profit (and other) lobbyists to report lobbying contacts with state agency officials that attempt to influence a decision on a regulatory rule or other decision.

State Solicitation Registration

Most states have charitable solicitation laws that require a non-profit organization to (1) register with a regulatory agency of the state (usually the Attorney General's office) prior to soliciting contributions from the general public and to (2) file annual financial statements with a state agency. Some states may require a connected political action committee (a Separate Segregated Fund) to register.

If a professional fundraiser is used, there may also be annual registration and bonding requirements. The definition of a professional fundraiser varies from state to state. If the 501(c)(4) organization's membership program solicits tax-deductible contributions for the 501(c)(3) organization, both organizations may have to register.

Many states use the IRS Form 990 as their annual financial reporting form, sometimes with additional schedules required. Many states require audited financial statements.

Call your Secretary of State's or State Attorney General's office to learn your state's requirements and which state office regulates charitable solicitation. You may want to consult a lawyer on these requirements.

Board Liability Insurance and Bonding

In recent years, many non-profit boards have investigated the cost of board liability insurance. Most small non-profit organizations have found the cost of insurance prohibitive and the likelihood of suits small. Given our litigious society, the need for liability insurance may increase, although the costs are unlikely to decrease. Some organizations have added "indemnification clauses" to their bylaws. It should be noted that they are to protect individuals, not the organization. These clauses indicate that as long as a board or staff member is acting in good faith, the organization will be responsible for any suits that might be filed against the individual for his or her work on behalf of the organization. Many organizations bond their staff people who handle money with what is called an employee "dishonesty" bond. This is not expensive unless lots of people handle money.

Summary of Agency Reporting Requirements

Internal Revenue Service

All of the following Internal Revenue Service publications and forms can be ordered by calling 1-800-424-FORM. Many of these forms are available at the IRS's Web site (www.irs.gov).

- *Form SS-4* is for requesting a Federal Employer Identification Number. (All organizations with staff must have an identification number.)
- *Forms 1023 and 1024* are for applying for tax exemption for a 501(c)(3) organization and a 501(c)(4) organization, respectively. Publication 557 describes in detail who can and should apply. Publication 557 also includes a good section on how to write Articles of

Incorporation that will suit the Internal Revenue Service.

- *W-4* is the Employee Withholding Allowance Form, which needs to be completed for new employees or when an employee's family circumstances change and the person's exemptions change. If any employee claims more than ten exemptions, the Internal Revenue Service must be notified.

- *I-9* is the Employment Eligibility Verification Form, required by the Immigration Reform Control Act of 1986. All new employees must complete it within three working days, and the form is kept in their personnel files.

- *Form 941* is the Quarterly Return of Withholding Tax Form for reporting on wages paid and federal income and social security taxes withheld. It must be submitted within thirty days after each quarter ends (January 31, April 30, July 31, and October 31).

- *Form 940* is the Employer's Annual Federal Unemployment (FUTA) Tax Return. A 501(c)(3) organization does not have to file. A 501(c)(4) organization does. It is due thirty days after the end of the calendar year (i.e., January 30 for the previous year).

- *Form 940-EZ* is a simplified version of Form 940. It may be used by organizations that pay unemployment contributions in only one state in a timely manner and do not have taxable FUTA wages that are exempt from state unemployment tax.

- *Form 990* is the Return of Organization Exempt from Income Tax. This annual financial information form must be filed by most 501(c)(3) and 501(c)(4) organizations that have revenues of $25,000 or more. A 501(c)(3) organization must also file Schedule A of Form 990. It is due on the fifteenth day of the fifth month after the end of the fiscal year (May 15 for calendar year organizations).

- *Form 990-EZ* is slightly shorter than Form 990 and can be used in place of Form 990 by organizations with gross receipts of less than $100,000 and end-of-year total assets below $500,000.

- *Form 990-T* is needed to report unrelated business income of more than $1,000. Unrelated business income is income that is unrelated to the organization's tax-exempt purposes or that is competitive with taxable enterprises in the marketplace. Unrelated business income includes unrelated advertising in your organization's magazine, rental incomes from other groups (if you own a building), gift shops, and bingo. Unrelated business income is not holding securities or conducting fundraising events. Holding one car wash is not unrelated business income, but setting up a regular car wash business is.

- *Form 2758* is used to extend the filing deadline for your Form 990, Schedule A, and Form 990T for up to two months. This form must be filed on or before the regular due date for Form 990.

- *Form 5678* is used by 501(c)(3) organizations for "electing" to expend a limited, but more than "insubstantial," amount of expenditures on lobbying.

- *W-2 Form* is the Wage and Tax Statement Form that is sent to employees about their previous year's wages and tax withholdings. These must be mailed to the employee by January 31 and to the IRS by February 28.

- *W-3 Form* is the Transmittal of Income and Tax Statements Form that summarizes the W-2 forms sent to employees. The W-3 form must be mailed to the Internal Revenue Service by February 28.

- *Form 1099* is used to report consulting payments of $600 or more. It must be sent to the individual consultants by January 31. This form is comparable to the W-2 form for employees.

- *Form 1096* is the Annual Summary and Transmittal of 1099 forms. This is comparable to the W-3 form and must also be mailed to the Internal Revenue Service by February 28.

State Agencies

The following documents and forms are those commonly required by states. Where you file each report varies from state to state.

- Incorporation papers, Articles of Incorporation.
- State payroll tax forms.
- Workers' Compensation, payments, and forms.
- Periodic corporate filings that may be required; these are unrelated to the above items.
- Out-of-state corporation filings for organizations operating in a state other than the one in which they are incorporated.
- *FEC Form 3X*, which must be filed by a political action committee in the state in which the candidate supported by the PAC was seeking office.
- For state and local elections, campaign finance reports by the 501(c)(4) organization or the political action committee.
- State lobby registration and annual report.
- Initial registration for solicitation in the state.
- Annual charitable solicitation financial report, sometimes including an audit.
- Professional fundraiser annual registration.

Federal Elections Commission

The following forms are required by the FEC:
- *FEC Form 1* is for filing the initial registration. This form must be filed within ten days of establishing a Separate Segregated Fund PAC to participate in federal elections.

- *FEC Form 3X* is for political action committees to report on receipts and disbursements. In election years, pre- and postelection reports, as well as quarterly reports, are due. In non-election years, semi-annual reports are due.

Running Non-Profit Organizations Is Serious Business

It is hard work to manage a non-profit organization efficiently and to stay abreast of all the necessary legal and financial matters. Take your responsibilities seriously. Make sure that adequate board and staff time and training are devoted to the financial and legal matters of the organization. You cannot claim ignorance and expect sympathy from the Internal Revenue Service or government agencies, let alone your membership and financial supporters.

The Director of every organization must devote a significant amount of time to managing the operation. All other staff must provide good records and draft reports or assist in other appropriate ways. Board members must not hesitate to ask questions to assure themselves that the legal and financial matters of the organization are in order.

Caution—this chapter is not meant to substitute for an attorney experienced in non-profit and election law. Our opponents will use our failure to meet legal requirements and reporting regulations to discredit us. Don't give them the chance.

Special thanks for contributions to this section go to Stuart Greenberg, author of *Citizen Action Financial Manager Handbook*; Rochelle Davis, Generation Green; and John Pomerantz, Alliance for Justice. The Alliance for Justice has more detailed publications on the legal requirements of not-for-profit organizations. See the bibliography.

25

Organizers aren't simply "discovered." Nor are they born with special "organizing genes." Rather, they're developed, cared for, and groomed, usually by other organizers.

The movement needs organizers who can hang in there for the long haul. Social change does not occur in a year or two. It is a lifetime occupation requiring lifetime commitments as well as lifetime support systems.

Organizing can be the most rewarding work we do. We are able to express our values through our daily work. We see people grow and develop and gain a sense of their own power. We also see powerful organizations built and real improvements made in the quality of life in society. We don't earn the highest salaries, but we are able to feel good about ourselves and our contributions to the world.

This chapter suggests a few ways that organizers can equip themselves to work for the long haul.

Setting and Meeting Goals

One of the best ways to "organize for the long haul" is to learn how to set and meet goals. Because organizing can seem illusive and unclear, organizers must set goals for themselves

Setting and Meeting Goals

Training and Supervision

Seeking Mentors and Trusted Colleagues

Achieving Balance in Your Life

Developing a Long-Term Vision

Personal Pressures on Organizers

Recognition and Building Partnerships

Working for the Long Haul

that provide structure and direction for the work and that can offer a sense of accomplishment.

Organizers should have two kinds of goals. The first are the direct work-related goals that include winning on issues, building organizations, and changing the relations of power.

In addition to the direct work-related goals, you should have some personal growth goals. For example, this year you might want to improve your public speaking skills, learn to supervise interns, or learn to use a database program. Your personal goals should be very practical and measurable so you can look back at the end of the year and see that you've met them. Being able to review your work of the last year and recognize that you've accomplished most of your goals will give you a sense of accomplishment. Such satisfaction helps us develop self-confidence and a sense of well-being, which in turn helps us continue organizing for the long haul.

Even though supervisors should help you set and meet these goals, they often do not. So take the initiative and help organize your supervisor. Outline both your direct work goals and your personal growth goals and how you plan to achieve them. Check in regularly on your progress toward meeting all your goals.

Training and Supervision

Making sure you receive adequate training and direction has been discussed in several other places in this manual, but it cannot be overemphasized. Ultimately, people can only develop a positive sense of their own abilities if they succeed in work situations. Who wouldn't wonder about themselves if everything they worked on failed? Amorphous jobs don't help one develop self-confidence. The only way most organizers can be successful is with good training and direction. You can't always control how you are feeling in a situation, but you can control what you do. Make sure that you seek out and insist upon the training and direction you need.

Both new and experienced organizers should consciously seek to know organizers working in other fields and other groups by joining formal networks or associating with informal ones. It helps to share war stories, learn from one another, and find out about the best organizing resources and support structures in your area.

Formal training opportunities, such as with the Midwest Academy, should be sought. If you are totally new to organizing, try to work for a few months before coming to a training session so you have more questions to ask.

Seeking Mentors and Trusted Colleagues

All new organizers need mentors, and all organizers need trusted colleagues that can help you evaluate projects and reflect on what you are doing. Such relationships should be developed with the full support of your supervisor, so talk with him or her about the need to have an organizing mentor. Make it clear that a mentor is not a supervisor but rather someone who helps you reflect on what you are doing. When the mentor is a more experienced person in your own organization, the line between mentoring and supervising can get blurred and lead to conflict.

Large social change organizations, such as unions or national organizations, usually have enough organizers on staff to ensure that new organizers can find mentors and trusted colleagues, although it may still be helpful to formally structure such relationships. The organizing networks, such as ACORN, USAction, or the Industrial Areas Foundation, structure training programs for staff, and networking meetings are held at which organizers can build relationships with colleagues. Consider if such a practice would be useful in your organization.

Unfortunately, it is harder to find a mentor in small, independent organizations with one or two organizers. If you work for such a group, you must find some other organizers to talk with regularly. In some cities, the National Organizers Alliance has set up a network of organizers. In other cities, there is an informal gathering of organizers. If such a grouping doesn't exist in your city, consider starting one. Don't make it complicated, just invite a handful of organizers to lunch on a monthly basis. Such meetings will help everyone and may lead to some organizational collaboration in the long run.

Some foundations will help pay for the consulting services of an organizing mentor. Review your financial supporters and see if one might provide some extra money to pay a mentor to meet with you. Having a little bit of money helps ensure that you will get the time you deserve. However, many experienced organizers are willing to mentor "pro-bono" if you demonstrate your commitment to learning organizing and if you make it easy on the mentor. Offer to take the mentor to lunch once a month near the mentor's office. Promise to keep your mentoring lunches to an hour and a half. Send written reports ahead of time covering your activities since the last meeting so the mentor doesn't have to remember everything.

Look around the field of experienced organizers. Approach one or two whom you admire and believe you would like to work with for a year or so. Outline your proposal for mentoring in writing to the person, and then call and discuss it with him or her.

Achieving Balance in Your Life

Social change doesn't occur overnight. We can't continually work in a frenzy expecting the revolution to come tomorrow. It won't. If we burn ourselves out today, we won't be around for tomorrow's struggles. Organizing is never a nine-to-five job. It often is fifty to sixty hours a week, but it shouldn't routinely be that. Yes, sometimes you will have to put in extremely long hours, but sometimes you need to work at a steadier, more leisurely pace and regroup.

If you find yourself blowing up at people, getting irritated over the littlest problem, or not enjoying your work, you need to review your work habits. If you are working excessive hours, you will become less effective in the time you do work and will begin thinking of yourself as a martyr (and everyone will avoid you). The social change movement of the 2000s does not need more martyrs. It needs effective, well-balanced organizers who are building power by involving people in winning real victories.

Friends and Families

In the past, too many organizers neglected their friends and families, only to regret it when they lost them. We all need personal support networks, families and close friends, who can share our joys and sorrows. Developing close relationships requires time. We can't ignore friends and families for long periods and then expect them to "be there" when we are ready or need them. Strong relationships provide organizers with a base of support for sustaining themselves for the long haul and assistance in developing self-confidence.

Interestingly enough, a large percentage of people who have been organizing for long periods of time, ten years or more, tend to have stable relationships. Although it's certainly not the case that if one has a good relationship, one becomes a good organizer, it does seem to be a factor in helping people survive for the long haul.

If we have children, we have to and want to spend time with them. Having children can help organizers relax and get away from their work—playing basketball with the kids or reading stories, for example. It can also be stressful trying to juggle work schedules and childcare responsibilities. Not all non-profits have policies geared toward family life, and you may need to consider proposing new policies.

Relaxing

As well as developing close relationships, organizers need to develop means for relaxing. Sometimes relaxing and developing relationships are the same thing. Many organizers find it important to exercise on a regular basis, particu-larly to release stress. Others find it helpful to practice hobbies, such as playing musical instruments, photography, singing, or reading history. The key is to find things to do that take your mind off your organizing work.

Vacations are important. If you are always "too busy" to take a vacation, something's wrong. Vacations help sustain you for the long haul and can be even more effective in the short haul. Organizers return from vacations with new ideas and renewed vigor and enthusiasm for their work. Even if you can't afford to "go" somewhere, you can find something totally different to do for several weeks. Take vacations!

If your organization does not have a sabbatical policy, consider trying to implement one. After a staff person has worked at an organization for seven to ten years, it is helpful for them to develop new skills and seek a fresh perspective. Sabbatical policies also encourage staff to stay with the organization for longer periods of time.

Developing a Long-Term Vision

Organizers who work for the long haul are not concerned solely about winning just this immediate issue, involving just those specific people, or building just that particular organization. Meeting the three principles of direct action organizing in any given context is important, but it is not enough. Organizers need a sense of vision that allows them to place their work in a more historical context and to understand that they are parts of the broader movement for social and economic justice in our society.

Organizing for the long haul demands a sense of political vision, a sense of where we are going. If we see only the short-term tasks before us, it is easy to become frustrated and discouraged. We must regularly review the ways in which our current work contributes toward meeting both short-term and long-term vision goals. A sense of vision grows out of a set of values, experiences, individual reflections, and organizational wisdom. As a result of these, organizers see their work in the broader context of efforts to make our society more just, more compassionate, and more egalitarian. Vision includes involving large numbers of people in the process of democracy and building accountable democratic institutions that can work for the good of humankind. It includes building active opposition to the greed and power of the wealthy few in their attempts to privatize and own the world.

We must remember our past successes by sharing our past victories with newcomers; otherwise, human nature leads us to forget past victories and dwell on our failures. And finally, we must celebrate change, success, and movement in the direction of a more just and fair society. Saul Alinsky used to say you can tell the caliber of an organization by the quality of its celebrations.

The book of Proverbs says, "Where there is no vision, the people perish." Hopefully we won't perish immediately without it, but we will be better equipped to sustain and encourage others and ourselves if we take time to reflect on where we've been and where we are going. The first decade of the new millennium will set the tone and direction for the kind of world that our children and grandchildren will live in. What happens in the United States matters not just for us and our communities but for people around the world.

Personal Pressures on Organizers

Most people do not find it natural to organize. We are taught to be polite and to accept situations as they are. Organizers sometimes need to push the limits of what is socially acceptable in order to bring about change. We are taught to respect authority. Organizers challenge authority when authority is unresponsive to people's needs. We are taught to value individualism. Organizers have to bring individuals together for group action and to build organizations. We are brought up to think of traditional occupations. How do you even explain what an organizer is to your parents?

It is not surprising that organizing puts some unusual personal pressures on organizers. These pressures, along with the many uncertainties of organizing, may increase an organizer's feelings of insecurity. Dealing with these pressures is central to being a good organizer, as well as a happy one. There are commonly two negative ways in which organizers and administrators respond to these pressures: the authoritarian response and the submission and falling victim response.

The Authoritarian Response

Some organizers respond to events that are seemingly out of their control by denying what they feel or by not being aware that they feel anything at all. This approach allows an organizer or administrator to charge ahead and get a great deal accomplished. By providing clear direction, such a person generates confidence and gives real staff leadership. But not acknowledging uncertainty can be detrimental to the organization, staff, and organizer alike. The organization, for example, may give too much control to the person who has all the answers and less to people learning leadership. This can forestall giving people a sense of their own power and team building since people may be directed but not trained to direct.

This style also holds the possible danger of an organizer or administrator becoming authoritarian and turning off people who are less clear, articulate, or self-confident. It rarely allows for building collegial relations as a group and instead substitutes one-on-one relations that are easier to handle. In short, it undermines the group's solidarity and spirit.

To members and staff, the administrator or organizer may convey impatience, especially with those who are less experienced or do not share this style. People who imply that they have all the answers and seek to maintain control belittle others' contributions. New ideas are rejected at first glance, and people who may want to offer new ideas are intimidated, as are people whose ideas diverge. Pushing opposition underground may make it go away for a while, but eventually confrontations erupt, challenging existing power and illegitimate authority. Often this style of behavior is combined with difficulty in giving praise or in admitting one's own mistakes. Others feel wary and critical in return.

For the administrator this creates enormous pressures, both personal and organizational. Because such a person feels a need to provide the staff leadership, he or she may force an inadequate division of labor. Others may not be "trusted" to produce or may withdraw from volunteering. At the personal or "internal" level, the organizer may become overburdened and stretched too thin. Filled with frustrations and few places to vent them, he or she may burst out with misdirected anger and complaints.

A person who is aware of this dynamic can take action to accommodate it. One way is to establish routine group review meetings, where the basic directions are discussed and problems shared. Someone who sets a positive group tone should chair these sessions. Problems related to control questions do not stem solely from insecurity. They can also be the result of overconfidence, a chaotic organizational structure, or staff conflicts.

The Submission and Falling Victim Response

A second common reaction to the demands and uncertainties of organizing is just the opposite of the first. Instead of becoming authoritarian, one is overwhelmed and responds with a kind of fear. The organizer or administrator may engage in very hard work and may work long hours, but his or her priorities will be off. In one way, this fear may provide a temporary basis for effective organizing because it makes the organizer particularly sensitive to the needs of others, able to respond generously and kindly to problems. But adapting the organizing to meet people's individual wants is seldom the best course. This kind of organizer may be very good at building others' confidence because of his or her "people" focus. But like the "controlling" organizer, this person can create problems organization-wide.

When an administrator's insecurity expresses itself by submission and falling victim to problems, he or she avoids making decisions, especially difficult ones such as firing someone, cutting the budget, or deciding on a risky course of action. But the life of a social change organization is bold and direct and involves timely action. To avoid making decisions is the kiss of death. Postponing decision making in order to avoid making the "wrong" decision or hurting someone's feelings makes the organization stumble for lack of strong leadership and allows outside forces to control situations.

For other staff, such indecisiveness leads to group insecurity. While relations between people may be fine under such an administrator, there may not be enough to challenge the staff to develop new skills and a broader vision. Not achieving enough, members and staff may drift off to more rewarding pursuits. An organization is designed to build collective power and, in doing so, to build individual power. Without models of self-confidence, the potential for gaining that power is undermined.

The person will simply end up feeling bad or worse as a result of his or her indecisiveness, taking issues personally and looking for personal, rather than organizational, solutions. The person's worst fears and anxieties will be heightened, creating a vicious cycle of self-criticism, less effective action, and more self-criticism. He or she may feel the victim of circumstances and blame others but fail to correct the problems, real or perceived.

Recognition and Building Partnerships

The healthier way to approach these problems is to acknowledge to yourself what you are feeling and to turn what might otherwise be a weakness into a strength.

Once you are in touch with your own feelings, you know what you know and what you don't. You know that building a team and an organization are primary goals. You understand the importance of developing others' confidence. You recognize that how you are feeling often mirrors the reality others are feeling. You trust people and you place your trust in a group process, thus freeing yourself from having to know every answer. You will have a new power if you use this insight to build a team that works together to solve problems.

Developing means for addressing our insecurities is important in learning to work more effectively with people and in enabling us to build powerful organizations that win real victories. Don't underestimate the importance of self-confidence in developing styles of behavior that are healthy and sustaining for the long term.

Care for yourself, learn to appreciate your abilities, and develop a vision that provides focus and meaning for your work. We've chosen this work—not as a job but as a commitment to a better world. We can change history. Justice can govern if we take the future into our own hands.

Our thanks to Heather Booth, founder of the Midwest Academy, for her contribution to the second half of this chapter. Heather has mentored dozens of people over the years.

26

The Myth of the Rising Tide

Our economic system continues to fail the majority of working Americans. This may seem an exaggeration coming as it does in the course of the longest economic recovery* in U.S. history.[1] Indeed, there is a widespread belief that the three-part combination of the new information economy, deregulation, and free markets has tamed the business cycle so that this economic recovery will not be followed by a serious recession. It is said that we are in a new and more productive kind of economy, free from unemployment and inflation. There is a growing belief, expressed in the passage of welfare reform legislation, that anyone with proper ambition can now find a job and make a decent living.

The truth is that as good as the recent years have been, they have been nowhere near good enough. In fact, the rising prosperity has done more to call

---

*The terms "economic expansion" and "economic recovery" are often used interchangeably to indicate periods of time in which the economy (gross domestic product) is growing. A recession, of course, is when it is shrinking. We use the word "recovery" because as of this writing, the economy has about returned to (recovered) the point it had reached before the last recession.

You Mean You're Not Getting Rich?
Economics in the New Millennium

into question the economic foundation of the country than would a recession. In a recession, it is always argued that times are exceptionally bad just now, but wait, there will be a recovery and then everything will be OK again. Well, there has been a recovery—the longest in history—with record low unemployment and inflation combined with rising wages and family income. The share of income going to the poorest families has, at least, stopped falling. The stock market has added enormous consumer purchasing power to the economy. Yet the best falls far short of what is needed. If this is indeed the historical high-water mark of the U.S. economy, as it may well be, then we must frankly appraise the point at which we have arrived. We will not soon be departing for some better place.

Nearly a Third of Working People Can't Find a Middle-Class Job

If there is one statistic that sums up the situation, it is this: One-third of the workforce is unable to find a job that will sustain a family at a middle-class standard of living. Roughly forty-five million decently paid jobs are simply missing from the economy. This figure represents the total of people who are either unemployed and looking for work, unemployed but gave up looking, or working part time but want a full-time job and those whose wages, on a full-time basis, would not lift a family of four above the poverty line.[2]

To be sure, in the closing years of the 20th century, some of the worst trends were reversed with real wages and family income ending a long period of decline and turning slowly upward. Average family income and real (after inflation) weekly pay have risen to just above where they were in 1989 at the start of the last recession. This was welcome news indeed, but from the standpoint of advancing the living standard of working families, it was as if the 1990s had never happened. Many families spent ten years of their working lives first going downhill economically and then, toward the millennium's end, arriving back where they started. For the working poor, even the most recent years of the boom have been a particular disappointment. Of all full-time year-round workers, the percentage living in poverty was virtually the same at the decade's end as it had been in the midyears. Worse, the actual number of such workers in poverty rose steadily and is now about three million. The situation stands in sharp contrast to the boom of the 1960s, when poverty among full-time workers actually dropped by 56 percent.[3]

As we went to press in September 2000, the 1999 Household Income figures had just been released by the Census Bureau. The median real household income showed a healthy rise of almost 3 percent from the previous year, putting it nearly $2,000 above the high point of the last recovery in 1989. Significantly, however, there was no decline in inequality, which has now remained unchanged for six consecutive years. The Economic Policy Institute (EPI) commented that the country seems to have leveled off at a historically high level of inequality and that where past economic expansions had reduced inequality, this one has not. EPI also notes that the rise in income is accomplished by a rise in working hours and that the average household worked thirty-three more hours in 1999 than in the previous year.[4]

Author and *Nation* columnist William Greider posed the question well when he asked, "In these best of times, how come typical Americans are still spending more than they earn to keep up?"[5] If the recovery continues well into the 2000s, some real progress might be seen, but if the peak comes in the early years of this decade, it will be necessary to conclude that this is about as good as it gets.

As the year 2000 approached, *The New York Times* raised a most interesting point. It reported that an otherwise spectacular economic picture was combined with the smallest wage increase on record. Actually wages had been rising at about 2.5 percent a year for the previous three years, but compared to profit growth this must have seemed small. *The Times* said, "With inflation dormant, the trend highlighted a conundrum that has economists and policy makers at the Federal Reserve scratching their heads: why has the combination of steady growth and low unemployment not forced a run-up in wages . . . as history and traditional economic models suggest it should?" A "run-up" in wages could be caused by a combination of workers changing jobs for higher pay elsewhere or by employers raising wages to hold or attract people. In part this is happening, but not to the degree the Federal Reserve had feared.

The Times reporter almost answered his own question by citing low inflation, which allows even small wage gains to put workers "ahead of the game." Then, almost as an afterthought, he hit a major reason when he quoted a corporate CEO as saying "wage increases are being held down, especially in manufacturing, by a persistent fear among workers about losing their jobs despite a strong economy."[6]

Six months later, *The Times* remained astonished: "What is amazing . . . is the failure of wages to rise, flatly contradicting the established economic theory. Most economists expected as unemployment fell below 5 percent that the scramble to find enough workers would force employers to bid up wages at an accelerating rate."[7] *The Times* made a useful observation: many of the people who are counted as being employed are actually temporary (or part-time) workers, and therefore, the job market may not be as tight as it appears. Seven months later, stagnant wages remained a mystery but a new insight emerged. Noting that while industrial companies traditionally moved to low-wage areas, *The Times* writer, Louis Uchitelle, cited recent studies showing that all types of service operations also change locations within the United States. Both the actual moves and the threat of them helps to quiet employee wage demands, he reasoned:

Various explanations have been offered by economists for the failure of labor shortages to give a bigger kick to wages in the record long expansion that started in 1991: weaker unions, the greater use of temporary workers, a minimum wage that has lost value, a flood of immigrant workers, layoffs and job insecurity, global competition. Often overlooked, however, has been the impact of the stepped-up rate of corporate migration, which adds another critical element to the mix.[8]

The article adds that corporate migration does help to spread the benefits of the economic expansion more evenly around the country.

Globalization: Lower Wages, Economic Instability, and New Organizing Opportunities

The role of globalization in keeping down wages is now widely recognized. Breakthroughs in technology, communications, and transportation allow products to be made profitably anywhere in the world, forcing American workers to compete with the lowest wage job markets. Indeed, the corporate approach is to demand complete freedom for products and money to move to any country while denying it to workers. Immigration policy prevents workers from coming to high-wage countries. At the same time, jobs are encouraged to leave for low-wage countries. "Commerce Dept. statistics imply that something like 1 million workers lose their jobs every year as a result of imports or job shifts abroad."[9] *Business Week,* which usually applauds free trade, concedes that "Globalization also

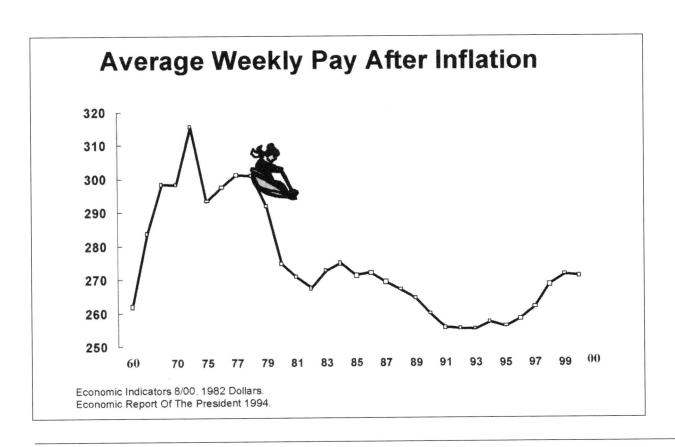

Average Weekly Pay After Inflation

Economic Indicators 8/00. 1982 Dollars.
Economic Report Of The President 1994.

helps push down U.S. wages. Studies show that trade accounts for roughly one quarter of the rise in U.S. income inequality since the 1970s. In addition, 62 percent of manufacturers use the threat of moving jobs abroad during union organizing drives.[10]

In addition to its impact on wages, globalization adds to the instability of the economic system itself. As William Greider put it:

> The core contradiction in the global economy—enduring over capacity and inadequate demand—is usually obscured by the more visible dramas of financial crisis because it is located in the globalizing production system, the long-distance networks of factories and firms that produce the goods and services flowing into global trade. Corporate insecurity—the fear of falling behind, the need to keep driving down costs, including labor costs—is what generates globalization's greatest contradiction.

> Yet each corporation decides (perhaps correctly) that it has no choice but to disperse and expand production for survival—moves that seem smart and necessary individually, but that collectively deepen the imbalances of over capacity and quicken the chase for new markets. So we witness the recurring episodes of giddy overinvestment by firms, investors and developing nations, followed by financial breakdown.[11]

Globalization is not as new as often supposed. Random examples include both the Jamestown, Virginia, and New York (New Amsterdam) colonies (1607 and 1621), which were the property of the privately owned British corporations that governed them and intended to make a profit from their activities. The British textile industry operated with American slave-produced cotton. The early American railroads were heavily financed by British capital. Adolf Hitler's Panzer divisions used tanks made by the Ford Motor Company.

Three aspects of globalization are new, however, and have an impact on the political and organizing climate:

- First, the extent to which the United States has become a net importer of foreign-made goods instead of an exporter is raising widespread concern over the impact of miserable working conditions on both foreign labor and American jobs. The record-setting American trade deficit, the amount by which imports outweigh exports, highlights the trade problem.

- Second, with the collapse of the Soviet Union there is no longer any competing economic or ideological system, and consequently there is no need to put a humane face on capitalism. In the past, agencies such as the International Monetary Fund and the World Bank would prop up the economies of poor countries in order to prevent revolutionary movements from aligning with the Soviets. Today, these agencies can devote their full efforts to making such countries produce profits for Western capitalists at the expense of the people and environment.

- Third—and this is the good news—certain kinds of global corporations are actually more vulnerable to citizen (consumer) pressure than in the past. This is because their products are virtually identical with those of other companies and only the brand names created by expensive advertising campaigns are distinctive. A Cadillac was always known as a quality car, and it came from a factory that made just one product, Cadillacs. Today, apparel, shoes, electronics, and even some cars often come from factories around the world that produce the same product for several different companies. The labels change but the products are virtually identical. Consumer loyalty is therefore to the brand logo, not to the product itself. This makes it possible to punish companies for their environmental, labor, or anti–human rights practices by using negative publicity. Once the logo loses its sparkle, consumers can switch to another brand name but still get the same or a very similar product. Nike shoes is a classic example. The company has about eight thousand employees, almost all of whom are in management and marketing. The tens of thousands of actual shoe workers who make Nikes are employees of subcontractors. Nike's Vice President for Asia put it succinctly: "We don't know the first thing about manufacturing. We are marketers and designers."[12]

Lives of Uncertainty in a Time of Plenty

Survey data confirms the astute observation that many people fear losing their jobs. In a poll asking people to guess the unemployment rate, respondents put it at 20 percent when the official figure was 5.3 percent.[13] (During the height of the Great Depression of the 1930s, the unemployment rate was 25 percent.) Over a period of nine years, another poll tracked responses to the question, "How likely [are you] to lose your job or be laid off in the next 12 months?" After nine years of economic growth, the number answering "not at all likely" actually decreased by 9 percentage points to 60 percent, although the already low unemployment rate was actually falling slightly. During the same period, the number of workers who said it would be "very easy" to find a new job with the same pay and benefits fell by 7 percentage points to only 27 percent of all workers.[14]

Why, for so many, does the greatest peacetime economic recovery in history evoke a sense of insecurity? One reason is that the employment situation is not really as good as it seems. Official unemployment figures are flawed. They count as unemployed only those people who have actually gone job hunting in the last four weeks.[15] (It used to be six weeks, but President Lyndon Johnson had it lowered to give the appearance that his War on Poverty was succeeding.) Another flaw is that part-time workers, those who want but can't find full-time jobs, are counted as employed with no distinction made. A better measure is the *under*employment rate that compensates for these errors. It is almost double the official rate.[16] A growing portion of the workforce is increasingly unaccounted for as U.S. policy drives immigrants into hiding. The official estimate of illegal immigration in 1999 was 275,000, but surveys of other data put the figure at 600,000, close to the number of legal permanent residents admitted at that time.[17] Unemployment among illegal immigrants is seldom counted.

Another problem with the employment figures is that they ignore the situation of a quarter of all workers who, although they are counted as being employed, have what are called "non-standard jobs" instead of regular full-time work.[18] These include part-time workers, temps, day laborers, independent contractors, and the self-employed. While many people prefer non-standard work, the fact remains that non-standard pay scales and benefits are, on the whole, lower than for people with comparable skills who work full time, and employment is less certain. The ranks of "non-standard" workers rose rapidly during the first half of the decade of the 1990s. For example, the number of temporary help jobs doubled between 1982 and 1989 and doubled again by 1997,[19] reaching

3.1 million, or 2.4 percent of the workforce, by 1999.[20] Indeed, the largest single employer in America is now Manpower Inc. It hires out 676,000 substitute workers a year.[21] In the final years of the 1990s, the rise in overall non-standard work slowed and regular full-time employment inched up from 73 percent in 1995 to 75 percent in 1999,[22] a very good trend if it continues.

The unemployment figures, as they are often quoted in the media, tend to conceal racial disparities. While African American and Hispanic unemployment rates have been falling, they are still about double the national average. For African American teenagers who looked for a job in the last four weeks, the current unemployment rate is actually higher than that of the Great Depression.

Not only are unemployment rates higher than they appear, but the instability of working life is increasing and with it the overall stress of trying to make a living and raise a family. For example, the number of workers with long-term jobs is steadily shrinking.[23] Even in times of low unemployment, job loss can have consequences. A fifteen-year study ending in the mid-1990s surveyed people who said that they had lost a job within the last three years of being interviewed. Of those, 35 percent had not found a new job when they were interviewed. Those who got new jobs (including part-time jobs) found that they were earning on average 14 percent less than before. Of those who previously had healthcare benefits, 29 percent got no coverage when they found a new job.[24]

Average Wages Are Moving Up, but Not Everyone Is Average

Many working people who do have decently paid jobs are finding that despite the general impression that everyone is getting ahead, they themselves are not. The truth is that most people are not getting ahead. In the midst of this unprecedented economic expansion, wage stagnation is a cause of rising debt, inequality, and an increase in working hours.

A feature article in *The New York Times* Business Section said:

> middle income families have been stuck in place for a decade, their incomes even losing ground to inflation through part of the 1990's according to data from the Census Bureau. Only last year did middle income families finally make significant progress; the median income rose more in 1998 than in any year since 1986. Yet, in contrast to earlier generations, these families don't see themselves as sharing in the national bounty. Instead, they wonder why they have to struggle so hard just to pay the bills.[25]

The previous period of expansion in the business cycle ended with the recession of 1989. After that year, real (inflation-adjusted) wages generally fell until 1996, when they slowly turned up again. Averages don't tell the whole story and they tend to conceal more than they explain. For middle-wage male workers, wages in 1999 were still below what they had been in 1989 partly because over half a million manufacturing jobs were lost in those years. Middle-wage women, on the other hand, did better. Their wages in mid-1999 were 3–5 percent higher, a small but definite improvement. In spite of gains, the economic gender gap continues. In 1999, the male middle-wage was $13 an hour and for women, $10.[26]

The chart below, "Percent Change in Number of People Earning $23 an Hour or Above," shows how the numbers of people holding very good jobs changed between 1989 and 1997.[27]

During those years, the percent of White men earning over $23 an hour remained the same, while that of Hispanic men declined slightly, probably because the figure includes a large number of new immigrants. Women in all groups moved ahead with White women leading. Keep in mind, however, that this chart is drawn to clearly state the differences between groups. The percentages on the left range only from –0.5 to 2.5 percent and show that the changes are really quite small and that the broad picture is one of overall wage stagnation. At the present rate, wage increases will have to continue for many years to make a real difference to working families.

The "Average Weekly Pay" chart on page 349 shows how average weekly pay rose, fell, and has risen again. Keep in mind that these averages conceal important differences between groups of working people.[28]

Economic Growth Won't Improve a Changing Job Structure

The factors that add uncertainty to working life stem from deeper structural changes in the nature of work. It is widely understood that more stable, unionized, and better paid manufacturing jobs have been disappearing from the economy. Many of them were sent abroad by American companies. While the projections from 1998 to 2008 show the loss slowing dramatically, still another 89,000 manufacturing jobs will be lost in that period. The lower paid service sector, after gaining 19 million jobs in the last decade, is projected to gain another 19 million by 2008.[29]

Of the top ten occupations projected by the Labor Department for the largest increase by the year 2008, only one, managers and top executives, is a highly paid category. Four more are decently paid occupations. They are shown in the table on the next page.

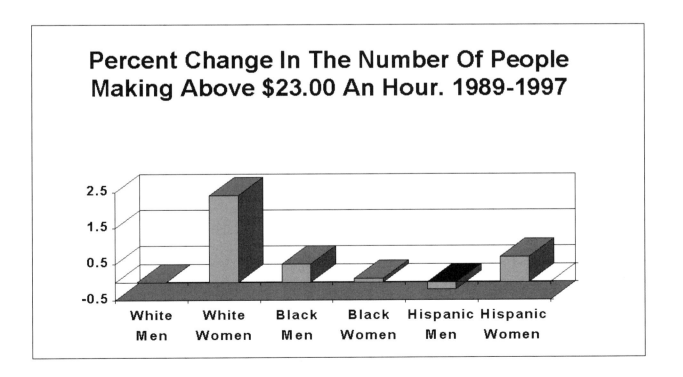

Percent Change In The Number Of People Making Above $23.00 An Hour. 1989-1997

High or Decently Paid Jobs by 2008

(Order of growth in parentheses)

Computer support specialists (1)

Systems Analyst (2)

Registered nurses (5)

Truck drivers (6)*

General managers and top executives (7)

The remaining five largest job growth occupations offer low pay and low benefits, and they are often part time as the table below indicates:

Lower Paid Jobs by 2008

(Order of growth in parentheses)

Home health aides (3)

Teachers aides (4)

Cashiers (6)*

Office clerks (8)

Retail sales (9)

* Both truck drivers and cashiers are numbered 6 because they are growing at the same rate.

It is not surprising that with the economic expansion driven by consumer spending, the two largest occupations among the top ten are retail sales people and cashiers. By the year 2008, jobs for over a million additional sales people and cashiers will have been created, jobs that average around $20,000 a year and have few benefits.[30] Interestingly, the third largest occupation in the top ten is bosses. Half a million new positions for managers and top executives will be added to the existing 3.5 million, a figure many working people feel is already far too high. Although there are fewer of them in number, the prize for the highest rate of job growth goes to computer support specialists.[31]

Another Day Older and Deeper in Debt

Another aspect of the economic insecurity facing America's families is the growth of what *Forbes* magazine called an "unprecedented burden" of consumer debt.[32] Although its growth has slowed in the most recent years, debt remains at record heights. "Working people are increasingly living beyond their means by borrowing in order to make ends meet (or in some cases in a desperate attempt to inch up their living standards). To a considerable extent, the current economic expansion has been built on consumer debt."[33] By the end of 1999, outstanding consumer debt had reached 100 percent of consumer disposable income,[34] up from 68 percent in 1980.

It is difficult to put debt figures in a context that makes them meaningful. Borrowing for a house or an education may be far better financially than not doing so. It is seldom clear how much debt is too much and how much is too little. However, debt, for whatever purpose, can become a factor in people's lives and shapes their options. The average family is now paying about $7,564 a year in interest payments.[35] What is particularly troubling is that 72 percent of household debt is secured by the family's home. In 1998 alone, money from mortgage refinancing and home-equity loans was used by consumers to pay off $34 billion in credit card debt. In part, the runup in house prices has made this extensive borrowing possible. In the event of an economic downturn, however, many families may be unable to make their payments and will lose their homes.[36] Why is this happening when the country seems awash with stock market profits? Between 1989 and 1998, average households, those in the middle of the income range, got 2.8 percent of the total growth in stock market holdings but 39 percent of the rise in household debt.[37]

A Little Rain May Fall—Vanishing Savings

Family savings can make living with uncertainty less stressful; however, the savings rate has been dropping steadily. By August 2000, the savings rate had fallen to its lowest level in the last four decades, and spending grew faster than incomes for the second consecutive month.[38]

Some analysts say that this is no cause for concern because the stock market has replaced conventional savings accounts. This is no doubt true for the upper middle class, but it raises the question, How wide is stock ownership? While the number of people owning stock directly or through pension plans and mutual funds has increased, by 1998 only 48 percent of families owned any stock at all and only 36 percent owned more than $5,000 worth. Indeed, the wealthiest 10 percent of the population own 88 percent of all the stock.[39] No doubt the 2000 census will show substantially wider stock ownership, but the overall picture will not change. Stock may be substituting for savings for some families, but many families have no stock for the same reason they have no savings: their income is too low.

Many Families Are Not Worth a Dime

Like savings, net worth is both a measure of how wealth is distributed and how secure families feel about being able to maintain their standard of living if something happens to their ability to work. Net worth is what a family has left after subtracting its debt from the total value of its assets. (Assets include items such as one's house, car, stock, savings accounts, and grandfather's antique watch.) If we arrange all of the families by income from low to high and then divide them into five groups of equal number, each group (or quintile) will contain 20 percent of all families. At decade's end, the poorest 20 percent of families had an average net worth of about minus $9,000. Their debts were much higher than their assets. The next poorest 20 percent of families had a net worth of $11,000, and the families in the middle 20 percent were worth somewhat above $61,000.[40] Even this is deceptive. The point of having assets is that the family can sell them to raise emergency cash. For working families, however, the biggest asset is usually their house, and selling it still leaves them with the problem of where to live. Selling the car complicates looking for a job.

When it comes to concentration of wealth, the United States is generally believed to occupy the world's number one position with the top 1 percent of the population holding roughly 40 percent of the nation's household wealth.[41]

"Nine to Five Isn't Working Anymore"

An additional source of stress stems from families having to work longer hours, often for less money. At an earlier time, "middle-class comforts" were available to single wage earner families, but to achieve them today a family must combine two or three incomes.

The combined annual weeks of paid work put in by families with children have risen steadily from 68 weeks at the end of the 1960s to 83 weeks in 1999. In the last two decades, the increase has been greatest among middle-income families. They added 12.5 weeks to their working year, just over three additional months of work out of what used to be family time for one or more members.

While working hours have increased dramatically for all racial groups, African American families have been hardest hit. In 1998, middle-income African American families with children worked 4,278 hours, which was 489 more hours than White families of comparable income and 228 more than Hispanics. A middle-class African American family and a White family may have the same income, but the African American family works 12 more weeks a year to get it. That is the meaning of the wage gap.[42] To all this, of course, must be added unpaid work in the home. For many years Americans were told that the reason the Japanese got ahead of us economically was that they worked longer hours than we do. As of 1999, we now work an hour and a half longer a week than do the Japanese and eight hours longer than the Swedes.[43] According to the Bureau of Labor Statistics, the increase is mainly in women's working hours. Those of men are not changing.[44]

As hours of paid work expand into what used to be family time, employers are seeking new money-saving efficiencies by promoting part-time schedules and work at home. The owner of a small business explained what his ideal labor arrangement would be: "I would want my employees to stay by their telephones . . . When a job comes into the shop, I would call them in to do the work and then send them home again." Of course, they would be paid only for the hours actually worked—perfect for him, but miserable for the employees. Today corporations are reaching for that ideal and convincing working parents that it is all for their benefit.

An *Business Week* article headed "9 to 5 Isn't Working Anymore"[45] described a company where the standard nine-to-five workday didn't coincide with the hours during which the company required the greatest number of workers. As a result, the overtime bill was very high. Then the company discovered flexible hours and now employees have the *privilege* of working the odd hours when they are most needed, and the overtime wage cost is down by 50 percent.

The same article featured an IBM supervisor who manages thirty-three employees from her home while she cares for an infant daughter. A charming photo depicts the mother on a conference call and the angelic nearly-two-year-old beaming from a highchair. But every parent knows that a "terrible twos" toddler won't sit still in a highchair for long and that trying to concentrate on something else while caring for one is nearly impossible. Nonetheless, the happy mother told *Business Week*, "This way I can give 120 percent to IBM and 120 percent to my newborn." Obviously, that equals 240 percent of something, but of what?

Polls indicate that other women see it differently. In response to the question, "Are time pressures on working families getting better or worse," 65 percent said "worse." Seventy-four percent thought government should do more about it, and 90 percent thought employers should do more. The figures for men were close to these.[46] It is also no doubt true that "new studies find that employees' top priority is gaining the flexibility to control their own time" and that in a recent poll, "56 percent of all managers say employees with flexible schedules are more productive per hour."[47] But is this really a win-win situation? It seems that wage stagnation actually forces families to put in more hours than they can sustain. Then, in the name of flexibility, employers add non-standard jobs in order to facilitate working the additional hours.

Shifts in the American family structure reflect these changes. A recent survey found that 62 percent of working-class adults reported being married in the 1994–98 period compared with 80 percent in the 1972–77 period. Both parents have jobs in two-thirds of families compared to just one-third in 1972, and about half of all children now live with their original parents, down from three-quarters in 1972.[48]

The payoff to employers is great. Gains in productivity have risen dramatically over the last decade, which means that while employers get more output from each worker, labor costs remain low. Such gains are often credited to computers and new technology, but they also come from flextime, telecommuting, and part-time work, all of which contribute to reduced labor costs. The extra profits should be shared with working people, but this has not been the case. In 1998, productivity was 33 percent higher than it had been in 1973, while weekly wages were actually 12 percent lower. If gains in wages had kept up with productivity gains, then the average wage in 1998 would have been $18.10 an hour instead of $12.77. That's a significant $11,000-a-year difference for a full-time worker.[49] Instead of going to higher wages, most of the productivity gains made by American workers over the decade of the 1990s went into corporate profits, which rose by 116 percent after taxes.[50]

At press time for this manual, the 1999 productivity figures were issued showing another year of strong growth. The gain in productivity was 2.9 percent, but inflation-adjusted pay per hour grew by only 2.6 percent, falling behind once again.[51] The business press was delighted. "As we close the books on 1999, it's clear that the boom in corporate profits will continue. Earnings for companies in the Standard and Poor's 500-stock index are projected . . . to increase 15.8 percent in 2000 on top of 1999's 14.4 percent gain. But many are expected to do better.[52]

Corporate economists were ecstatic over the productivity gains: "That's using every worker just about as efficiently as possible," commented Joel Naroff of Naroff Economic Advisors, while Wells Fargo economist Sung Won Sohn said, "we're continuing to enjoy the thrust of computers and other information technologies. That is really the primary driver of productivity gains."[53]

These views represent the conventional wisdom, but a very different and undoubtedly more accurate picture is painted by Stephen S. Roach, the Chief Economist and Director of Global Economics for Morgan Stanley, Dean Witter. Roach says that instead of doing more work in the same number of hours, the traditional measure of productivity, what is really happening is that many people are just working longer hours that don't register in the official figures.[54]

Noting that the fastest productivity gains are coming in the service sector, which employs 77 percent of the non-government, non-agricultural workers, Roach observes, "And this is precisely the kind of work where traditional measures of productivity may be least reliable."

Roach argues that the service sector is not just "hamburger flippers" but that two-thirds of it is white collar, and of those half are managers or professionals. In other words, they are knowledge workers says Roach, and no matter how good the computers get, jobs that require thought still take time. Roach says it is "ludicrous" to believe that the average workweek in the service sector is really 32.9 hours and hasn't risen in thirteen years as the Labor Department claims.

Courtesy of laptops, cell phones, home fax machines and other appliances, knowledge workers are now online in cars, planes, trains and homes, virtually tethered to their offices. The "24/7" culture of nearly round-the-clock work is endemic to the wired economy. No one doubts that hard-working people in the service sector are getting more done than they used to. But improving productivity is not about working longer, it's about adding more value per unit of work time.

Absent genetic re-engineering, workers who think for a living may simply not be able to boost their efficiency like workers on the factory floor, no matter how sophisticated their tools.

Acceleration of productivity through hard work alone isn't sustainable: people simply can't work harder and harder indefinitely. That's a lesson that should not be lost on America and its brave new economy.[55]

The Prosperity Gap: One Nation, Two Economies, and a Rising Tide of Inequality

Perhaps the most disappointing aspect of the current situation is that it has disproved the old proverb "A rising tide raises all ships." For a very long time, this bit of folk "wisdom" stood as the justification for trickle-down economics, the practice of making the rich richer in the belief that the money would eventually trickle down to poor and working people. Feeding the horse to feed the sparrows leads to tax breaks and public spending that benefit wealthy corporations and individuals.

In recent years, a rising tide hasn't raised all ships, or as *U.S. News* aptly put it, "yachts still float higher than dinghies."[56] The rich have gotten richer while everyone else has either stayed in place or fallen behind. Adjusting for inflation, between 1989 and 1999 there was a drop from $54,600 to $49,900 in the net worth of the household in the middle of the American income scale, the median household. In other words, the midpoint between the poorest and the richest households has been moving toward the poorer end.[57]

The chart, "Income Bonanza at the Top," shows the change in average income between the years 1988–90 and 1996–98. Over those years, the average family income of the poorest 20 percent of all families rose by $100. This is certainly better than had it continued to go down, but the big

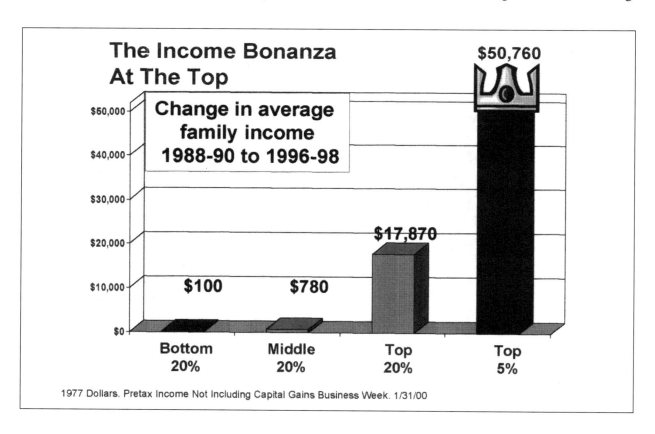

Organizing for Social Change

gains went to the top 20 percent and within that group to the richest 5 percent of families.

**Percentage Change in Income
1998–90 to 1996–98**

Bottom fifth of families	0.8 percent
Middle fifth of families	1.7 percent
Richest fifth of families	15 percent
Richest 5 percent of families	27 percent

Center on Policy and Budget Priorities, 1977 Dollars

Why Part of the Middle Class Is Getting Richer

It is not difficult to understand why the poor are showing only the smallest gains in recent years. What is less obvious is why one portion of the middle class is getting richer while another portion is not. *Business Week* offers a unique and important analysis of what it calls the "The Prosperity Gap":[58]

If you work in a "New Economy" industry such as software, financial services, media or consulting, you have probably seen your earnings skyrocket in recent years. But if you work in an "Old Economy" industry, it is more likely than not that your wages, after adjusting for inflation, have not gone up much. If you stay at a job in an Old Economy industry, you are destined to become relatively poorer and poorer in a richer and richer society.

According to *Business Week*, in the "New Economy" the basic product is information, and "no physical product or personal services change hands." With the focus on "information" and not physical products or services, the New Economy is also referred to as the "Information Economy"

or "Digital Economy." This describes the situation, but there is still the question of how information becomes as valued as physical products.

Not all information has value. High-value information can be thought of as a message that reduces the possibility that a product, once created, might not be sold at a profit. The "Information Economy" is formed as information technologies are employed to shorten the time and distance between the consumer, the producer, and the profit. Corporate and individual consumers, shopping on the Internet, now have vastly more information, such as the names and prices of thousands of suppliers for basically the same products. They have greater choices and can make a more informed decision due to the technology. Businesses benefit greatly from better information on consumer demand and preferences. It is this information flow between the consumer and the chain of suppliers that can reduce market uncertainties and lead to more efficient and profitable production.

While in the recent past, "data processing" technology helped businesses reduce internal operating costs, the convergence of information, computing, telecommunications, and global networks are remaking business and world economics. Businesses in the information technology (IT) industry recognize that their competitive advantage is dependent on skilled IT workers who can turn information into profitable knowledge. For example, in a multibillion-dollar manufacturing company, more accurate information about future sales demand can allow a one-week reduction in finished-goods inventory. This might well translate into saving millions of dollars in inventory holding costs every week! A $10 million advanced planning system pays for itself in a few weeks. With the explosion in demand and a worldwide labor shortage, the salaries of information technology workers have risen dramatically.

As *Business Week* notes, the information industries are profiting from the ever-increasing speed and falling costs of data processing, as well as opportunities in new fields, such as Internet marketing. Money is pouring in, and companies can afford to pay high wages to the technically trained people they need. For example, sales representatives selling telecom equipment saw their incomes rise by 30 percent between 1995 and 1999, while their counterparts in traditional manufacturing got only a 3 percent increase.[59] In the Old Economy, where people work in fields such as construction, transportation, utilities, manufacturing, healthcare, retail/wholesale sales, and education, wages are lagging behind.

Overall, New Economy real wages are up by 11 percent since 1994, while Old Economy wages are up by only 3 percent.[60] This is not just a matter of better-educated workers versus less-educated workers. Primary and secondary schoolteachers, a well-educated but Old Economy group, have seen real salaries rise only 2.3 percent from 1995 to 1998.[61]

Those joining the IT job market, 350,000 in 1996 alone,[62] do so at a high personal cost. They have accepted a life of continuous learning—to keep up they learn the next-generation programming language while they put the current one to use. The environment is far from stable; the world-wide employee turnover rate is 15 percent, and "hot" areas such as the "silicon valley" approach double that amount.[63]

How many people are in each sector of the economy? *Business Week* estimates the division to be as follows:

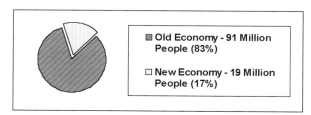

Old Economy - 91 Million People (83%)

New Economy - 19 Million People (17%)

Noting that "the wage gap between New Economy and Old Economy workers seems likely to widen for years to come," *Business Week* compares the situation to that at the end of the nineteenth century when the Old Economy was agriculture and the New Economy was

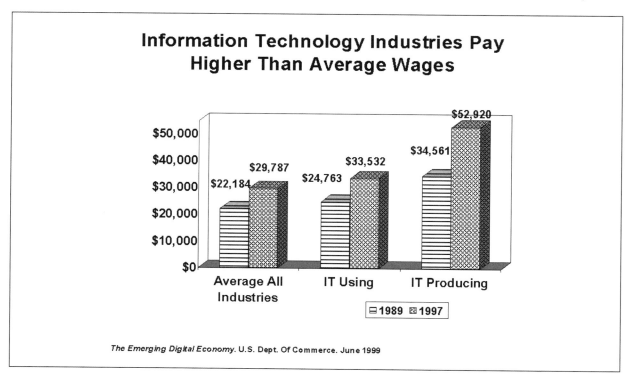

Information Technology Industries Pay Higher Than Average Wages

$50,000
$40,000
$30,000
$20,000
$10,000
$0

Average All Industries: $22,184 / $29,787
IT Using: $24,763 / $33,532
IT Producing: $34,561 / $52,920

☐ 1989 ▨ 1997

The Emerging Digital Economy. U.S. Dept. Of Commerce. June 1999

manufacturing. "Spurred by the advent of such innovations as automobiles, telephones, and electrification, the industrial sector quickly caught up and far surpassed the farming sector in jobs, output and productivity."

To compare the rise of information industries to a transformational economic revolution of the magnitude of the Industrial Revolution is an exaggeration. During the Industrial Revolution, increased farm productivity combined with constantly expanding manufacturing made it possible for almost the whole workforce to shift into what was then the New (industrial) Economy. (Indeed, in England and Scotland, agricultural workers were literally forced into industry by the Enclosure Acts and in Ireland by the potato famine.) But can today's New Economy absorb a comparably high percentage of traditional Old Economy workers? If it does, then what will the information they process be about if it no longer concerns the real goods and services economy? Someone has to go on building and flying airplanes if a Web site selling airline tickets is to be useful.

The existence of the New Economy depends on the continuation of the Old. Not all, or even most, workers will be able to transfer into the more highly paid sector. This assertion is supported by the Labor Department's projection that by 2008, the percentage of all jobs requiring at least an associate (two-year) college degree will rise from 25 percent to only 27 percent.[64] Indeed, it is reasonable to suppose that eventually competition and overinvestment will slow New Economy growth, and will bring its profits and wages back toward the average. Something similar occurred during the industrial revolution in Europe. The early nineteenth century industries based on newly developed steam power grew at an astounding rate and rapidly produced great wealth for their owners. After the first rounds of

mechanization, the process slowed and later innovations took far longer to develop and to become profitable.[65]

The changing job picture helps to explain why one group of working people loses income while another group gains; however, there are not two groups in the equation but three. The third consists of the richest 1 percent of the population, who own 40 percent of all the wealth. Often, they are the employers of the other two groups. The average net worth of households in the top 1 percent is over $10 million each,[66] but as we know from the example of Bill Gates, it goes up into the billions. (To be exact, Gates had $58 billion in 1998, an amount that now fluctuates daily.[67]) Interestingly, of the ten richest individuals in America in 1998, three were from Microsoft and one was Michael Dell of Dell Computers.[68]

If the era were the 1890s instead of the 2000s, if the names were those of the robber barons Frick and Carnegie instead of Dell and Gates, and if the industry were steel and not computers, then we would have images of men working in stifling mills, digging at smoking slag piles, and turning over red-hot slabs of metal twelve to fourteen hours a day, six days a week. We might remember that it was Andrew Carnegie, the founder of U.S. Steel, who hired a private army to massacre his own workers when they went on strike at Homestead, Pennsylvania.[69] We would then see why it was widely understood that the exploitation of working people had built the great fortunes amassed by the rich.

However, when the product is information, not steel, and the workers drive expensive cars to air-conditioned offices, it is easy to think that the process has fundamentally changed and that the new wealth just appears or results from the pure thought and good luck of certain gifted individuals. It is easy to believe that labor no longer plays a role in producing wealth and therefore has no claim to it. It is just as easy to forget that the Internet itself is a social product, developed under the auspices of the Defense Department with public money and sustained by a network of institutions both private and public.

The creation of wealth, as much now as in the past, is the result of the efforts of millions of people who are nurtured, are educated, live, and work within the fabric of a whole society. When social problems develop as a result of the unequal distribution of wealth, society has the right, indeed the obligation, to use that wealth to correct them.

Will the Good Times Last?

If these are indeed the best of times, then how long will they last?

There have been six recessions and, not counting the present one, five periods of recovery since 1960. Not counting the shortest (one-year) recovery, the average recovery length has been roughly six and a half years. The present recovery is now about nine years old, and the two other longest lasted about eight years each. If the economic system has not fundamentally changed, and there are those who think that it has, then according to the law of averages the next recession ought to be starting as this is being written. However, at present, economic growth and employment are holding up splendidly.

There are nonetheless two additional troubling trends: The first is the slowdown in the rise of weekly earnings. The second is the negative trade balance in which America's imports greatly outpace exports.

The first trend is shown in the "Changing Weekly Pay, Month by Month" chart.[70] The chart does not show actual weekly wages. It shows average wage *changes* adjusted for inflation. Wages rose rapidly from 1996 to the middle of 1998, but then the increases began getting smaller. If this trend continues, it will mean that consumers will not be able to keep up the current spending pace that sustains the recovery.

The second trend involves the new records that are being set in the U.S. trade deficit, a

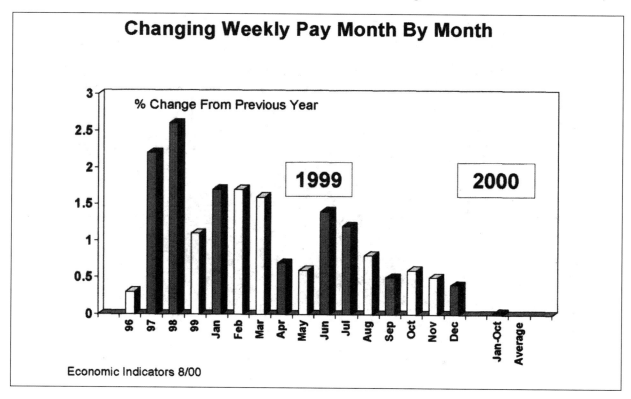

Changing Weekly Pay Month By Month

% Change From Previous Year

1999   2000

Economic Indicators 8/00

measure of how much more we are buying from other countries than we sell to them. Low-priced imports do help to keep inflation low, but they also account for some of the loss of better paid manufacturing jobs. Says *Business Week*,

> The value of imported goods and services is more than 30 percent greater than that of exports. As a result the U.S. is now in an unsustainable international financial position that will only get worse over the coming year. At some point, when the financial markets deem this burden to be too high, changing investor sentiment will hurt the dollar, interest rates and the prices of U.S. financial assets.[71]

The U.S. trade deficit hit an all-time record in February 2000,[72] breaking its highest annual record in 1999 and causing columnist William Greider to comment in *The Nation*, "Since early 1998 the United States has provided roughly half the total demand growth in the entire world, according to the International Monetary Fund. The more ominous fact is that America's status as a debtor nation has deteriorated rapidly during the booming prosperity of the past three years."[73]

Jeff Faux, Director of the Economic Policy Institute, comments:

> As U.S. growth slows relative to a reviving Europe, and as the emerging markets and perhaps even Japan recover, short-term capital that was parked in the U.S. safe haven will begin traveling to foreign lands once more. This will put further pressure on U.S. interest rates to rise in order to attract enough funds to finance the trade deficit.

In a mature expansion with a growing debt burden, pauses or dips in growth that might have been shaken off in the early stages of the cycle become more problematic. Thus, for example, with so many Americans working at the maximum to make their monthly payments, a rising unemployment rate—or even a cutback in hours—could dramatically undercut consumer confidence. Reform of the welfare system, which used to provide countercyclical support of purchasing power, adds to the vulnerability. Having the poor more dependent on a paycheck for their income will magnify the depressing impact of a rising unemployment rate. Throw in negative investor reaction to a financial landscape strewn with dot-com bankruptcies, plus an unluckily timed spike in the price of oil, and we have a somewhat new recipe for an old-style recession.[74]

In addition to these trends and probably more serious, the underlying problem of all market economies continues to exist in America. During boom times, investment expands and companies increase production in order to maximize profits and edge out their competitors. As profits increase, which they have dramatically in recent years, corporations face the "problem" of how to reinvest all that money when investing means creating still more productive capacity (factories and services). With every effort being made to hold down wages, the need to reinvest capital eventually leads to the creation of so much excess productive capacity that there is not a sufficient market at prices that will maintain profits. As production is cut back, unemployment rises and demand falls, necessitating further cutbacks.

It is significant that as of the 108th month of the current expansion (May 2000), the economy is being driven by consumption, not by investment. Consumption is about five percentage points above the average in postwar expansions, while investment is slightly below the average.[75] The fact that so much money has flowed into stock market speculation suggests that the limits of actual productive investment have been reached. This is why there have been six recessions since 1960 and why there will eventually be a seventh.

And Then, There's the Fed

The Federal Reserve Board can't create prosperity, but it can certainly bring it to a halt. The "Fed" is the closest thing we have to economic regulation in America. Its mission is to insure the stability and profits of the banking system. To some extent this coincides with the public interest, but only up to a point. By moving interest rates up and down, the Fed can control the cost of borrowing money from American banks. In theory, the cheaper it is to borrow, the more money will be invested and the faster the economy will grow.

Banks, like any other business, make a product and sell it at a profit. In this case, the product is loans. The interest charged for the loan is the profit. Unlike a shoe store that gets paid before the clerk will hand you your shoes, the bank might not get paid in full for thirty years. Therefore, banks have a worry that shoe stores don't have, that is, the impact that price increases occurring next year will have on the profit from loans made last year. This is the problem of inflation.

Here is an example: You borrow a dollar from the bank. The dollar will buy a pound of beans. In four years, you pay back the dollar plus six cents a year interest for a total of $1.24.* But over the four years prices have risen, including the price of beans, so that now one dollar buys only three-quarters of a pound of beans. That means that because prices have risen, the dollar is worth only seventy-five cents in purchasing power. Add in the twenty-four cents interest, now worth only eighteen cents, and instead of making a profit, the bank has lost seven cents. Every older person says, "I can remember when a candy bar was a nickel and look at it now." Multiply that by billions and you see the problem that banks have. Loan officers are hoping that when you pay back the dollar, it will buy more than a pound of beans, not less, in which case the banks will get a real profit. They therefore make full use of the regulatory structure that they control, the Federal Reserve, to stop prices from rising.

On behalf of the banks, the Fed tells the business community that raising prices is bad. Businesses raise prices anyway, and then say, "The Devil made me do it!" According to the prevailing ideology, the Devil is always the rising wages of working people—never rising profits. So the Fed raises interest rates to slow business activity and create unemployment. The way the Fed sees it, unemployment helps hold down wages and thus prices. For years the magic number was 6 percent unemployment. Below that, the Fed would put on the brakes. It no longer seems to have a magic number, but the Fed watches and worries. As this is written, the Fed is very worried and has started slowing down the economy.

---

*To keep it simple we omit compounding. The bank would really make you pay twenty-six cents, and these aren't even magic beans.

The strains on the economy might soon become evident in the labor market [Greenspan] said, where a rapidly declining pool of jobless workers could force employers to begin raising wages at a pace that could ignite a widespread and destabilizing rise in prices. The nation is also bumping up against the limit of what it can import from other countries, he said.[76]

But are wages really to blame? As inflation watchers start to see alarming indications, *Business Week* announced "The Return of Pricing Power."

The roaring economy means producers of everything from beef and paper goods to houses and medicines can raise prices and still keep sales brisk. Even home personal computers . . . are sporting higher tickets.

Of course the good news for Corporate America may not be good for the economy as a whole. The widespread ability to raise prices is worrying some inflation watchers. . . .

In many sectors, price hikes are helping to fuel surprisingly strong profits. For instance price gains helped boost income at Smurfit-Stone Container Corp., a big maker of corrugated boxes, to $40 million in the first quarter compared with a $92 million loss in the same period a year ago.

. . . in many areas of the economy, emboldened executives find they can command more for even fairly common goods. Surging demand for the kind of steel used in cars, for instance, is driving up long dormant prices. After dropping

to as little as $340 a ton in early 1998, cold-rolled sheet steel has rebounded to as much as $450 a ton.

Competition certainly hasn't gotten any easier. . . . But for now, the pricing party rumbles on—and companies are rushing to get in on the fun while it lasts.[77]

Why is it that when companies raise prices they are just "getting in on the fun," but when workers ask for higher wages, it's a threat to the economy?

The Wall Street Journal adds:

Yet many sectors [of the business community] have responded to deflationary pressure by curbing supply—by closing old plants, refusing to build new ones or buying out competitors. Now they are reaping the rewards of less supply by increasing prices.[78]

So much for free markets!

Consider again the necessity that corporations have of finding ways of reinvesting profits. Now we learn that companies are trying to cut back on supply in order to raise prices/profits. But don't they still need to reinvest the profits? How can they simultaneously limit supply and wages in order to sustain profits, while reinvesting their profits in the creation of still more supply? Something has to give, and herein lies the basic instability of the economic system.

The Worst of Politics in the Best of Times

Even mainstream economists generally believe that despite the apparent health of the economy, the current economic expansion will "inevitably"[79] come to an end. *Business Week* suggests that when it does, the wage gap between New Economy and Old Economy workers will turn into a political gap. The first group will be supporting the free trade and deregulation policies that benefit the corporations for which they work. The second group will demand security, benefits, and protectionism for more traditional manufacturing.

Both Democrats and Republicans have become increasingly dependent on New Economy industries for campaign funds. That's not surprising since that's where most of the new wealth is being created. But it does mean that there could be an opening for a new party that addresses the concerns of Old Economy workers.[80]

Unlike *Business Week*'s projection of conflict between the rival defenders of the New and the Old Economies, Lester Thurow, the liberal economist and author, sees the lines drawn more between the upper and lower classes. Thurow comments:

At some point, those who are losing economically have to use their political power to vote in a government that reverses the outcome of the market. No one knows where this point is. In the United States there have now been over 25 years of rising inequality in income and wealth with no observable political backlash. Perhaps our society could move much farther along the continuum toward inequality, perhaps not. But it is a stupid society that runs an experiment to see where its breaking points are.[81]

More than likely, there will not be neat points of cleavage between either the Old and New Economies or the upper and lower classes. This is America, after all, and every issue becomes intertwined with race, ethnicity, and gender as well as with class and income. New Economy knowledge workers are disproportionately White, at least the better paid of them are, and those are the ones most likely to identify with the interests of their employers. Old Economy workers, while majority White, include a disproportionately high number of People of Color.

What is new in the situation is that a portion of the better paid, more skilled industrial workers, those who have tended to be conservative and to identify with the Republican Party, may now be up for grabs politically if neither party will address their needs. At the same time, people in the knowledge industries, though better paid and even wealthy, are not necessarily conservatives; however, they may not identify themselves with the traditional constituencies of the Democratic Party. Digital-age workers who are economically conservative but socially tolerant make up about one-third of registered voters according to estimates by the Pew Research Center. They are "most likely to be under the age of fifty, college educated, upwardly mobile and overwhelmingly white."[82] They are probusiness, proenvironment, and prochoice. They favor gun control, campaign-finance reform, and a higher minimum wage. Oddly, they are projected by Pew to favor Bush over Gore in the 2000 election; however, "Neither candidate has the precise platform New Economy workers want."[83]

New Economy workers may be probusiness, but anticorporate sentiment is also on the rise. Seventy-two percent of Americans say that business has too much power over too many aspects of American life. Seventy-four percent say that companies have too much political influence. "Put simply," says *Business Week*, "it is becoming fashionable to be anticorporate."

If today's anticorporate backlash is more low-key than the counterculture revolution of the 1960s, it may be even more dangerous for corporate America. Back then, antibusiness attitudes were restricted mostly to youth and college students. And they were just one element of a broader generation gap that led baby boomers to reject the entire Establishment from its sexual mores to the Vietnam War and military-industrial complex. Today, those Americans angry at corporations cut across generations, geography and even income groups.[84]

The changing economy combined with growing inequality is creating the social base for a political realignment whose dimensions are only now starting to emerge. This realignment can reshape the politics of the new century just as the realignments of the New Deal, the Civil Rights, and the Reagan eras reshaped the politics of the Twentieth Century.[85] As political realignment unfolds, bringing new parties and maverick candidates within the old parties, there may well be support for a long-overdue revamping of the election system to include instant runoff voting that enables minor party candidates to run without being spoilers.[86] Such developments are as likely on the Right as on the Left. While liberal Democrats promote free trade, globalization, and deregulation, it remains for individuals such as the conservative columnist and sometimes presidential hopeful Patrick Buchanan to say,

Unbridled capitalism is an awesome force that creates new factories, wealth and opportunities that go first to society's risk takers and holders of capital. But unbridled capitalism is also an awesome destructive force. It makes men and women obsolete as rapidly as it does the products they produce and the plants that employ them.[87]

Not that Buchanan shares progressive values—*just the opposite*. Nor is he offering an alternative to unbridled capitalism that goes beyond his opposition to free trade, but he understands that unbridled capitalism is the problem and not the solution—something that cannot be said for the leading Democrats. In past periods of history, this type of Right Wing anticapitalism attracted large numbers of the economically threatened middle class.

Social conservatives now appear ready to punish the Republicans for being too liberal on social issues *and* too conservative, as they see it, on economic issues. A party can tell its committed followers only so long that it knows they are unhappy with its policies but "face it, you have no place else to go." They will find a place to go.

As old political alignments break up, a key group will be the midwage White men and their families, the people whose incomes have been stagnant or in decline throughout these best of times. It would be a major political mistake to write them off or to think that their numbers are not needed to form a progressive political majority. The big question facing progressives is how to win over the majority of these workers and show them that their real interests are linked to those of lower-wage workers and the poor who are disproportionately non-White.

Failed Policies of the 1990s— Battlegrounds of the Millennium

At the beginning of the new millennium, it is becoming clear that many of the policy solutions implemented in the closing decades of the last century were never workable. It is by attacking on these points that progressives can start to shape a new majority consensus.

- A rising tide does not raise all ships—at least it doesn't raise them all equally. The nation must aggressively use tax and wage laws to redistribute income.[88] Here is a case in point: Agriculture Secretary Dan Glickman said in 1999, "During this, the most prosperous economy in decades, it should shock Americans to learn that hunger persists and it is in every state." He released a USDA study showing that 10 percent of all households are going hungry.[89] America will not simply grow out of the many social and economic problems that have been caused by discrimination, exploitation, and wealth inequality. Growth can make these problems easier to solve but only if they are directly addressed.

- Managed Care has not been the answer to unaffordable health insurance, and Health Maintenance Organizations (HMOs) are not the low-cost alternative to independently practicing physicians. They can't provide better service at lower cost. Headlines say "Premiums are Climbing by as Much as 30 percent."[90] After rising relentlessly for eleven years, the number of Americans without health insurance declined in 1999 to 42.6 million, a drop of 1.7 million, or .8 of a percentage point, from 1998. This is the first reduction since the height of the previous recovery in 1987. It is remarkable that so great an improvement in the economy has brought so small an improvement in medical coverage.[91] Medical Associations discuss forming unions to protect doctors from HMO management, and it is clear that universal national health care or Medicare for All and real prescription drug coverage need to be on the national agenda again.[92]

- Deregulation, in banking, airlines, and utilities, hasn't led to cheaper and improved service. Instead, it has often led to immense bailouts for corporations at public expense. The idea that deregulated companies will be more environmentally responsible or safety conscious is proving to be a myth, and reregulation is already being discussed by legislators in states where utility deregulation has lead to rapidly rising prices.[93]

- Free trade agreements such as the North American Free Trade Agreement (NAFTA) and its various extensions haven't saved American jobs. NAFTA destroyed 440,172 American jobs between 1994, when it took effect, and the first half of 1999. Though comparatively small, the number is astonishing given the exaggerated claims of NAFTA backers and the Clinton Administration that it would dramatically increase American jobs. NAFTA is making the U.S. trade deficit worse. Before NAFTA, in 1993, the trade deficit with NAFTA partners Mexico and Canada was $18.2 billion. NAFTA was supposed to fix that, but instead the deficit rose to $47.3 billion, a rise of 160 percent.[94] It wasn't supposed to happen.

- Throwing people off welfare has not gotten them out of poverty and into the middle class.[95] In an article headed "From Welfare to Worsefare?" *Business Week* says, "The recent data show that while millions of former welfare mothers have jobs, their incomes are often lower than before the reforms were enacted."[96]

- Record low unemployment has not provided a job for everyone. There are still roughly 5.5 million unemployed people of whom about 1.2 million have been looking for work for over 15 weeks.[97] As noted, non-White unemployment is roughly double that of White unemployment. If the best of times still cannot provide enough jobs, then the free market can't be the only answer. It is time to revive the idea of government-sponsored work projects with meaningful training and living wage pay scales.

- If conservatives are right that the free market really is the solution, why does corporate welfare continue in boom times when it clearly isn't needed? "Federal corporate tax expenditures—special exclusions, exemptions, deductions, credits, deferrals or tax rates—totaled more than $76 billion in fiscal year 1999, according to conservative estimates by the Office of Management and Budget. For the five-year period 2000–2004, the government will spend more than $394 billion on corporate tax subsidies."[98] Tax subsidies only scratch the surface of corporate welfare.

- The free market is not producing affordable housing for people with lower and moderate incomes. As the cities are awash with stock market money, there has been a boom in luxury housing. Developers are moving into traditionally low-income urban areas and forcing people out to distant suburbs.

- Weakening environmental and consumer protection laws has not resulted in greater self-policing and responsibility by industry. In fact, as we write, industry is demanding the right to treat food with radiation without even labeling it for consumer awareness and to recycle radioactive waste from nuclear reactors into consumer products, including children's toys.

- It has not been the case that union busting and union-free workplaces lead to productivity gains that are shared with the workers. Actually, organized workers continue to do better, but government agencies refuse to enforce the laws that protect organizing.[99]

Are the Best of Times Good Enough?

The question remains. Even if these best of times continue, are they good enough? For some people the answer is a resounding yes. A single

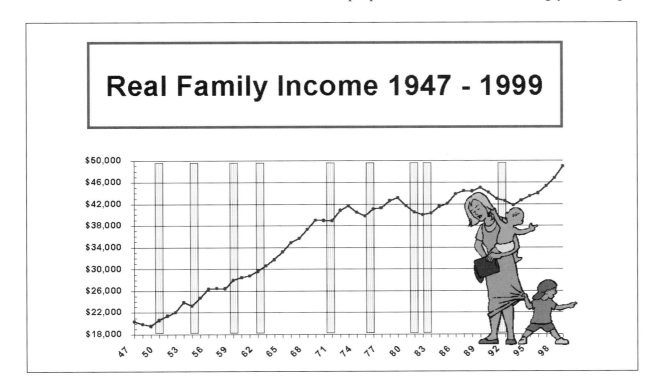

Real Family Income 1947 - 1999

You Mean You're Not Getting Rich? Economics in the New Millennium

369

bottle of wine was recently sold at auction for $44,000, and for those who were bidding, these must be good times indeed.[100]

The "Real Family Income, 1947–1999" chart[101] tells a somewhat different story. Starting after World War II, average inflation-adjusted income rose dramatically, less so for People of Color, but dramatically nonetheless.

Those good years, ending around 1973, came to be considered typical of how the system works. Many people have fond memories of "the good old days" and expect that the country will return to them if we can just figure out what went wrong in the 1970s. They don't know what went wrong but feel that it must have something to do with marijuana, sexual freedom, and civil rights.

Actually, nothing went wrong in the seventies. That decade and the years since are the rule, not the exception. It was the twenty-year period after the WW II that was the exception. The war destroyed the industry of Europe and Asia. Countries that had been prewar competitors lay in smoking ruins awaiting American industry and capital to come and rebuild them. Through the Marshall Plan, America loaned Europe the money to buy our goods and machinery, and then, for twenty years, we supplied Europe and Asia's needs.[102] When Volkswagens and Hondas appeared on our streets, that era ended. The rapid rise in the living standard ended with it. Since then, income has moved up or down within a fairly narrow range.

The postwar years were also exceptional because of the high levels of government spending that kept the economy moving. In addition to the Marshall Plan, the GI Bill of Rights provided today's equivalent of $125 billion for higher education. In addition, during the war years (1941–1945), Americans had accumulated $1.1 trillion in savings (1999 dollars), which was quickly spent when factories returned to peacetime production. The birth of the baby boomers combined with suburbanization added greatly to spending at all levels of the economy.[103]

When looking at the "Real Family Income" chart, keep in mind that *income* is different from

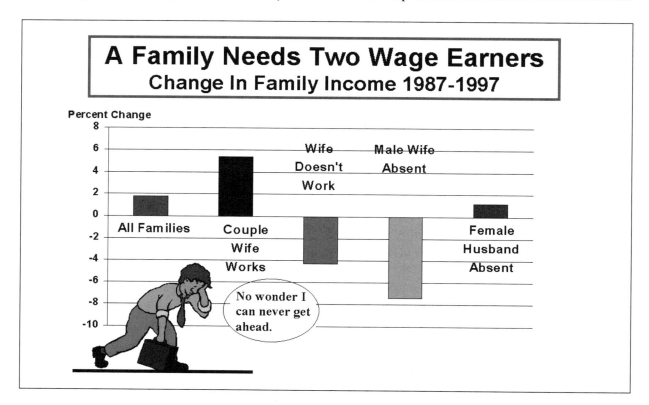

Organizing for Social Change

wages. Income includes wages and also money from sources that typical families don't have, such as investments, executive bonuses, and the like, all of which pulls up the high end. Consider also that "An increase in the number of married women in the workforce contributed to a 150 percent increase in the real median income of married couple families. In 1997, the median (middle) income for all families was $44,568 but for married couple families with the wife working, it was $60,669.[104]

The chart "A Family Needs Two Wage Earners"[105] shows that looking beyond the averages produces a different picture. Only families with two wage earners were really able to make any progress over the last ten years. Their average income rose by almost 6 percent. For everyone else, except families headed by women, average income actually fell. Single women managed to get their income up to $21,023, not that far above the poverty wage of $16,600.[106]

What it all comes down to is this. Assuming that a family needs an income of at least $45,000 to live a modest middle-class lifestyle,[107] then 60 percent of White families are making it or doing better, as are 40 percent of Black and almost 40 percent of Hispanic families. Everyone else is not![108] Provided that the best of times continue, unless you are a knowledge worker, a manager,

or a member of a two-income family, your chance of getting to this level is uncertain at best. Your chance of getting beyond it is doubtful.

The alternatives, therefore, are either to hope for dramatically better times than these or to start organizing for fundamental social and economic change. We recommend organizing. Never before has our country shown that it can produce such abundance so productively. There is no reason why more than half our people should have to struggle just to get by. The problems, rooted in the economic system, can be solved through political action to change that system.

October 5, 2000

It is unacceptable to claim that after the fall of communism, capitalism is the only alternative.

—**Pope John Paul II**[109]

Our thanks to John Curtis, an Information Technology Consultant, for his advice on the technology section of this chapter.

Notes

1. The Bureau of Economic Research dates this recovery from March of 1991.

2. The number of workers making a poverty wage of $8.19 and hour or less in 1999 was 35.6 million, or 26.8 percent of the workforce. See *The State of Working America 2000–2001*, issued by the Economic Policy Institute. (There may be a small amount of double counting between poverty wage workers and involuntary part-time workers, 2.6 percent of the workforce in 1999). **Note:** The references in this chapter to *The State of Working America* refer to the 1998–1999 edition. At press time, the 2000–2001 edition was issued, allowing us to update much material. This most valuable book is updated regularly and can be ordered by calling 800-EPI-4844 (202-331-5510). Visit EPI's Web site at http://www.epinet.org.

3. *Business Week.* July 10, 2000. "A New Economy But No New Deal." Gene Koretz. Online edition. The story cites a report from the business-oriented think tank, The Conference Board. From 1966 to 1978, poverty among full-time year-round workers dropped by 56% from 4.8% to 2.1%. Between 1986 and 1998, however, the rate rose to 3%. The actual number of poor, full-time workers rose by 40%. In explaining the situation, the report, written by Linda Barrington, noted the rise of low-paid retail and service sector jobs. The article concludes that the high-tech boom is creating unskilled jobs as well as skilled, for example, cashiers who don't need to know how to add, and it may be reducing the number of better paid mid-skilled jobs as well.

NOTE: *poverty wages* and *workers in poverty* are two separate concepts. A poverty wage, $8.19 in 1999, is one that will not lift the family of four of a single wage earner above the poverty line. But, not everyone earning this amount, or less, is the sole support of a family of four, and poverty definitions change with family size. Therefore not all poverty wage workers actually live in poverty at the official definition. A worker in poverty is someone who actually lives below the poverty line either because of low wages, family size, or both. This article refers to workers who live in poverty while working 35 hours or more a week for fifty weeks a year. The 1999 poverty line was $8,500 a year for a single person, $10,869 for a two-person family, $13,290 for a family of three, and $17,028 for a family of four. Of course, these levels are ridiculously low and indicate that public policy makers have no conception of what real life is like.

4. Income and Poverty 1999. Press Briefing. www.census.gov. 09/26/00. Economic Policy Institute Analysis. 09/26/00. www.epinet.org. 1999 real median household income was $40,800. Poverty fell from 12.7% the previous year to 11.8%.

5. "Unfinished Business—Clinton's Lost Presidency. William Greider. *The Nation.* 2/14/00.

6. "Wage Growth in '99 Below Expectations." *The New York Times.* 4/30/99, by Richard W. Stevenson.

7. *The New York Times.* 11/6/99. "Jobless Rate Drops to 4.1 percent As Wages Rise By 1¢ an Hour." By Louis Uchitelle. Business Week. Pg. 1.

8. "Renewed Corporate Wanderlust Puts a Brake on Salaries and Prices." *The New York Times.* 07/04/00. Louis Uchitelle. Pg. 1.

9. "Backlash." *Business Week.* 04/24/00. Pg. 42.

10. As above and Pg. 43.

11. "Shopping till we Drop." William Greider. *The Nation.* As above. 04/12/00. Pg. 12.

12. *Monthly Review.* April 2000. "Monopoly Capital at the Turn of the Millennium." John Bellmy Foster. Pg. 10. The author cites David Korten *The Post-Corporate World: Life After Capitalism.* 1999. Pp. 77–78.

13. Cited in "The Hidden Side Of The Clinton Economy." John E. Schwartz. *Atlantic Monthly.* 10/98. The poll was conducted in 1996.

14. Cited in *The State of Working America,* Pg. 240. The poll covered the period from 1978 to 1996.

15. Many people think that the unemployment figure is based on claims for Unemployment Insurance. This is not so. The Labor Department does a monthly survey of a representative sample of the population. People who say that they are not working, want to work and have applied for a job, or visited an employment agency in the last four weeks are counted as unemployed. If a person applied for a job in the last five weeks, that person is not counted as unemployed, but instead is placed in the category "Not In Labor Force." It is a very convenient method, but at least has the virtue of being consistent from year to year and is accurate in that respect.

16. Example for the month of August, 2000: Labor force = 140.7 million. Unemployed = 4.2%. Unemployed

plus discouraged workers = 4.4%. Unemployed, plus discouraged, plus workers only marginally attached to the workforce = 5%. All of the above plus those working part-time who want full-time jobs = 7.3% total *under*employment, or about 10.2 million people. Bureau of Labor Statistics. 9/8/00.

17. "Keeping the Hive Humming." *Business Week.* 04/24/00. Pg. 51. 700,000 legal residents were admitted in fiscal 1998. The study was done by Neal S. Soss, chief economist at Credit Suisse First Boston. The Urban Institute estimates that the foreign-born will be 12% of the population by 2020, up from 6.2% in 1980.

18. *The State of Working America.* Pg. 242

19. *Monthly Review.* 10/99. "Downsizing of America." By Andy Merrifield. Pg. 41

20. *The New York Times.* " 11/6/99. "Jobless Rate Drops…."

21. "Downsizing of America." *Monthly Review.* 10/99 Pg. 41.

22. *State of Working America 2000–2001.* From the executive summary on the Web.

23. Between 1979 and 1996, the number of workers who had been on the current job for ten years or more fell from 41 percent to 35.4 percent. The drop for those who hadn't finished high school was 7.3 percentage points, for those with college and beyond, it was 6.9 points. *The State of Working America.* Pg. 233.

24. *The State of Working America.* Pg. 238.

25. *The New York Times.* Money & Business section. Pg. 1. "The American Middle, Just Getting By." Louis Uchitelle. 8/1/99.

26. *Tax Cut No Cure for Middle Class Economic Woes.* Briefing Paper. Economic Policy Institute. 9/99. Bernstein, Rasell, Schmitt, and Scott.

27. Data from *The State of Working America.* Pg. 140–142

28. *Economic Indicators. Various years.* Data in 1982 dollars.

29. *Monthly Labor Review.* Nov. 1999. Pg. 34.

30. *The Wall Street Journal Almanac.* 1999. Pg. 234. Based on Bureau of Labor Statistics data.

31. All figures except wages noted above are from the BLS November 1999 Employment Outlook Projections.

32. March 6, 2000, Quoted in *Monthly Review,* May 2000.

33. *Monthly Review.* "Working-Class Households and the Burden of Debt." Pg. 3.

34. *The State of Working America 2000–2001.* Introduction from the Web.

35. *Los Angeles Times.* "Household Debt Grows Precarious As Rates Increase." "Total liabilities have passed after-tax incomes for the first time, especially among lower-earning families. Interest hikes weigh heaviest on those maxed out on cards."

36. *Monthly Review.* May 2000. Pg. 7. "Mortgage delinquencies are almost certain to rise in the near-term due to three factors: rising interest rates on adjustable-rate mortgages; the rapid growth of high-risk mortgage lending with down payments of 10 percent or less; and an expansion of predatory or subprime lending within the home-secured lending market. *MR* Pg. 9.

37. *State of Working America 2000–2001.* From the Web (which means no page numbers). The term "middle" means the middle 20% or middle quintile. Average household debt for this group was $45,800 in 1998. Personal bankruptcy in 1999 was six out of every 1,000 adults, almost twice the rate at during the height of the previous business cycle peak in 1989.

38. *The New York Times.* "Savings Rate Hits 4-Decade Low As Consumer Spending Increases" September 30, 2000. Pg. C-3. The savings rate, the amount of income left after spending, became a negative (0.4%). As a whole, consumers spent more money than they earned in August, and had nothing left to save. The measure of income used here does not include capital gains such as the sale of stock. The averages cited here no doubt conceal very different experiences between the rich and working people.

39. *The State of Working America 2000–2001.*

40. The State of Working America 2000–2001. Pg. 260. The most recent figures for the year 1998 follow

Wealth Class	Average Net Worth in 1998
Top 1 percent	$10,203,700
Next 4 percent	$ 1,115,000
Next 5 percent	$ 623,500
Next 10 percent	$ 344,900
Fourth 20 percent	$ 161,300
Middle 20 percent	$ 61,000
Second 20 percent	$ 11,100
Bottom 20 percent	$ -8,900

41. "The Rich Get Richer." By James Lardner. *U.S. News.* Online edition. 02/21/00 (Cover story.)

42. *The State of Working America 2000–2001.* Economic Policy Institute.

43. *The Birmingham News.* 10/10/99. Report of a study by the International Labor Office, a public policy organization.

44. As above. The BLS says that women worked an average of 36 hours a week in 1998, compared to 34 hours in 1997. The average for men is unchanged at 42 hours. The article quotes a time management consultant who suggests spending less time checking e-mail!

45. "9 to 5 Isn't Working Anymore." *Business Week.* 9/24/99.

46. *Business Week.* 9/20/99. "Wooing Minivan Moms." Pg. 83. Celinda Lake conducted the poll. The article says that politicians of both parties are wooing suburban women on these issues.

47. *Business Week.* Working Life. Commentary by Michelle Conlin. Pg. 94. 10/20/99.

48. Reuters dispatch. "Two-Parent Families Growing Scarcer—U.S. Study. The study was done by the National Opinion Research Center at the University of Chicago and was directed by Timothy Smith. 11/24/99.

49. *Shifting Fortunes.* Pg. 27. Based on data from *The State of Working America 1998–99.*

50. Council of Economic Advisors *Economic Indicators.* July 1999. Data from the U.S. Dept. of Commerce. (This monthly publication is prepared for the Joint Economic Committee of Congress by the Council of Economic Advisors.)

51. "U.S. Productivity Growth In '99 Is Best in 7 Years." By Stuart Silverstein. *The Los Angeles Times.* 02/10/00. Online edition.

52. *Business Week.* "Making The Most of a Good Situation." 12/27/99.

53. Associated Press dispatch 2/9/00

54. "Working Better or Just Harder." Stephen S. Roach. *The New York Times.* 2/14/00. Pg. A-21.

55. As above.

56. *U.S. News and World Report.* 5/24/99. Cover story.

57. *Shifting Fortunes.* United for a Fair Economy. Pg. 6. Note that the 1997 figure is preliminary. 37 Teple Place, Boston, MA 02117. (617) 423-2148.

58. *Business Week.* The Prosperity Gap. 9/27/99. Michael J. Mandel.

59. The Prosperity Gap. Pg. 100.

60. The Prosperity Gap. Pg. 90.

61. The above article notes that in the second quarter of 1999, profits in New Economy industries rose by 58 percent while those in Old Economy industries showed a gain of only 9 percent.

62. *The Emerging Digital Economy.* U.S. Dept. of Commerce. June 1999. Pg. 38.

63. Meta Group, Stamford, CT. 2000

64. "America's Jobs Are Changing." *Business Week* 1/24/00. Pg. 32. Based on the November 1999 *Monthly Labor Review.*

65. For a useful discussion of the industrial revolution and the information revolution, see "Beyond the Information Revolution" by Peter Drucker in the 10/99 *Atlantic Monthly.*

66. *The State of Working America 2000–2001.* Pg. 260. Year 1998.

67. *Shifting Fortunes.* Pgs. 6 and 16.

68. *Shifting Fortunes.* Pg. 16. Bill Gates, Microsoft $58.4 Billion. Paul Allen, Microsoft $22.1 Billion. Michael Dell, Dell Computer $12.8 Billion. Steven Ballmer, Microsoft $12.2 Billion. Source: *Forbes 400.* Oct. 12, 1998

69. See *The Rise of American Civilization.* Charles Beard. Macmillan Co. New York. 1930. Vol. II. Pg. 235

70. Council of Economic Advisors *Economic Indicators,* August 2000, and Bureau of Labor Statistics press release of 10/15/99. 1982 dollars.

71. *Business Week.* 10/4/99. Pg. 31. "Business Outlook"

72. "The U.S. trade deficit shot up to a record $29.2 billion in February as Americans' demand for foreign oil hit an all time monthly high while sales of exports dipped." "For all of last year, the deficit soared to an all-time high of $267.6 billion, 62.9 percent above the previous record an imbalance of $164.3 billion in 1998." Associated Press report. 4/19/00.

73. *The Nation* 04/10/00. "Shopping Till We Drop." Pg. 11.

74. *The American Prospect.* "The Next Recession." Aug. 31, 2000.

75. *Monthly Review.* May 2000. Pg. 2. "The share of consumption expenditures in Gross Domestic Product (GDP) during the current expansion has risen nearly five percentage points above the average for all previous post–Second World War expansions, while the

share of total fixed investment in GDP has fallen 1.4 percentage points below the average for all earlier expansions. Hence, investment remains semi-stagnant when compared with earlier expansions - reflecting that powerful tendency toward stagnation that continues to characterize the capital accumulation process."

76. "Greenspan Warns of Another Rise in Interest Rates." *The New York Times*. 02/18/00. Pg 1. Col. 6

77. "The Return of Pricing Power." *Business Week*. May 8, 2000. Page 50. Joseph Weber.

78. "Firms Start to Raise Prices, Stirring Fear in Inflation Fighters." *The Wall Street Journal*. 5/16/00. Pg 1. "Many executives confess that they would be happy to see an easing of the brutal anti-inflationary culture of the 1990s."

79. *Business Week*. 9/27/99. Pg. 100. It should be noted, however, that the International Monetary Fund and the Federal Reserve are both optimistic that the global and American economies will sustain current growth rates through the year 2000. Associated Press reports of 9-23-99. But IMF officials warned that unforeseen shocks, such as a sudden plunge in America's high flying stock marker, or a precipitous drop in the value of the dollar could disrupt the newfound optimism.

80. *Business Week*. 9/27/99. Pg. 102.

81. *Shifting Fortunes*. Pg. 1. Lester Thurow is a professor of management and economics at the MIT Sloan School of Management.

82. *Business Week*. 8/7/00. "The Politics of Prosperity." Pg. 96.

83. As above. "While New Republicans and New Democrats vie to craft issues for prosperous times, . . . the current debate fails to even hint that today's techno-boom could become tomorrow's techno-bust." Pg. 106.

84. *Business Week*. 9/11/00. "Too Much Corporate Power?" Pg. 144. The *Business Week* poll was conducted between August 25 and 29, 2000. The article noted that "56% of workers feel that they are underpaid, especially as wages since 1992 have topped inflation by 7.6% while productivity is up 17.9%."

85. As this is written, the 2000 elections are still ahead of us. The reader is invited to collect the results and compare them to the situation in 1992 when Clinton was first elected. At that time, the Democrats had 57 Senators and House majority of 266. They held 28 governorships and a majority of state legislatures.

How well they do in the midst of the "best of times" will make a very interesting story. Figures from *The Nation*. 2/14/00. Pg. 12.

86. Instant runoff voting, long in use in England, Ireland, and Australia allows voters to rank candidates by first choice, second choice, etc. When no candidate receives a majority, the lowest is dropped, and that candidate's ballots are distributed among the remaining candidates according to the voter's second choice.

87. "Did Success Ruin the Right? By Patrick Buchanan. *The New York Post*. 3/25/98

88. "Whether measured by wages, income or wealth, for 25 years the share of the privileged has increased, and everyone else (a roughly 80 percent majority) has become relatively worse off." Juliet Schor, economist and senior lecturer on women's studies at Harvard University. *Shifting Fortunes*. Pg. 5.

89. Associated Press Report from *The Evansville Courier & Press*. The USDA expressed the situation in a phrase of wondrous subtlety, It found that 9.7 percent of households were considered "food insecure."

90. *The New York Times*. "HMO Costs Spur Employers To Shift Plans." 9/6/00. Pg. 1. "The rising premiums suggest that apart from the most restrictive bare-bones Health Maintenance Organizations, Managed Care is no longer keeping medical costs down. The industry has also been consolidating recently, increasing profits, but weakening the ability of employers to bargain on rates.

91. *The New York Times*. 9/29/00. Pg. A16. The President commented, " I believe it validates our health care and economic policies." But, the Census Bureau reports that the overall proportion of the population covered by government insurance programs remained unchanged. The reduction was due to an expansion of employer insurance programs, a response to the now low unemployment rate of 4.1%.

92. *Business Week*. 9/27/99. Pg. 52, reports that HMO contracts for employee health benefit plans are being signed with rate increases "as much as 15 percent or six times the overall rate of inflation." "The magnitude of expected increases for next year, on top of hikes this year well above inflation suggest that Managed Care has done much of what it can do to trim costs, some experts say. That means that consumers of health care will no longer be insulated from the rising costs of providing care." HMOs lost $1.25 billion in 1997 and 1998 says the article.

93. See "A Dwindling Faith in Deregulation." *The New York Times.* 09/15/00. Pg. C1. The California legislature has already acted to cap utility prices in its first city to go to free market prices, San Diego. The cost of electricity immediately doubled and the sponsor of the state's deregulation bill is now calling for reregulation. Prices are rapidly rising in deregulated markets a cross the country. See also "California Electrical System Is on the Verge of Failure." *The New York Times on the Web.* Aug. 3, 2000. "Four years after it led the nation into a sweeping deregulation of the electric industry, California is at the brink of a breakdown in its power supply."

94. "NAFTA's Pain Deepens. Job Destruction Accelerates in 1999." An Economic Policy Institute briefing paper. By Robert E. Scott. November 1999.

95. "A new study by the Center on Budget and Policy Priorities reports that the worst off families (the poorest of the poor) have become even more impoverished in the wake of welfare reform. And a closer tie between growth and poverty entails the risk that poverty could soar during a downturn. *Business Week.* 9/6/99. Pg. 26.

96. *Business Week.* 10/09/00. Pg. 104. Average annual income of single mothers in the lowest 20% of families equaled $8,759 in 1995. Welfare reform was enacted in 1996. In 1998, the average income of this group of mothers was $8,410. (Constant dollars.)

97. *Economic Indicators.* 6/00. Pg. 13.

98. Nader Congressional Testimony. June 30, 1999.

99. Comparing workers of similar experience, education, region, industry, occupation, and marital status a study by the Economic Policy Institute finds that overall, combined wages and benefits are 15 percent higher for union members. *The State of Working America* 1998–1999. Pgs. 184–185.

In a recent poll by Peter Hart Associates, 43 percent of employees say that they would vote for a union at their workplace. Yet, only about 14 percent of workers are organized. Why? According to a National Labor Relations Board study, a third of all companies where union elections are held illegally fired union supporters, half threatened to close facilities and 91 percent required workers to meet one-on-one with supervisors on the issue. *Business Week. 7/19/99. Pg. 43.*

100. *Business Week.* 9/6/99. "What Am I Bid For This Well Aged Bottle?" Pg. 106. All right, so the wine was 1870 Chateau Lafite Rothschild, but Christie's recently sold three bottles of 1994 California Screaming Eagle Cabernet for $3,335. "'The market is hot,' says Christie's director of wine sales."

101. US Census Bureau. Historical Income Tables - Families. Table F-7. (www.census.gov/hhes/income/histinc/f07.html).

102. "[The] Marshall Plan boosted export demand. The United States committed over $13 billion ($115 billion in 1999 dollars) to help rebuild Europe ... . As much as 80 percent of this aid came back to the United States in the form of orders for American exports ... ." *Growing Prosperity.* Bluestone and Harrison. A Century Foundation Book. 2000. Pg. 35.

103. Above. Pgs. 34-35.

104. *Measuring Fifty Years of Economic Change.*

105. The Census Bureau definition of "family" is two or more people related by blood or marriage. The Census Bureau has different figures for "households," which include single and unrelated people.

106. U.S. Census Bureau. Historical Income Tables - Families. Table F-7. *The New York Times* of Oct. 18, 1999, reports in a front-page story by Louis Uchitelle that the Census Bureau is considering revising the unrealistically low definition of poverty. Poverty is now defined as an income below $16,600 a year for a family of four. The revised estimate would put it at $19,500, raising the percentage of families in poverty from the 12.7 percent announced last month to 17 percent. The author cautions that making this change is up to the Administration in power and is a highly sensitive political decision which President Clinton intends to pass on to his successor. The current calculation, developed in the '60s, takes the minimum amount of money needed for enough food to sustain life, and multiplies it by three to reach an amount that is supposed to cover all the families expenses. The new method would make separate estimates for food, housing, health care, transportation and personal expenses.

107. A study released on September 13, 2000, by the Woman's Center for Education, The NY Community Trust and the United Way of New York, found that a "Self Sufficiency Budget" the minimum amount a family of three would need to live without public assistance was $38,088 in the Bronx and $46,836 in Queens. In New York State's least expensive location, the town of Plattsburgh in Clinton County, the amount is $28,900. These amounts do not allow for savings,

insurance, self-paid education, movies or eating in restaurants. From *The New York Times.* 9/13/00.

108. Census Historical Income tables. In 1997, the average income for people in the third quintile of White families was $46,755. The average income in the forth quintile of Black families was $45,806, and for Hispanic families it was $43,075. We regret that the Census Bureau does not make a corresponding figure available for Asian families.

109. Quoted in *The New York Times,* "Poland's Glossy Capitalism Display's a Darker Side." Pg. 1, 9/30/99. By Roger Cohen. "And Poland, like the rest of central Europe has discovered that a rising capitalist tide does not lift all boats. Some are bound to sink, not necessarily in silence."

PART IV
Selected Resources

This list of resources is just a beginning point. Many worthy publications and organizations have been left out due to constraints of time and space.

Introduction to Organizing

Saul D. Alinsky, *Rules for Radicals: A Practical Primer for Realistic Radicals* (New York: Vintage Books, 1989), and *Reveille for Radicals* (New York: Vintage Books, 1991). The classic organizing handbooks, originally published in 1946 (*Reveille*) and 1971 (*Rules*).

Robert Bellah et al., *Habits of the Heart: Individualism and Commitment in American Life,* (Berkeley: University California Press, 1996). A thought-provoking text read by many organizers. Helpful distinctions between private and public life.

Gary Delgado, *Beyond the Politics of Place: New Directions in Community Organizing in the 1990s* (Oakland, Calif.: Chardon Press, 1999). A short, insightful book.

Leigh Dingerson and Susan H. Hay, *The Co/Motion Guide to Youth-Led Social Change*

Resources for Organizing

(Washington, D.C.: Alliance for Justice, 1998). This user-friendly training manual is designed to engage young people in action by giving them the tools, skills, and strategies to solve problems and improve their communities.

Ed Hedemann, ed., *War Resisters League Organizer's Manual* (War Resisters League, 1981). An excellent compilation of organizing tips. The chapters on designing leaflets and organizing street fairs are particularly good supplements to this manual.

Si Kahn, *Organizing: A Guide for Grassroots Leaders* (Washington, D.C.: National Association of Social Workers, 1999). A solid introduction to organizing.

John P. Kretzmann and John L. McKnight, *Building Communities from the Inside Out: A Path Toward Finding and Mobilizing a Community's Assets* (Chicago: ACTA Publications, 1997). The sourcebook for asset-based community development. Additional related manuals and reports are also available from ACTA, (800) 397-2282.

Midwest Academy, *Organizing for Social Change*, 4th ed. (Santa Ana, Calif.: Seven Locks Press, 2001). The ultimate and definitive work on all aspects of direct action organizing. This book meets the needs of every organization from the most local neighborhood groups to national legislative coalitions. Available from Seven Locks Press, P.O. Box 25689, Santa Ana, CA 92799, (800) 354-5348, (714) 545-2526.

Lee Staples, *Roots to Power: A Manual for Grassroots Organizing* (Westport, Conn.: Greenwood Publishing Group, 1991). Based on ACORN's model of neighborhood organizing. Instructive for all organizers. Good chapters on the role of organizers, group maintenance, and dealing with details.

Building Coalitions

Cherie R. Brown, *Art of Coalition Building: A Guide for Community Leaders* (New York: The American Jewish Committee, 1984). An excellent guide to coalition-building, including a good chapter on building unity across ethnic, religious, and class divisions.

The National Assembly of National Voluntary Health and Social Welfare Organizations, *Community Collaboration Manual* (Washington, D.C.: National Collaboration for Youth, 1991). A helpful manual for social service agencies interested in working together to solve common problems.

Recruiting Volunteers

Several good chapters on this subject are also in the books listed above under "Introduction to Organizing."

Michael J. Brown, *How to Recruit People to Your Organization*. Order from Michael J. Brown (Jewish Organizing Institute, 37 Temple Place 5th Floor, Boston, MA 02111, (617) 350-9994 or MBrown7387@aol.com). A forty-page practical manual to help organizations increase and strengthen the commitment of members.

Marlene Wilson, *How to Mobilize Church Volunteers* (Minneapolis: Augsburg Fortress Publications, 1990). A superb book on mobilizing volunteers. Most of the author's suggestions are applicable in non-church settings.

Working with Community Boards

John Gillis, ed., *Board Member Manual* (Frederick, Md.: Aspen Publishers, Inc., 1999), 7201 McKinney Circle, Frederick, MD 21701, (800) 368-8437. This manual helps boards improve long-range planning, run more effective committees, strengthen fundraising, and develop a sense of a team. Aspen Publishers has produced two training videos for board members. The videos can be purchased only if one purchases a manual.

John Paul Dalsimer, *Understanding Nonprofit Financial Statements: A Primer for Board Members* (Washington, D.C.: National Center for Nonprofit Boards, 1996). Especially helpful for board members who are new to financial responsibilities or to non-profit accounting. Critical for community board members of large social service agencies or community development corporations.

Joan Flanagan, *Successful Volunteer Organization: Getting Started and Getting Results in Nonprofit Charities, Grassroots and Community Groups* (Chicago: Contemporary Books, Inc., 1984). One of the best overviews of what it takes to develop a successful volunteer organization.

Kim Klein and Stephanie Roth, *The Board of Directors* (Inverness, Calif.: Chardon Press). Ten clear articles on recruiting, developing, and using board members effectively. Good sections on how board members can help raise funds.

Charles N. Waldo, *A Working Guide for Directors of Not-for-Profit Organizations* (Westport, Conn.: Quorum Books, 1986). A very helpful guide. Geared toward larger non-profits, but useful for others.

Planning and Facilitating Meetings

Robert C. Biagi, *Working Together: A Manual for Helping Groups Work More Effectively*, (Amherst, Mass.: Center for Organizational and Community Development, University of Massachusetts, 1978). A helpful resource for community organizations and citizen boards.

Michael Doyle and David Straus (contributor), *How to Make Meetings Work: The New*

Interaction Method (New York: Berkley Publishing Group, 1993). This book is a classic in meeting design and facilitation.

George M. Prince, *The Practice of Creativity; A Manual for Dynamic Group Problem Solving,* 1972. Out of print, but worth looking for in libraries. Excellent suggestions on extracting creativity from a group.

Sam Kaner et al, *Facilitator's Guide to Participatory Decision-Making* (Philadelphia: New Society Publishers, 1996). A useful training manual covering a variety of facilitation skills.

Media Relations

American Federation of Teachers, *An Activist's Guide to the Media* (Washington, D.C.: American Federation of Teachers); 555 New Jersey Ave., NW, Washington, DC 20001 (202) 879-4400. A simple, incredibly information-packed brochure on using the media.

Jason Salzman, *Making the News: A Guide for Nonprofits & Activists* (Boulder, Colo.: Westview Press, 1998). A comprehensive and detailed how-to guide, from determining what is newsworthy and shaping your message to planning events, contacting reporters, and creating press releases and visuals, including how to influence cartoonists.

Nancy Brigham, with Maria Catalfio and Dick Cluster, *How to Do Leaflets, Newsletters & Newspaper*s (Annapolis, Md.: Union Communication Services); 165 Conduit Street, Annapolis, MD 21401-2512, (800) 321-2545, www.unionist.com. Very practical suggestions that don't assume you have unlimited resources.

Designing and Leading a Workshop

Duane Dale, Robin Miller, and David Magnani, *Beyond Experts: A Guide for Citizen Group Training* (Amherst, Mass.: Center for Organizational and Community Development, University of Massachusetts, 1979).

William A. Draves, *How to Teach Adults* (Manhattan, Kans.: The Learning Resources Network, 1997); (800) 678-5376. An excellent introduction to working with adults.

William A. Draves, *How to Teach Adults in One Hour* (Manhattan, Kans.: The Learning Resources Network). Another useful book, especially if you conduct short sessions.

Jane Vella, *Learning to Listen, Learning to Teach: The Power of Dialogue in Educating Adults* (San Francisco: Jossey-Bass Publishers, 1997). A great introduction to adult education techniques.

Working with Religious Groups

Eileen W. Lindner, ed., *Yearbook of American and Canadian Churches,* (Nashville: Abingdon Press, published annually). An invaluable resource book for groups working with state and national religious bodies. Lists the bishops and comparable religious leaders and their addresses for each denomination.

Samuel G. Freedman, *Upon This Rock: The Miracles of a Black Church* (New York: Harper Collins, 1994). An inspirational book about organizing with churches.

C. Eric Lincoln, *Race, Religion, and the Continuing American Dilemma* (New York: Hill and Wang, 1999). The leading scholar on Black religion, Lincoln examines the ways race and religion have shaped American society. Helpful background for organizing with the religious community.

Gregory F. Pierce, *Activism That Makes Sense: Congregations and Community Organization* (Chicago: ACTA Publications, 1997). A good introduction to church-based community organizing.

Albert Vorspan and Rabbi David Saperstein, *Jewish Dimensions of Social Justice: Tough Moral Choices of Our Time* (New York: Union of American Hebrew Congregations, 1999); (888) 489-8242.

Working with Labor Organizations

R. Emmett Murray, *The Lexicon of Labor: More than 500 Key Terms, Biographical Sketches, and Historical Insights Concerning Labor in America* (Annapolis, Md.: Union Communication Services); 165 Conduit Street, Annapolis, MD 21401-2512, (800) 321-2545, www.unionist.com. Invaluable resources for union and non-union folks alike.

Martin Jay Levitt with Terry Conrow, *Confessions of a Union Buster* (Annapolis, Md.: Union Communication Services); 165 Conduit Street, Annapolis, MD 21401-2512, (800) 321-2545, www.unionist.com. Best book out for understanding how vicious union-busting firms are.

Tactical Investigations

Larry Makinson, *Follow the Money Handbook* (Washington, D.C.: Center for Responsive Politics, 1994). Explains how to trace campaign contributions from special interest groups.

Includes a helpful discussion of reforming campaign financing.

Shel Trapp, *Who, Me a Researcher? Yes You!* (Chicago: National Training and Information Center). A great guide to grassroots community research. NPA/NTIC, 810 N. Milwaukee, Chicago, IL 60622, (312) 243-3035

U.S. General Services Administration and U.S. Department of Justice, *Your Right to Federal Records: Questions and Answers on the Freedom of Information Act and the Privacy Act* (Washington, D.C., 1992). This twenty-five-page booklet describes how to use the Freedom of Information Act and Privacy Act to obtain records from the federal government. Order from R. Woods, Consumer Information Center-N, P.O. Box 100, Pueblo, CO 81002, www.pueblo.gsa.gov.

Grassroots Fundraising

Joan Flanagan, *The Grass Roots Fundraising Book: How to Raise Money in Your Community* (Chicago: Contemporary Books, Inc., 1992). The most popular how-to book on grassroots fundraising.

Joan Flanagan, *Successful Fundraising: A Complete Handhook for Volunteers and Professionals* (reprint, Chicago: Contemporary Books, 1999). Practical guide on raising big money.

The Grantsmanship Center, *The Whole Nonprofit Catalog* (P.O. Box 17220, Los Angeles, CA 90017). Available free because it advertises the center's training courses. Frequently includes excellent fundraising articles.

Kim Klein, *Fundraising for Social Change,* 3d ed. (Inverness, Calif.: Chardon Press, 1996). Excellent chapters on direct mail, telephone solicitation, and major donor campaigns.

Mellon Bank, *Discover Total Resources: A Guide for Nonprofits,* (Pittsburgh: Community Affairs Division, Mellon Bank Corporation); One Mellon Bank Center, Pittsburgh, PA 15258, (412) 234-5000 www.mellon.com. Free. Available in quantity to groups.

Eileen Paul, ed., *Religious Funding Resource Guide 1997/1998,* (Inverness, Calif.: Chardon Press, 1997). The guide includes application forms and grant lists from 37 religious funding sources.

Andy Robinson, *Grassroots Grants: An Activist's Guide to Proposal Writing* (Inverness, Calif.: Chardon Press, 1996). Useful, hands-on techniques for successful grantwriting for social change.

Supervision

David L. Bradford, Allan R. Cohen (contributor), *Managing for Excellence: The Guide to Developing High Performance in Contemporary Organizations* (Wiley Management Classics) (reprint, New York: John Wiley & Sons, 1997). A recent classic management book.

Andre Delberg, Van De Ven Delberg, *Group Techniques for Program Planning: A Guide to Nominal Group and Delphi Processes* (Middleton, Wis.: Green Briar Press, 1986). A helpful book, despite the confusing title.

Beth Gilbertsen and Vijit Ramchandani, *Developing Effective Teams: Proven Methods for Smoother and More Productive Teamwork* (St. Paul: Amherst Wilder Foundation, 1999); 919 Lafond Avenue, Saint Paul, MN 55104, (800) 274-6024, www.wilder.org, Basic principles on helping staff work well as a team. Good for lead organizers.

Paul Hersey, Kenneth H. Blanchard (contributor), and Dewey E. Johnson, *Management of Organizational Behavior: Utilizing Human Resources,* 7th ed. (Englewood Cliffs, N.J.: Prentice Hall, 1996). Explains in great detail the need to use different kinds of management and supervisory styles with different personnel.

Gracie Lyons, *Constructive Criticism: A Handbook* (Berkeley, Calif.: Wingbow Press, 1988). A good book, especially for those who find it hard to give criticism well.

Anne Wilson Schaef and Diane Fassel (contributor), *The Addictive Organization: Why We Overwork, Cover Up, Pick up the Pieces, Please the Boss, and Perpetuate Sick Organizations* (Harper San Francisco, 1990). Helps explain addictive behavior in non-profit organizations and steps that can be taken toward recovery. Fascinating reading for people who work in non-profit organizations.

Financial and Legal Matters

ProChoice Resource Center, *(C)(3)s, (C)(4)s, & PACs: A Primer on Political Activities and Tax Exempt Organizations* (Oakland, Calif.: Chardon Press, 1999); 3781 Broadway, Oakland, CA 94611, (888) 458-8588, www.chardonpress.com. A full thirty-eight pages on this cheery subject.

Alliance for Justice, *Worry-Free Lobbying for Nonprofits: How to Use the 501(h) Election to Maximize Effectiveness*, (Washington, D.C.: Alliance for Justice, 1999). No charge. Describes how non-profits and the foundations that support them can take advantage of the clear and generous provisions in federal law encouraging their lobbying activities via the 501(h) election.

American Institute of Certified Public Accountants, *Audits for Not-Profit Organizations,* (Jersey City: American Institute of Certified Public Accountants); Customer Service, 201 Plaza 3, Jersey City, NJ 07311, (888) 777-7077, www.aicpa.org. A standard guide for most organizations.

Thomas R. Asher, *Foundations and Ballot Measures: A Legal Guide* (Washington, D.C.: Alliance for Justice, 1998). $10. Helps foundations navigate the federal rules regarding both support of public charities that engage in ballot measure campaigns and the role foundations themselves may play in supporting or opposing ballot measures.

Thomas R. Asher, *Myth v. Fact: Foundation Support of Advocacy* (Washington, D.C.: Alliance for Justice, 1998). $20. Dispels the myths associated with funding advocacy organizations and offers a full range of advocacy activities that foundations can support.

Gregory L. Colvin and Lowell Finley, *The Rules of the Game: An Election Year Legal Guide for Nonprofit Organizations* (Washington, D.C.: Alliance for Justice, 1996). $20. Reviews federal tax and election laws that govern non-profits in an election year and explains the right (and wrong) ways to organize specific voter education activities.

Gregory L. Colvin and Lowell Finley, *Seize the Initiative* (Washington, D.C.: Alliance for Justice, 1996). $20. Answers frequently asked questions by non-profit organizations about work on ballot measures.

CPAs for the Public Interest, *The Audit Process: A Guide for Not-for-Profit Organizations* rev. (Chicago: CPAs for the Public Interest, 2000); 222 South Riverside Plaza, Chicago, IL 60606, (312) 993-0393. Covers the audit process from the initial decision of whether or not to have an audit to planning for next year's audit.

John Paul Dalsimer and Susan J. Ellis, ed., *Self-Help Accounting for the Volunteer Treasurer* (Philadelphia, Pa.: Energize Books, 1989). Simple guide for volunteer treasurers.

Gail M. Harmon, Jessica A. Ladd, and Eleanor Evans, *Being a Player: A Guide to the IRS Lobbying Regulations for Advocacy Charities* (Washington, D.C.: Alliance for Justice, 1995). $15. This primer provides a detailed, plain-language road map of IRS lobbying regulations.

Elizabeth Kingsley, Gail Harmon, John Pomeranz, and Kay Guinane, *E-Advocacy for Nonprofits: The Law of Lobbying and Election-Related Activity on the Net* (Washington, D.C.: Alliance for Justice, 1998). $25. Discusses the law governing Internet advocacy—from voter-education Web sites to e-mail action alerts.

Maryland Bar Association, ed., *Starting a Nonprofit Organization: A Practical Guide to Organizing, Incorporating and Obtaining Tax Exempt Status,* 4th ed. (Baltimore: The Community Law Center and The Maryland Association of Nonprofit Organizations, 1999); 190 W. Ostend St., Baltimore, MD 21230,

(410) 727-6367/(800) 273-6367. A very practical short book.

Arnold J. Olenick and Philip R. Olenick, *A Nonprofit Organization Operating Manual: Planning for Survival and Growth* (New York: Foundation Center, 1991).

B. Holly Schadler, *The Connection: Strategies for Creating and Operating 501(c)(3)s, 501(c)(4)s, and PACs* (Washington, D.C.: Alliance for Justice, 1998). $25. Explains the advantages and issues to be considered in establishing more than one type of exempt organization to expand activists' influence on the policy process.

United Way of America, *Accounting and Financial Reporting: A Guide for United Ways and Not-for-Profit Human-Service Organizations* (Alexandria: United Way of America, 1989); 701 North Fairfax St, Alexandria, VA 22314-2045 (800)772-0008 www.unitedway.org. An excellent introduction to accounting for non-profits.

Recent U.S. Social Change History

Taylor Branch, *Parting the Waters: America in the King Years 1954-1963* (New York: Touchstone Books, 1989). A superb history, filled with the kind of details organizers are interested in.

Taylor Branch, *Pillar of Fire: America in the King Years 1963–1965* (New York: Simon & Schuster, 1999). The sequel.

Sara Evans, *Personal Politics: The Roots of Women's Liberation in the Civil Rights Movement and the New Left* (New York: Random House, 1980). An insightful look at women's development during their involvement in the civil rights movement and the new left.

Susan Ferriss and Ricardo Sandoval, *The Fight in the Fields: Cesar Chavez and the Farmworkers Movement* (San Diego: Harcourt, 1997). Based on the inspiring video by Ray Telles and Rick Tejada-Flores, this is a lively and detailed accounting of the work of Cesar Chavez and the farmworkers' movement.

Robert Fisher, *Let the People Decide: Neighborhood Organizing in America (Social Movements Past and Present)* (Boston: Twayne Publications, 1997). A good, detailed history of organizing from the perspective of neighborhoods. Focuses on the interconnection between the social and political context and the possibilities for activism.

Eric Foner, *The Story of American Freedom from Colonial Times to the Present* (New York: W.W. Norton, 1998). Foner analyzes how the American idea of freedom—what it is and to whom it should apply—has changed through the course of our history.

Helen Garvy (producer-director), *Rebels with a Cause* (New York: Zeitgeist Films, 2000). A feature-length film history of Students for a Democratic Society in the 1960s. The film combines historic footage with present-day interviews of SDS activists. Essential to understanding how those turbulent times shaped the years that followed. Released in 2000 by Zeitgeist Films, 247 Centre St., 2nd Floor. New York, NY 10013, (212) 274-1989, mail@zeitgeistfilm.com.

Alex Haley (contributor), *The Autobiography of Malcolm X* (reprint, New York: Ballantine Books, 1992). A classic book that every American should read.

Sanford D. Horwitt, *Let Them Call Me Rebel: Saul Alinsky, His Life and Legacy* (New York: Vintage Books, 1992). A long but readable history of Alinsky's life and work, with exactly the kind of behind-the-scenes details that organizers will appreciate.

Maurice Isserman, *The Other American: The Life of Michael Harrington* (New York: Public Affairs, 2000). Harrington was a leading socialist author, teacher, and leader.

Peter Medoff and Holly Sklar*, Streets of Hope: The Fall and Rise of an Urban Neighborhood,* (Cambridge, Mass.: South End Press, 1994). The story of the organizing of the Dudley Street Neighborhood Initiative, which transformed a neighborhood in Boston through community efforts.

James Miller, *"Democracy Is in the Streets": From Port Huron to the Siege of Chicago* (Boston: Harvard University Press, 1994). An intellectual history of the student movement of the 1960s, from which came the leadership of many of today's organizations.

Charles M. Payne, *I've Got the Light of Freedom: The Organizing Tradition and the Mississippi Freedom Struggle* (Berkeley: University of California Press, 1995). The story of the organizing that went on at the grassroots level, behind the headlines.

Frances Fox Piven and Richard Cloward, *The Breaking of the American Social Compact* (New York: New Press, 1998). Piven and Cloward analyze the assault over the last three decades on America's social compact, including the impact of devolution and welfare "reform." One of many useful books by these authors.

Mary Beth Rogers, *Cold Anger: A Story of Faith and Power Politics* (Denton, Tx.: University of North Texas Press, 1990). The story of the Industrial Areas Foundation organizing in Texas.

Juan Williams, *Eyes on the Prize: America's Civil Rights Years 1954–1965* (New York: Penguin USA, 1988). Another excellent history of the civil rights struggle.

Howard Zinn, *A People's History of the United States, 1492–Present.* (New York: Harper Trade, 1995). The story behind the usual story of American history.

Howard Zinn, *The Twentieth Century: A People's History* (New York: Harper Trade, 1998).

Power, Politics, Issues

Dean Baker and Mark Weisbrot, *Social Security: The Phony Crisis* (Chicago: University of Chicago Press, 1999). This book examines the dire forecast for social security and separates the misinformation, disinformation, and political motivations behind it. The authors believe that the system as it is currently constituted offers the best opportunity for financial security for future retirees.

Donald L. Barlett and James B. Steele (contributor), *America: What Went Wrong?* (Kansas City, Mo.: Andrews McMeel Publishing, 1992). A description of how corporate influence in Washington has undermined the middle class.

Harry Boyte, Heather Booth, and Steve Max, *Citizen Action and the New American Populism* (Philadelphia: Temple University Press, 1986). Analyzes the rise of grassroots progressive activity during the 1980s and its Right Wing counterpart.

Citizens for Tax Justice, *Tax Expenditures: The Hidden Entitlements* (Washington, D.C.: Citizens for Tax Justice, 1995); 1311 L St, NW, Washington, DC, 20005 (202) 626-3780. Explains how the tax structure is set up to give billions to the rich and corporations.

G. William Domhoff, *The Power Elite and the State: How Policy Is Made in America (Social Institutions and Social Change)* (New York: Aldine de Gruyter, 1990). Domhoff leads the way on documenting the relationship between monied interests and politics.

William Greider, *One World, Ready or Not: The Manic Logic of Global Capitalism* (New York: Touchstone Books, 1998). Greider looks at the human cost of globalization and proposes a number of steps that could be taken to avoid the disastrous consequences of economic exploitation.

William Greider, *Who Will Tell the People: The Betrayal of the American Democracy* (reprint, New York: Touchstone Books, 1993). A widely read book on how politicians are "bought" and the consequences for American democracy.

Michael Harrington, *Socialism Past and Future* (Denver: Mentor Books, 1997). Harrington's last book analyzes past strengths and weaknesses of the socialist movement and argues that socialism is still the best hope for a decent livable world.

Sylvia Hewlett, Cornel West, and Eric West, *The War against Parents*, (Boston: Mariner Books,

1999). The authors dissect the lip service that has been given to family values and propose that parents organize to overcome the real obstacles that are thrown in the way of raising children—lack of access to health care, affordable day care, and so on. Family values from a progressive perspective.

Jim Hightower, *If the Gods Had Meant Us to Vote, They'd Have Given Us Candidates* (New York: Harper Collins, 2000). Hightower dissects both the Republicans and Democrats and the wealthy multinational corporations that provide so much of the money for elections and makes the case for changing the system.

Charles Lewis, *The Buying of the President 2000* (New York: Avon Books, 2000). Another excellent contribution by Lewis discusses the cash flow between special interests and the candidates (Bush, McCain, Gore, and Bradley) and offers insight into the others (Forbes, Dole, Keyes, and Bauer), proving that campaign cash is a non-partisan issue.

Kevin P. Phillips, *Boiling Point: Republicans, Democrats, and the Decline of Middle-Class Prosperity* (New York: Harper Collins, 1994). Describes the concentration of wealth and its political consequences and why the middle class is squeezed.

Sam Pizzigati and Howard Saunders (illustrator), *The Maximum Wage: A Common Sense Prescription for Revitalizing America—By Taxing the Very Rich* (New York: Apex Press, 1992). A popular book on one approach to addressing the increasing concentration of wealth.

The Public Health and Labor Institute, *Corporate Power and the American Dream: Toward an Economic Agenda for Working People*

(New York: Apex Press, 1997). A workbook and discussion guide on jobs, earnings, mergers, corporate welfare, and the economy. Written with a trade union audience in mind, but good for wider groups.

Theda Skocpol, *Boomerang: Health Care Reform and the Turn against Government* (New York: W.W. Norton, 1997). Skocpol uses the defeat of President Clinton's health care initiative to analyze the success of the Right Wing's attack on government itself as the problem.

Introduction to Economics

Barry Bluestone and Bennett Harrison, *The Battle for Growth with Equity in the 21st Century* (Boston: Houghton Mifflin Company, 2000).

Chuck Collins and Felice Yeskel, *Economic Apartheid in America: A Primer on Economic Inequality and Security* (New York: New Press, 2000). An activist guide to closing the growing gap in income and wealth distribution.

Bob Hulteen and Jim Wallis, eds., *Who Is My Neighbor? Economics as If Values Matter* (Washington, D.C.: Sojourners, 1994). A study guide that helps groups understand the current economic choices, dream of a different world, and make plans to change the world. Good for religious or peace/social action groups.

Robert Lekachman and Borin Van Loon, *Capitalism for Beginners,* (New York: Pantheon Books, 1981). Out of print. Highly readable and illustrated with cartoons. Explains the theories of Adam Smith, Karl Marx, John Maynard Keynes, Milton Friedman, and others.

Robert Pollin and Stephanie Luce, *Living Wage: Building a Fair Economy* (New York: New Press,

1998). This book provides a history and analysis of the living wages campaigns that have been waged across the country to provide a decent standard of living for low-wage workers.

United for a Fair Economy, *The Activist Cookbook: Creative Actions for a Fair Economy* (Oakland, Calif.: Chardon Press, 1997); www.chardonpress.com. Step-by-step guides on how to creatively educate people about the economy. Includes the best training exercises from United for a Fair Economy, an organization that really knows how to bring economics to life.

William Julius Wilson, *The Bridge over the Racial Divide: Rising Inequality and Coalition Politics* (Berkeley: University of California Press, 1999). Wilson concludes that inequality is rising and suggests the need for a broad-based coalition to combat it.

Jobs and the Industrial Base

Barry Bluestone and Irving Bluestone (contributor), *Negotiating the Future: A Labor Perspective on American Business* (reprint, New York: Basic Books, 1994). A good overview of the relationship between U.S. business and jobs in the economy.

Sam Bowles, David Gordon, and Thomas Weisskopf, *After the Wasteland: A Democratic Economics for the Year 2000* (Armonk, N.Y.: M.E. Sharpe, Inc., 1991). A democratic alternative to economic decline.

Harry Braverman and John Bellamy Foster (introduction), *Labor and Monopoly Capital: The Degradation of Work in the Twentieth Century* (New York: Monthly Review Press, 1999). A classic theoretical work on the changing nature of work and the people who do it.

Draws parallels between the deskilling of craft work, and the present-day deskilling of white-collar and managerial work.

Michael Brower, *Cool Energy: Renewable Solutions to Environmental Problems* (Cambridge, Mass.: MIT Press, 1992). Authoritative discussion of renewable energy sources. Includes policy recommendations and further reading sources.

David Dembo and Ward Morehouse, *The Underbelly of the U.S. Economy: Joblessness and Pauperization of Work in America* (special edition, New York: Apex Press, 1999). *A* most useful pamphlet on jobs, wages, and the pauperization of work. Calculates the true jobless rate, as distinct from the government unemployment rate. Updates previous editions of this valuable research.

Public Health Institute and The Labor Institute, *Jobs and the Environment*, 4th ed. (New York: Apex Press, 1994). A workbook and discussion guide mainly for union members but good for more general audiences. Covers why environmentalism is not the cause of unemployment, basic and workplace environmental issues.

William Julius Wilson, *When Work Disappears: The World of the New Urban Poor* (New York: Vintage Books, 1997). Wilson examines the disappearance of jobs in the urban ghetto in the wake of a globalized economy.

Periodicals

The American Prospect was founded in 1990 as a forum for progressive policy debate. It provides a bimonthly discussion of politics and policy issues from a clearly progressive, if somewhat scholarly, viewpoint; a recent change in format makes the magazine more lively and accessible than in the past. Subscriptions are available at www.prospect.org or by calling (888) 687-8732.

ColorLines, a quarterly publication of the Applied Research Center and the Center for Third World Organizing, has as its goal to "bring together the leading organizers of color and the leading writers on race to speak on the issues, the organizing, the arts, the ideas of our time." Subscriptions may be ordered through Chardon Press at (888) 458-8588.

Dollars and Sense, 1 Summer St., Somerville, MA 02143, (616) 628-8411 www.igc.apc.org/dollars/. An easy-to-read progressive bimonthly magazine on economics.

Grassroots Fundraising Journal, 3781 Broadway Oakland, CA 94611, (888) 458-8588, www.chardonpress.com. Best current nuts-and-bolts advice on grassroots fundraising for community organizations.

In These Times, Institute for Public Affairs, 2040 N Milwaukee Ave., Chicago, IL 60647, (800)827-0270, www.inthesetimes.com. A weekly newspaper of use to all organizers. Covers the news not covered in regular daily papers.

Labor Notes, 7435 Michigan Ave, Detroit, MI 48210, (313) 842-6262, www.labornotes.org. A monthly publication providing short stories on progressive labor struggles around the United States.

*Monthly Review,*122 W. 27th St., New York, NY 10001, (212) 691-2555. An independent

Socialist magazine written more for the academic community than for organizers. Invaluable analysis of American and international economic conditions.

New Perspectives Quarterly, Center for Study of Democratic Institutions, 10951 West Pico Blvd., Third Floor, Los Angeles, CA 90064, (310) 474-0011, www.npq.org Examines social and political thought on economics, religion, politics, and culture.

The Nation. First published in 1865, *The Nation* comes out weekly and is the country's oldest continuously published progressive news magazine: www.thenation.org, (800) 333-8536.

The Nonprofit Times, 240 Cedar Knolls Road, Suite 318, Cedar Knolls, NJ 07927, (973) 734-1700, www.nptimes.com. Monthly tabloid full of good ideas and case studies. Available free to full-time, non-profit directors.

Shelterforce is a publication of the National Housing Institute and focuses on issues of affordable housing and community development. It includes a highly readable combination of how-to, policy, and news and information about community organizing and development: www.nhi.org, (973) 678-9060

Too Much: A Quarterly Commentary on Capping Excessive Income and Wealth, United for a Fair Economy, 37 Temple Place, Second Floor, Boston, MA 02111, (617) 423-2148, www.ufenet.org. A lively publication from a very lively organization organizing against rising economic inequality.

WorkingUSA, a quarterly journal of labor and society, covering current labor issues: M.E. Sharpe, (800) 541-6563, or www.mesharpe.com.

World Policy Journal, World Policy Institute, 65 Fifth Avenue, Suite 413, New York, NY 10003, (212) 229-5808, www.worldpolicy.org. Contains essays, interviews, and forum debates on current U.S. foreign policy, international economics, regional political developments, and domestic U.S. policy.

Useful Organizations, Resources, and Web Sites

The danger of making a list like this is that inevitably we will have left someone out. However, using the organizations listed below as a jumping-off point should take you far and wide, and hopefully you will run into the ones we omitted along the way.

AFL-CIO, the American Federation of Labor and Congress of Industrial Organizations, the federation labor unions in the country, has a Web site that provides a variety of news about working conditions and union organizing around the country, information about workers' rights, discussion of policy issues of concern to working people and their families, links to training for union members as well as people interested in learning more about the work of unions, links to union affiliates, and much more: 815 16th Street, NW, Washington, DC 20006, (202) 637-5000, www.aflcio.org

Applied Research Center is a public policy, educational, and research institute whose work emphasizes issues of race and social change. Its Web site includes downloadable reports and many supporting materials on education, race, and a variety of other topics, as well as links to training and to *ColorLines* magazine, which the center copublishes with the Center for Third World Organizing: 3781 Broadway, Oakland, CA 94611, (510) 653-3415 www.arc.org

Center for Community Change helps poor people to improve their communities and change policies and institutions that affect their lives by developing their own strong organizations. It conducts policy analysis and provides technical assistance and campaign coordination on a variety of issues of concern to low-income people, including housing, community development, jobs and economic development, and welfare "reform." Its Web site features many useful resources, publications, and news updates: 1000 Wisconsin Ave., NW, Washington, DC 20007, (202) 342-0567, www.communitychange.org.

Center for Labor and Community Research conducts research and produces publications "to assist labor, communities, and business to pursue the High Road of economic development guaranteeing the building of a strong, participative and productive economy, social justice and the equitable distribution of wealth." Its Web site includes publications and an extensive list of links to organizations working on related issues: 3411 W. Diversey Parkway, Suite 10, Chicago, IL 60647, (773) 278-5418, www.clcr.org.

Center for Responsive Politics is a non-partisan, non-profit research group based in Washington, D.C., that tracks money in politics and its effect on elections and public policy. The center conducts computer-based research on campaign finance issues for the news media, academics, activists, and the public at large. Via the searchable database on the center's Web site, you can find out how much money particular candidates have raised, how much particular donors have given, and other very useful information: 1101 14th St., NW, Suite 1030, Washington, DC 20005-5635, (202) 857-0044, www.opensecrets.org.

The Center for Third World Organizing (CTWO) links communities of color with organizing skills, political education, and visions of a just society. CTWO seeks to galvanize public support for policies that both advance racial justice and promote equity in the arenas of gender, economics, and sexuality. It provides training and consultation to community organizers and organizations, including its well-known Minority Activist Apprenticeship Program, and a variety of other sessions. The center is copublisher of *ColorLines*, along with the Applied Research Center: 1218 E. 21st Street, Oakland, CA 94606, (510) 533-7583, www.ctwo.org.

Center on Budget and Policy Priorities (CBPP) is a non-partisan research organization and policy institute that conducts research and analysis on a range of government policies and programs, with an emphasis on those affecting low- and moderate-income people. Its Web site includes an extensive and useful set of articles and studies on budget-related issues. CBPP provides assistance to state organizations as well as to international NGOs, and the Web site includes many links around the country and the world: 820 First, NE, Suite 510, Washington, DC 20002, (202) 408-1080, www.cbpp.org.

Chardon Press publishes and/or distributes lots of relevant publications on many useful topics relating to social change, from nitty-gritty topics like fundraising to combating racism to movement history: 3781 Broadway, Oakland, CA 94611, (888) 458-8588, www.chardonpress.com.

Citizens for Tax Justice is a non-partisan non-profit research and advocacy organization dedicated to fair taxation at the federal, state, and local levels. It conducts extensive analysis of tax-related legislative proposals. Its Web site includes extensive information on current tax issues, including updates and analysis, as well as a list of publications and links to organizations working on related issues. Citizens for Tax Justice, 1311 L Street NW, Washington, DC 20005, (202) 626-3780, www.ctj.org.

comm-org is a Web site and list server offering many useful resources, including an extensive list of links to other organizing Web sites and organizations. It posts job and conference announcements, papers, course syllabi, research and policy links, as well as a variety of other materials related to community development and organizing: http://comm-org.utoledo.edu.

The Economy Policy Institute is a non-profit, non-partisan think tank that seeks to broaden the public debate about strategies to achieve a prosperous and fair economy. It produces many useful economic policy analyses on issues like the minimum wage, the living wage, social security, the state of the economy, and others. 1660 L Street, NW, Suite 1200, Washington, DC 20036, (202) 775-8810, www.epinet.org.

The Electronic Policy Network is a consortium of over sixty generally progressive public policy organizations and advocacy groups, sponsored by *The American Prospect*. Its Web site provides many useful links: www.epn.org.

Families USA is a national non-profit organization dedicated to the achievement of high-quality, affordable health and long-term care for all Americans through work at the national, state, and community levels. It provides research, public information, technical assistance, and coordination of policy campaigns. Its Web site includes extensive information of a variety of health care policy issues, both nationally and by state, as well as legislative alerts, job

listings, a list server, and much more: 1334 G Street NW, Washington, DC 20005, (202) 628-3030, www.familiesusa.org.

The Joint Center for Political and Economic Studies is a national, non-profit institution that conducts research on public policy issues of special concern to Black Americans and other minorities. Founded in 1970, the Joint Center provides independent analyses through research, publications, and outreach programs. It publishes a monthly policy magazine, *Focus*. The Web site includes extensive publications and research data: 1090 Vermont Avenue, NW, Suite 1100, Washington, DC 20005, (202) 789-3500, www.jointctr.org.

The Foundation Center provides useful resources to both funders and grant seekers. Its Web site includes publications and links to training as well as to over 1,500 foundation Web sites. Very useful for researching funding sources. The center has libraries full of resources in five cities, as well as cooperating collections in more locations around the country: 79 Fifth Avenue/16th Street, New York, NY 10003-3076, (800) 424-9836, http://fdncenter.org/.

Highlander Research and Education Center. Founded in 1932, the Highlander Center has a long history of working with people struggling against oppression, in Appalachia and beyond. It conducts residential trainings and is an excellent source of materials on trainings in the popular education tradition: 1959 Highlander Way, New Market, TN 37829, (423) 933-3443, www.hrec.org.

The Institute for Global Communications was established to advance the work of progressive organizations and individuals for peace, justice, economic opportunity, human rights, democracy, and environmental sustainability through strategic use of online technologies. Its Web site includes news about a variety of progressive organizing, action alerts, and extensive links to other progressive organizations. Areas of special focus include PeaceNet, WomensNet, AntiRacismNet, and EcoNet: www.igc.org.

The Labor Heritage Society is an excellent source for music, videos, books, art, and other cultural materials related to labor history: 1925 K Street, Washington, DC 20006, www.laborheritage.org.

The Midwest Academy is one of the nation's oldest and best known schools for community organizations, citizen organizations, and individuals committed to progressive social change. In addition to being the authors of this book, we offer five-day training sessions for leaders and staff of citizen and community groups, as well as training and consultation to a wide variety of action organizations. The Web site lists upcoming training dates and provides a sample training agenda, an introduction to direct action organizing, and job listings: 28 E. Jackson, #605, Chicago, IL 60604, (312) 427-2304, www.midwestacademy.com.

The National Center for Nonprofit Boards is dedicated to strengthening non-profit boards and the organizations it directs. It provides a variety of resources on board development and the various functions of boards, through workshops, publications, networking, and consulting. Numerous publications are available through the Web site: 1828 L Street, NW, Suite 900, Washington, DC 20036-5104, (800) 883-6262, www.ncnb.org.

The National Housing Institute is an organization that examines housing policy issues and produces reports, along with its well-known journal, *Shelterforce*, which is published bimonthly and covers issues in community development and community organizing as well as housing. The Web site contains the online edition of *Shelterforce* as well as a number of housing policy studies and other useful information: National Housing Institute, 439 Main Street Suite 311, Orange, NJ 07050, (973) 678-9060, www.nhi.org.

The National Interfaith Committee for Worker Justice was founded to call upon religious values in order to educate, organize, and mobilize the religious community on issues and campaigns that will improve wages, benefits, and working conditions for workers, especially low-wage workers. It is an excellent source for faith-based materials on workers' rights from a wide variety of faith traditions, as well as devotional materials and booklets explaining labor unions, the living wage campaign, and other issues to a faith-based audience: 1020 W. Bryn Mawr, Chicago, IL 60660, (773) 728-8400, www.nicwj.org.

National Organizers Alliance (NOA) is a membership organization of community and labor organizers and allied workers whose mission is to nurture and sustain the people who work in the field of progressive organizing. The Web site includes a jobs listing (for NOA members only), links to a variety of organizations, and information about the NOA Pension Plan, a portable, multiple employer pension plan for organizers: 715 G Street SE, Washington DC 20003, (202) 543-6603, www.noacentral.org.

The National Training and Information Center, the research and education arm of National People's Action (NPA), has an excellent list of publications on organizing and issues such as redlining, community reinvestment, FHA housing, and many other issues. It also publishes

Disclosure, a periodical that reports on the activities of organizations in the NPA network: 810 N. Milwaukee, Chicago, IL 60622, (312) 243-3035.

The Northland Poster Collective is a great source for bumper stickers, T-shirts, posters, buttons, and other materials on labor themes, current as well as historical. It is the source for many classic designs. Materials can be purchased in bulk for fundraising; the collective also does custom printing. P.O. Box 7096, Minneapolis, MN 55407, (800) 627-3082, www.northlandposter.com.

United for a Fair Economy is a very creative group dedicated to addressing the growing income and wealth gap. It has excellent resources, training, and materials on economic inequality. The Web site includes information as well as action alerts and links to organizations working on related issues: 37 Temple Place, Second Floor, Boston, MA 02111, (617) 423-2148, www.ufenet.org.

USAction is a national coalition of organizations including over twenty-six statewide affiliates, three labor unions, the US Student Association, and a variety of other organizations whose mission is to strengthen progressive political power to win social, racial, economic and environmental justice for all and to serve as a national voice amplifying the voices of grassroots organizations for progressive values. Issues include public education, campaign finance reform, social security, health care, and the environment. The Web site includes links to affiliate organizations as well as other organizations working on the same issues: 1341 G St., NW, 10th Floor, Washington, DC 20005, (202) 661-0216, www.usaction.org.

Training Videos

Board Member Manual and Videos, Aspen Publishers, Inc., 7201 McKinney Circle, Frederick, MD 21701, (800) 368-8437, Manual: $29.00, Videos: vol. I $49.00 and vol. II $51.00. Aspen Publishers has produced two training videos for board members. The videos can be purchased only if one purchases a manual: www.aspenpublishers.com.

Chicago Video Project, *Accessing the Media,* ACTA Publications, 4848 N. Clark Street, Chicago, IL 60640, (800) 397-2282, $24.95. This twelve-minute video trains groups how to focus their messages, pitch stories or events, follow up on press releases, and deal with journalists on-site to maximize the coverage received.

Chicago Video Project, *The Democratic Promise: Saul Alinsky and His Legacy,* Chicago Video Project, 800 W. Huron, Ste. 3 South, Chicago, IL 60622, (312) 666-0195, www.chicagovideo.com, $15.00 + $3.00 for shipping.

Chicago Video Project, *Running Good Meetings,* ACTA Publications, 4848 N. Clark Street, Chicago, IL 60640, (800) 397-2282, $24.95. Excellent twelve-minute video that teaches the basic elements of running good meetings, including preplanning, starting and ending on time, developing and sticking to agendas, and dealing with naysayers.

Joan Flanagan, *Fund-Raising Training Videotapes.* These three tapes sell for $30.00 each or $75.00 for all three. The topics are Getting Started, Asking for Money, and Fund Raising Forever. Checks should be made payable to the Bowman Gray School of Medicine and sent to Partners in Caregiving Program, The

Bowman Gray School of Medicine, Medical Center Blvd., Winston-Salem, NC 27157, or call (910) 716-4941.

Grassroots Fundraising, The Kim Klein Video Series, Headwaters Fund, 122 W. Franklin Ave., Ste. 518, Minneapolis, MN 55404, (612)879-0602. A six-video series. The six topics are The Basics of Fundraising, The Role of the Board, Asking for Money, Major Gifts, Direct Mail, Special Events, Donor Loyalty.

Sources for Progressive Audiovisuals

Below are sources for films and videos on organizing and progressive issues. Call or write for their free catalogues.

Cambridge Documentary Films, Inc.
P.O. Box 390385
Cambridge, MA 02138-0004
(617) 484-3993
www.shore.net/–cdf
e-mail: cdf@share.net

Canadian Labour Congress
2841 Riverside Drive
Ottawa, Ontario, Canada KIV 8X7
(613) 521-3400
www.clc-ctc.ca

The Video Project
200 Estates Drive
Ben Lomond, CA 95005
(831) 336-2160 or (800) 475-2638
www.videoproject.org
e-mail: videoproject@video.org

Public Media Home Vision
4411 N. Ravenswood Avenue
Chicago, IL 60640

(312) 878-2600
Outside of Illinois: (800) 323-4222

First Run/Icarus
153 Waverly Place, Sixth Floor
New York, NY 10014
(800) 876-1700

Fusion Video
100 Fusion Way
Country Club Hill, IL 60478
(708) 799-2350 or (800) 338-7710

Kartemquin Films
1901 W. Wellington
Chicago, IL 60657
(773) 472-4366
www.kartemquin.com
e-mail: kartemquin@aol.com

Media Network of New York
39 W. 14th Street, Suite 403
New York, NY 10011
(212) 929-2663

Media Process Group
770 N. Halsted, Suite 507
Chicago, IL 60622
(312) 850-1300
www.mediaprocess.com
e-mail: info@media process.com

New Day Films
22-D Hollywood Avenue
Hohokus, NJ 07423
(201) 652-6590
e-mail: tmcndy@aol.com

Camera News, dba Third World Newsreel
Distribution Production Organizing
545 Eighth Ave., Tenth Floor
New York, NY 10018

(212) 947-9277

www.twn.org

e-mail: twn@twn.org

Videos for a Changing World

Turning Tide Productions

P.O. Box 864

Wendell, MA 01379

(800) 557-6414

In addition, audiovisual resources are available at public, university, and union libraries.

SONGS

Lift Every Voice

Lift ev'ry voice and sing, til earth and heaven
    ring,
Ring with the harmonies of liberty;
Let our rejoicing rise, high as the list'ning skies.
Let it resound loud as the rolling sea.
Sing a song full of the faith that the dark past
    has taught us,
Sing a song full of the hope that the present has
    brought us:
Facing the rising sun of our new day begun,
Let us march on till victory is won.

Stony the road we trod, bitter the chast'ning
    rod,
Felt in the days when hope unborn had died;
Yet with a steady beat, have not our weary feet,
Come to the place for which our fathers sighed?
We have come over a way that with tears has
    been watered,
We have come, treading our path thro' the blood
    of the slaughtered,
Out of the gloomy past, till now we stand at
    last,
Where the white gleam of our bright star is cast.

God of our weary years, God of our silent tears,
Thou who hast brought us thus far on the way;
Thou who hast by Thy might led us into the
    light,
Keep us forever in the path, we pray,
Lest our feet stray from the places, our God,
    where we met Thee,
Lest our hearts, drunk with the wine of the
    world, we forget Thee;
Shadowed beneath Thy hand, may we forever
    stand,
True to our God, true to our native land.

Let us keep onward still, keep our resolve until,
We achieve brotherhood for all mankind;
Look to the rising sun, new work each day is
    begun,
Daily we strive til we true freedom find.
Save our hope that we so long and so dearly did
    cherish,
Lest our hearts weary with cruel disillusion
    should perish;
Stretch forth a loving hand, you who in power
    stand,
Lose not our faith, lose not our native land.

-James Weldon Johnson (v.4 Henrietta McKee)

It Could Have Been Me

Students in Ohio and down at Jackson State
Shot down by a vicious fire one early day in
    May
Some people cried out angry "You should have
    shot more of them down"
But you can't bury youth my friend. youth
    grows the whole world round

It could have been me but instead it was you
So I'll keep doing the work you were doing as
    if I were two
I'll be a student of life, a singer of songs, a
    farmer of food and a righter of wrongs
It could have been me but instead it was you
And it may be me dear sisters and brothers
    before we are thru
But if you can die* for treedom - freedom (3x)
If you can die for freedom, I can too
*(other v. substitute: sing, live, fight)

The junta took the fingers of Victor Jara's hands
They said to the gentle poet "Play your guitar
now if you can"
Well, Victor started singing til they shot his
body down
You can kill a man but not a song when it's
sung the whole world 'round

A woman in the jungle so many wars away
Studies late into the night, defends a village in
the day
Altho' her life and struggle are miles away from
me
She sings a song and I know the words and I'll
sing them til she's free

One night in Oklahoma, Karen Silkwood died
Because she had some secrets big companies
wanted to hide
Well they talk of nuclear safety, they talk of
national pride
But we all know it's a death machine and that's
why Karen died

Our sisters are in struggle, from Vietnam to
Wounded Knee
From Mozambique to Puerto Rico and they
look to you and me
To fight against the system that kills them off
and takes their land
It's our fight too if we're gonna win, we've got
to do it hand in hand

It's gonna be me and it's gonna be you
So we'll keep doing the work we've been doing
until we are thru
We'll be students of life, singers of song, farm-
ers of food and fighters so strong
It's gonna be me and it's gonna be you
But it will be us dear sisters and brothers before
we are thru

'Cause if you can fight for freedom, freedom
(3x)
If you can fight for freedom, we can too!

-Holly Near

1974 Hereford Music (ASCAP). New verses
1983. Used by permission.

Mountain Song

I have dreamed on this mountain
Since first I was my mother's daughter
And you can't just take my dreams
Away - not with me watching
You may drive a big machine
But I was born a great big woman
And you can't just take my dreams
Away - without me fighting

(bridge) This old mountain raised my many
daughters
Some died young, some are still living
If you come here for to take our mountain
Well, we ain't come here to give it

I have dreamed on this mountain
Since first I was my mother's daughter
And you can't just take my dreams
Away - not with me watching

No, you can't just take my dreams
Away - without me fighting
No, you can't just take my dreams away

-Holly Near

1978 Hereford Music (ASCAP). Used by permission.

No More Genocide

Why do we call them the enemy
This struggling nation that's won independence
    across the sea?
Why do we want these people to die?
Why do we say North and South, o why, o why,
    o why?

Well, that's just a lie! One of the many and
    we've had plenty
I don't want more of the same/no more geno-
    cide in my name!

Why are our history books so full of lies
When no word is spoken of why the Indian dies
    and dies?
Or that the Chicanos love the California land
Do our books all say it was discovered by one
    white man?

Why are the weapons of the war so young?
Why are there only rich ones around when it's
    done?
Why are so many of our soldiers black or
    brown?
Do we think it's because they're good at cutting
    other people down?

Why do we support a colony
When Puerto Rican people are crying out to be
    free?
We sterilize the women and rob the copper
    mines
Do we think that people will always be so
    blind?

Nazi forces grow again, ignorance gives them a
    place
The Klan is teaching children to hate the human
    race

Where once there was a playground, now an
    MX missile plant
Do they think it's fun to see just how much we
    can stand?

-Holly Near

1972 Hereford Music (ASCAP). Used by permission.

Union Maid

There once was a union maid who never was
    afraid
Of goons and ginks and company finks and the
    deputy sheriffs who made the raids
She went to the union hall when a meeting it
    was called
And when the company boys came 'round she
    always stood her ground

Chorus:
O you can't scare me, I'm sticking to the union
I'm sticking to the union, I'm sticking to the
    union
O you can't scare me, I'm sticking to the union
I'm sticking to the union til the day I die

This union maid was wise to the tricks of com-
    pany spies
She never got fooled by a company stool, she'd
    always organize the guys
She always got her way, when she struck for
    higher pay
She'd show her card to the company guard and
    this is what she'd say:

Chorus

You women who want to be free, take a little tip
    from me

Break outa that mold we've all been sold, you
   got a fighting his-to-ree
The fight for women's rights with workers must
   unite
Like Mother Jones, move those bones to the
   front of every fight!

Chorus

-w: Woody Guthrie (new v. anon.) m: trad.
("Redwing")
TRO _1961 and 1963 Ludlow Music, Inc. NY,
NY. International copyright secured. Made in
USA. All rights reserved, incl. public perform-
ance for profit. Used by permission.

This Land Is Your Land

This land is your land, this land is my land
From California to the New York Island
From the redwood forest to the Gulf Stream
   waters
This land was made for you and me

As I was walking that ribbon of highway
I saw above me that endless skyway
I saw below me that golden valley
This land was made for you and me

I've roamed and rambled and I followed my
   footsteps
To the sparkling sands of her diamond deserts
And all around me, a voice was sounding: /
   This land...

When the sun came shining and I was strolling
And the wheat fields waving and the dust
   clouds rolling
As the fog was lifting, a voice was chanting/
   This...

As I went walking, I saw a sign there
On the sign it said "No Trespassing"
But on the other side it didn't say nothing
That side was made for you and me!

In the shadow of the steeple I saw my people
By the relief office, I seen my people
As they stood there hungry I stood there asking
Is this land made for you and me?

Nobody living can ever stop me
As I go walking that freedom highway
Nobody living can make me turn back/ This...

-Woody Guthrie

TRO_ 1956 (renewed 1984), 1958 (renewed
1986), 1979 Ludlow Music, Inc. NY, NY.
International copyright secured. Made in USA.
All rights reserved, incl. public performance for
profit. Used by permission.

If I Had a Hammer

If I had a hammer, I'd hammer in the morning
I'd hammer in the evening, all over this land
I'd hammer out danger, I'd hammer out a warning
I'd hammer out love between my brothers and
   my sisters all over this land

2. If I had a bell, I'd ring it in the morning . . .
3. If I had a song, I'd sing it in the morning . . .
4. Well I got a hammer and I got a bell
   And I got a song to sing all over this land
   It's the hammer of justice, it's the bell of
   freedom
   It's a song about love between...

-Lee Hays and Pete Seeger

Amazing Grace

Amazing grace! How sweet the sound
That saved a wretch (soul) like me
I once was lost and now am found
Was blind but now I see

'Twas grace that taught my heart to fear
And grace my fears relieved
How precious did that grace appear
The hour I first believed

The Lord has promised good to me
His word my hope secures
He will my shield and portion be
As long as life endures

Thru many dangers, toils and snares
I have already come
'Tis grace that brought me safe thus far
And grace will lead me home

When we've been here 10,000 years
Bright shining as the sun
We've no less days to sing God's praise
Than when we first begun

Allelujah (3x) Praise God! (repeat)

Amazing grace has set me free
To touch, to taste, to feel
The wonders of accepting Love
Have made me whole and real

w: John Newton m: trad (v.5 by John P. Rees.
v.6 by New York YM Quakers)

Bread and Roses

As we go marching marching in the beauty of
    the day
A million darkened kitchens, a thousand mill
    lots gray
Are touched with all the radiance that a sudden
    sun discloses
For the people hear us singing: bread and roses,
    bread and roses!

As we go marching marching, we battle too for
    men
For they are women's children and we mother
        them again (for men can ne'er be free til
        our slavery's at an end)
Our lives shall not be sweated from birth until
    life closes
Hearts starve as well as bodies, give us bread
        but give us roses

As we go marching, marching, unnumbered
    women dead
Go crying thru our singing their ancient call for
    bread
Small art and love and beauty their drudging
    spirits knew
Yes it is bread we fight for, but we fight for
    roses, too

As we go marching, marching, we bring the
    greater days
The rising of the women means the rising of the
    race
No more the drudge and idler, ten that toil
    where one reposes
But a sharing of life's glories - bread and roses,
    bread and roses!

w: James Oppenheim

O Freedom

O freedom, O freedom
O freedom over me!
And before I'd be a slave I'll be buried in my
    grave
And go home to my Lord and be free

No more killin's (3x) over me...
No more fear...
No more hunger...
There'll be joy...
There'll be singing...
There'll be peace...

trad. (adapted by SNCC)

Solidarity Forever

When the union's inspiration, thru the workers'
    blood shall run,
There can be no power greater anywhere
    beneath the sun.
Yet what force on Earth is weaker than the fee-
    ble strength of one,
But the union makes us strong.

Chorus:
Solidarity forever! (3x)
For the union makes us strong.

Is there aught we hold in common with the
    greedy parasite,
Who would lash us into serfdom and would
    crush us with his might?
Is there anything left to us but to organize and
    fight?
For the union makes us strong.

It is we who plowed the prairies, built the cities
    where they trade,
Dug the mines and built the workshops, endless
    miles of railroad laid.
Now we stand outcast and starving 'mid the
    wonders we have made,
But the union makes us strong.

All the world that's owned by idle drones is
    ours and ours alone.
We have laid the wide foundations, built it sky-
    ward stone by stone.

It is ours not to slave in, but to master and to
    own,
While the union makes us strong.

They have taken untold millions that they never
    toiled to earn.
But without our brain and muscle not a single
    wheel can turn.
We can break their haughty power, gain our
    freedom when we learn
That the union makes us strong.

In our hands is placed a power greater than their
    hoarded gold,
Greater than the might of armies magnified a
    thousand-fold.
We can bring to birth a new world from the
    ashes of the old,
For the union makes us strong.

- w: Ralph Chaplin m: Battle Hymn of the
Republic

People Like You

Old fighter, you sure took it on the chin.
Where'd you ever get the strength to stand
Never giving up to giving in.
You know, I just want to shake your hand,
Because. . .

Chorus:
People like you help people like me
Go on, go on
People like you help people like me
Go on, go on

Old Battler, with a scar from every town,
Thought you were no better than the rest.
You wore your colors every way but down.
All you ever gave was your best.
But you know that...

Chorus

Old dreamer, with a world in every thought
Where'd you get the vision to keep on?
You sure gave back as good as what you got
I hope that when my time is almost gone
They'll say that...

Chorus

-Si Kahn

_ Flying Fish Records. All rights reserved. Used by permission.

This Little Light of Mine

This little light of mine, I'm gonna let it shine
    (3x)
Let it shine (3x)

Everywhere I go...etc.

Shine on people everywhere...etc.

'Til we all get organized..etc.

Equal rights for everyone...etc.

All around the neighborhood...etc.

All around the universe...etc.

This little light of Mine, I'm gonna let it shine
    (3x)
Let it shine (3x)

-trad.

Study War No More

Gonna lay down my sword and shield down by
    the riverside
Down by the riverside, down by the riverside,
Gonna lay down my sword and shield down by
    the riverside
And study war no more

Chorus: I ain't gonna study war no more (6x)

2. Gonna put on that long white robe, down by
    the riverside . . . etc.
3. Gonna put on that starry crown . . .
4. Gonna walk with the Prince of Peace . . .
5. Gonna shake hands around the world . . .
6. Gonna lay down those atoms bombs . . .

Gonna lay down my income tax/I ain't gonna
    pay for war no more
Gonna lay down my GE stock/and live off war
    no more
Gonna lay down my Honeywell job/and work
    for war no more
Gonna lay down those Congressional
    hawks/and vote for war no more

trad. (new v. anon.)

We Shall Not Be Moved

We shall not, we shall not be moved (2x)
Just like a tree that's standing by the water
We shall not be moved

1. The union is behind us, we shall not be
   moved (2x)
   Just like a tree...
2. We're fighting for our freedom . . .
3. We're fighting for our children . . .
4. We'll build a mighty union . . .
5. _____ is our leader . . .
6. Black and White together . . .
7. Young and old together . . .

No nos, no nos moveran (2x)
Como un arbol firme junto al rio
No nos moveran

1. Unidos en la lucha, no nos moveran...
2. Unidos en la huelga, no nos moveran...

-w: textile workers (Spanish v: from a
Salvadoran union organizer)

Will the Circle Be Unbroken

I was standing by my window on a cold and
   cloudy day
When I saw the hearse come rolling for to carry
   my mother away

Will the circle be unbroken by and by, Lord, by
   and by?
There's a better home a-waiting in the sky,
   Lord, in the sky

Lord I told that undertaker "Undertaker, please
   drive slow
For this body you're a hauling, Lord I hate to
   see her go"

I followed close behind her, tried to hold up and
   be brave
But I could not hide my sorrow when they laid
   her in the grave

-Charles H. Gabriel

Will the circle be unbroken, by and by Lord by
   and by?
There's a better way to live now, we can have it
   if we try

I was singing with my sister, I was singing with
   my friends
And we all can sing together, cause the circle
   never ends

I was born down in the valley where the sun
   refused to shine
But I'm climbing up to the highland gonna
   make that mountain mine!

-Cathy Winter, Betsy Rose and Marcia Taylor.

New words _1988 Authors. Used by permission.

We Shall Overcome

We shall overcome, we shall overcome
We shall overcome someday
Oh, deep in my heart I do believe
We shall overcome someday

1. We'll walk hand in hand . . . etc .
2. We shall live in peace . . .
3. Black and White together . . .
4. We are not afraid . . .
5. We will organize . . .
6. The union makes us strong . . .

-trad.

Joe Hill

I dreamed I saw Joe Hill last night
Alive as you and me
Says I, But Joe, you're ten years dead
I never died, says he
I never died, says he

In Salt Lake, Joe, by God says I
Him standing by my bed
They framed you on a murder charge
Says Joe, but I ain't dead
Says Joe, but I ain't dead

The copper bosses killed you, Joe
They shot you, Joe, says I
Takes more than guns to kill someone
Says Joe, I didn't die
Says Joe, I didn't die

And standing there as big as lite
And smiling with his eyes
Says Joe, What they forgot to kill
Went on to organize
Went on to organize

From San Diego up to Maine
In every mine and mill
Where workers strike and organize
That's where you'll find Joe Hill
That's where you'll find Joe Hill

I dreamed I saw Joe Hill last night
Alive as you and me
Says I, But Joe, you're ten years dead
I never died, says he
I never died, says he

-1938, Earl Robinson and Alfred Hayes

E.R.A. SONG

What's gonna happen in 2004
When your grandchildren ask
What you did before
Before you get all old and grey
There's gonna be your judgement day

Were you there in the olden days, Grampa?
Were you there when they tried to say Grandma
Wasn't equal to you in every way
Tell us how you helped pass the E.R.A.

It'll sure sound funny when you tell those kids
Just what their grandpa really did
'Cause they just won't believe their own
        grandpa
Tried to keep down their own grandma

(Chorus)

What you gonna tell 'em on Judgement Day,
That their grandpa voted no on the E.R.A.?
What you gonna tell those little kids?
How you gonna tell them what you did?

- 1980, Jackie Kendall

I Woke Up This Morning

(women) I woke up this mornin with my mind
(men)   Where was your mind?
(women) Centered on justice.
(women) I woke up this mornin with my mind.
(men)   Where was your mind?
(women) Centered on justice.
(women) I woke up this mornin with my mind.
(men)   Where was your mind?
(women) Centered on justice.

(men)   Say it on.
(women) Say it on.
(men)   Say it on.
(women) Say it on.
(all sing) Justice will be won
            And when your mind's on the right
            We'll win the fight
            Our minds're on justice, forevermore.

w: slightly adapted by Kimberley Bobo m: traditional

Workers and Health Care

There once was a working maid, who really was
        afraid. To tell her
boss her health care costs were not within her
        means to pay.
This maid is not alone; all workers long have
        known:
If health's a perk that comes with work employ-
        ers must be shown . . .

Chorus:
That the time has come, we're going for health
        care
We're going for health care! We're going for
        health care!
That the time has come, we're going for health
        care!
We're going for health care! Health care for all!

There's many an employee, to raise a family,
Must toil all day at minimum pay to still wind
        up in poverty.
It's also all-too-rare, for them to get health care.
The boss, you see, gets off scot free and doesn't
        pay her share.

w: Jeff Kirsh; m: "Redwing" ("Union Maid")

Open the Doors! (To Health Care for All)

There's a crisis in this country that's affecting
        you and me.
The doors that lead to health care, don't open
        easily.
The costs are astronomical; no care if you are
        poor.
It's time we organize ourselves to open up the
        doors !

Chorus:
Open the doors! Open the doors!
Hear the people knocking loudlyheed their call.
Open the doors! Open the doors!
The time has come for health care for all!

Medicare has passed despite the fight of doctors
        and their friends
To give the seniors health care, on which they
        could depend.
But who knew the docs who fought it, would
        make a mint instead,
And leave the seniors' pocketbooks forever in
        the red.

Many women having babies do without
        pre-natal care.
We let that crime go forward, as if we're not
        aware,
That the children are our future, our real security;
Instead of building missiles we should make all
        health care free.

There are thirty seven million who are outside
        looking in.
They are workers, they are children; they're our
        neighbors and our kin.
They need universal health care, to keep them
        safe and sound;

We're mad about those health care doors and
    aim to knock 'em down.

Oh, those doors are artificial and they ain't
    made out of steel.
They are put there by a system that's forgotten
    how to feel.
All the fear that people live with when an ill-
    ness comes to call.
The system needs some changin' and its called
    health care for all!

-Jeff Kirsch

Midwest Academy Fight Song

Mine eyes have seen the power of our coalition
    board.
We are tramping on the targets who want all the
    wealth to hoard.
We have loosed a great constituency and
    brought new folks aboard,
Through concrete victories!

Chorus:
Plan the strategy together.
Work the strategy together.
Win the strategy together.
Organizing makes us strong!

On the newsprint at the meetings, we our goals
    articulate.
Coalition building strategies we must succinctly
    state.
We identify the forces to whom we can best
    relate,
Through concrete victories!

We identify the people who can give us what
    we need.
We develop all the actions that will make
    THEM pay us heed.
And give back to common people what
    THEY'VE stolen in THEIR greed!
Through concrete victories!

w: Peter Shuchter and other participants in the
spring, 1990 Midwest Academy training session
in Philadelphia

m: Battle Hymn of the Republic

INDEX

("b" indicates boxed material; "i" indicates an illustration; "n" indicates a note)

The Midwest Academy, a training institute for progressive organizers and activists, conducts regularly scheduled week-long training sessions throughout the year. The Academy also provides ongoing consulting and training for organizers and organizations. If your current staff is not able to provide this we recommend that you contract with an experienced organizer for at least a year to provide ongoing support and training. New organizers who come to a Midwest Academy training session and have someone back home to provide ongoing help are much more likely to succeed than those who return to fend for themselves. Some foundations that support your organization may be willing to provide additional technical assistance funds for your organizing staff.

The Midwest Academy also leads on-site training and planning sessions for boards, staff, and leaders of organizations across the country. Training and planning sessions are adapted to meet the specific needs of the contracting organizations.

For more information about the Midwest Academy and its programs, visit our Web site at www.midwestacademy.com or use the mail-in card below.

Please send me information about the following Midwest Academy programs and resources:

❑ Week-long intensive organizer training sessions

❑ On-site training sessions

❑ Promotional flyers describing this manual

❑ Other organizing resources

Name: _____

Organization: _____

Address: _____

Phone (Daytime): _____

Mail to: **Midwest Academy,** 28 East Jackson Blvd., Suite 605, Chicago, IL 60604
Phone: 312-427-2304 Fax: 312-427-2308 mwacademyl@aol.com

Please send me information about the following Midwest Academy programs and resources:

❑ Week-long intensive organizer training sessions

❑ On-site training sessions

❑ Promotional flyers describing this manual

❑ Other organizing resources

Name: _____

Organization: _____

Address: _____

Phone (Daytime): _____

Mail to: **Midwest Academy,** 28 East Jackson Blvd., Suite 605, Chicago, IL 60604
Phone: 312-427-2304 Fax: 312-427-2308 mwacademyl@aol.com